LAUREL

THE MOON OF THE CARIBBEES
Eugene O'Neill's smoldering one-act drama of sailors aboard a docked freighter in a Caribbean port.

WHAT PRICE GLORY?
Anderson and Stalling's searing, fast, and bawdy portrayal of soldiers in combat that broke barriers by using battlefield profanities on the stage.

THEY KNEW WHAT THEY WANTED
Sidney Howard won the Pulitzer Prize for this drama of an aging winegrower, his young bride, and a hired hand, later produced as Broadway's smash musical, *The Most Happy Fella*.

PORGY
America's greatest folk drama, DuBose and Dorothy Heyward's moving play was later adapted as the libretto of George Gershwin's now classic *Porgy and Bess*.

STREET SCENE
Elmer Rice's realistic look at life in New York's tenements during two explosive summer days—later a musical play with music by Kurt Weill and lyrics by Langston Hughes.

HOLIDAY
Philip Barry's sophisticated comedy about America's elite in which a self-made young man must choose between marriage into high society and happiness.

Selected and introduced by

KENNETH MACGOWAN

FAMOUS
AMERICAN PLAYS
OF THE
1920s

Foreword by Gordon Davidson

A LAUREL BOOK
Published by
Dell Publishing
a division of
The Bantam Doubleday Dell Publishing Group, Inc.
666 Fifth Avenue
New York, New York 10103

ISBN: 0-440-32466-1

Printed in the United States of America
Published simultaneously in Canada

New Dell Edition

September 1988

10 9 8 7 6 5 4 3 2 1

KRI

Contents

Foreword

When I first scanned the Famous American Plays series, I felt somewhat awed by the task of composing a foreword to all the volumes. The idiosyncratic nature of the series—an attribute I find quite appealing—dictates that each volume not only embody the temperament of a decade but also reflect the spirit of the editor selecting the plays. These editors, an assortment of distinguished critics and theater practitioners including Kenneth Macgowan, Harold Clurman, Henry Hewes, Lee Strasberg, Ted Hoffman, and Robert Marx, define "the best" differently with each decade, each volume, even from play to play.

Yet somehow, despite the bent of the individual editor and with all the regrettable omissions—many choices shaped by the limitation of plays available for publication at the time (where, for example, is arguably the most famous and continuously developing twentieth-century American playwright Neil Simon?)—I still believe that the series comprises a living document to a crucial aspect of this century's American theater: the evolution and shifting emphasis in theme, approach, and even location. American theater has been on the move from Broadway to off-Broadway, from off-Broadway to off-off-Broadway, and finally from the singular concentration in and among the streets of New York to what has become the most exciting transformation of this century— the decentralization of American professional theater to include virtually every state in the union. The plays in these volumes reveal this journey and reflect the incredible changes not only in the theater but in our culture. The process of decentralization has affected and will continue to affect the very nature of the plays being written and the audiences attending them.

In the volumes covering the 1920s through the 1950s, all the plays—except for Eugene O'Neill's *The Moon of the Caribbees*—were Broadway plays. In the 1960s, only two plays included made it to Broadway from off-Broadway and from a regional theater. In the 1970s, only one did, although two others later moved to or reappeared briefly on Broadway. In the 1980s, *all* the plays started either off-Broadway, off-off-Broadway, or in regional theaters around the country, and three of them subsequently have appeared on Broadway.

The shifting emphasis in theme can be seen through the eyes of those who introduce each volume. In the 1920s the theater was considered a scene of "curious conflict" between realism and a freer form of theatricality. In the next decade, attention to the socioeconomic details of an individual's psychological condition became what Harold Clurman called "the most significant difference" between the theater of the twenties and the thirties. What informs many of the plays in that collection is a sense of political alertness married to an almost naive inexperience with actual events. Many of these plays, from *Idiot's Delight* to *End of Summer*, show what Clurman described as *interest* in subject matter rather than any authentic familiarity with it.

In the forties, we find a drama that reveals a new sense of history and a new relationship to it. As the editor of that volume reflects, "History is no longer regarded as a clear and orderly process of cause and effect, but rather as a series of traffic snarls and collisions of many people and forces moving in different directions." Plays written prior to the tragedy at Pearl Harbor give none-too-buried warnings of the imminence of danger, yet all the while they continued to reassure audiences that all would be well as long as everybody maintained faith in American hope and glory. But the theater, like the country, was trying to learn some very hard lessons by sidestepping the mistakes of past generations, on and offstage. *Home of the Brave* and *All My Sons* were both cautionary tales as much as they were realistic studies of the cost and consequences of war. The end of the conflict overseas brought renewed optimism on the boards, a response to victory that led to enthusiastic, if slightly ill-informed, ideas about theatrical innovation. But the audience for early ex-

perimental theater turned out to be far smaller than antici-
pated, although directors like Elia Kazan were making great
and subtle strides in discerning authorial personality—what
editor Henry Hewes calls "subconscious searchings"—in the
work of newly discovered playwrights like Tennessee
Williams.

Lee Strasberg found "numerous important playwrights
[but] fewer important plays in the 1950s." Yet Strasberg,
himself an innovator in modern acting technique, discerns a
uniquely modern thematic perspective in these plays in the
fusing of present, past, and future time and in the revelation
of psychological insight. Strasberg anticipates the founding
of a "new theater" that would "broaden the vision of man on
the stage" by its "awareness and perception of drama in
characters to which drama had never been previously at-
tributed, more subtle and more varied sense of relationship
between people, and a deeper penetration of their motiva-
tion." It was an exciting time for the actor, the first generation to be influenced by Strasberg's ideas. Unfortunately, too
few of the plays chosen for that volume proved of lasting
importance. Even Strasberg seems to have suspected this—
he ends his introduction, written in 1962, with a poignantly
optimistic look to the impending creation of a repertory
theater at Lincoln Center, under the guiding spirit of then-
President and Mrs. Kennedy.

Thus, as illustrated by the impressive list of plays collected
in these volumes, the plays of the twenties, thirties, forties,
and fifties embody the evolution of the theater on many
levels. In the sixties, however, was *revolution*. A remarkable
transformation had its true beginning in the early 1960s.

With the help of the Ford Foundation and the vision of W.
MacNeill Lowry, Vice President for the Arts, the theater and
theater professionals began to venture out from New York
City—not as they used to, tied to a rubber band that snapped
them back at the end of a tour or summer stock engagement
in time for the "new season on Broadway"—but as pioneers
and adventurers to new lands, eager to set down roots and
create some sense of permanence in cities all across the
United States, and to explore and reflect those communities
onstage. In 1963 the Tyrone Guthrie Theater opened its

doors in Minneapolis, in 1965 the Long Wharf in New Haven, Connecticut. In 1965 ACT traveled from Pittsburgh to Chicago and finally set up a permanent home in San Francisco. In 1964 the Actors Theatre of Louisville opened its doors. In 1963 the Seattle Repertory Theatre began, and in April 1967 the Mark Taper Forum in Los Angeles welcomed audiences for the first time. All in all, since that time 309 theaters have been established in 43 states and 150 cities. They were founded by individual artists, by partners, and by collectives. Some have inherited the structure of not-for-profit corporate entities with boards of directors, some have built buildings, some have established local, regional, and national profiles, and all have together produced an enormous body of work in less than thirty years. The Theatre Communications Group was formed in New York City as a service organization to bind this far-flung community together through meetings, publications, and advocacy.

I felt the excitement of this revolution firsthand; in fact, my career echoes the movement of the times. While when I first began looking for work in the theater in 1958 (I was still in the army), I thought about the possibility of finding work outside of New York, it was *in* New York that my life in theater had really begun: seeing Laurence Olivier in that famous double bill *Oedipus the Critic* (that memorable offstage howl); seeing the Lunts, Laurette Taylor, Gertrude Lawrence, Lee J. Cobb, Ray Bolger, John Gielgud, Judith Anderson, Melvyn Douglas, Paul Muni, Ralph Richardson. What performers! But, at that time, my options outside New York were limited. There was summer stock; there was college theater (my dad taught and directed at Brooklyn College). There was Nina Vance and the Alley Theatre in Houston; Margo Jones in Dallas; Zelda Fichandler at the Arena Stage in Washington, D.C.; the Cleveland Playhouse under K. Elmo Lowe; and a couple of theaters in San Francisco, including The Theatre of the Golden Hind and Herbert Blau and Jules Irving's Actors Workshop. And that was about it.

I felt compelled to start in New York. I chose a position as an apprentice stage manager at the American Shakespeare Festival. I worked with and under the mentorship of John Houseman, Jack Landau, Jean Rosenthal, Bernard Gersten,

Marc Blitzstein, David Hays, Dorothy Jeakins. It was as an assistant to Houseman that, finally, in 1964, I made my way to Los Angeles, where John was directing a production of *King Lear* starring Morris Carnovsky for The Theatre Group, a professional theater on the campus of UCLA. Three years later I opened the Mark Taper Forum, a 750-seat thrust stage in the Los Angeles Music Center. In April 1987 we celebrated the twentieth anniversary of our continuous production of plays: world and American premieres, classic revivals, young people's theater, and a host of developmental programs. The Taper is one of a network of theaters, a *family* of theaters that, though situated differently, still have many similarities: in structure, in attempts at creating subscription audiences, in nurturing artists, in revealing the life of the community they serve.

The regional theater movement began as an alternative to the commercial pressures of Broadway and as an alternative to living in New York City. It therefore initially concerned itself with the presentation of classics, modern and ancient, that were done commercially only sporadically. Dedicated to the development of companies of actors, designers, directors, these theaters preserved and reinterpreted the living library: Shakespeare, Shaw, Molière, Ibsen, Pirandello, the Greeks, as well as the American giants of the thirties, forties, and fifties. In fact, many of the plays reproduced in this series were and are the staples of regional theater programming. Audiences were willing to go to a theater with a recognizable, and to some extent familiar, list of plays performed and produced well. Actors and directors and designers searched for ways to make these plays come alive for contemporary audiences. These same audiences tended to shy away from new plays or unknown authors, unless they had the imprimatur, the stamp of approval, of a Broadway success (or at least a decent enough run on Broadway). Work on the "great plays" gave actors and directors a chance to stretch themselves and refine their skills (voice, movement, diction).

Then, to borrow from a book popular in the sixties, something happened. Concurrent with the social and cultural revolution with which we are all so familiar, Broadway really began to decline. (The "fabulous invalid," as it was known, began to look terminal.) Simultaneously, New York became a less hospitable or even challenging environment for artistic creativity. The reasons for this have been documented; they include soaring production costs, escalating ticket prices, urban blight, urban flight, expense account theatergoing and the loss of the regular audience; competition for attention and talent from TV and movies; and, to varying degrees, the usurpation by other media (including popular music) of the content, subject matter, and even form that was previously the territory and province of the theater.

And in the sixties the artists took to the streets, lofts, basements, churches, and parks to write the plays that began to speak of their horror, outrage, and pain over war, assassination, and the gradual corruption of the spirit exemplified by Saran Wrap and defense budgets. As Edward Parone wrote in his introduction to a collection of plays entitled *Collision Course*, these plays were "written on impulse in short bursts that seem to want to impinge directly upon their audiences without the barrier of intellect or manners or preconceptions." And in turn the regional theater began to turn its attention to the presentation of new plays (note: some, like the Mark Taper Forum and the New York Public Theater, did this from the beginning), and with this came the creation of a system for developing new theater pieces through commissions, readings, laboratories, workshops, festivals, conferences, and the use of small venues (second spaces) as homes for venturesome work.

Like many revolutions, these changes grew of necessity; only in retrospect do we see their far-reaching effects. Not only did these developments allow audiences throughout the United States to participate in the adventure and excitement of creating and discovering new works of art, but they changed or reversed the flow of material and talent (plays, playwrights, actors, directors, and designers) both out of New York and back. Broadway is no longer the generator of material and the source of personnel for the theater. It is a grand and heady as well as pain-inducing receiver of the fruits of theater from elsewhere—traditionally London and now more and more the rest of the United States.

The decentralization of the American theater is the most

challenging and enduring transformation of the last three decades. It's both the best and worst thing that could have happened, because it also makes it that much more difficult to see, taste, judge, be influenced by, and know one another's work, and it puts an extra pressure on the need to share and find some ground upon which artists and audience have common experiences. The lack of a center or single pulse makes the gift of a collection like this one, a compilation of all our work, that much more valuable.

The decentralization also has brought to the surface a whole new set of problems, questions, esthetics, and challenges for the theater of the future. First and foremost is the need for a belief in the theater as an art form rather than as a business that produces a product which is either a success (a hit that makes money) or a failure (a flop and a financial disaster). The theater searches for survival as an institution, with all of the responsibilities an institution has to itself and its community. It serves a community and must be aware of the cultural, ethnic, and social diversity of its artists and its audience. It can speak to the specifics of a city, state, region, and to a nation. It can give voice to the needs of the community as well as reflect the hopes and aspirations of a wide cross-section of its population. It can be a place that nurtures, trains, and develops talent. It can nurture the soul.

Some challenges are immediate, even practical. These resident regional theaters are housed in buildings as diverse in size and shape as their location. We have birthed in this same time period thrust stages, arena stages, small theaters, black boxes, *and very few* conventional proscenium theaters. Our writers are therefore exploring ways to create new forms of realism, naturalism, expressionism, and theatricality that let us know we are in a theater and not in front of a movie or television screen.

Other challenges are intellectual or spiritual. The "death of Freud" and the journey through the Jungian jungle may lead us to a more mythic search to satisfy our spiritual hunger and needs. The desire to better come to grips with our political and social realities can lead writers to explorations and insights unattainable on *Nightline*, but possible also because of the new access to information that even Johnny

Carson's nightly monologue provides.

Language and metaphor, technology in the service of (revealing, not dehumanizing) the individual, and acting that examines both the truth of human behavior and the extraordinary capacity of humans to perform with style, skill, and bravery—these are the possibilities that challenge the leadership of this network of theaters today in the United States.

Finally, the theater has to face its relationship and responsibility to the changing multicultural essence of this country. The challenges of nontraditional casting, of cross-cultural writing and nonhomogeneous audiences are the big questions for the future. These volumes American famous plays, impressive and important as they are, still reflect a harsh reality: in over seven decades, the collection contains only two black playwrights, no Hispanic or Asian-American writers, and only three women. These plays therefore reflect a theater in desperate need to get in touch with its own heart and the heartbeat of the society in which it dwells. One can only imagine what future volumes will contain and what extraordinary leaps of imagination, heart, and mind they will reveal. One hopes the series will continue long into the twenty-first century as a tribute to a theater that reflects a diversity of ideas, a wealth of voices, and a fervent belief in the centrality of the art to all our lives.

—Gordon Davidson

Introduction

This book might have been called *The American Drama Comes of Age*. Perhaps these plays aren't as famous as they once were. I would be the last to say that they're the best of their decade. But they are—to borrow an apt adjective from other anthologies—representative. They carry something of the flavor and the promise of our burgeoning theater of the twenties. And they record the birth of a new sort of American playwright.

The ten years from the end of World War I to the fatal fall of 1929 seemed to us who watched the stage in New York, the Big Decade. Broadway boomed, along with Wall Street. Why not? The country was turning out new novelists and poets, new painters and composers. New publishers and new art galleries appeared. Why not new playwrights and new theaters? Mr. and Mrs. Joe Doakes were getting a kick out of culture, and were ready to pay for it. In the twenties the playhouses along Broadway almost doubled, and also the plays to fill them. The silent movies had taken over some of the theaters on what was still the Great White Way, but many new ones shot up. In 1928 there were almost 60 legitimate Broadway playhouses against 35 in 1920. The number of productions—including new plays, revivals, and musicals—waxed from 196 in 1920–1921 to 270 in the peak season of 1927–1928. Even in 1920 there were often as many first nights in ten weeks as in any full year of the fifties; two or three productions would open on the same Monday or Tuesday. On Nov. 1,

1920, for example, the critics had to choose between *Just Suppose* by A. E. Thomas, noted for a number of hits; *The Prince and the Pauper,* the Mark Twain story with the then-potent star William Faversham; a musical comedy; and *The Emperor Jones.* (We all chose wrong, for the Provincetown Players, who had nurtured O'Neill, got less attention than what we now call "off Broadway.")

Yes, Broadway boomed like Wall Street in the twenties, but it didn't bust. As the theaters shrank in number in the thirties and forties, they presented better and better plays. The "fabulous invalid" lived on, and ever more heartily. There were two reasons. The movies, instead of Broadway, served the mass audience that wanted melodrama and farce, and served it better. Also, they served it more cheaply—an important matter in the thirties when the pocketbook of the mass audience was as flat as a thin dime. But more important to the future of our stage was the effect of the teeming twenties on Broadway. What was largely a show shop had been turned into the image of a true theater. Broadway producers found that there was a fine audience for fine plays, and they found—a discovery of even greater significance—that there were Americans who could write some of these plays.

Perhaps Burns Mantle was a bit clairvoyant when he launched his yearbooks of the theater with *The Best Plays of 1919–1920.* More likely he saw, that season, a clear portent in the production and success of Eugene O'Neill's *Beyond the Horizon,* Zoë Akins' *Déclassée,* Booth Tarkington's *Clarence,* John Drinkwater's *Abraham Lincoln,* the Arthur Hopkins–John Barrymore–Robert Edmond Jones *The Jest,* and St. John Ervine's *Jane Clegg.* And yet Mantle could hardly have foreseen the many and more brilliant triumphs of American playwriting, acting, and producing that were to distinguish the twenties.

Let me name only a few. The season of 1920–1921 brought O'Neill's *The Emperor Jones* and his *Diff'rent,* and Gilbert Emery's sound tragedy *The Hero.* The next season gave New York *Anna Christie, The Hairy Ape,* Owen Davis's play of frustration *The Detour,* and Sidney Howard's poetic drama *Swords; Dulcy* began the fecund collaboration of George S. Kaufman and Marc Connelly; and the Broadway career of George Kelly started auspiciously with *The Torch-Bearers.* In terms of acting and production, between November, 1923, and the tenth of January, 1924, New York saw the players of the Moscow Art Theater, Eleanora Duse, and Max Reinhardt's *The Miracle,* as well as Maxwell Anderson's first play, *White Desert.* The fall of 1924 brought *What Price Glory?* by Anderson and Laurence Stallings, O'Neill's *Desire Under the Elms,* and Sidney Howard's *They Knew What They Wanted.* The last half of the decade saw more plays by Howard, Kelly, and Anderson, O'Neill's *Strange Interlude,* the Heywards' *Porgy,* and Elmer Rice's *Street Scene,* as well as the emergence of Robert E. Sherwood with *The Road to Rome* and *Waterloo Bridge,* and the success of Philip Barry with *Paris Bound* and *Holiday.* Not to mention such effective blends of comedy and drama as *Broadway, Burlesque, Chicago,* and *The Front Page.*

As I happened to be a drama critic from 1910 to 1924 and a producer in New York until the end of 1931, I saw most of the plays of the two decades and all of the outstanding ones. In many cases I can check recollections by reviews, and through rereading the published plays I can reappraise my comments and also my memories of later productions. In the light of the printed page, what I wrote and what I remembered sometimes seem a trifle too roseate. Also, until O'Neill and Kelly and Howard appeared on Broadway, I'm afraid I was a bit too absorbed in the wonders of the new stagecraft that had begun with Robert Edmond Jones in 1915 and progressed with Lee Simonson and Norman Bel Geddes until half a dozen scene designers could, all too often, outdo directors and actors.

The season of 1919–1920 seems the turning point. In the *Evening Globe* and *Theatre Arts Magazine,* I hailed it as the best that New York had ever had. In the January, 1920, issue of *Theatre Arts*—then a quarterly —I wrote: "These months the American theater is passing through the most interesting and significant period of its history. . . . It seems about to bring forth theater organizations to match its producers and designers. And there are signs of plays and playwrights to justify them all." By July, 1921, the work of new American playwrights and the successful production of foreign plays such as Molnar's *Liliom,* Shaw's *Heartbreak House,* Barrie's *Mary Rose,* Milne's *Mr. Pim Passes By,* and Galsworthy's *The Skin Game* made me see "a better season than last—which was itself the best season the New York theater had ever known." I wish I had added: "This doesn't imply that the previous seasons had been hard to beat."

Between 1905 and 1920 there had been American plays of some merit, but they were lost in a welter of mediocrity. There had been revivals of classics, but without benefit of the new stagecraft.

The year of 1906 promised more from American playwrights than the next fifteen years fulfilled. Minnie Maddern Fiske presented Langdon Mitchell's brilliant comedy *The New York Idea.* Clyde Fitch—theatrical tailor to Charles Frohman's stars—reversed his field and wrote a bitter study of a lying woman in *The Truth;* he turned to verity only once again, in *The City.* The same year saw Henry Miller and Margaret Anglin in William Vaughn Moody's mixture of the daring and the conventional, *The Great Divide.* In 1906, with *The Three of Us,* Rachel Crothers began to write an earnest combination of problem play and comedy that she was to exploit for thirty years. E. H. Sothern and Julia Marlowe produced *Jeanne d'Arc,* one of a number of poetic dramas by Percy MacKaye, who did his best work somewhat later in the prose fantasy *The Scarecrow.*

In 1908 came Edward Sheldon's *Salvation Nell,* and soon his *The Nigger* and *The Boss,* all a blend of realism and the theatric style that he exploited a little later in *Romance.* In 1914 a playwright who was to bulk large in the twenties won success with his first play; he was Elmer Rice and his play, *On Trial,* was a clever melodrama of flashbacks. Jesse Lynch Williams also bridged the two decades with his light comedy *Why Marry?* of 1917, to be followed by *Why Not?* five years later.

The rest of the productions of those fifteen years included, besides many musicals, plays of little significance. Melodramas with long runs ranged from Porter Emerson Browne's *A Fool There Was*—which, as a film, immortalized Theda Bara—to Bayard Veiller's *Within the Law* and J. Hartley Manners' *Peg o' My Heart,* while Catherine Chisholm Cushing's *Pollyanna* sold sentimentality. There were a few obvious attempts at near-tragedy, beginning with Eugene Walter's *Paid in Full* in 1908. His *The Easiest Way*—borrowing a bit from Pinero's *Iris*—won a *succès de scandale* with the story of an actress who chose the primrose path. Some other plays—*The Fourth Estate, Leah Kleschna,* and *Fine Feathers,* for example—found it wise to change tragic endings into happy ones.

There was popular comedy of many kinds. At the top were the plays of Clare Kummer, *Good Gracious, Annabelle* and *A Successful Calamity.* A bit below in style but skillfully tailored to much greater popular success came some of the many plays by Winchell Smith —with or without collaborators—*The Fortune Hunter, Turn to the Right,* and *The Boomerang. Lightnin',* which he wrote with Frank Bacon, broke all long-run records with 1,291 performances. George M. Cohan turned from musicals to *Get-Rich-Quick Wallingford* and *Hit-the-Trail Holiday;* his best job of play carpentry was *Seven Keys to Baldpate,* deftly contrived from Earl Derr Biggers' mystery novel.

There is an important difference in style between the better playwrights of the twenties and those who wrote between 1905 and 1920. The newer men could make their dialogue seem natural without losing dramatic effectiveness. The realism of the older writers often faltered. There were a few plays of the earlier period in which characters seemed to speak as they might in real life—Mitchell's *The New York Idea,* Fitch's *The Truth,* and Williams' *Why Marry?* But remember that these were comedies. In drama, even the best of the playwrights sacrificed true realism by overplaying emotion. Until they came to the climactic scene, their dialogue would be natural enough. Then they wrote the "big speech." This emotional tirade, this cataract of words, had been so much a part of drama that James A. Herne had used it in his pioneering piece of realism, *Margaret Fleming,* in 1890. Even a fine poet like William Vaughn Moody could be guilty of this kind of theatricalism. In the first act of *The Great Divide* three drunken men corner Ruth Jordan in a lonely ranch house. Object: rape. She agrees to marry the best of the lot, a prospector named Stephen Ghent, if he will save her from the others. He shoots it out with one and buys off the other with a chain of gold nuggets. In the last act we learn that Ruth has made enough money to redeem the golden chain, and "free herself" by giving it to Stephen. As she confronts him, she cries:

> I held myself so dear! And you bought me for a handful of gold, like a woman of the street! You drove me before you like an animal from the

market. . . . Since then this has been around my neck, around my limbs, a chain of eating fire. Link by link I have unwound it. You will never know what it has cost me, but I have paid it all. Take it and let me go free. Take it, take it, I beseech you!

To which Stephen replies, a few speeches later:

. . . your price has risen. This is not enough. (*He throws the chain about her neck and draws her to him by it.*) You are mine, mine, do you hear? Now and forever.

I could quote much the same sort of thing from the work of Edward Sheldon and lesser men. In the twenties, too, you will find such highfalutin talk, but only in the plays of Channing Pollock and a few other sensation seekers. Never in the plays of the newer playwrights.

There are other stylistic differences, but they are merely a matter of vocabulary. Just as sex now raises its sometimes ugly head from the Freudian couch and provides our stage with words once heard only where two or three men were gathered together in the name of ribaldry, many plays of the twenties used more profanity than the stage had ever known before. Their authors couldn't claim the dubious distinction of filling in for the first time the blank in "you son of a ——"; that was the work of Clyde Fitch in *The City* back in 1915. Yet, if the playwrights of the twenties used less violent cuss words, the language was violent enough to spawn the story of the dowager who, as the curtain fell on *What Price Glory?*, muttered to her companion: "Where the hell are my goddam overshoes?" By contrast the slang of those days now seems as old-fashioned as a pen wiper: "Hi, peaches and cream," "You're a brick," "Not on your gay young life," "We could hit it up to beat the band," or "on the q.t."

In both comedy and drama, the plays of this collection should demonstrate how the American drama came of age in the twenties through the work of new writers with more ability, integrity, and imagination than Moody, Sheldon, Fitch, or even Mitchell. In the main, we see an upsurge of skill and veracity, vitality and power. The twenties not only brought a new sort of realism to the American theater. They also saw the beginnings of a movement away from realism and toward a freer form of drama, a movement that has been a potent force in the past fifteen years. Though no play in the present volume—for reasons that will appear later—is an example of this new trend, its genesis is clear enough in *The Emperor Jones, The Hairy Ape, Desire Under the Elms, The Great God Brown, Strange Interlude,* and in certain plays by men of less talent than O'Neill.

Now as to the plays I have chosen for this volume. By the rules of the game—as established for this collection and for two more Laurel Editions which will cover the thirties and the forties—my choice is restricted to the calendar years of 1920 through 1929. I might wish that the area had been set by theatrical seasons. If the field had been 1919–1920 through 1928–1929, I might have included Booth Tarkington's solo comedy, the highly amusing *Clarence.* If the bounds had been 1920–1921 to 1929–1930, I would certainly have chosen Connelly's *The Green Pastures.*

But, you may ask, if I don't include *Clarence* why should I choose O'Neill's *The Moon of the Caribbees,* which was produced in 1918? And why is there no example of O'Neill's experiments in a freer form of drama? If the publishers of O'Neill's plays had released one of his longer plays, I would have chosen *The Emperor Jones* or *Desire Under the Elms; The Emperor Jones* because it was not only his first attempt to escape the bonds of realism, but the first successful one by any

American; the other play because I think that in it he wrote his best tragedy and came closest to perfection of dialogue. *The Moon of the Caribbees* is a tragedy *in petto,* though the only death is the living one of the broken little gentleman "Smitty, the Duke." O'Neill told Smitty's story again in *In the Zone,* but he told it more theatrically and without the poignant beauty of the tropic night in which the drunken sailors and the native girls riot around the lonely Smitty.

There were other tragedies beside O'Neill's in the twenties—Zoë Akins' Pinerotic *Déclassée;* Owen Davis's rather obvious *The Detour;* Theodore Dreiser's failure in *The Hand of the Potter,* and Anderson's in the verse play *White Desert;* Patrick Kearney's greater success in *An American Tragedy;* Gilbert Emery's *The Hero;* Arthur Richman's very limited *Ambush;* Martin Flavin's not too important *The Criminal Code;* and *Gods of the Lightning,* Maxwell Anderson's and Harold Hickerson's not too effective version of the Sacco-Vanzetti case—but not one of these was both famous *and* good enough to include here.

As for comedy, I rather wish I might have included *Clarence,* which is full of Tarkington's special talent for picturing—not unsympathetically—some of the absurder aspects of the adolescents of his day. I wish, too, that something from George S. Kaufman and one of his various collaborators seemed suitable. From *Dulcy,* his first venture with Connelly—which might have been played by Gracie Allen or modeled upon her instead of on the women caricatured by F.P.A.—to *The Royal Family* and *June Moon,* fun and success marked Kaufman's plays. Though sophisticated and satiric, he was more successful than most playwrights in pleasing the widest public. He achieved this unlikely union of success and sophistication by adding to his observant humor deft turns of plot that seemed obviously tricky only after they had surprised and beguiled the audience. This was the kind of trick that George Kelly pulled as a comic coda to *The Show-Off*. It was artifice of a cheaper sort that spoiled Don Marquis's otherwise entrancing portrait in *The Old Soak* of the man who had an aversion to "wine and beer and them soft drinks." Among the not quite enduring comedies of the twenties I must regretfully include Jesse Lynch Williams' mild Shavianism *Why Not?* Salisbury Field's slight but deft *Wedding Bells*, and two highly successful but somewhat obvious plays, Floyd Dell's and Thomas Mitchell's *Little Accident* and Frank Craven's *The First Year*.

I must confess that I was sorely tempted by two plays of George Kelly's—less by *The Torch-Bearers*, that satire on the exhibitionists in our little theaters, than by *The Show-Off*. A writer and actor of vaudeville sketches, uncle of the Princess of Monaco, and brother of Walter Kelly, the celebrated "Virginia Judge" of variety, Kelly was by instinct a man of the theater. His braggart Aubrey Piper in *The Show-Off* is a most effective figure, but plot-wise the play leaves something to be desired.

Kelly gave up such easy twists of comedy to write more seriously, especially in *Craig's Wife*. That play, however, like Sidney Howard's *The Silver Cord*, seems to me just a bit too pat and obvious in its intent. Owen Davis's *Icebound* and Gilbert Emery's *The Hero* are sound enough but lacking in stature. I prefer *Street Scene* because of Elmer Rice's ability to create varied characters, to feel their inward life, and to bring it forth in natural yet stage-worthy dialogue. The mechanics of his plot—a husband's discovery of his wife's love affair and his murderous revenge—may be too obviously foreshadowed early in the play. But the emotions and drives of his people seem true and significant. Some of Rice's later plays, *We, the People* and *American Landscape* are perhaps more penetrating, and

Counsellor-at-Law is better built, but *Street Scene* still seems a bold piece of reportage, both effective and affecting.

There were playwrights of the twenties whose work was only a foreshadowing—sometimes a weak one—of what they were to do later. In the thirties, Thornton Wilder went far beyond *The Trumpet Shall Sound* of 1926. Marc Connelly's solo effort *The Wisdom Tooth* was outdistanced by *The Green Pastures,* and Paul Green's *In Abraham's Bosom* by *The House of Connelly.* Edwin Justus Mayer and Samson Raphaelson were to write better plays than theirs of the twenties. John Van Druten's *Young Woodley* is not to be compared with his later work. Maxwell Anderson was to rise above *White Desert,* the comedy of *Saturday's Children,* and the hilarious violence of *What Price Glory?* to the verse plays *Elizabeth, the Queen, Mary of Scotland,* and *Winterset.*

Robert Sherwood wrote better plays in the thirties than in the earlier decade. *Reunion in Vienna, Idiot's Delight,* and *Abe Lincoln in Illinois* have more stature than *Waterloo Bridge* or *The Road to Rome.* Yet I should have been glad to include the historical satire that was his first success. Like Mark Twain and Bernard Shaw, in *The Road to Rome* Sherwood did something more than debunk history. In the first act he may have cut down Fabius from the inventor of the war of attrition—and the godfather of the Fabian Society—to a rather silly husband, but in the rest of his play Sherwood made Hannibal an arresting and significant figure, and he gave his heroine many finely phrased speeches to turn back the conqueror from the sack of Rome.

The twenties offered at least two high comedies of distinction—S. N. Behrman's *The Second Man* and Philip Barry's *Holiday.* I chose *Holiday* because it seemed less reminiscent of Old World posturings on the upper crust. In the thirties Barry may have written more ambitiously in *Hotel Universe, The Animal Kingdom,* and *The Philadelphia Story,* but *Holiday* shows all the essential skills of this deft writer of upper class comedy. Some critics have objected to his concentration on the "ever-so-rich and ever-so-sophisticated," yet it is hard to quarrel with a man who wrote of what he knew best, who recognized the Achilles heels in high society, and who had the style and the wit that could present and then mercilessly puncture the pretensions of the men and women who worshiped success and correctitude in the boom years. And Barry could wisecrack with ingenuity and occasionally write such perfect nonsense as Nick Potter's description of his fictitious youth that begins: "I arrived in this country at the age of three months, with nothing in my pockets but five cents and an old hat-check. . . . When I came down the gangplank of that little sailing vessel—steam was then unknown, except to the very rich— Friends, can you picture that manly little figure without a tug at your heart strings and a faint wave of nausea?"

I have included *What Price Glory?* partly because it is lively and effective theater, and partly because Laurence Stallings' and Maxwell Anderson's comedy was the forerunner of a peculiarly American type of play. A curious collaboration resulted in a curious product. As a fighting Marine, Laurence Stallings had lost a leg in France. As a pacifist, Anderson had lost two jobs. Stallings was—and still is—a lusty, swashbuckling fellow, *l'homme qui rire;* Anderson was sober, earnest, not given much to humor. In writing the first draft of the play, one man chose acts one and three, the other act two. You would have expected Anderson to take on the job of building act two, since it is the only wholly dramatic scene in the play. Here in a cellar of an embattled town, there is no lusty wench for Captain

Flagg and Sergeant Quirt to fight over; just the bloody business of war and the moment in a cellar at the front when a lieutenant goes to pieces and says he'll order his platoon out even if Flagg shoots him: "What price glory now? Why in God's name can't we all go home? Who gives a damn for this lousy, stinking little town but the poor French devils who live here." This would seem to be just the meat for the pacifist, Anderson. Actually, however, he wrote the first and last acts, which showed the violent, bawdy, and hilarious battle of Quirt and Flagg for possession of the peasant Charmaine. After Stallings had finished the second act, he used his intimate acquaintance with doughboy talk to revise Anderson's dialogue. The result was not so much a direct attack on war as a picture of both its ribald violence and its futility. *What Price Glory?* is unromantic about war and women. It is neither patriotic nor respectable. Plot-wise it may be rudimentary, but it is fast and funny.

This comic slant on serious material, this mixing of realism and hokum violence, along with a good deal of very frank language, appeared in a number of other successes of the twenties—*Broadway* by Philip Dunning and George Abbott, *Chicago* by Maurine Watkins, *Burlesque* by George Manker Waters and Arthur Hopkins, *The Front Page* by Ben Hecht and Charles MacArthur. Curiously enough, it was this kind of drama, instead of O'Neill's work, that opened up the German stage to a flood of American plays. The success of *Broadway* and *What Price Glory?* broke the way for more serious material. Beginning with the twenties, our better plays have become more and more popular from England and Scandinavia to Turkey.

Within a fortnight in November, 1924, New York saw the premières of two plays with the same plot. In O'Neill's *Desire Under the Elms* and Howard's *They Knew What They Wanted,* an old farmer marries a girl from far away. In O'Neill's play the wife has a child by the man's son, in Howard's by a hired man. But there the resemblance ends. Howard made his play a comedy of character. Because his old man was an Italian grape grower in California instead of a New Englander piling stone on stone, Howard was able to end his play with Tony Patucci's accepting his unfaithful wife and "his" son: "We tellin' evrabody he's Tony's baby. Den evrabody say Tony is so goddam young and strong he's break both his legs an' havin' baby just da same! *(To Amy)* What you done was mistake in da head, not in da heart. . . . Mistake in da head is no matter." It did matter forty years before, when the playwright Bronson Howard—no kin to Sidney Howard—told an audience at Harvard, "The wife who has once taken the step from purity to impurity can never reinstate herself in the world of art this side of the grave." This was true enough in the artificial drama to which the elder Howard contributed *The Banker's Daughter*, the subject of his lecture, as well as *Saratoga* and *Shenandoah*. But when playwrights began to observe humbler people and use their qualities with honesty and sympathy, a different and a kinder sort of drama became possible.

American folk drama—which seems to mean plays about the flavorsome common people of the Appalachians and the Deep South—began to flourish in the twenties, and it reached its peak in *Porgy*. Pulitzer Prizes went to two folk plays—Hatcher Hughes' *Hell-Bent fer Heaven*, perhaps a bit obvious, and to Paul Green's *In Abraham's Bosom*, painful but not powerful enough. When Percy MacKaye wrote *This Fine Pretty World*, he flooded the stage with a torrent of "mountain white" argot that drowned out comprehension. Lulu Vollmer's *Sun-Up* ran even longer than *Porgy*, but in smaller theaters. Dorothy and DuBose Heyward's play of life in Catfish Row was not only honest and earnest. It was so colorful, so poignant, and so powerful that in George Gershwin's *Porgy and Bess* it became an opera which—without benefit of the "Met" —slowly grew in popularity until it conquered even Moscow.

Our theater of the twenties was the scene of a curious conflict. It was the battleground of opposing forces, yet these forces were united in a common end. Playwrights and producers sought more intensity of expression, but they sought it in conflicting ways. Most of them tried to achieve it through more realism; some through an escape from realism by way of splendid theatricalism on the one hand or symbolic distortion on the other. The result was a wide variety of plays and of production styles.

The case for and against realism was clear enough. In the course of half a century this type of drama had won a dominant place in the theater, but it seemed to many of us that it held this place legitimately only when it was uncompromisingly truthful and vigorously dramatic. Realism became art only if it achieved the high emotion of the theater within the narrow confines of its form, as in Ibsen's *Rosmersholm;* or if it took some human problem on which men felt intensely and presented this with naked truth as well as power, as in Hauptmann's *The Weavers*. In the first half of the twenties, I applauded the realism of *Anna Christie, What Price Glory?*, and *They Knew What They Wanted,* but I cheered louder for the freer form of *The Emperor Jones, The Hairy Ape, The Great God Brown,* and *Strange Interlude*. While I recognized that realism was natural and inevitable, I thought—and wrote—that there was something in the nature of the theater that made realism a difficult and sometimes an unsatisfactory method of expression. Its principal material, the actor, was too near actuality. Was it a triumph of art to make a flesh-and-blood actress named Pauline

Lord into a flesh-and-blood woman named Anna Christie—especially when the heart of the whole business was the elaborate pretense that there really wasn't any actor, there really wasn't any theater, and we were really looking through the fourth wall of a river-front saloon? Today I would be inclined to say that through this esthetic limitation Eugene O'Neill, Arthur Hopkins, the director of the play, and Robert Edmond Jones, the designer, proved their mastery of the theater.

For those who rebelled at realism, expressionism seemed, for a time, a way out. Born in a Germany racked by war and defeat, this distortion of reality, this making of men into emotional stereotypes, won critical acclaim—too much from me in *Continental Stagecraft* —but never complete success on the American stage. *The Hairy Ape* and Elmer Rice's *The Adding Machine* came nearest to accomplishment, but there was little power in their tragedy because it was limited by the special nature of the victims. Sophie Treadwell came nearer the mark in *Machinal* but, again, the tragic figure wasn't great enough. After some routine caricature in *Pinwheel*, Francis Faragoh wrote a fine and moving finish—but too late. There was considerable praise for John Howard Lawson's *Processional*, and for *Beggars on Horseback*, which George S. Kaufman and Marc Connelly took from a German source. But these plays —together with Lawson's *Roger Bloomer* and some of the work of his confreres among the New Playwrights group of 1927 and 1928—seemed to suggest that satire, rather than tragedy, might be the fruit of expressionism in America. And, as Kaufman himself once remarked, "Satire is what closes Saturday night."

Except for the adventurers in expressionism, all but two of our notable playwrights stuck pretty close to the realism of Ibsen. The dissenters were Marc Connelly, who thrust some fantasy into *Wisdom Tooth,* and O'Neill, whose eight experiments ranged from dire failure to outstanding success. The other playwrights played it safe. Perhaps they had never heard of the success of Belasco's production of Molnar's *The Phantom Rival* in 1914—four dreams in an envelope of reality. The huge hit of *Liliom* in 1921, with its seven scenes—one of them in heaven—couldn't lure our realists away from the three- and four-act play. They may have been deterred by the failure of such rather freakish imports from Europe as Shaw's *Back to Methuselah,* Čapek's *The World We Live In,* and Meinhard's and Bernauer's *Johannes Kreisler.* As beginners, the new writers may have felt instinctively—and perhaps wisely —that they had better master old-fashioned realism before they tried experiments like Connelly's daring and triumphant *The Green Pastures* and Sidney Howard's *Yellow Jack,* both produced in the thirties. The only successful experimenter was O'Neill, and we must remember that he had had some years of realistic writing before he tackled *The Emperor Jones.* He had his failures—*The Fountain, Dynamo, Lazarus Laughed,* and *Days Without End*—as he doggedly tried new ways to achieve heightened vitality. *The Emperor Jones, The Great God Brown,* and *Marco Millions* had fairly long runs, but they were nursed to success through economies of production that more commercial managements than the Provincetown Players, the Greenwich Village Theater, and the Theatre Guild couldn't have achieved. It was only the spring of 1928 that O'Neill won complete and unquestioned popularity for the soliloquy in the nine-act drama *Strange Interlude.* But, whether or not his earlier experiments could have achieved success in the ordinary competition of Broadway, there can be no question that they blazed the trail for later adventurers.

I think it is equally certain that O'Neill's *Beyond the Horizon* and *Anna Christie*—both produced by commercial managers—blazed the trail for the realists. True, the first of these had to invade Broadway by way of special matinees; but though it went into the evening bill only late in February, it totted up 111 performances; Arthur Hopkins put *Anna Christie* before well-filled houses for 177. Through these two plays Broadway managers discovered that they had a maturer audience than they had suspected, an audience eager for the exceptional realism of *What Price Glory?*, *They Knew What They Wanted, Street Scene, Craig's Wife,* and others to come.

But who blazed the trail for O'Neill himself from 1915 to 1920? Who—or, rather, what—gave him the encouragement to write in the years before Broadway discovered new playwrights and new audiences? And who and what made it possible for the Theatre Guild to come into existence, and to insure a successful hearing on Broadway for the best European playwrights as well as O'Neill? The men and women who made all this possible were amateurs—the founders of the Provincetown Players and the Washington Square Players. They were the off-Broadway producers of their day.

The Washington Square Players had a bit of a lead on the Provincetown. They opened at the Bandbox Theater on West Fifty-Seventh Street in February, 1915. O'Neill and his fellow writers, artists, and amateur actors used a Cape Cod drawing room in the summer of 1915, produced *Bound East for Cardiff* and other one-act plays in the Wharf Theater of Provincetown in 1916, and didn't bring O'Neill's sea-play to Greenwich Village until the fall. Both groups began with short pieces by American writers, but their objectives soon became clearly different. The Washington Square Players had Maeterlinck's *Interior* on its first bill and turned to European dramas when they tried long plays. The Provincetown group called its playhouse the Playwrights Theater, but the phrase might better have been the American Playwrights Theater, for in its seven years of activity it never produced anything but native—and new—drama.

The Washington Square Players, as an organization, was a World War I casualty, but most of its leaders reunited in 1919 to form the Theatre Guild. The record of its first ten years was indeed impressive. The only "art theater" that ever competed successfully on Broadway, it gave 9,000 performances of 70 productions, worked up a subscription list of 32,000, and built a theater. Yet the Guild produced only four American plays in its first four years and it rejected some by O'Neill. It lost $20,000 bravely on Shaw's *Back to Methuselah,* but its subscription list carried the costly *Marco Millions* to success in 1929.

If the Provincetown Players hadn't stood ready to produce all that O'Neill wrote from 1915 to 1920, would our outstanding dramatist have gone on writing for a non-existent stage; would he ever have written *Beyond the Horizon*? And who but the group in the converted stable on Macdougal Street would have produced *The Emperor Jones* and done it so superbly by engaging the Negro actor Charles S. Gilpin and by building a plaster sky-dome to bring the sinister night of the jungle in upon him? But without the plays of O'Neill, one may perhaps ask, could the Provincetown Players have endured as long as they did? Barely two months after *The Hairy Ape*—produced in association with Arthur Hopkins—the Village venture took a long vacation.

O'Neill himself credited yet another force with playing a major part in his career and in giving our stage new playwrights. This was Professor George Pierce Baker of Harvard. When the first successful teacher of playwriting died, his most famous pupil wrote:

Only those of us who had the privilege of membership in the drama class of George Pierce Baker back in the dark age when the American theater was still, for playwrights, the closed shop, star system, amusement racket, can know what a profound influence Professor Baker, who died last Sunday, exerted toward the encouragement and birth of modern American drama.

There were Harvard playwrights before Baker taught playwriting; some came under his influence in a course on early English drama that he began to teach in 1890. The list is variegated enough: Royall Tyler, class of 1776, whose *The Contrast* was the first American comedy produced in New York; Moody, 1893; MacKaye, '97; Charles T. Dazey, '81, who wrote the hardy perennial *In Old Kentucky;* popular hit-makers like Jules Eckert Goodman, '99, of *The Man Who Came Back* and half a dozen Potash and Perlmutter comedies; Edward Knoblock, '96, author of *Kismet;* and Owen Davis, '93, who concocted nearly a hundred and thirty melodramas such as *Bertha the Sewing Machine Girl* and *Nellie the Beautiful Cloak Model* before he wrote the tragedy *The Detour* and won a Pulitzer Prize with *Icebound.* Other men of the theater from Baker's earlier days included critics John Corbin, '92, and Walter Prichard Eaton, 1900, director and manager Winthrop Ames, '95, and John D. Williams, '03, who produced *Beyond the Horizon.*

Fortune smiled on Baker. His first playwriting class, in the spring of 1906, included not only critic Van Wyck Brooks, philosopher Horace Kallen, and Theatre Guild wheel-horse Maurice Wertheim, but also a playwright who was to score a Broadway success while still a graduate student. He was Edward Sheldon. When Baker returned from a European sabbatical in 1908, he found, as his biographer, William Payne Kinne, puts it, "Mrs. Fiske's continuing success with *Salvation Nell* had made the playwriting course as alluring as a gold field." But, though Baker had plenty of students in the next few years, their output wasn't remarkable. Fred Ballard's *Believe Me, Xantippe,* with John Barrymore, and Cleves Kinkead's *Common Clay,* with Jane Cowl, were run-of-the-mill plays. Like O'Neill, Baker's best writers—Robert E. Sherwood, S. N. Behrman, George Abbott, Philip Barry, and Sidney Howard—didn't show their wares on Broadway until the twenties. After Baker went to Yale his output was chiefly notable for Maurine Watkins, who wrote *Chicago;* George Sklar and Albert Maltz, who turned out agitprop ("agitation propaganda," a term applied to some overtly left-wing literature of the thirties) plays for the Theater Union in the thirties; and the stage director Elia Kazan. While Baker was still at Harvard, other men felt his enthusiasm for the theater and responded to it—the future critics Heywood Broun, Gilbert Seldes, Brooks Atkinson, and John Mason Brown, and the scene designers Lee Simonson, Robert Edmond Jones, and Donald Oenslager. We must remember, too, that Baker's work in production as well as in playwriting did much to create the university theater that now brings drama to more than two hundred cities across America.

Looking backward from *Death of a Salesman* and *J. B.,* I must emphasize again what a vitalizing role O'Neill played in leading our drama away from narrow realism and into the freer form of expression that distinguishes it today. It is all too true that after the failure of *Days Without End* in 1933, O'Neill returned to realism in the final and tragic decade of his life as a writer. Nevertheless, from *The Emperor Jones* through *Strange Interlude,* his work in the twenties broke great gaps in the "fourth wall" of realism. And through these gaps—aided by the ingenuity of new designers like Jo Mielziner and Boris Aronson—other men found their way to such plays as Rice's *Lady in the Dark,* Wilder's

Our Town and *The Skin of Our Teeth*, Williams' *Glass Menagerie* and *A Streetcar Named Desire*, Archibald MacLeish's *J. B.*, and above all, Miller's *Death of a Salesman*. To the O'Neill of the twenties we owe, I believe, a drama truer to life as the playwright sees it and a theater truer to the high art of frank make-believe.

KENNETH MACGOWAN

THE MOON
OF THE CARIBBEES

by Eugene O'Neill

*First production, December 20, 1918,
at the Playwright's Theatre, New York City,
with the following cast:**

Seamen on the GLENCAIRN:

YANK, *Harry Winston*
DRISCOLL, *Hutchinson Collins*
OLSON, *William Forster Batterham*
DAVIS, *W. Clay Hill*
COCKY, *O. K. Liveright*
SMITTY, THE "DUKE," *Charles Ellis*
PAUL, *Percy Winner*
LAMPS, THE LAMP LIGHTER, *Phil Lyons*
CHIPS, THE CARPENTER, *Fred Booth*
OLD TOM, THE DONKEYMAN, *William Stuart*

Firemen on the GLENCAIRN:

BIG FRANK, *Howard Scott*
MAX, *Jimmy Spike*
PADDY, *Charles Garland Kemper*
THE FIRST MATE, *Lewis B. Ell*
BELLA, *Jean Robb*
SUSIE, *Bernice Abbott*
PEARL, *Ruth Collins Allen*

**The cast of the later version of this play,
reprinted here, also includes Dick, a fireman;
Violet, a West Indian Negress; two other seamen,
Scotty and Ivan; and several other members
of the stokehole-engine-room crew.*

SCENE—*A forward section of the main deck of the British tramp Steamer* Glencairn, *at anchor off an island in the West Indies. The full moon, half-way up the sky, throws a clear light on the deck. The sea is calm and the ship motionless.*

On the left two of the derrick booms of the foremast jut out at an angle of forty-five degrees, black against the sky. In the rear the dark outline of the port bulwark is sharply defined against a distant strip of coral beach, white in the moonlight, fringed with coco palms whose tops rise clear of the horizon. On the right is the forecastle with an open doorway in the center leading to the seamen's and firemen's compartments. On either side of the doorway are two closed doors opening on the quarters of the Bo'sun, the ship's carpenter, the messroom steward, and the donkeyman—what might be called the petty officers of the ship. Near each bulwark there is also a short stairway, like a section of fire escape, leading up to the forecastle head (the top of the forecastle)—the edge of which can be seen on the right.

In the center of the deck, and occupying most of the space, is the large, raised square of the number one hatch, covered with canvas, battened down for the night.

A melancholy Negro chant, faint and far-off, drifts, crooning, over the water.

Most of the seamen and firemen are reclining or sitting on the hatch. PAUL *is leaning against the port bulwark, the upper part of his stocky figure outlined against the sky.* SMITTY *and* COCKY *are sitting on the edge of the forecastle head with their legs dangling*

*over. Nearly all are smoking pipes or cigarettes. The
majority are dressed in patched suits of dungaree.
Quite a few are in their bare feet and some of them,
especially the firemen, have nothing on but a pair of
pants and an undershirt. A good many wear caps.*

*There is the low murmur of different conversations
going on in the separate groups as the curtain rises.
This is followed by a sudden silence in which the singing from the land can be plainly heard.*

DRISCOLL [*a powerfully built Irishman who is sitting on
the edge of the hatch, front—irritably*]. Will ye listen
to them naygurs? I wonder now, do they call that
keenin' a song?

SMITTY [*a young Englishman with a blond mustache.
He is sitting on the forecastle head looking out over
the water with his chin supported on his hands.*] It
doesn't make a chap feel very cheerful, does it? [*He
sighs.*]

COCKY [*a wizened runt of a man with a straggling gray
mustache—slapping* SMITTY *on the back*]. Cheero, ole
dear! Down't be ser dawhn in the marf, Duke. She
loves yer.

SMITTY [*gloomily*]. Shut up, Cocky! [*He turns away
from* COCKY *and falls to dreaming again, staring toward the spot on shore where the singing seems to
come from.*]

BIG FRANK [*a huge fireman sprawled out on the right of
the hatch—waving a hand toward the land*]. They
bury somebody—py chiminy Christmas, I tink so
from way it sound.

YANK [*a rather good-looking rough who is sitting beside* DRISCOLL]. What d'yuh mean, bury? They don't
plant 'em down here, Dutchy. They eat 'em to save
fun'ral expenses. I guess this guy went down the
wrong way an' they got indigestion.

COCKY. Indigestion! Ho yus, not 'arf! Down't yer know

as them blokes 'as two stomacks like a bleedin' camel?

DAVIS [*a short, dark man seated on the right of hatch*]. An' you seen the two, I s'pect, ain't you?

COCKY [*scornfully*]. Down't be showin' yer igerance be tryin' to make a mock o' me what has seen more o' the world than yeself ever will.

MAX [*a Swedish fireman—from the rear of hatch*]. Spin dat yarn, Cocky.

COCKY. It's Gawd's troof, what I tole yer. I 'eard it from a bloke what was captured pris'ner by 'em in the Solomon Islands. Shipped wiv 'im one voyage. 'Twas a rare treat to 'ear 'im tell what 'appened to 'im among 'em. [*Musingly.*] 'E was a funny bird, 'e was—'ailed from Mile End, 'e did.

DRISCOLL [*with a snort*]. Another lyin' Cockney, the loike av yourself!

LAMPS [*a fat Swede who is sitting on a camp stool in front of his door talking with* CHIPS]. Where you meet up with him, Cocky?

CHIPS [*a lanky Scotchman—derisively*]. In New Guinea, I'll lay my oath!

COCKY [*defiantly*]. Yus! It *was* in New Guinea, time I was shipwrecked there. [*There is a perfect storm of groans and laughter at this speech.*]

YANK [*getting up*]. Yuh know what we said yuh'd get if yuh sprung any of that lyin' New Guinea dope on us again, don't yuh? Close that trap if yuh don't want a duckin' over the side.

COCKY. Ow, I was on'y tryin' to edicate yer a bit. [*He sinks into dignified silence.*]

YANK [*nodding toward the shore*]. Don't yuh know this is the West Indies, yuh crazy mut? There ain't no cannibals here. They're only common niggers.

DRISCOLL [*irritably*]. Whativir they are, the divil take their cryin'. It's enough to give a man the jigs listenin' to 'em.

YANK [*with a grin*]. What's the matter, Drisc? Yuh're as sore as a boil about somethin'.

DRISCOLL. I'm dyin' wid impatience to have a dhrink; an' that blarsted bumboat naygur woman took her oath she'd bring back rum enough for the lot av us whin she came back on board to-night.

BIG FRANK [*overhearing this—in a loud eager voice*]. You say the bumboat voman vill bring booze?

DRISCOLL [*sarcastically*]. That's right—tell the Old Man about ut, an' the Mate too. [*All of the crew have edged nearer to* DRISCOLL *and are listening to the conversation with an air of suppressed excitement.* DRISCOLL *lowers his voice impressively and addresses them all.*] She said she cud snake ut on board in the bottoms av thim baskets av fruit they're goin' to bring wid 'em to sell to us for'ard.

THE DONKEYMAN [*an old gray-headed man with a kindly, wrinkled face. He is sitting on a camp stool in front of his door, right front*]. She'll be bringin' some black women with her this time—or times has changed since I put in here last.

DRISCOLL. She said she wud—two or three—more, maybe, I dunno [*This announcement is received with great enthusiasm by all hands.*]

COCKY. Wot a bloody lark!

OLSON. Py yingo, we have one hell of a time!

DRISCOLL [*warningly*]. Remimber ye must be quiet about ut, ye scuts—wid the dhrink, I mane—ivin if the bo'sun is ashore. The Old Man ordered her to bring no booze on board or he wudn't buy a thing off av her for the ship.

PADDY [*a squat, ugly Liverpool Irishman*]. To the divil wid him!

BIG FRANK [*turning on him*]. Shud up, you tamn fool, Paddy! You vant make trouble? [*To* DRISCOLL.] You und me, ve keep dem quiet, Drisc.

DRISCOLL. Right ye are, Dutchy. I'll split the skull av

the first wan av ye starts to foight. [*Three bells are heard striking.*]

DAVIS. Three bells. When's she comin', Drisc?

DRISCOLL. She'll be here any minute now, surely. [*To PAUL, who has returned to his position by the bulwark after hearing DRISCOLL's news.*] D'you see 'em comin', Paul?

PAUL. I don't see anyting like bumboat. [*They all set themselves to wait, lighting pipes, cigarettes, and making themselves comfortable. There is a silence broken only by the mournful singing of the Negroes on shore.*]

SMITTY [*slowly—with a trace of melancholy*]. I wish they'd stop that song. It makes you think of—well—things you ought to forget. Rummy go, what?

COCKY [*slapping him on the back*]. Cheero, ole love! We'll be 'avin our rum in arf a mo', Duke. [*He comes down to the deck, leaving SMITTY alone on the forecastle head.*]

BIG FRANK. Sing someting, Drisc. Den ve don't hear dot yelling.

DAVIS. Give us a chanty, Drisc.

PADDY. Wan all av us knows.

MAX. We all sing in on chorus.

OLSON. "Rio Grande," Drisc.

BIG FRANK. No, ve don't know dot. Sing "Viskey Johnny."

CHIPS. "Flyin' Cloud."

COCKY. Now! Guv us "Maid o' Amsterdam."

LAMPS. "Santa Anna" iss good one.

DRISCOLL. Shut your mouths, all av you. [*Scornfully.*] A chanty is ut ye want? I'll bet me whole pay day there's not wan in the crowd 'ceptin' Yank here, an' Ollie, an' meself, an' Lamps an' Cocky, maybe, wud be sailors enough to know the main from the mizzen on a windjammer. Ye've heard the names av chanties but divil a note av the tune or a loine av the words do ye know. There's hardly a rale deep-water sailor lift on the seas, more's the pity.

YANK. Give us "Blow the Man Down." We all know some of that. [*A chorus of assenting voices:* Yes!—Righto!—Let 'er drive! Start 'er, Drisc! *etc.*]

DRISCOLL. Come in then, all av ye. [*He sings:*] As I was a-roamin' down Paradise Street—

ALL. Wa-a-ay, blow the man down!

DRISCOLL. As I was a-roamin' down Paradise Street—

ALL. Give us some time to blow the man down!

CHORUS

Blow the man down, boys, oh, blow
the man down!
Wa-a-ay, blow the man down!
As I was a-roamin' down Paradise
Street—
Give us some time to blow the
man down!

DRISCOLL. A pretty young maiden I chanced for to meet.

ALL. Wa-a-ay, blow the man down!

DRISCOLL. A pretty young maiden I chanced for to meet.

ALL. Give us some time to blow the man down!

CHORUS

Blow the man down, boys, oh, blow
the man down!
Wa-a-ay, blow the man down!
A pretty young maiden I chanced
for to meet.
Give us some time to blow the
man down!

PAUL [*just as* DRISCOLL *is clearing his throat prepara-tory to starting the next verse*]. Hay, Drisc! Here she come, I tink. Some bumboat comin' dis way. [*They all rush to the side and look toward the land.*]

YANK. There's five or six of them in it—and they paddle like skirts.

DRISCOLL [*wildly elated*]. Hurroo, ye scuts! 'Tis thim right enough. [*He does a few jig steps on the deck.*]

OLSON [*after a pause during which all are watching the approaching boat*]. Py yingo, I see six in boat, yes, sir.

DAVIS. I kin make out the baskets. See 'em there amidships?

BIG FRANK. Vot kind booze dey bring—viskey?

DRISCOLL. Rum, foine West Indy rum wid a kick in ut loike a mule's hoind leg.

LAMPS. Maybe she don't bring any; maybe skipper scare her.

DRISCOLL. Don't be throwin' cold water, Lamps. I'll skin her black hoide off av her if she goes back on her worrd.

YANK. Here they come. Listen to 'em gigglin'. [*Calling.*] Oh, you kiddo! [*The sound of women's voices can be heard talking and laughing.*]

DRISCOLL [*calling*]. Is ut you, Mrs. Old Black Joe?

A WOMAN'S VOICE. Ullo, Mike! [*There is loud feminine laughter at this retort.*]

DRISCOLL. Shake a leg an' come aboard thin.

THE WOMAN'S VOICE. We're a-comin'.

DRISCOLL. Come on, Yank. You an' me'd best be goin' to give 'em a hand wid their truck. 'Twill put 'em in good spirits.

COCKY [*as they start off left*]. Ho, you ain't arf a fox, Drisc. Down't drink it all afore we sees it.

DRISCOLL [*over his shoulder*]. You'll be havin' yours, me sonny bye, don't fret. [*He and Yank go off left.*]

COCKY [*licking his lips*]. Gawd blimey, I can do wiv a wet.

DAVIS. Me, too!

CHIPS. I'll bet there ain't none of us'll let any go to waste.

BIG FRANK. I could trink a whole barrel mineself, py

chiminy Christmas!

COCKY. I 'opes all the gels ain't as bloomin' ugly as 'er. Looked like a bloody organ-grinder's monkey, she did. Gawd, I couldn't put up wiv the likes of 'er!

PADDY. Ye'll be lucky if any of thim looks at ye, ye squint-eyed runt.

COCKY [*angrily*]. Ho, yus? You ain't no bleedin' beauty prize yeself, me man. A 'airy ape, I calls yer.

PADDY [*walking toward him—truculently*]. Whot's thot? Say ut again if ye dare.

COCKY [*his hand on his sheath knife—snarling*]. 'Airy ape! That's wot I says! [PADDY *tries to reach him but the others keep them apart.*]

BIG FRANK [*pushing* PADDY *back*]. Vot's the matter mit you, Paddy. Don't you hear vat Driscoll say—no fighting?

PADDY [*grumblingly*]. I don't take no back talk from that deck-scrubbin' shrimp.

COCKY. Blarsted coal-puncher! [DRISCOLL *appears wearing a broad grin of satisfaction. The fight is immediately forgotten by the crowd who gather around him with exclamations of eager curiosity.* How is it, Drisc? Any luck? Vot she bring, Drisc? Where's the gels? *etc.*]

DRISCOLL [*with an apprehensive glance back at the bridge*]. Not so loud, for the love av hivin! [*The clamor dies down.*] Yis, she has ut wid her. She'll be here in a minute wid a pint bottle or two for each wan av ye—three shillin's a bottle. So don't be impashunt.

COCKY [*indignantly*]. Three bob! The bloody cow!

SMITTY [*with an ironic smile*]. Grand larceny, by God! [*They all turn and look up at him, surprised to hear him speak.*]

OLSON. Py yingo, we don't pay so much.

BIG FRANK. Tamn black tief!

PADDY. We'll take ut away from her and give her nothin'.

THE CROWD [*growling*]. Dirty thief! Dot's right! Give her nothin'! Not a bloomin' 'apenny! etc.

DRISCOLL [*grinning*]. Ye can take ut or lave ut, me sonny byes. [*He casts a glance in the direction of the bridge and then reaches inside his shirt and pulls out a pint bottle.*] 'Tis foine rum, the rale stuff. [*He drinks.*] I slipped this wan out av one av the baskets whin they wasn't lookin'. [*He hands the bottle to* OLSEN *who is nearest him.*] Here ye are, Ollie. Take a small sup an' pass ut to the nixt. 'Tisn't much but 'twill serve to take the black taste out av your mouths if ye go aisy wid ut. An' there's buckets more av ut comin'. [*The bottle passes from hand to hand, each man taking a sip and smacking his lips with a deep "Aaah" of satisfaction.*]

DAVIS. Where's she now, Drisc?

DRISCOLL. Up havin' a worrd wid the skipper, makin' arrangements about the money, I s'pose.

DAVIS. An' where's the other gels?

DRISCOLL. Wid her. There's foive av thim she took aboard—two swate little slips av things, near as white as you an' me are, for that gray-whiskered auld fool, an' the mates—an' the engineers too, maybe. The rist av thim'll be comin' for'ard whin she comes.

COCKY. 'E ain't 'arf a funny old bird, the skipper. Gawd blimey! 'Member when we sailed from 'ome 'ow 'e stands on the bridge lookin' like a bloody ole sky pilot? An' 'is missus dawn on the bloomin' dock 'owlin fit to kill 'erself? An' 'is kids 'owlin an' wavin' their 'andkerchiefs? [*With great moral indignation.*] An' 'ere 'e is makin' up to a bleedin' nigger! There's a captain for yer! Gawd blimey! Bloody crab, I calls 'im!

DRISCOLL. Shut up, ye insect! Sure, it's not you should be talkin', an' you wid a woman an' childer weepin' for ye in iviry divil's port in the wide worrld, if we can believe your own tale av ut.

COCKY [*still indignant*]. I ain't no bloomin' captain, I

ain't. I ain't got no missus—reg'lar married, I means.
I ain't—

BIG FRANK [*putting a huge paw over* COCKY's *mouth*].
You ain't going talk so much, you hear? [COCKY *wriggles away from him.*] Say, Drisc, how ve pay dis
voman for booze? Ve ain't got no cash.

DRISCOLL. It's aisy enough. Each girl'll have a slip av
paper wid her an' whin you buy anythin' you write
ut down and the price beside ut and sign your name.
If ye can't write have some one who can do ut for ye.
An' rimimber this: Whin ye buy a bottle av dhrink
or [*With a wink.*] somethin' else forbid, ye must
write down tobaccy or fruit or somethin' the loike
av that. Whin she laves the skipper'll pay what's
owin' on the paper an' take ut out av your pay. Is
ut clear to ye now?

ALL. Yes—Clear as day—Aw right, Drisc—Righto—Sure.
etc.

DRISCOLL. An' don't forgit what I said about bein' quiet
wid the dhrink, or the Mate'll be down on our necks
an' spile the fun. [*A chorus of assent.*]

DAVIS [*looking aft*]. Ain't this them comin'? [*They all
look in that direction. The silly laughter of a woman
is heard.*]

DRISCOLL. Look at Yank, wud ye, wid his arrm around
the middle av wan av thim. That lad's not wastin'
any toime. [*The four women enter from the left,
giggling and whispering to each other. The first
three carry baskets on their heads. The youngest and
best-looking comes last.* YANK *has his arm about her
waist and is carrying her basket in his other hand.
All four are distinct Negro types. They wear light-
colored, loose-fitting clothes and have bright bandana handkerchiefs on their heads. They put down
their baskets on the hatch and sit down beside them.
The men crowd around, grinning.*]

BELLA [*she is the oldest, stoutest, and homeliest of the*

four—grinning back at them]. 'Ullo, boys.

THE OTHER GIRLS. 'Ullo, boys.

THE MEN. Hello, yourself—Evenin'—Hello—How are you? etc.

BELLA [*genially*]. Hope you had a nice voyage. My name's Bella, this here's Susie, yander's Violet, and her there [*Pointing to the girl with* YANK] is Pearl. Now we all knows each other.

PADDY [*roughly*]. Never mind the girls. Where's the dhrink?

BELLA [*tartly*]. You're a hawg, ain't you? Don't talk so loud or you don't git any—you nor no man. Think I wants the ole captain to put me off the ship, do you?

YANK. Yes, nix on hollerin', you! D'yuh wanta queer all of us?

BELLA [*casting a quick glance over her shoulder*]. Here! Some of you big strapping boys sit back of us on the hatch there so's them officers can't see what we're doin'. [DRISCOLL *and several of the others sit and stand in back of the girls on the hatch.* BELLA *turns to* DRISCOLL.] Did you tell 'em they gotter sign for what they gits—and *how* to sign?

DRISCOLL. I did—what's your name again—oh, yis— Bella, darlin'.

BELLA. Then it's all right; but you boys has gotter go inside the fo'castle when you gits your bottle. No drinkin' out here on deck. I ain't takin' no chances. [*An impatient murmur of assent goes up from the crowd.*] Ain't that right, Mike?

DRISCOLL. Right as rain, darlin'. [BIG FRANK *leans over and says something to him in a low voice.* DRISCOLL *laughs and slaps his thigh.*] Listen, Bella, I've some-thin' to ask ye for my little friend here who's bash-ful. Ut has to do wid the ladies so I'd best be whis-perin' ut to ye meself to kape them from blushin'. [*He leans over and asks her a question.*]

BELLA [*firmly*]. Four shillin's.

DRISCOLL [*laughing*]. D'you hear that, all av ye? Four shillin's ut is.

PADDY [*angrily*]. To hell wid this talkin'. I want a dhrink.

BELLA. Is everything all right, Mike?

DRISCOLL [*after a look back at the bridge*]. Sure. Let her droive!

BELLA. All right, girls. [*The girls reach down in their baskets in under the fruit which is on top and each pulls out a pint bottle. Four of the men crowd up and take the bottles.*] Fetch a light, Lamps, that's a good boy. [LAMPS *goes to his room and returns with a candle. This is passed from one girl to another as the men sign the sheets of paper for their bottles.*] Don't you boys forget to mark down cigarettes or tobacco or fruit, remember! Three shillin's is the price. Take it into the fo'castle. For Gawd's sake, don't stand out here drinkin' in the moonlight. [*The four go into the forecastle. Four more take their places.* PADDY *plants himself in front of* PEARL *who is sitting by* YANK *with his arm still around her.*]

PADDY [*gruffly*]. Gimme thot! [*She holds out a bottle which he snatches from her hand. He turns to go away.*]

YANK [*sharply*]. Here, you! Where d'yuh get that stuff? You ain't signed for that yet.

PADDY [*sullenly*]. I can't write me name.

YANK. Then I'll write it for yuh. [*He takes the paper from Pearl and writes.*] There ain't goin' to be no welshin' on little Bright Eyes here—not when I'm around, see? Ain't I right, kiddo?

PEARL [*with a grin*]. Yes, suh.

BELLA [*seeing all four are served*]. Take it into the fo'castle, boys. [PADDY *defiantly raises his bottle and gulps down a drink in the full moonlight.* BELLA *sees him.*] Look at 'im! Look at the dirty swine! [PADDY *slouches into the forecastle.*] Wants to git me in trouble. That settles it! We all got to git inside, boys, where we won't git caught. Come on, girls. [*The girls pick up their baskets and follow* BELLA. YANK *and* PEARL *are the last to reach the doorway. She lingers behind him, her eyes fixed on* SMITTY, *who is still sitting on the forecastle head, his chin on his hands, staring off into vacancy.*]

PEARL [*waving a hand to attract his attention*]. Come ahn in, pretty boy. Ah likes you.

SMITTY [*coldly*]. Yes; I want to buy a bottle, please. [*He goes down the steps and follows her into the forecastle. No one remains on deck but the* DONKEYMAN, *who sits smoking his pipe in front of his door. There is the subdued babble of voices from the crowd inside but the mournful cadence of the song from the shore can again be faintly heard.* SMITTY *reappears and closes the door to the forecastle after him. He shudders and shakes his shoulders as if flinging off something which disgusted him. Then he lifts the bottle which is in his hand to his lips and gulps down a long drink. The* DONKEYMAN *watches him impassively.* SMITTY *sits down on the hatch facing him. Now that the closed door has shut off nearly all the noise the singing from shore comes clearly over the moonlit water.*]

SMITTY [*listening to it for a moment*]. Damn that song of theirs. [*He takes another big drink.*] What do you say, Donk?

THE DONKEYMAN [*quietly*]. Seems nice an' sleepy-like.

SMITTY [*with a hard laugh*]. Sleepy! If I listened to it long—sober—I'd never go to sleep.

THE DONKEYMAN. 'Tain't sich bad music, is it? Sounds kinder pretty to me—low an' mournful—same as listenin' to the organ outside o' church of a Sunday.

SMITTY [*with a touch of impatience*]. I didn't mean it was bad music. It isn't. It's the beastly memories the damn thing brings up—for some reason. [*He takes another pull at the bottle.*]

THE DONKEYMAN. Ever hear it before?

SMITTY. No; never in my life. It's just a something about the rotten thing which makes me think of—well—oh, the devil! [*He forces a laugh.*]

THE DONKEYMAN [*spitting placidly*]. Queer things, mem'ries. I ain't ever been bothered much by 'em.

SMITTY [*looking at him fixedly for a moment—with quiet scorn*]. No, you wouldn't be.

THE DONKEYMAN. Not that I ain't had my share o' things goin' wrong; but I puts 'em out o' me mind, like, an' fergets 'em.

SMITTY. But suppose you couldn't put them out of your mind? Suppose they haunted you when you were awake and when you were asleep—what then?

THE DONKEYMAN [*quietly*]. I'd git drunk, same's you're doin'.

SMITTY [*with a harsh laugh*]. Good advice. [*He takes another drink. He is beginning to show the effects of the liquor. His face is flushed and he talks rather wildly.*] We're poor little lambs who have lost our way, eh, Donk? Damned from here to eternity, what? God have mercy on such as we! True, isn't it, Donk?

THE DONKEYMAN. Maybe; I dunno. [*After a slight pause.*] Whatever set you goin' to sea? You ain't made for it.

SMITTY [*laughing wildly*]. My old friend in the bottle here, Donk.

THE DONKEYMAN. I done my share o' drinkin' in my time. [*Regretfully.*] Them was good times, those days. Can't hold up under drink no more. Doctor told me I'd got to stop or die. [*He spits contentedly.*] So I stops.

SMITTY [*with a foolish smile*]. Then I'll drink one for you. Here's your health, old top! [*He drinks.*]

THE DONKEYMAN [*after a pause*]. S'pose there's a gel mixed up in it someplace, ain't there?

SMITTY [*stiffly*]. What makes you think so?

THE DONKEYMAN. Always is when a man lets music

bother 'im. [*After a few puffs at his pipe.*] An' she
said she threw you over 'cause you was drunk; an'
you said you was drunk 'cause she threw you over.
[*He spits leisurely.*] Queer thing, love, ain't it?

SMITTY [*rising to his feet with drunken dignity*]. I'll
trouble you not to pry into my affairs, Donkeyman.

THE DONKEYMAN [*unmoved*]. That's everybody's affair,
what I said. I been through it many's the time.
[*Genially.*] I always hit 'em a whack on the ear an'
went out and got drunker'n ever. When I come home
again they always had somethin' special nice cooked
fur me to eat. [*Puffing at his pipe.*] That's the on'y
way to fix 'em when they gits on their high horse
I don't s'pose you ever tried that?

SMITTY [*pompously*]. Gentlemen don't hit women.

THE DONKEYMAN [*placidly*]. No; that's why they has
mem'ries when they hears music. [SMITTY *does not
deign to reply to this but sinks into a scornful silence.* DAVIS *and the girl* VIOLET *come out of the forecastle and close the door behind them. He is staggering a bit and she is laughing shrilly.*]

DAVIS [*turning to the left*]. This way, Rose, or Pansy,
or Jessamine, or black Tulip, or Violet, or whatever
the hell flower your name is. No one'll see us back
here. [*They go off left.*]

THE DONKEYMAN. There's love at first sight for you—an'
plenty more o' the same in the fo'c's'tle. No mem'ries
jined with that.

SMITTY [*really repelled*]. Shut up, Donk. You're disgust-
ing. [*He takes a long drink.*]

THE DONKEYMAN [*philosophically*]. All depends on how
you was brung up, I s'pose. [PEARL *comes out of the
forecastle. There is a roar of voices from inside. She
shuts the door behind her, sees* SMITTY *on the hatch,
and comes over and sits beside him and puts her arm
over his shoulder.*]

THE DONKEYMAN [*chuckling*]. There's love for you,
Duke.

PEARL [*patting* SMITTY's *face with her hand*]. 'Ullo, pretty boy. [SMITTY *pushes her hand away coldly.*] What you doin' out here all alone by yourself?

SMITTY [*with a twisted grin*]. Thinking and,—[*He indicates the bottle in his hand.*]—drinking to stop thinking. [*He drinks and laughs maudlinly. The bottle is three-quarters empty.*]

PEARL. You oughtn't drink so much, pretty boy. Don' you know dat? You have big, big headache come mawnin'.

SMITTY [*dryly*]. Indeed?

PEARL. Tha's true. Ah knows what Ah say. [*Cooingly.*] Why you run 'way from me, pretty boy? Ah likes you. Ah don' like them other fellahs. They act too rough. You ain't rough. You're a genelman. Ah knows. Ah can tell a genelman fahs Ah can see 'im.

SMITTY. Thank you for the compliment; but you're wrong, you see. I'm merely—a ranker. [*He adds bitterly.*] And a rotter.

PEARL [*patting his arm*]. No, you ain't. Ah knows better. You're a genelman. [*Insinuatingly.*] Ah wouldn't have nothin' to do with them other men, but [*She smiles at him enticingly.*] you is diff'rent. [*He pushes her away from him disgustedly. She pouts.*] Don' you like me, pretty boy?

SMITTY [*a bit ashamed*]. I beg your pardon. I didn't mean to be rude, you know, really. [*His politeness is drunkenly exaggerated.*] I'm a bit off color.

PEARL [*brightening up*]. Den you do like me—little ways?

SMITTY [*carelessly*]. Yes, yes, why shouldn't I? [*He suddenly laughs wildly and puts his arm around her waist and presses her to him.*] Why not? [*He pulls his arm back quickly with a shudder of disgust, and takes a drink.* PEARL *looks at him curiously, puzzled by his strange actions. The door from the forecastle is kicked open and* YANK *comes out. The uproar of shouting, laughing and singing voices has increased in violence.* YANK *staggers over toward* SMITTY *and* PEARL.]

YANK [*blinking at them*]. What the hell—oh, it's you, Smitty the Duke. I was goin' to turn one loose on the jaw of any guy'd cop my dame, but seein' it's you—[*Sentimentally.*] Pals is pals and any pal of mine c'n have anythin' I got, see? [*Holding out his hand.*] Shake, Duke. [SMITTY *takes his hand and he pumps it up and down.*] You'n me's frens. Ain't I right?

SMITTY. Right it is, Yank. But you're wrong about this girl. She isn't with me. She was just going back to the fo'c's'tle to you. [PEARL *looks at him with hatred gathering in her eyes.*]

YANK. Tha' right?

SMITTY. On my word!

YANK [*grabbing her arm*]. Come on then, you, Pearl! Le's have a drink with the bunch. [*He pulls her to the entrance where she shakes off his hand long enough to turn on* SMITTY *furiously.*]

PEARL. You swine! You can go to hell! [*She goes in the forecastle, slamming the door.*]

THE DONKEYMAN [*spitting calmly.*] There's love for you. They're all the same—white, brown, yeller 'n' black. A whack on the ear's the only thing'll learn 'em. [SMITTY *makes no reply but laughs harshly and takes another drink; then sits staring before him, the almost empty bottle tightly clutched in one hand. There is an increase in volume of the muffled clamor from the forecastle and a moment later the door is thrown open and the whole mob, led by* DRISCOLL, *pours out on deck. All of them are very drunk and several of them carry bottles in their hands.* BELLA *is the only one of the women who is absolutely sober. She tries in vain to keep the men quiet.* PEARL *drinks from* YANK'S *bottle every moment or so, laughing shrilly, and leaning against* YANK, *whose arm is about her waist.* PAUL *comes out last carrying an accordion.*

He staggers over and stands on top of the hatch, his instrument under his arm.]

DRISCOLL. Play us a dance, ye square-head swab!—a rale, Godforsaken son av a turkey trot wid guts to ut.

YANK. Straight from the old Barbary Coast in Frisco!

PAUL. I don' know. I try. [*He commences tuning up.*]

YANK. Ataboy! Let 'er rip! [DAVIS *and* VIOLET *come back and join the crowd.* THE DONKEYMAN *looks on them all with a detached, indulgent air.* SMITTY *stares before him and does not seem to know there is any one on deck but himself.*]

BIG FRANK. Dance? I don't dance. I trink! [*He suits the action to the word and roars with meaningless laughter.*]

DRISCOLL. Git out av the way thin, ye big hulk, an' give us some room. [BIG FRANK *sits down on the hatch, right. All of the others who are not going to dance either follow his example or lean against the port bulwark.*]

BELLA [*on the verge of tears at her inability to keep them in the forecastle or make them be quiet now they are out*]. For Gawd's sake, boys, don't shout so loud! Want to git me in trouble?

DRISCOLL [*grabbing her*]. Dance wid me, me cannibal quane. [*Some one drops a bottle on deck and it smashes.*]

BELLA [*hysterically*]. There they goes! There they goes! Captain'll hear that! Oh, my Lawd!

DRISCOLL. Be damned to him! Here's the music! Off ye go! [PAUL *starts playing "You Great Big Beautiful Doll" with a note left out every now and then. The four couples commence dancing—a jerk-shouldered version of the old Turkey Trot as it was done in the sailor-town dives, made more grotesque by the fact that all the couples are drunk and keep lurching into each other every moment. Two of the men start dancing together, intentionally bumping into the others.* YANK *and* PEARL *come around in front of*

SMITTY *and, as they pass him,* PEARL *slaps him across the side of the face with all her might, and laughs viciously. He jumps to his feet with his fists clenched but sees who hit him and sits down again smiling bitterly.* YANK *laughs boisterously.*]

YANK. Wow! Some wallop! One on you, Duke.

DRISCOLL [*hurling his cap at* PAUL]. Faster, ye toad! [PAUL *makes frantic efforts to speed up and the music suffers in the process.*]

BELLA [*puffing*]. Let me go. I'm wore out with you steppin' on my toes, you clumsy Mick. [*She struggles but* DRISCOLL *holds her tight.*]

DRISCOLL. God blarst you for havin' such big feet, thin. Aisy, aisy, Mrs. Old Black Joe! 'Tis dancin'll take the blubber off ye. [*He whirls her around the deck by main force.* COCKY, *with* SUSIE, *is dancing near the hatch, right, when* PADDY, *who is sitting on the edge with* BIG FRANK, *sticks his foot out and the wavering couple stumble over it and fall flat on the deck. A roar of laughter goes up.* COCKY *rises to his feet, his face livid with rage, and springs at* PADDY, *who promptly knocks him down.* DRISCOLL *hits* PADDY *and* BIG FRANK *hits* DRISCOLL. *In a flash a wholesale fight has broken out and the deck is a surging crowd of drink-maddened men hitting out at each other indiscriminately, although the general idea seems to be a battle between seamen and firemen. The women shriek and take refuge on top of the hatch, where they huddle in a frightened group. Finally there is the flash of a knife held high in the moonlight and a loud yell of pain.*]

DAVIS [*somewhere in the crowd*]. Here's the Mate comin'! Let's git out o' this! [*There is a general rush for the forecastle. In a moment there is no one left on deck but the little group of women on the hatch;* SMITTY, *still dazedly rubbing his cheek;* THE DONKEYMAN *quietly smoking on his stool; and* YANK *and* DRISCOLL, *their faces battered up considerably, their*

undershirts in shreds, bending over the still form of
PADDY, *which lies stretched out on the deck between*
them. In the silence the mournful chant from the
shore creeps slowly out to the ship.]

DRISCOLL [*quickly—in a low voice*]. Who knoifed him?

YANK [*stupidly*]. I didn't see it. How do I know? Cocky,
I'll bet. [*The* FIRST MATE *enters from the left. He is*
a tall, strongly-built man dressed in a plain blue uni-
form.]

THE MATE [*angrily*]. What's all this noise about? [*He*
sees the man lying on the deck.] Hello! What's this?
[*He bends down on one knee beside* PADDY.]

DRISCOLL [*stammering*]. All av us—was in a bit av a
harmless foight, sir,—an'—I dunno— [*The* MATE
rolls PADDY *over and sees a knife wound on his*
shoulder.]

THE MATE. Knifed, by God. [*He takes an electric flash*
from his pocket and examines the cut.] Lucky it's
only a flesh wound. He must have hit his head on
deck when he fell. That's what knocked him out.
This is only a scratch. Take him aft and I'll bandage
him up.

DRISCOLL. Yis, sor. [*They take* PADDY *by the shoulders*
and feet and carry him off left. The MATE *looks up*
and sees the women on the hatch for the first time.]

THE MATE [*surprised*]. Hello! [*He walks over to them.*]
Go to the cabin and get your money and clear off.
If I had my way, you'd never— [*His foot hits a*
bottle. He stoops down and picks it up and smells of
it.] Rum, by God! So that's the trouble! I thought
their breaths smelled damn queer. [*To the women,*
harshly.] You needn't go to the skipper for any
money. You won't get any. That'll teach you to
smuggle rum on a ship and start a riot.

BELLA. But, Mister—

THE MATE [*sternly*]. You know the agreement—rum—no
money.

BELLA [*indignantly*]. Honest to Gawd, Mister, I never brung no—

THE MATE [*fiercely*]. You're a liar! And none of your lip or I'll make a complaint ashore tomorrow and have you locked up.

BELLA [*subdued*]. Please, Mister—

THE MATE. Clear out of this, now! Not another word out of you! Tumble over the side damn quick! The two others are waiting for you. Hop, now! [*They walk quickly—almost run—off to the left.* THE MATE *follows them, nodding to* THE DONKEYMAN, *and ignoring the oblivious* SMITTY.]

[*There is absolute silence on the ship for a few moments. The melancholy song of the Negroes drifts crooning over the water.* SMITTY *listens to it intently for a time; then sighs heavily, a sigh that is half a sob.*]

SMITTY. God! [*He drinks the last drop in the bottle and throws it behind him on the hatch.*]

THE DONKEYMAN [*spitting tranquilly*]. More mem'ries? [SMITTY *does not answer him. The ship's bell tolls four bells.* THE DONKEYMAN *knocks out his pipe.*] I think I'll turn in. [*He opens the door to his cabin, but turns to look at* SMITTY—*kindly.*] You can't hear it in the fo'c's'tle—the music, I mean—an' there'll likely be more drink in there, too. Good night. [*He goes in and shuts the door.*]

SMITTY. Good night, Donk. [*He gets wearily to his feet and walks with bowed shoulders, staggering a bit, to the forecastle entrance and goes in. There is silence for a second or so, broken only by the haunted, saddened voice of that brooding music, faint and far-off, like the mood of the moonlight made audible.*]

[THE CURTAIN FALLS]

WHAT PRICE GLORY?

*by Maxwell Anderson
and Laurence Stallings*

*First production, September 3, 1924,
at the Plymouth Theatre, New York City,
with the following cast:*

CORPORAL GOWDY, *Brian Donlevy*
CORPORAL KIPER, *Fuller Mellish, Jr.*
CORPORAL LIPINSKY, *George Tobias*
FIRST SERGEANT QUIRT, *William Boyd*
CAPTAIN FLAGG, *Louis Wolheim*
CHARMAINE DE LA COGNAC, *Leyla Georgie*
PRIVATE LEWISOHN, *Sidney Elliott*
LIEUTENANT ALDRICH, *Fay Roppe*
LIEUTENANT MOORE, *Clyde North*
LIEUTENANT SCHMIDT, *Charles Costigan*
GUNNERY SERGEANT SOCKEL, *Henry G. Shelvey*
PRIVATE MULCAHY, *Jack MacGraw*
SERGEANT FERGUSON, *James A. Devine*
A BRIGADE RUNNER, *John J. Cavanaugh*
MONSIEUR PETE DE LA COGNAC, *Luis Alberni*
ANOTHER BRIGADE RUNNER, *Arthur Campbell*
BRIGADIER GEN. COKELEY, *Roy La Rue*
A COLONEL, *Keane Waters*
A CAPTAIN, *William B. Smith*
A LIEUTENANT, *Fred Brophy*
ANOTHER LIEUTENANT, *Thomas Buckley*
A CHAPLAIN, *John C. Davis*
TOWN MAYOR, *Alfred Renaud*
SPIKE, *Keane Waters*
A PHARMACIST'S MATE, *Thomas Sullivan*
LIEUTENANT CUNNINGHAM, *J. Merrill Holmes*
LIEUTENANT LUNDSTROM, *Robert Warner*

SCENES

ACT I *Company Headquarters in a French village in the
zone of advance.*
ACT II *A cellar in a disputed town.*
ACT III *The bar at Cognac Pete's.*

Act one

SCENE I

A room in a French farmhouse—now a U.S. Marine company headquarters. A couple of desks covered with maps and papers. Several scattered chairs. Three runners sit talking and smoking, very much at ease. LIPINSKY *is seated at one end of bench,* KIPER *at the other;* GOWDY *is sitting on a stool near* KIPER.

GOWDY. Well, where the hell did you come from?

KIPER. Who, me? I come from every place I've been to.

GOWDY. Yeah, well, where you been to?

KIPER. Me? I've been to China, Cuba, the Philippines, San Francisco, Buenos Ayres, Cape Town, Madagascar . . . wait a minute—Indiana, San Domingo, Tripoli, and Blackwell's Island.

LIPINSKY. Ever going home?

KIPER. Who, me? I can't go anywhere without going home.

GOWDY. By the time this war's over you ought to be pretty near ready to marry and settle down.

KIPER. There ain't going to be any after-this-war. Anyway, I got married after the last two wars and when I get through paying my debt to Lafayette, I'm through settling down. I never have settled down in so many hick towns in my life.

LIPINSKY. What became of them two broads?

KIPER. My wives?

LIPINSKY. Yeah.

KIPER. The first one never knew my last name, and when I left town she was out of luck.

GOWDY. And the next one?

KIPER. Ain't I signing the payroll for her every month? A twenty-dollar allotment, and she gives it to a fireman in Buffalo. Here I am saving democracy, and he's turning in a twenty-bell alarm the first of every month.

GOWDY. That's a waste of cash, the way I look at it. It stands to reason when a girl gets rid of one bozo she's looking for another. Now why does the late unlamented finance that little game? There's no justice in that.

KIPER. Who said it was justice? It ain't justice; it's alimony.

GOWDY. Well, alimony's all right if you're well fixed; hell, a girl ought to have some fun! I don't want a girl to quit living just because she ain't living with me, but the guy that's getting his ought to pay for it. What do you want to pay alimony for?

KIPER. What did you want to come to France for? It's the same reason why I pay alimony. So's to see the rest of the girls. Join the Marines and see the girls —from a porthole.

GOWDY. God! I came to France because I had a brainstorm one day and signed on the dotted line.

LIPINSKY. There ain't but one man in the world that came to France to see the mam'selles, and that's the skipper. When there's women around the skipper's got trick eyes like a horsefly.

KIPER. The old man? Say, he can't look at a mam'selle without blushing. Compared to me he's an amateur. He don't know the difference between a Hong-Kong honky-tonk and a Santo Domingo smoongy.

LIPINSKY. No, oh, no! I suppose women is an open book to you. You're damn well right—a code book.

KIPER. Yeah, you're damn well right. When I was in

Turkey with that landing party the Sultan had to hunt through his harem with a flashlight to find a decent-looking girl, and when I left China the Yangtse was full of the bodies of virgins that drowned their beautiful selves because I was shipping over. And when I was in Spain the king of Spain put an ad in the paper offering a reward for the return of the queen.

GOWDY. What did you do?

KIPER. Took her back for the reward.

LIPINSKY. Huh! I notice you've got Cognac Pete's daughter, too.

KIPER. If I had the skipper's uniform and his Sam Browne belt, I could take that little wench away from him before you could say squads right! You ain't never seen it done. The skip's full of wind.

GOWDY. Anyway, Flagg's got Pete's kid sewed up—and she's as pretty a little frog as ever made a dish of frog's legs.

KIPER. Pete's kid! The poor little tart! What could she do? Ain't the skipper billeted there? God! I guess even Lippy could make a kid if she slept on the other side of a paper wall.

LIPINSKY. God! I don't know. Ain't it the truth some guys just naturally walk away with women? Damned if I could ever do it!

KIPER. Take one good long look at yourself and you'll see why. There ain't many as unfortunate as you are. I guess there ain't anybody handicapped with features like them there.

LIPINSKY. Sometimes I think it's features, and sometimes I think it's luck. Once I spent three hundred dollars on a dame at Asbury Park in two days, and she keeping her damn chum with her all the time. Finally I got the extra one so drunk she couldn't tell her own name, and I ditched her. Then this broad I was trying to make insisted on riding on the merry-go-round. . . . God! the merry-go-round. Nothing else would satisfy her. She'd rung ducks till it rained ducks. She'd shot up more powder in shooting galleries than's been shot in this war, and she wanted to ride on the merry-go-round! So we got on the merry-go-round, and I threw her into a chariot and I piled on a horse. She hollers, "Whoopee, whoopee, let's do it again!" Jeez, I had spent three hundred bucks and I said, "Now, honey, let's not ride any more. Come on, let's do what you promised." She said she would after one more turn on the merry-go-round. So I, like a bloody fool, tries to save twenty cents by catching a brass ring. Son-of-a-bitch! I fall off and break my leg!

KIPER. My God!

LIPINSKY. Yes, sir. I broke my leg.

GOWDY. You certainly have had your share of tough luck.

LIPINSKY. So when the captain walks off with the top soldier's girl I say to myself, maybe there's luck in it. Maybe the breaks favored him. They never did favor me.

GOWDY. Any skipper can walk off with any top soldier's girl in my opinion. Say, maybe that's the lowdown on why the sergeant left.

KIPER. Naw—he was too damn good. Regimental took him. We'll probably get a lousy replacement. Probably get a corporal with ten years' experience chasing prisoners at Portsmouth. Soon's the new sergeant gets here the skip's going on ten days' leave.

LIPINSKY. Yeah? Where?

KIPER. Paris.

LIPINSKY. You going with him?

KIPER. Yep.

LIPINSKY. Some guys have all the luck.

[*The door opens,* SERGEANT QUIRT, *the very picture of an old-timer, enters and looks quickly around. All rise.*]

QUIRT. L. Company?

KIPER. Company Headquarters.

QUIRT. Where's the company commander?

KIPER. Just stepped down the street. Will be back soon.

QUIRT. He's going on leave?

KIPER. Right.

QUIRT. What's his name?

KIPER. Captain Flagg.

QUIRT. Whew!

KIPER. You know him?

QUIRT. Do you?

KIPER. Yes, sir!

QUIRT. Company Headquarters. Looks like a God damn reception room to me.

KIPER. We aim to please.

QUIRT. Yeah, to please yourself. Well, listen, I'm the new top soldier here. Who's the company clerk?

LIPINSKY. I am, sir.

QUIRT. Clear this jam out of here and let's have a look at what you're doing.

LIPINSKY. Will you get the hell out?—and don't come back till you're sent for. [KIPER *and* GOWDY *go out.*]

QUIRT. I've been ten kilometers west of you. Took the wrong turn.

LIPINSKY. Here's the map. That's the only road there is, and we can't use it. The damn thing is one long shell-hole from last May.

QUIRT. Jeez!

LIPINSKY. That's what they all say.

QUIRT. Don't you ever clean these galleys?

LIPINSKY. We don't do anything else.

QUIRT. You haven't got a police sergeant, I suppose?

LIPINSKY. We've got an acting corporal. Old Hennessey was bumped off last time up.

QUIRT. Spud Hennessey?

LIPINSKY. That's the soldier.

QUIRT. Tough for Spud to go. A grand soldier. Too damn finicky, though.

LIPINSKY. We've gone to hell for chow since he left.

QUIRT. That's queer. I never knew Flagg to let his men go to hell.

LIPINSKY. Not his fault. These cooks are no good. Hennessey was acting mess sergeant, too.

QUIRT. That's like old times.

LIPINSKY. Yeah?

QUIRT. Say, if the skipper's going ashore they'd better get him out of here before he gets too drunk to navigate. I've seen him shove off with a liberty party and spend a forty-eight-hour leave sleeping it off on the beach.

LIPINSKY. It's the same skip, all right. You know him.

QUIRT. I'll say I do . . . I think I'll look him up. Where's he likely to be?

LIPINSKY. Damned if I know. He might be at Pete's place. Anybody can tell you where that is—just this side of the river.

QUIRT. All right. I'll find it. [*Goes out briskly. After he has gone* LIPINSKY *goes to the door and whistles.* KIPER *and* GOWDY *come in.*]

LIPINSKY. Did you take a slant at the amphibian?

GOWDY. Yeah.

KIPER. What of it?

LIPINSKY. He's our new papa.

KIPER. So he says.

LIPINSKY. He's soldiered with the skipper before. Says he never saw the chief sober.

KIPER. Is he hard-boiled?

LIPINSKY. There's only one place in the world they boil them as hard as that, and that's the Tropic of Cancer.

KIPER. What does he know?

LIPINSKY. This God damn army's going to run right from now on or get off on its ear.

GOWDY. He must have used some language on you?

LIPINSKY. Not a word, and I'm not going to give him a chance, either.

KIPER. Scared, huh?

LIPINSKY. You meet a top with two glass eyes, a slit across his face for a mouth and a piece out of his ear, and you might just as well heave out and lash up. That bird could curse the hide off a whole Senegalese regiment.

[CAPTAIN FLAGG *enters and comes to chair above table. He is a fine, magnificently endowed man.*]

FLAGG. 'Tenshun! [*Reading report which he picks up from table.*] Where's that first sergeant?

KIPER. Went out looking for you, sir.

FLAGG. Scatter and find him, a couple of you. [LIPINSKY, GOWDY, *and* KIPER *start out.*] Stay here, Kiper. [KIPER *comes back.*] Damn him, why couldn't he sit still? [LIPINSKY *and* GOWDY *go out.*] What's he like?

KIPER. Tough.

FLAGG. Yeah? I hope he damn well hangs the whole damn company up by the thumbs. About time we had a little discipline around here.

KIPER. Yes, sir.

FLAGG. "Yes, sir!" "Yes, sir!" Shut your trap, will you?

KIPER. Oh, yes, sir.

FLAGG. Go to hell! Everything packed?

KIPER. Absolutely.

FLAGG. Bike working? Side-car trimmed?

KIPER. Tuned it up this morning.

FLAGG. Well, we're going ashore as soon as I see the new top soldier, you understand? And we don't stop for anything smaller than shell-holes!

KIPER. Ay, ay, sir!

FLAGG. Go sit down! Go read a book! You make me nervous. [KIPER *sits.* CHARMAINE *slips in. She is a drab.* FLAGG, *who is busy at the desk, does not see her at first. He looks up impatiently.*] Well, hello! hello! What are you doing here? You better run along back to your papa. Listen, *mon amie,* you better beat it back to *le père,* understand?

CHARMAINE. Why? [*She comes nearer.*]

FLAGG. Well, I'm busy.

CHARMAINE. You are going away.

FLAGG. So that's it. Kiper, did you tell the kid I was going away?

KIPER. No, sir, she saw me with your *musette* bag.

CHARMAINE. The sergeant went away. He is not coming back. Now you go away. You are not coming back.

FLAGG. As far as the sergeant's concerned, you're quite right, dearie; but as far as I'm concerned, you're dead wrong. The sergeant isn't coming back. We have a new sergeant, see? But I am coming back.

CHARMAINE. *Oui?*

FLAGG. *Oui, oui, oui!*

CHARMAINE. No. You are such a lovely liar. You don't want to make me cry. So you lie a little—*n'est-ce pas?*

FLAGG [*takes her by shoulders*]. I'm not lying, Charmaine. I don't know how I can prove it to you, but I'm telling the solemn truth. [*A knock on the door.*] See who that is, and keep him out, whoever it is.

KIPER [*opens the door, goes out, and returns*]. It's Lewisohn, third platoon replacement. He wants permission to speak with you, sir.

FLAGG. What about?

KIPER. Lost something, sir.

FLAGG. Let him in. [LEWISOHN *enters. He is a pale little boy.*] Let's have it quick, soldier.

LEWISOHN [*saluting*]. Beg pardon, sir. [*Very much scared.*]

FLAGG. What do you want?

LEWISOHN. The truth is, sir, I've lost my identification tag.

FLAGG. What? What? Lost what?

LEWISOHN. My identification tag.

FLAGG. Well, I thought I'd been around a good deal, and I've had 'em ask me to show 'em where they live and button up their pants for them and put on their little night-drawers, but I'm a son-of-a-gun if this isn't the first time anybody has ever asked me to help him find his identification tag!

LEWISOHN. Sorry, sir. I—I thought it was—I. . . .

FLAGG. What did you think?

LEWISOHN. I thought it was important, sir.

FLAGG. And what, may I ask, made you think it was important?

LEWISOHN. In case I was—ah—hit, sir. They wouldn't know who I was. I thought maybe it would matter.

FLAGG. Matter?—to whom?

LEWISOHN. Well—to keep the records—or to my folks.

FLAGG. Listen, boy, why did you ever leave your home and come over here?

LEWISOHN. Why, to fight, sir.

FLAGG. Yeah. Well, you'll get a chance, don't you worry, and for God's sake learn to act like a man. Never mind your identification tag. If you want to know what your name is look in your hat.

LEWISOHN. Yes, sir.

FLAGG. By the way, what is your name?

LEWISOHN. Louis Lewisohn.

FLAGG [*to* KIPER]. Make a note of that, Kiper. [KIPER *makes a note in the book he carries in his pocket.*] Now, anything else? Hope you got a good room with a view and running water and everything.

LEWISOHN. No, sir. [*Swallowing a lump in his throat.*]

FLAGG. No? I'm surprised. Well, go on outside and swear at me a while. It'll do you good, and that's what I'm here for. I'm here to keep you in hot water till you're hard-boiled. See? You can go.

LEWISOHN. Yes, sir. [*He salutes and goes.*]

FLAGG. Make a note of that, Kiper, and get him a new tag if they have to build a new factory in Hoboken to turn it out. The God-forsaken fool's dying of grief away from mother. Got it?

KIPER. Yes, Captain Flagg.

FLAGG. Then step outside and guard the door a minute. [KIPER *salutes and goes out, closing the door carefully.* FLAGG *then turns to* CHARMAINE.] Now, you little she-woman, what do you want?

CHARMAINE. You are going away.

FLAGG. Damn it, I'm not going away. I'm going to Paris
—coming back in eight days. Eight days in Paris, see,
then I come back.

CHARMAINE. The sergeant did not come back.

FLAGG. My God, child, get this! The sergeant is not
coming back. I am coming back. We have a new
sergeant, see?

CHARMAINE. *Oui?*

FLAGG. *Oui, oui.*

CHARMAINE. No. I think the captain does not love me,
not any more?

FLAGG. Girlie, I love you fit to kill. I love you no end,
same as always. Come here. [*She puts her arms
around his neck.* FLAGG *takes her in his arms.*] You're
as sweet as Burgundy, and you've got a kick like
triple sec. Sure I love you. Everybody loves you. I
love you, dearie girl, but I don't trust you.

CHARMAINE. You take me to Paris? Yes? Take me to
Paris?

FLAGG. No. I guess not.

CHARMAINE. But I'm so unhappy when you go away.

FLAGG. Yes, you are! I wish you were. Why, you little
Geisha. [*Chucking her under the chin.*] If I didn't
wear captain's stripes you wouldn't know me from
the K.P.'s.

CHARMAINE. No, dear Captain Flagg. [*Her arms on his
shoulders. She runs a hand through his hair.*] It is
true, I shall be so lonesome. I shall be all alone at
the inn, crying every day to break your heart.

FLAGG. You'll be dancing all night and flirting all day
with the Y.M.C.A. boys, you mean. Ain't it so?

CHARMAINE. *Oui.* But you could take me. I can't be
good—unless you take me. I want to be good for you.
We could have so good time—in Paris.

FLAGG. No, I can't take you. But listen. [*Takes hold of
her shoulders.*] While I'm gone you wait for me. Re-

member, you're my girl, see? Just my girl, and you wait for me, see?

CHARMAINE. *Oui*, I will.

FLAGG. And listen to this. [*Putting her away.*] If I find out you've been running with some one else, I'll break you in two, see? [*He makes the motion of breaking something.*] Now, will you be good while I'm gone?

CHARMAINE [*coming into his arms*]. *Oui, monsieur.*

FLAGG. That's better. You know what I mean?

CHARMAINE. *Oui.*

FLAGG. That's right, little kitten, purr. . . . And remember, I don't trust you any further than I can see you. Now run along. [FLAGG *turns to table, but* CHARMAINE *follows him.*]

CHARMAINE. But you will take me to Paris?

FLAGG [*seating himself on edge of table, he beckons her with his finger and takes her on his knee, between his legs*]. You ever been to Paris?

CHARMAINE. *Non* . . .

FLAGG. Well, there's a river in Paris.

CHARMAINE. *La Seine.*

FLAGG. Yeah, the Seine. That's where they drown little girls like you. Every time the police catch a little girl in Paris, they drown her in the Seine. You can't go there. They'd drown you.

CHARMAINE. It is not true.

FLAGG. It is true. I'll tell you another thing. There's nothing to eat in Paris, no food but horses; no wine, only water. No young girls, only old women. Some of the girls they drown in the Seine; some they make into sausages for the generals. Paris is full of generals that won't eat anything but young girls. You can't go to Paris.

CHARMAINE. You are full of lovely lies. Oh, it is not true.

FLAGG. Uh, you don't know Paris.

CHARMAINE. Oh, but I know these captains and ser-

geants! They do not ever put anything, what you
say, past me. But, oh, I love you for a lovely liar!
[*Embraces him.*] And I will be good; I will, *vraiment!*

FLAGG. That's a good girl. Now you go back to Papa
Pete's. Stay home nights. Wait for Captain Flagg.
Kiss me good-bye. [*She kisses him.*] Now run along.
[*She goes.*] Kiper!

KIPER [*coming in*]. Yes, sir.

FLAGG. Have you found that sergeant yet?

KIPER. He's coming with Lipinsky, sir.

FLAGG. Tell him to damn well get a wiggle on.

KIPER [*to* QUIRT, *outside*]. He's waiting for you, sir.
[LIPINSKY *enters with* QUIRT.]

QUIRT [*saluting*]. Captain Flagg?

FLAGG [*returning salute and remains seated, not even
glancing at* QUIRT]. Hello, Sergeant. Where've you
been all day?

QUIRT. Ten kilometers west by mistake.

FLAGG. Do you know our lay-out?

QUIRT. I've got a general idea.

FLAGG. What kind of a hole were you in over there?

QUIRT. Much the same as yours, only we had a road.

FLAGG. Do you think you can handle this company? It's
a rough crowd of old men and little baa-lamb re-
cruits. [*He still does not look up.*]

QUIRT. It's an army, ain't it? Sure.

FLAGG. I damn well hope you can. We're in a devilish
sector here, and it's going to be worse when we move
up again. We just hold half a town; the Heinies hold
the other half. It rains grenades most of the time.
About half our men are green replacements. They
damned near ruined us in that last tour of duty.
You'll have to whip some of 'em into shape before
we go up. Close order drill is best.

QUIRT. Half of 'em raw?

FLAGG. Over half.

QUIRT. Well, I've seen worse.

FLAGG. Now, I'm going on leave, you see. Eight days.

While I'm gone you feed 'em up and give 'em hell.
Teach 'em where they are. Make 'em so bad they'll
eat steel rather than get another dressing from you.
Make 'em hard, but don't break 'em. Give 'em eats
and about eight hours of drill and guns a day.
They're mostly Bible Class boys, and God knows
most of 'em haven't got long to live.

QUIRT [*takes step toward table*]. Cut the comedy, Captain. You must know me.

FLAGG [*rising, looks at* QUIRT *for the first time*]. Yeah?
I'm a cuckoo if it ain't the old Hoppergrass!

QUIRT. Thought you didn't know me. Well, I'm glad
to meet you again, Captain Flagg.

FLAGG. Kiper—

KIPER. Yes, sir.

FLAGG. Step out and tell all platoon commanders to report here at once.

KIPER. Ay, ay, sir. [*Exits.*]

FLAGG. Well, Quirt, I'm glad to see you, because if there
was ever a good soldier needed I need one here, and
you're as good as there is; but I'm damned if I take
any particular joy in meeting you again. You've been
poison to me everywhere I've served with you.

QUIRT [*at right of table*]. Same to you, I'm sure, and
many of 'em. Personally I'd as soon meet a skunk in
a dugout, and officially I don't think much of your
crew. I broke you the first time in China, and you
broke me in Cuba. You're in a position to break
me now, and if you didn't need me worse than the
wildcat needed what he didn't have, you'd break
me again.

FLAGG. I'd see you in hell before I'd break you, and
you know it. I'll give you exactly what you deserve,
and as long as you're straight we'll get along, always
providing we don't have to shake hands. If that's
understood, why, take hold. The company's yours.

QUIRT. Well, before I take hold, let me get one more
remark in the record. I wish to God I could jump

your damn gang. I've heard of it all along the line.
You've got a rabble, and I know it. I saw it coming
into Is-sur-Tille once when you didn't see me. A
shambling bunch of hams that wouldn't salute anything under a general.

FLAGG. All right, and what's my outfit's rating at regimental?

QUIRT. Oh, I got to hand it to you. You can hypnotize
'em. They'd start out to cut their way to Berlin if you
gave the word. But, my God, they ain't much to
look at, Captain Flagg.

FLAGG. Well, teach 'em to salute if it'll make you feel
any happier, Hoppergrass. And before the platoon
commanders get here, there's one thing I'd like to
ask you. What did you do with the little girl?

QUIRT. What little girl?

FLAGG. You damn well know what little girl.

QUIRT. It's a small world, Captain Flagg, but the number of soldiers' sluts is numerous.

FLAGG. I was a corporal under you in China. You broke
me to get her.

QUIRT. You were a damn fool. You'd have married her
if it hadn't been for me, and be running a laundry
now with the seat of your pants hanging down between your knees.

FLAGG. What happened to her?

QUIRT. What happened to the battleship *Maine?*

FLAGG. My God. . . .

QUIRT. I broke you in China. I admit I broke you for
that little Chink. And when I served under you in
Cuba you got even. That's why I'm still a sergeant.
[*A knock at the door from* KIPER.] Let it go at that.

FLAGG. Kiper?

KIPER [*outside*]. Ay, ay, sir!

FLAGG. Bring 'em in. [KIPER *opens the door and follows
into the room* LIEUTENANTS ALDRICH, MOORE, *and*
SCHMIDT, *and* GUNNERY SERGEANT SOCKEL. *They salute.
They line up.*] Gentlemen, this is First Sergeant

Quirt, who is in charge. This is Lieutenant Aldrich; this is Lieutenant Moore, and this is Lieutenant Schmidt, and you'll remember Sockel from Cuba. He's commanding the fourth platoon.

QUIRT [*turns to* SOCKEL]. Hello, Joe. How's tricks?

SOCKEL. Pretty good. How's yourself.

[*They smile broadly, two old-timers among green lieutenants.*]

QUIRT. Ticking like a clock.

FLAGG. Aldrich, you're senior here, aren't you?

ALDRICH. Yes, sir. Two days ahead of the others.

FLAGG. You'll be in command here. Ask Quirt for any advice you need. I'll be back Wednesday week. . . . Now, men, Sergeant Quirt here is one of the best God damn soldiers that ever destroyed a memorandum receipt. I've soldiered with him around the world, and there isn't a finer, cleaner, smarter Marine afloat than Quirt—when he's sober. As long as he's sober, he'll run this outfit—whether I'm here or absent; but Quirt loves the bottle; and when he's drunk he's the lousiest, filthiest bum that ever wore a uniform. When drunk, he's worse than I am, and you know damn well I don't allow anybody to get as bad as that. If he tanks up I'll break him. I've broken him once, and he knows I'll do it again. The first raw crack he makes will find him drilling in the rear rank of Sockel's platoon, drilling like a tramp with a broom for a rifle. Get that, Aldrich; the first time you find him down in the square with a face in the dirt in front of all these young nipple-nursers, you lock him up and keep him locked up till I return.

ALDRICH. Yes, sir.

FLAGG. Give him his head, and let him have anything he wants, and don't forget he's forgotten more about being a soldier than any of you college boys will ever know. But if you're wise you won't play cards with him, and before you lend him any money you'd bet-

ter kiss it a last long farewell. That's all. Kiper, have
you got the waterproofs in that side-car?

KIPER. Ay, ay, sir.

FLAGG. Give her a spin, and we'll shove off. [*Picks up
cap and stick from table and goes out, followed
by all save* QUIRT. *Off stage, the motorcycle clatters. The* LIEUTENANTS *shout farewell.* QUIRT *goes
up to right window, looks out, and then sits at table,
takes out dice, and practices a few turns. He holds
the dice up to his eyes and then spins.* QUIRT *whistles
"Pretty Baby."*]

QUIRT. Seven, baby. [*He smiles with satisfaction.*] Look
at those acrobats act. You got to treat the old man
right, now. [*There is a light tap on the door to left.*
QUIRT *puts dice in pocket and looks at map.*] Come
in.

[CHARMAINE *enters.*]

CHARMAINE. *Le capitaine—il est parti?*

QUIRT. Just left. Don't cry, little one.

CHARMAINE. *Le nouveau sergeant. N'est-ce pas?*

QUIRT. *N'est-ce pas* is right.

CHARMAINE. I wanted to see the captain.

QUIRT. Just too late, sorry to say. [*Looks at her for first
time.*] You one piecie captain's fella boy? You captain's fella?

CHARMAINE. *Le capitaine? Mais non!*

QUIRT. I'll bet it's *mais non.* Say, ain't you Cognac
Pete's daughter?

CHARMAINE. *Oui.* You stay at Pete's?

QUIRT. Sure. [*Pause.*] *Et vous?*

CHARMAINE. *C'est mon père.*

QUIRT. Uh-huh. I thought so. [*Rises; crosses to her.*]
Well, baby, you better stick to me, and you'll have
another papa.

[*A terrific commotion begins outside. A vociferous
Irish voice is heard shouting over and over again,
"I'll get that lousy German son-of-a-bitch, I'll get the*

German bastard," while LIPINSKY *and* GOWDY *yell,*
"Cut it out, you loafer. Dry up, dry up or you'll get
yours." LIPINSKY *opens the door.* CHARMAINE *steps*
back. The shouting is audible only when door is
open.]

LIPINSKY. Sergeant, there's a drunken Mick named Mulcahy raising hell outside. Can't do a thing with him.
Got blood in his eyes for a guy from Cincinnati.

QUIRT [*sternly out of the corner of his mouth, not looking at him*]. Tell him to pipe down. [LIPINSKY *goes
out. Door closes; shouting stops.* CHARMAINE *goes toward door.*] Better not go out there now, honey.
Some rough language is taking place out there.

[LIPINSKY *re-enters. Shouting is started again.*]

LIPINSKY. Sergeant, the Mick's sitting on Gowdy, and
I can't pull him off.

QUIRT [*quietly, as before*]. Tell him to pipe down. [LI-
PINSKY *goes out. Shouting stops.* QUIRT *crosses to*
CHARMAINE.] You going to promenade *avec moi* to-
night? Down by the canal? Under the lime trees?

CHARMAINE. No. [*She is trembling.*]

QUIRT. No? Captain's own private darling, huh? Say,
you're a damned pretty frog. For a frog, I don't know
as I ever saw a prettier.

[*The hullabaloo redoubles outside.* LIPINSKY *comes in
again.*]

LIPINSKY. Shall we lock him up, Sergeant?

QUIRT. Drag him in. [LIPINSKY *and* GOWDY *drag in a
huge, red-faced Irishman and stand him groggily on
his feet below* QUIRT.]

MULCAHY. That damn Nussbaum from Cincinnati is a
German spy, and I'll have his guts out of him before
I'm through.

QUIRT [*quietly*]. Mulcahy, pipe down.

MULCAHY. I tell you that Nussbaum is a German spy!
I'll get the lousy German and every German out of
Cincinnati. . . . [*The* SERGEANT *plants one squarely*

on MULCAHY's *jaw. He goes down like a log.*]
QUIRT [*still out of the corner of his mouth*]. Drag him
out.
[LIPINSKY *and* GOWDY *take him by arms, turn him
around, and drag him out.* QUIRT, *rubbing his knuck-
les, crosses back of table to* CHARMAINE, *who is smiling at her wonderful hero with the powerful punch.*]
QUIRT. Why, hello, Pittsburgh, you love me?
[*They embrace and hold a long kiss.*]

CURTAIN

SCENE II

*Late afternoon, eight days later. The scene is un-
changed.* LIPINSKY *is lying along bench, smoking a cigarette and trying to sleep at the same time.* KIPER
enters, singing at the top of his voice. LIPINSKY's *cap is
down over his eyes.* POLICE SERGEANT FERGUSON *is at
table toward back, working over papers; he is smoking
a pipe.*

KIPER. "Mademoiselle from Armentiere, parlez-vous?
Mademoiselle from Armentiere, parlez vous?
Mademoiselle from Armentiere—"
Hullo, hullo—Jeezus. [*Puts musette bags in corner.*]
LIPINSKY. Knock off that chat. [*On bench; doesn't
move.*]
KIPER. Say, are you running this God damn army?
LIPINSKY. You're damn well right, I'm running this
army.
KIPER. Well, you had better God damn well snap out
of it. You're relieved.
LIPINSKY [*sitting up*]. Skipper come back?
KIPER. Almost. He's at the Last Chance.
LIPINSKY. Still soaked?

KIPER. He ain't soaked. He's just the drunkest bum you ever saw in your life.

LIPINSKY. Trying to whip the world?

KIPER. Naw, just quiet drunk. Looks out of those eyes of his like two red holes in the snow.

LIPINSKY. How's Paris?

KIPER. Never got that far. Washed ashore at Bar-le-Duc.

LIPINSKY. Yeah? Good time?

KIPER. Pretty good the first day.

LIPINSKY. What'd you do the rest?

KIPER. You see, it was this way. The skip and me was promenading, and he was swinging that damn little Pekin swagger-stick of his when up comes an M.P. "Sorry, sir," says the M.P.; "Corps commander's regulations, sir, no swagger-sticks." The skip says, "Well, and who, may I ask, is the corps commander? Tell him he can take his lousy army and sell it for cheese." "Sorry, sir," says the M.P. "Corps commander's regulations, sir, and I'll have to take that stick away from you." "All right," says the skip, whirling the stick around his head, "pitch in, soldier, pitch in!"

LIPINSKY. Did he take it away?

KIPER. Aw, take it away! Listen to the poor nut. I spent the next six days of my leave detained as a material witness for attempted manslaughter.

LIPINSKY. I guess the skip didn't draw much.

KIPER. Draw hell! Didn't I swear this yellow-bellied M.P. came up and knocked him into the road?

LIPINSKY. Yeah?

KIPER. And the court looks at this M.P. and says, "Right face! Take him away and give him ten days, bread and water."

LIPINSKY. Serve him right, the Boy Scout! They ought to take away those guys' whistles before they blow themselves to death. And speaking of whistles, this new top of our's don't do nothing else at all besides blow a whistle. It's been one bloody formation after another ever since you left.

KIPER. Is that the kind of hombre he is?

LIPINSKY. He's a sea-going son-of-a-bitch. He ain't sit down since he was here. He's got the first platoon down in the village now taking up the dirt from the courtyard with teaspoons. You can't get in the chow line until you catch twenty horse-flies. He seen Cooper pulling a fag at reveille this morning. What's Cooper doing now? Boy, following the ponies, following the ponies. *He's* out collecting apples.

KIPER. Well, the skip will make him cut that stuff. Me and the skip ain't going to see the little boys bullied.

LIPINSKY. You and the skip, yeah. But say, the skip and this top soldier are going to tangle pant-legs over another little matter before they have been together one day.

KIPER. What t'hell!

LIPINSKY. This horny pelican is going aboard the skip's old hooker every night.

KIPER. Down at Cognac Pete's house?

LIPINSKY. Parking his dogs in Pete's kitchen every night with that little black-eyed frog sitting in his lap lighting his pipe.

KIPER. If the skip finds that out there'll be a noise like you'd throw a tomcat in a dog-pound.

[*Enter* SERGEANT QUIRT.]

QUIRT [*to* KIPER]. Where's Captain Flagg?

KIPER. Last Chance.

QUIRT. What the hell do you mean, coming in here without him? What do you think you're paid for?

KIPER. I tried to argue with him, Sergeant, and he picked me up and threw me out the window. Lucky for me it was open.

QUIRT. Go get him. Don't argue. Get him. Take Lippy along.

[LIPINSKY *and* KIPER *start, hesitate, and talk.* QUIRT *starts toward chair above table.* LIEUTENANT ALDRICH *enters.*]

ALDRICH. Heard the skipper was aboard.

QUIRT [*turning to* ALDRICH]. Grounded on the last bar.

ALDRICH. Yeah?

QUIRT [*to* KIPER *and* LIPINSKY, *who hurry off*]. Cast off, will you? Travel! Hit the deck! [*To* ALDRICH.] Sending out a salvage party. He's full to the scuppers.

ALDRICH. All I hope is he comes in mild and goes to sleep. He's got too damn much talent for raising hell to suit me.

QUIRT. You ought to seen him in China. Straight as a mast, muscled like a gorilla, Christian as hell. Good deal of liquor has flowed under his belt since then.

ALDRICH. Expect any trouble?

QUIRT. What do you mean?

ALDRICH. This here now little wild woman.

QUIRT. I don't know what's your game.

ALDRICH. Oh, all right! Just the same, you'd be a damn sight wiser to lay off, in my opinion.

QUIRT. Lay off what?

ALDRICH. Charmaine.

QUIRT [*turning to* ALDRICH]. Are you thinking of making this a three-handed game?

ALDRICH. I am not.

QUIRT. Because if you are, all I got to say is, help yourself to whatever you can get. It's love in a manner of speaking, and it's certainly war. Everything dirty goes.

ALDRICH. Suit yourself. You've known him longer than I have.

QUIRT. He's got a grudge against me, I don't mind telling you. And I ain't wasting any ardent affection on him. If it hadn't been for him, I'd had a company of my own. I didn't know she was his meat when I first saw her. But when I found out, d'you think I'd apologize and back out the door out of deference to him? I says, Kippy-dope, you're mine!

ALDRICH. Yeah—but do you know what I heard at mess to-day?

QUIRT. Nope.

ALDRICH. Well, now listen. I didn't intend to mix into this unless it was necessary, but Schmidt got it straight yesterday that old Cognac Pete was going to prosecute some soldier or other for corrupting Charmaine's morals.

QUIRT. Charmaine's what? Jeez, that's good!

ALDRICH. Maybe so. Just the same, he's got a case.

QUIRT. He has not.

ALDRICH. No? Suppose he gets you before a court martial? It's a hanging matter if he wants to push it. You know the regulations.

QUIRT. You mean he's after me?

ALDRICH. I don't know who he's after. You—or Flagg. Has Cognac anything on you?

QUIRT. Well, they might hang me once as a sort of lesson to me.

[*Motorcycle clatters outside.*]

ALDRICH. Well, there you are. Suppose he takes it to headquarters? Where's Quirt then? Sitting pretty?

QUIRT. Well, I just resign all rights and interests in the mam'selle and avoid possible complications.

ALDRICH. Fine. There's Kiper already. If Flagg's with him, for God's sake use a little diplomacy.

[*Outside,* FLAGG *in drunken voice says, "Get out of my way, Kiper." Noise of* KIPER *being pushed.*]

QUIRT. Diplomacy, with that?

[FLAGG *enters, coat in hand and hair mussed. He still carries stick.* LIPINSKY *and* KIPER *follow. All stand at attention until the* CAPTAIN *is seated.*]

ALDRICH [*saluting*]. How are you, Captain Flagg?

FLAGG. I'm a wreck, that's what I am! I'm an epoch-making disaster! You see before you, Mr. Aldrich, one of the seven great calamities of the world!

QUIRT. Hope you had a pleasant leave, sir.

FLAGG. Well, I didn't. Held for carrying a stick. Picked up the second day by one of Pershing's Sunday-School teachers. By God, he must think he's running a day nursery! . . . What's happened?

QUIRT. Not a thing.

FLAGG. Boys in shape?

QUIRT. They'll do. Three more days, and I'd risk them on the line.

FLAGG. Try and get three days. If we aren't digging in somewhere before then, I'll pay the Russian national debt out of my salary. How much do you think I spent in Bar-le-Duc?

QUIRT. How much did you have?

FLAGG. Eight hundred francs, and I got a chance to get rid of thirty. Here's the whole roll. Does anybody want it? Just my luck to have to move in again with seven hundred and seventy francs on me and get bumped off. [*A knock at the door by* BRIGADE RUNNER.] Come in.

[*A* BRIGADE RUNNER *enters.*]

THE RUNNER. Captain Flagg?

FLAGG. Right here.

THE RUNNER. From Captain Simpson, sir. He wanted you to know the "G One" crowd is on the way over.

FLAGG. Tell him I'm much obliged. Anything else?

THE RUNNER. That's all. How do I get to the Twelfth?

FLAGG. Show him, Kiper. [KIPER *and* THE RUNNER *salute and go out.* FLAGG *starts to button his coat.*] Damn headquarters! It's some more of that world-safe-for-democracy slush! Every time they come around here I've got to ask myself is this an army or is it a stinking theosophical society for ethical culture and the Bible-backing uplift! I don't want that band of Gideons from headquarters. Now you watch that door. Watch it! In ten minutes we're going to have another of these round-headed gentlemen of the old school here giving us a prepared lecture on what we're fighting the war for and how we're to do it— one of these bill-poster chocolate soldiers with decorations running clear around to his backbone and a thrilling speech on army morale and the last drop of fighting blood that puts your drive over to glorious victory! . . . The side-whiskered butter-eaters! I'd like to rub their noses in a few of the latrines I've slept in, keeping up army morale and losing·men because some screaming fool back in the New Jersey sector thinks he's playing with paper dolls. [*A knock.*] Well, come in, come in. [LIEUTENANT MOORE *enters.*] Hello.

MOORE. How are you, Captain Flagg? Hope you liked Bar-le-Duc?

FLAGG. Ever been there?

MOORE. Once.

FLAGG. Ever put in much time in the re-decorated chicken stable where they detain the A.W.O.L.'s?

MOORE. Afraid I never saw it, sir.

FLAGG. Well, you haven't missed a great deal. They whitewashed the damn shanty right over the hen manure. Phew! I can smell it yet. If I'd stayed there another day I'd have laid an egg.

MOORE. Tough luck! But what I really wanted to say, sir, was there's an old fellow outside here who wants to see you about his daughter. He seems to think somebody's taken advantage of her.

FLAGG. Somebody in this outfit?

MOORE. Yes, sir.

FLAGG. Took advantage of the girl, huh?

MOORE. That's what he says.

FLAGG. He means she took advantage of her opportunities and now he's taking advantage of his. What's the old boy's name?

MOORE. Can't quite make it out, but it seems to be Pete something or other. Are there any Pete's in France? Sounded like Cognac Pete.

FLAGG. Yeah?

MOORE. Sounded like it.

FLAGG [*rising, perturbed*]. Well, wait a minute. Cognac Pete's, huh? Is the girl with him?

MOORE. No.

FLAGG. Hell!

QUIRT. Think fast, Captain. Think fast.

FLAGG. Quirt, do you know anything about this?

QUIRT [*starting to leave*]. Not a thing.

FLAGG. You leaving us?

QUIRT [*unembarrassed*]. A few orders to make out, sir. [*He grins.*] Can't very well work here, you see.

FLAGG. I'm damned if I see. Sit down and spill your ink. And if you've put up a game on me, you crawling crab. . . .

QUIRT. Me? What have I got to do with it? Think fast, Captain, think fast.

FLAGG. Damn it, send him in, and we'll see. [MOORE *goes out.*] Hell!

QUIRT [*laughing*]. Think fast, Captain. Don't forget to think fast.

FLAGG. You sit where you are, you hyena; and laugh, damn you, laugh. [*Enter* COGNAC PETE, *an ancient nut-brown Frenchman, very polite and humble, followed by* MOORE *and* KIPER. MOORE *and* PETE *stand by the table.* KIPER *sits on bench.*] Pete, what's this I hear about a complaint? What's the matter, huh? One of my men, huh?

PETE. *Oui, mon capitaine.*

FLAGG. I'm damned if I can leave this damn army half a day without hell breaking loose somewhere. Come on, let's have it; spit it out.

MOORE. Allay, Pete.

PETE [*speaking in an unintelligible rush of French*]. *Ah, monsieur le capitaine, je suis un vieillard; mais j'ai vécu heureusement, et mes enfants on été toujours honnêtes, mais hélas, mon capitaine, quelque chose de terrible vient de passer, une calamité monstrueuse.* . . .

FLAGG [*to* MOORE]. What's on the menu? Do you get anything out of that?

MOORE. He says something has happened.

FLAGG [*distressed*]. Does it take all that vocabulary to

say something has happened in French? Well, keep going, keep going.

MOORE. Allay, Pete.

PETE. *Mains, mon capitaine, voilà que les américains ar-rivent. Ils sont grands et forts, et ils demandent tou-jours ce qu'ils veulent. Ils ne s'accoutument pas à nos mœurs ni à nos habitudes, mais—nom de Dieu!— pourquoi choisissent—ils la seule fleur de ma vie, quand ils peuvent trouver n'importe où qu'ils vont des poules qui les desirent? Ma seule fleur, ma fleur Charmaine, ma fleur délicate!*

FLAGG. What language is he talking now?

MOORE. He says the soldiers take what they want, and they have trampled the one flower of his life.

FLAGG. Is that all he said?

MOORE. The rest is poetry.

FLAGG [*impatiently*]. Well, tell him to omit flowers, see, omit flowers.

MOORE [*to* PETE]. *Brèvement.*

PETE. *Ma fille. Ma fille bien-aimée. Elle est défleurée. Elle est dans la boue, elle est déshonorée.*

FLAGG [*to* MOORE]. More flowers?

MOORE. No, sir. He says his daughter's been—ah— ruined. [*Pause.*] . . . so to speak.

FLAGG. Ruined, huh? Rape or seduction?

MOORE [*to* PETE]. *C'est-elle soumise, ou l'a-t-on forcée?*

PETE. *Les américains sont si forts. Ils se forcent sur elle, ils ferment sa bouche de façon qu'elle ne peut don-ner l'alarme. Que peut faire la petite fille? L'améri-caine est forte, elle peut se défendre, mais la Fran-çaise, elle est gentille et modeste et craintive et ne sait se défendre.*

FLAGG [*to* MOORE]. Now what's all that?

MOORE. Rape, sir.

FLAGG. Does he allude to any specific girl, or is he speak-ing of French wenches in general?

MOORE [*to* PETE]. *Comment s'appelle ta fille?*

PETE. Charmaine.

MOORE. Charmaine, sir.

FLAGG [*very seriously*]. Look here, Moore. You know as well as I do, this same little baggage has been pretty free with me. What's the old boy's game? And for God's sake, what do you think you're up to, bringing him in here?

MOORE. You mean you're . . . God, I didn't know that!

FLAGG. You didn't! You must go around here wearing blinders. You see the fix you've got me in?

QUIRT. Think fast, Captain, think fast.

MOORE. To tell the truth, I got the impression it was somebody else. Honest to God, I thought he said it was a soldier. . . . [FLAGG *hesitates and then gives* MOORE *a quick look.* MOORE *is embarrassed.*] I wasn't sure, but I got that impression.

FLAGG. Did he name anybody?

MOORE. No.

FLAGG [*turning away*]. Well, damn her little soul. No, I know damn well it wasn't anybody else. [*Turns to* MOORE.] Ask him how much he wants.

MOORE. How much what?

FLAGG. Money, you highbrow, money! What else do you think he wants?

MOORE. I don't know, but if I thought he wanted money I certainly would not have listened to him.

FLAGG. You're just a bleating babe in the woods, you are. That's what they all want.

MOORE. He told me he wanted the man to marry the girl.

FLAGG. Marry her!

PETE. *Elle était une petite enfant innocente, une fleur à demiouverte.*

FLAGG. What's that? Flowers again?

MOORE. He says she was an innocent child.

FLAGG. Listen. You tell him I'm sure she's still an innocent girl. Tell him Charmaine is one of the most virtuous and respectable ladies I've ever had the pleasure of meeting.

MOORE [*to* PETE]. *Monsieur le capitaine dit que c'est impossible et que vous vous trompez, monsieur, parce que Charmaine est tout à fait honnête and vertueuse.*

PETE [*shaking his head*]. *Non! non! non!—je ne me trompe pas—malheureusement c'est bien la vérité.*

MOORE. He's sure of it.

FLAGG. Ask him if he wants to bring charges.

MOORE. *Désirez-vous le faire passer au conseil de guerre?*

PETE. *Conseil de guerre? Ça se peut.*

MOORE. He says perhaps.

FLAGG. What does he mean, "perhaps"? Ask him how much he wants.

MOORE. *Il demande ce que vous voulez.*

PETE. *Mais la petite qui est défleurée—il faut qu'on la fasse honnête, et moi—est-ce donc que l'honneur de ma famille ne vaut rien? Il faut qu'ils se marient, et quant à moi—il faut me payer si je ne le fais pas passer devant le conseil de guerre. Il me faut cinq cent francs.*

FLAGG. Flowers?

MOORE. No, he wants the fellow to marry the girl—and he wants five hundred francs.

FLAGG. I see. That's better. Tell him he can have three hundred. Tell him he can pick any son-in-law he wants out of the whole damn army.

MOORE [*to* PETE]. *Elle peut choisir n'importe qui qu'il soit de toute la compagnie—et vous—vous aurez trois cent francs.*

PETE [*suddenly wildly angry*]. *Ça ne va pas! vous vous moquez de moi, vous officiers américains. je connais le truc—moi—de vous voir m'insulter quand il s'agit de la rapace. Alors, messieurs, j'irai aux G.H.Q. et vous verrez. C'est la mort, et gare à votre peau! Me voilà qui vient vous voir ici, malheureux mais amical, et je ne reçois que des insultes. Cinq cent francs! Rien de moins, et il la marie.* [*He starts for door.*]

FLAGG. Wait a minute. [ALDRICH *bars the door*.] What's wrong?

MOORE. He's insulted. Going to Headquarters. Five hundred, he wants; and it's a certain man, he says.

FLAGG. What man?

MOORE. *Quel homme?*

PETE [*turning, crosses in front of table; to* QUIRT, *dramatically*]. *Le voilà! Alors je m'en vais. Vous vous moquez de moi! Laissez-moi partir.*

[QUIRT *rises, knocking over chair.*]

FLAGG [*taking a step toward* QUIRT]. Quirt, what's the meaning of this?

QUIRT. Sorry, sir, I don't quite catch the drift myself.

FLAGG. Have you been around with Charmaine?

QUIRT. Charmaine? I don't think so, Captain. But I've got a poor memory for names.

FLAGG. You're a liar. You knew Charmaine was mine, and you couldn't keep your hands off her.

QUIRT. Yeah? It's getting to be a habit of mine, huh? Whaddye going to do about it, Captain Flagg?

FLAGG. Oh? What [*Walks to table.*] am I going to do about it?—I'm going to marry you to Charmaine and let you make an honest woman out of her! Quirt, you've taken the detail right off my shoulders, and it's your turn to think fast! [*Turns to* MOORE.] Mr. Moore, now tell the old man that the sergeant was making honest proposals and desperate love! Ask what church he belongs to, or whether he wants 'em married by the cashier of the bank. [*Turns to* QUIRT. MOORE *turns to* PETE; *they start toward the door.*] Sergeant, you arrived in the nick of time with replacements! You saved the day! The Marines have landed and have the situation well in hand! We're going to decorate you! We're going to let you hold the bag!

QUIRT. All very interesting, Captain. But how are you going to do it? I may have landed, but I don't remember seeing any article in what I signed saying

you could pick my woman for me. Seems to me you'd
learned that I pick my women for myself.

FLAGG. Quirt, you've signed on for a cruise with this
woman, and you can't jump ship. I can tell Aldrich
to stand out of the way and let that old man go to
headquarters with his story about you . . . and what
chance has a lousy Marine sergeant got before an
army court-martial when ten majors start the iron
ball rolling? Ten army majors back in Paris, who
ain't going to let anybody do any seducing but themselves. Don't be a hayshaker, Quirt. You can't play
guardhouse lawyer in this country. You're in the
army now, with a lot of western shysters sitting in the
judge advocate general's room.

QUIRT. And who's going to be witness against me? You
couldn't get that little frog to swear anything. I'm
too damned handsome a soldier. I'm strong with this
little French broad. Told me last night, just before
you come back, she never loved a soldier who loved
like me. Said she wished the whole damned outfit
would move away and leave us in peace. Why, she's
jealous every time I have to go to formation.

FLAGG. Sergeant, in about five minutes you're going to
be married; in about eight you're going to please this
old man by leaving an allotment here for about two-
thirds of your pay in regular army style. The more
you talk, the more you hang yourself up by the
thumbs.

QUIRT. This ain't talk. What do you say I go get this
little baby and you ask her if she'll say anything
about me that ain't praise and admiration? What do
you say I go get her? What do I care a whoop in hell
what this old bozo says about me? I ain't seduced
him! He's after money. Well, I ain't got money. I
don't have to carry money around in my love affairs.
What do you say I go get her?

FLAGG. Of course, you'll go get her. And propose marriage to her on the way, because you'll meet the wed-

ding detail when you get here. Gowdy, go to the Y tent and get the chaplain. [GOWDY *goes out.*] Aldrich, accompany Sergeant Quirt to the tavern and tell Charmaine that I'm giving away in marriage the handsomest sergeant in the corps. Tell her she's a woman in a thousand, because Quirt has already run away from a thousand; and if it weren't for my seeing justice done him, he'd run away from that many more. All right, Quirt, we'll be waiting for you. [QUIRT *and* ALDRICH *go out.* FERGUSON *fixes chair, returns to seat, and* FLAGG *turns to* MOORE.] Mr. Moore, tell papa the wedding bells are going to ring, and there's money in it for him, money in it!

[MOORE *seats* PETE *on stool at window; then whispers. A knock at the door.* LIPINSKY *opens it.*]

LIPINSKY. Brigade runner, Captain Flagg.

FLAGG. Send him in.

[*The* RUNNER *enters.*]

RUNNER. Company commander?

FLAGG. What is it—shoving off?

RUNNER. Moving in an hour, sir.

FLAGG. In an hour?

RUNNER. Please initial. [*Offers pencil and paper.*]

FLAGG [*signing*]. You hear that, Moore?

MOORE. Yes, sir.

FLAGG [*up, and business-like*]. Going in an hour. You know what that means.

MOORE. Yes, sir.

FLAGG. Pass the word to our platoon commanders to stand in heavy packs in thirty minutes. The *camions* are waiting at the crossroads with ammunition. [MOORE *goes out.*] Kiper, tell Quirt to salvage all rations in the square. [KIPER *starts for door but stops as* FLAGG *says, "Wait a minute."*] Don't let on to Quirt we're going in. We'll marry him to Charmaine and march the blushing bridegroom off to war. [*Walks up and down.*]

FERGUSON. Afraid you can't marry them this evening,

Captain Flagg. Chaplain very sticky on that point. Have to be married in the morning.

FLAGG. Well, then, the mayor could marry them, couldn't he? Lipinsky, go get the mayor. Who's seen the mayor to-day?

KIPER. Just saw him down by the bridge on a load of manure.

FLAGG. There you are, Lipinsky—load of manure, near the bridge. Get the mayor, dust him off, and bring him here toot pronto. If the chaplain can't do it, the mayor can.

[LIPINSKY *starts to go out but halts and calls* "Ten-shun." PETE *still sits on stool. In walks a* BRIGADIER-GENERAL, *one* COLONEL, *one* CAPTAIN, *and two* LIEU-TENANTS.]

THE GENERAL. Hello, Flagg. Haven't you received that order yet? Not a soul stirring on your damned street. [*All salute.*] Flagg, you run the most disreputable outfit of the brigade. I come into town to hold a staff conference and find the whole shebang asleep. What kind of platoon commanders have you got, anyway, sitting round here like a nest of hoboes when you're moving in forty-five minutes? [*The staff remains standing at attention.*]

FLAGG. Just got the order, General. We'll get off in time. Never missed a train in my life.

THE GENERAL. Well, I don't see how you do it. *Camions* back two miles at the crossroads. Your men will have ammunition there, and I want every man to carry two extra bandoliers.

FLAGG. If you don't mind my saying so, General, we're the refuse of the brigade back of the line and we carry extra bandoliers into it.

THE GENERAL. Well, I'll tell you why. Division wants a line straightened that we're going to take over. Isn't straight enough for him. Where's that map? Map, Davis!

THE COLONEL [*turns*]. Map, Tolbert!

THE LIEUTENANT. Map, Price.

THE CAPTAIN. Where's that map? [*Looks wildly around. The last* LIEUTENANT *to enter hands map to* PRICE.] Here's the map, sir. [*Hands map to* GENERAL.]

THE GENERAL. Good boy, good boy. A map, after all, among you soldiers. Now, see here, Flagg. [*Pointing to map, which he spreads out on table.*] There she is, and here's the line. The corps wants it straightened out. It will take the steel, the cold steel. But they've got to have it straightened out. Give them the steel and you can do it. You'll hold the town—our half of it—and you'll get these fellows out if it takes a week. Your men are a bunch of tramps, but they can do this sort of thing.

FLAGG. Individualists, General, individualists.

THE GENERAL. Well, it's the penalty you pay for laxity. I admit it has its compensations. But you've got to give 'em the steel. You've got to run 'em down like rats. You give them the old cowering point. We've got to get them out. We want to go in there and run 'em out. We want to give 'em steel.

FLAGG. We? Staff going in there too, General?

THE GENERAL [*disconsolately*]. No—they won't risk us fellows, curse the luck.

FLAGG. That's too bad, General.

THE GENERAL. But we'll be behind you, Flagg.

FLAGG. How far, General?

THE GENERAL. We'll probably be at Cemetery Farm. We haven't studied the indirect fire properly yet, but we'll be behind you.

THE COLONEL [*handing bundle of posters to* GENERAL]. Beg pardon, sir; these posters.

THE GENERAL. And, Flagg, some Yankee Doodle back in Hoboken sends you some posters with his compliments.

FLAGG. Posters? What for?

THE GENERAL. To post behind the German lines—sent to all companies of this brigade.

FLAGG. My God! What are we advertising? Camels?

THE GENERAL. Oh, no! It's intelligence work. Explaining our mission over here to the German soldier. There are three hundred posters. Send a small detail through the German lines some night and tack 'em up all over the place.

FLAGG. How many men am I supposed to lose on that job?

THE GENERAL. Not one. We don't want to lose a man. But tack 'em up.

FLAGG. Yeah, that's easy to say. I'd like to tack up a few in Hoboken containing my sentiments on two-starred idiots who waste men on that kind of monkey-business.

THE GENERAL. Well, here is another thing, Flagg, the big G. one wants a prisoner out of that town of yours. Wants an officer from one of those Alsatian regiments where the deserters are filtering through. And I've got to get him.

FLAGG. Oh, don't say that, General, don't break our hearts. I've got to get him. I knew damn well you had a bolt of black crepe up your sleeve when you came in the door.

THE GENERAL. Hold down the losses, Flagg . . . and listen. If you send me one of those Alsatian officers in good condition I'll send your whole company back for a month's rest.

FLAGG. You mean it?

THE GENERAL. Mean it! You know me, Flagg. I'll do more if you get me an officer without a scratch. I'll give you eight days in any hotel in France. If you weren't such a bum, Flagg, I'd put you on staff.

FLAGG. I've been a bum, General, but I'm damned if I'd go on staff.

THE GENERAL [*at the door*]. Hold down the losses, Flagg, and give 'em the steel—and don't forget those posters, for they're damned important—and if you fetch me that prisoner you get a month's rest and eight days'

leave. [*The door opens. In walk the* CHAPLAIN, CHAR-
MAINE *and* QUIRT, MAYOR, KIPER, *and* LIPINSKY.]
Hullo! My God, what's this? A wedding party?

FLAGG. Why, yes, General. I don't suppose we ought to
wait for it, but it's a sort of special case and won't
take long.

THE GENERAL. *You* aren't getting married, are you,
Flagg?

FLAGG. Not this trip; no, sir. It's Sergeant Quirt.

THE GENERAL [*turning to* QUIRT]. Oh, yes, I remember
Sergeant Quirt very well.

FLAGG. I didn't like to intrude company matters when
you were in haste, General, but the truth is, Sergeant
Quirt has expressed a wish to marry the inn-keeper's
daughter here, and her father was waiting to press
charges; so, you see—

THE GENERAL. Oh! Charges? . . .

FLAGG. Personally, I'm opposed to Quirt's marrying at
all, but he insists his intentions were honorable, and
he's such a fine soldier I should hate to carry this
old man to H.Q. with a complaint.

THE GENERAL. What's this, Sergeant?

QUIRT. A courtship, General; a love match from the
start. Honorable intentions on both sides.

THE GENERAL. Sounds a little fishy to me, I must say, but
go right ahead. Don't waste time.

[FERGUSON *comes forward.*]

PETE. *Monsieur le général, les Américains sont si forts
—ils m'ont déshonoré—ma petite fille—ma fleur char-
monte—ma fleur délicate* . . .

FERGUSON. In case of a marriage, Captain Flagg, a little
allotment is regulation.

FLAGG. Thanks, Fergy; I almost forgot the allotment.

QUIRT. Hell, we don't need no allotment. This is a love
match.

FLAGG. Of course, it holds us up a bit, but if the General doesn't mind?

FERGUSON. A little allotment is regulation, sir.

THE GENERAL. Go ahead, go ahead.

FLAGG. Ferguson, where are those allotment blanks?

FERGUSON. Right here, sir.

THE GENERAL [*to* FERGUSON]. Make it out for two-thirds of the sergeant's pay, Ferguson.

FERGUSON [*sits and fills papers*]. Yes, sir.

QUIRT [*standing, with* CHARMAINE]. I don't know about this, General.

THE GENERAL. It's for your own good, Quirt. How do you plan to get out of it, otherwise?

QUIRT. Get out of it? Didn't I tell you it was a love match?

THE GENERAL. No more talk, Sergeant; sign up or stand trial.

FLAGG. For your own good, Quirt.

QUIRT. For whose good, Captain Flagg?

THE GENERAL. Sign up, Quirt.

[FERGUSON *gives paper to* FLAGG. QUIRT *reluctantly signs.*]

FLAGG. All in order. [*Looks over paper.*] Shipshape, Sergeant Quirt. Beautiful hand you write, sir. And now, Chaplain, Sergeant Quirt is next.

THE GENERAL. Let's get it over with. And here's her father ready to give her away.

PETE. *Merci, mon général.*

THE GENERAL. A regular church wedding, and Captain Flagg can be best man.

FLAGG. Get that, Sergeant Quirt? Charmaine—[*He crosses and hands her allotment papers with a bow.*] keep this in a good safe place. It means money to you the first of every month.

CHARMAINE. *Merci.*

THE GENERAL. Turn on the ceremony.

CHAPLAIN. This is a little irregular.

THE GENERAL. Run it through. Sorry we can't wait to kiss the bride, Quirt. You have about twenty minutes, Flagg.

FLAGG. Right, sir.

THE GENERAL. One word, Quirt. You're going in to-night. You're going in in twenty minutes. If you take your men into the line in first-rate condition, looking like soldiers, you'll square yourself with me. Keep that in mind.

QUIRT. We're going in in twenty minutes?

THE GENERAL. Yes. We're off, men. So long, Flagg. Twenty minutes.

FLAGG. Good-bye, General.

[*All salute.* THE GENERAL *and his retinue file out at door.*]

CHAPLAIN. Do you, Charmaine, take this man for your husband, to love, honor—

QUIRT. She does not, I do not, we do not. So we're going in in twenty minutes, eh—and you were going to tie me up before I knew anything about it? And I suppose if I don't marry her you'll lock me up. If you think you can take your men in to-night without a first sergeant, you lock me up. I would like to see you take this gang of tiny tots across that last two miles without a sergeant. Well, if this sergeant goes in, he goes in single; so you God damn well better make up your mind what you're going to do.

FLAGG. Well, skunk, you've got me. You win. Hit the deck.

QUIRT. Sorry, Charmaine, but I've got work to do. I can't marry you to-night, I can't marry you any God damn time at all, and if I never see you again—why, then I never see you again, understand? What's more, don't you try cashing that allotment, or by God I'll pull something that'll stop my pay for good. Get out of my way. [*He goes out. Instantly a whistle blows.*]

FLAGG. Sorry, Charmaine, but I need that sergeant. Shake a leg, you hayshakers. Pass the word for inspection in five minutes, and they'd better be ship-

shape. *Camions* at the crossroad. Extra bandoliers
and V. B. grenades for the outside ranks. Don't let
Quirt do all the work.

THE RUNNERS. Ay, ay, sir. [*They go out hastily.*]

PETE [*angrily*]. *Sont-ils mariés? Ou votre sergeant, se
moque-t-il de moi?*

FLAGG. Sure, they're married.

PETE [*beats on table*]. *Prenez garde! Je viendrai!*

FLAGG [*turns—speaks ominously*]. Don't bother me.
Don't get in my way, see? We're fighting a war with
Germany. I don't give a damn whether he's married
or not. Run along outside. [*Turns* PETE *around;
spanks him.*] I'm busy. [PETE *goes out, stops near*
CHARMAINE *and says, "Sale vache"; then goes out.*
FLAGG *goes to table, gets his hat, turns toward the
door.*] So long, Fergy. Take care of the stuff.

FERGUSON. Yes, sir. [*Turns to desk.* FLAGG *starts out.*
CHARMAINE *crosses to him.*]

CHARMAINE [*her hand on his arm*]. I'm so sorry. You
should have taken me to Paris. I told you to take me
to Paris. I could not be good all alone.

FLAGG [*takes her by shoulders*]. That's all right, Charmaine. You're a damn fine little animal. Go right on
having a good time. It's a great life, and you've got
a genius for it.

CHARMAINE. But you do not love me, not any more!

FLAGG. Sure I love you! Everybody loves you.

CHARMAINE. You think I am *pas bonne*?

FLAGG. Listen, Charmaine. Don't you worry any more
about Quirt and me. It's a thousand to one you'll
never see either of us again. I'm damned sorry I have
to take your sergeant away, but this war's lousy with
sergeants. There'll be thirty along in thirty days.
Anyway you'll probably never see us again. Kiss me
good-bye. [*They kiss.*] Now you forget me!

CHARMAINE. I never forget you.

[*A whistle blows outside.*]

FLAGG. You won't forget me? Well, if I get leave, Charmaine . . . you never can tell. [*The whistle blows twice.*] It's a hell of a war, but it's the only one we've got. [*He goes out. She stands staring after him.*]

FERGUSON [*from his table; turning*]. Well, little missy. You're a single woman *with* an allotment. There ain't many as fortunate as that.

CHARMAINE. He will come back?

FERGUSON. Which one?

CHARMAINE. The captain.

FERGUSON. Not likely. Not likely either of them will. A soldier hardly ever doubles on his trail in this war.

CHARMAINE. No?

FERGUSON. Hardly ever. And you're just as fortunate you didn't marry a soldier, darling. They're a bad lot to keep house for. I know. I've been keeping house for one regiment or another since I was as young as you are.

CHARMAINE. Oh, but they are beautiful.

FERGUSON. The girls always like them. I don't know why.

CHARMAINE. They go into hell to die—and they are not old enough to die.

FERGUSON. I shouldn't think it would matter much to you, dear. Some get killed, but plenty more come in to relieve them. Never any shortage of soldiers.

CHARMAINE. It's terrible!

FERGUSON. It's their business. Some of 'em get killed at it, same as in any trade.

CHARMAINE [*crosses to back of* FERGUSON's *chair; leans over him.*] Can I help you?

FERGUSON. No.

CHARMAINE. To-morrow?

FERGUSON. No.

CHARMAINE. You are unkind.

FERGUSON. Just because I'm the only man around here do you think I'm going to let you bother me? You run along home and pray God to keep you out of mischief a few days. It won't do you any harm. [*He bends over his work.*]

CHARMAINE. *Bon soir.* [*He does not hear her.*] *Bon soir!*

FERGUSON. What?

CHARMAINE. *Bon soir.*

FERGUSON. Oh, yes, good night. [*She slowly crosses to door, looking back at him all the way. She quietly closes door, and just as she does so,* FERGUSON *very loudly says,* "Good night." *He bends over his desk, alone, writing and sings.*]

"The French they are a funny race, parlez-vous,
The French they are a funny race, parlez-vous . . ."

CURTAIN

Act two

A cellar in a disputed town, a typical deep wine cellar of a prosperous farmhouse on the edge of a village in France. It resembles half of a culvert thirty feet in diameter, with a corresponding curved roof and walls. One end is open, and the other is walled up, admitting a narrow and rather low door in the center, through which a flight of stairs extends to the ground floor above. This cellar is lit dimly by two candles placed at either side of the front stage and held in bottles on small bully-beef boxes. The rear wall can only barely be discerned. Along the sides of this culvert are dirty white ticks stuffed with straw for sleeping quarters, the sort of ticks headquarters detachment men carry about with them. There are four on each side, arranged with all the litter of miscellany a soldier carries about tucked at their heads, and with the foot of these pallets extending into the center of the cul-

vert. The effect is not unlike in design that of a hospital ward, with feet toward the center aisle. Back of FLAGG'S *bunk all manner of stuff—first-aid kits, bandages, chocolates, sticks, pistols and rifles, notes, books of memoranda, etc.*

Two men are asleep, snoring gently—gas masks at alert on chests, tin hats on back of heads, and heads on floor. They are indescribably dirty, and with six or eight days' beard.

The two men are SPIKE *and* KIPER. KIPER *is on second bunk at left,* SPIKE *on third bunk at right.* GOWDY *enters. Stirs* SPIKE *with his foot.*

GOWDY. All right. Heave out and lash up. Lively now. Rations are in. Go draw for ten. At the gray stable to-night. Take that sack there. [*Points to a muddy sack on the floor near by.*]

SPIKE. What time is it? Rations in?

GOWDY. You heard me, Spike. Shake a leg and go draw rations for ten men, at the gray stable near the square. It's after two o'clock.

SPIKE. Where's Captain Flagg.

GOWDY. Down tying up Mr. Aldrich.

SPIKE. So they got him. Bad?

GOWDY. I'll say they did. A ticket home. Right arm torn all to hell.

SPIKE. A damned dirty shame. He's lucky, though, to get out with an arm. I'd sell 'em mine, and at the same price. What was it—that one-pounder again?

GOWDY. No. Fuse cap from a grenade. Made a hell of a mess on Mr. Aldrich. He was crawling on the embankment near the railway station, and somebody inside threw him a present.

SPIKE [*now up and re-winding a spiral legging*]. A damned swell officer, if you ask me. Taking him out to-night.

GOWDY. No. The skipper is bringing him here. Send him out to-morrow night. He's lost too much blood to walk it before dawn. God, it's getting on my nerves.

KIPER [*who has been awakened*]. Who? Mr. Aldrich hit bad?

GOWDY. Pretty bad. Arm. Make a bunk for him, willya? Shake it down and pile another in the back. He'll want to sit up with it. Make up Harry's bunk.

SPIKE [*at door, about to go upstairs, turns at this*]. Harry's bunk? Why Harry?

GOWDY. Harry's through with bunks.

SPIKE. Bumped off?

GOWDY. Worse. In the belly crossing the square.

[SPIKE *goes out.*]

KIPER. Where is he?

GOWDY. The skipper rushed him back an hour ago. No use, though; Harry was unconscious—halfway—holding half his guts in his bare hands and hollering for somebody to turn him loose so he could shoot himself.

KIPER. Captain Flagg want me?

GOWDY. He said not to wake you. Might need you later on.

KIPER. A good job for me, I suppose. Jeez, with this daylight saving I ain't going to live forever, that's sure. I think I'll go crazy and get the doc to gimme a ticket.

GOWDY. Flagg's crazy now. Raving crazy. Hasn't slept for five nights. We'll be sitting on him in another night like he's had to-night.

KIPER. The whole damned universe is crazy now.

[KIPER *has come forward to* FLAGG'S *bunk, smoking. Enter* PHARMACIST'S MATE, *with a large clothing roll trussed up in leather straps with a portmanteau handle. He is young, pink-faced, but horribly callous, probably some kid from a medical school of 1917.*]

MATE [*looking about in the dark as he approaches* KIPER]. Flagg's company P.C.?

KIPER [*hostile;* GOWDY *sits up*]. Yeah.

MATE. Where'd I better set up shop, soldier? [*He looks about the cellar.*]

KIPER [*worried*]. What do you want to set up shop for, sailor?

MATE [*sitting down on bunk; starts unpacking, takes off helmet*]. How'd I know? This ain't my party. Flagg wants it here.

KIPER. What's he want it for to-night?

MATE. He's going to put on a little party before morning. [*He uncovers a litter of blue-rolled bandages on bunk; absorbent cotton, a jar of iodine which he unscrews, and some wooden sticks around which he begins to twist wisps of cotton for daubs.*] A little party.

KIPER. The whole damn company, I suppose, and all the engineers he can find to boot.

MATE [*professionally*]. Oh, no. He ain't got arrangements here for that many. I'd say a small party, according to the stuff they gave me at the dressing station.

KIPER [*incredulous*]. How small?

MATE [*with immense indifference, busy about his detail*]. Oh, I'd say about two operating tables . . . [*A pause as he enjoys the effect on* KIPER.] A small party. About four couples for bridge.

KIPER. Yeah. [*Rather miserable.*] Low bridge around that lousy railroad station.

MATE. I guess so. They were passing out V. B. grenades down by the street to the station when I came through.

KIPER [*immensely friendly all of a sudden*]. Look here, sailor. You are smarter than me. . . .

MATE [*interrupting*]. Oh, no!

KIPER [*insistently*]. Oh, hell, yes! Any man smart enough not to join in them four couples is smarter than I am. Even you're smarter. Now that being the case, tell me why the hell we want the Heinies out of that God damn railway station. Leave 'em there, I say. Let 'em sit where they damned well are. They ain't going anywheres.

MATE. I can't tell you.

KIPER. Nobody can. Like as not General Pershing himself couldn't tell you about it . . . and . . . oh, sweet baby, but last night down there I swore to God so long as I lived I'd never let another German in that railroad station throw a potato masher at me.

MATE. You can throw a grenade at him.

KIPER. Sure I can. But I don't want to no more. I pitched yesterday, and my arm is sore. I know I can do it, and it ain't fun any more. I know all about Flagg's invitations to parties. I know why they all got R.S.V.P. on 'em. Right smart of V.B. grenades provided. . . .

[*Enter* LIPINSKY, *who comes down; looks first at* KIPER.]

LIPINSKY [*immediately perceiving the litter*]. Jeez, Kiper, I wish you'd keep the undertakers out of here. What's all this, Jack? [*He waves to the mate's stuff.*]

MATE [*selecting a small bandage*]. Well, this one is yours, and the rest is for your friends.

LIPINSKY [*cheerily*]. Don't try to put the bug on me. I ain't no queen bee. They ain't made one that could burst alongside of me. If they'd made it, I'd be down with the daisies long ago. I'm proof now. It's down in the cards that I'll live to see the navy at Mare Island again. [*He lights a cigarette which he has taken from* FLAGG'S *bunk.*] Yes, sir, I'll live to beat the pants off that bird that sold me the wrist watch down by the main gate.

KIPER. How do you know you're going to live? Said your prayers, I suppose, and got an answer.

LIPINSKY. And who'd send me an answer?

KIPER. The great cosmic top sergeant who runs this world.

LIPINSKY. Well, I don't want any answer from that bird. He'd send the answer collect, and it would say, "Fall in and get the manure outa the French angels' back-yards. Clean up heaven, you low-down Marine, so's the National Guard won't get typhoid when they all die and come here."

KIPER. There ain't any heaven. Paris is heaven enough. If I ever get outa hell, I'm certainly going to stay in heaven until I die.

LIPINSKY. Of course, there's a heaven.

MATE. On the level, now. You birds know your souls go somewheres. You've seen too many men die. A fellow is walking along, blood in his face and breath in his lungs, and whizz - eeee - zzzz, boommmmm . . . he's down on the ground and something's gone. Something's gone, I tell you. Something that was in that bird a minute before has left, and all you've got is a pack of bloody rags and a lot of dirt. Well, for the want of a better name, you call that something a soul . . . and you can't kid me . . . the soul's gone somewheres.

KIPER. What of it? That soul ain't any of my business. It ain't got to eat, it ain't got to run; it ain't got to stand in line ten days a week to sign the payroll. I should get on my ear about where this doodlebug in my chest is going after I die. It ain't never helped me none. It can go to hell for all I care.

LIPINSKY. Jeez, Kiper, don't talk that way around me. [*Raises eyes.*] It wasn't me, God; it wasn't your little Vladysek Lipinsky. Not him. He knows too damn well if he was to talk that way you would certainly make him cover up and yell for mercy before morning.

KIPER. And you were the one wasn't going to be hit a while ago.

LIPINSKY. That's why I ain't going to be hit. My little soul's all ready to turn out for every formation, boots blacked and buttons shined. A little sea-going soul that knows its top sergeant can give it a kick in the pants any time he gets ready.

KIPER. Well, if there is a God, he ain't got medicine big
   enough to worry me. Why the hell doesn't he win the
   war for one side or the other and get this mess over?
   I know plenty of men could win it. Flagg probably
   could, if you gave him the army and a barrel of
   whisky.

LIPINSKY. But you like the chaplain, Kiper. You said he
   was a swell bird the other day.

KIPER. Sure I like the chaplain. Gimme two packs of
   Camels two nights ago. If God was to show himself,
   now—come down with a bunch of angels driving a
   wagon-load of cigarettes, that would be something
   like it. The chaplain said my folks was all praying
   for me to come through, and for God to spare me
   after hearing their prayers. God, I ain't that dirty a
   coward! That's a case of saying, "Oh, God, don't kill
   our child. Kill every kid in the neighborhood, but
   bring the one marked Kiper safe back home. . . ."
   No, I don't want none of that for mine. . . . And
   you can take all your New Testaments with the
   khaki backs and throw 'em in the incinerator so far
   as I want anything out of 'em. I'd rather have a book
   of cigarette papers any time. . . . I ain't asking anybody for a damned thing in this war. And you can
   take all your Bible backers and psalm singers and
   hitch 'em to the ration wagons, if you ask me.

MATE. Well, this is all very pleasant, but I got business
   over in the next company now. Bad curve in the position there, and 'long toward daybreak they start hollering "First Aid" as regular as a clock. If I was you
   fellows I'd go out and sleep in different shell-holes
   to-night . . . see which one of you is right. . . . Tell
   your skipper I'll be back around three-thirty. [*He
   steps on his cigarette and prepares to go out after
   QUIRT enters, which he does. QUIRT enters. SERGEANT
   QUIRT is tired.*]

QUIRT. Captain Flagg here?

GOWDY. Still in the orchard . . . digging those new rifle

pits. We've got nine captured Maxims there. Those birds can't change the belts, but they can tap a thousand rounds apiece by pressing the buttons in the dark. Fifteen men could hold this half of the town, the way he's got the positions staked out.

QUIRT. There'll be about fifteen holding it if this business of reconnoitering patrols keeps up. I'd like to have that divisional staff in this town one night. Still bad in the square?

GOWDY. Pretty bad. Rifles in box rest in the railway station . . . light automatics.

QUIRT. I thought Flagg got 'em out last night.

GOWDY. They filtered back in at dusk to-night. Our cross-fire couldn't stop 'em. The skipper says they are working them from pulleys from the first floor, and the railroad embankment covers them from us.

QUIRT [*stretching out and sighing as he takes off his tin hat and mops his forehead*]. Running rations down that ravine every night is the toughest job I've ever soldiered.

GOWDY. Lucky to-night?

QUIRT. Pretty lucky. Six out of ten come back. Them two Jameson boys got it from the same shell going down. Dutchy and the little Jew were hit right at the dump. Easy ones though. They'll be back in ten days.

[*A commotion at head of stairs. Enter* CAPTAIN FLAGG *supporting* ALDRICH *by gripping* ALDRICH'S *uninjured wrist over his shoulder and easing him gently down steps.* ALDRICH *is not groaning. After all, it won't hurt for fifteen minutes or so. But he is weak from loss of blood and soaked through, and is in an indescribable mess of dried blood and dirt, which appears black.* FLAGG, *who is unkempt, has no leggings or laces in his breeches, these flapping in the most disillusioning fashion about his bare legs. His blouse, an old army blouse many sizes too big and without a sign of any insignia, is tied with a piece of twine. He is bare-*

headed—*no tin hat and no accoutrements of any sort. He is a very weary-looking man. He wears belt and holster with automatic bound to leg. As* FLAGG *enters, followed by* MATE, GOWDY *jumps up and spreads blanket on bunk.*]

FLAGG. Right here, Aldrich. [*Lowers him down on bunk. The* PHARMACIST'S MATE *follows him.* FLAGG *kneels above* ALDRICH. *The* MATE *stands.*] Gimme a stick of that dope, Holsen.

MATE. They are quarter grains, Captain.

FLAGG [*to* ALDRICH, *lying down*]. Take these two now. [*He puts two tablets from a tiny vial in the wounded officer's mouth.*] I'm putting these in your blouse. Get somebody to give you one every three hours until you are carried out.

ALDRICH. What are they?

FLAGG. Morphine—quarter grains—

ALDRICH [*not dramatic, just casual*]. What if I take them all when your back is turned?

FLAGG [*turning his back and crossing to his own bunk down left; sits on bunk*]. Go ahead. It's your affair.

[*After* FLAGG *is seated on his bunk a strange sob is heard at the head of the stairs.* LIEUTENANT MOORE, *last seen in company headquarters, rushes in and goes straight over to* ALDRICH, *where he stands and looks down at his arm, and not his face.*]

MOORE. Oh, God, Dave, but they got you. God, but they got you a beauty, the dirty swine. God DAMN them for keeping us up in this hellish town. Why can't they send in some of the million men they've got back there and give us a chance? Men in my platoons are so hysterical every time I get a message from Flagg, they want to know if they're being relieved. What can I tell them? They look at me like whipped dogs—as if I had just beaten them—and I've had enough of them this time. I've got to get them out, I tell you. They've had enough. Every night the same way. [*He turns to* FLAGG.] And since six o'clock

there's been a wounded sniper in the tree by that orchard angel crying *"Kamerad! Kamerad!"* Just like
a big crippled whippoorwill. What price glory now?
Why in God's name can't we all go home? Who gives
a damn for this lousy, stinking little town but the
poor French bastards who live here? God damn it!
You talk about courage, and all night long you hear
a man who's bleeding to death on a tree calling you
"Kamerad" and asking you to save him. God damn
every son of a bitch in the world who isn't here! I
won't stand for it. I won't stand for it! I won't
have the platoon asking me every minute of the
livelong night when they are going to be relieved.
. . . Flagg, I tell you you can shoot me, but I won't
stand for it. . . . I'll take 'em out to-night and kill
you if you get in my way. . . . [*Starts sobbing again.*
GOWDY *and* KIPER *sit up.*]

FLAGG [*rising quickly as though he might kill the man,
and then putting his arm around the chap, who has
clearly gone smash for a few minutes. He speaks in a
quiet, chastening tone, with a gentility never before
revealed.*] Here, boy, you can't do this before all
these men. [*Walks him.*] They are rubbed up, too.
You are all tuckered out with your side of the line.
Don't worry about your platoon. We'll get them out.
You turn in here. [*Walks him to bunk on the left
side of the room.* KIPER *crosses and throws blanket on
him; stops at bunk nearest entrance.*] And dope off
for a little while . . . that's it, give him a blanket,
Kiper . . . and now take it easy a while, and you can
go back to your platoon in time to stand to. Sleep it
off, boy, sleep it off. . . . You're in a deep wide hole,
and shells can't get you. Sleep it off. [FLAGG *crosses
to his own bunk, lights cigarette at candle, seats himself on bunk.* GOWDY *rests head on arm.* QUIRT *kneels
on floor, gets a piece of chocolate out of his pocket;
rises, as though his legs were asleep. He carries his
helmet. He crosses and tosses candy to* MOORE.]

QUIRT. Just a little chocolate I bought off a Y.M.C.A. wagon down at the base. [QUIRT *is sympathetic and begins to talk nervously.*] I got hit myself once. In Nicaragua. We were washed up before we made a landing. I was a corporal, and when we were scrubbing down and putting on clean uniforms—doctors' orders, you know, so they wouldn't have to wash us when we were hit—[*Turns to* GOWDY.]—A bird said to me—it was old Smoke Plangetch, who was killed in 1913 in a chippie joint in Yokohama—Smoke said to me: "You'd better swab down, you son of a sea-bitch, because I dreamed last night they wrote your name on a bullet." I said to him, "The bullet ain't been cast that can shoot Micky Quirt." He said, "If your name is on one, it will turn the corner and go upstairs to find you." Jeez! That afternoon when we made a landing and hit the beach, the spigs was on a hill five hundred yards off shore. We started up the hill—they weren't many of us dropping—and I came to a log I had to jump [QUIRT *illustrates this.*] and I lost my balance and threw my hand up in the air. [QUIRT *extends his wrist.*] Look, right through the God damn fin, as pretty as a pinwheel . . . Smoke saw it. "Oh, yeah, you wisenheimer son of a Chinese tart," he says to me, "your name was on that one and you had to reach up for it." [GOWDY *laughs.* QUIRT *is obviously embarrassed by having spoken of himself so much. He turns and recollects his business and goes over to* FLAGG. *Crosses to the foot of* FLAGG'S *bunk.*] Rations detail in, sir. Lost the two Jameson boys in the ravine going down. Both badly hit. Lost Fleischman and Rosenthal in the dump. Both slight. Brought back all the ammunition and two sacks of bread, one of canned willie, French; I carried a sack of beet sugar on my back. Got a piece of shrapnel in it where they are shelling the crossroads —stopped it square. In the next war, I'm going to wear a suit of beet sugar and stand forest fire watch in the Rocky Mountains. [*He turns, and then remembers and comes back.*] Oh, I brought up two of these thirty-day wonder lieutenants from a training camp. Sent up by divisional for instruction.

FLAGG. By God, I won't stand for it. They wipe their damned dirty feet on this company. They can give my men all their damned good jobs. They can keep us in the line all during the whole damned war. But I'll be damned if my sergeants have got time to teach army lieutenants how to button their pants in the dark.

QUIRT. They are in my hole now, sir. Pretty badly shaken up by the ravine. First time up, you know. Shall I send them to you, sir?

FLAGG. Send them to me, and for God's sake, don't call me sir any more to-night.

QUIRT [*to* GOWDY]. All right. You heard him. Hit the deck. You'll find 'em in my hole. [GOWDY *goes.*] Those Huns in the railway station again?

FLAGG. Try to cross the town square when there's a flare up, and you'll see.

QUIRT. You get a visit from brigade headquarters to-night. I saw their party in the ravine as we were going down to the dump.

FLAGG. The old man says we've got to drive them off the embankment. Huh! He can give me five general courts and I'll not waste another man at that business. It will take a brigade action to get them out for good.

QUIRT. Do you mind if I take a look around there now? I'd like to see this damned war some. For six days I've been a lousy bakery wagon—haven't seen a spiggoty yet, except stinking dead ones—I never see soldiers stink like these Heinies.

FLAGG. All right. Go get your blooming can blown off. But bury yourself, while you're about it. The burying detail is in for the night.

QUIRT. Gosh, I wish to hell I was home.

FLAGG. Go get one of those Alsatian lootenants then, and you'll get a leave.

QUIRT. I don't want to die yet, thanking you just the same. Well, here goes. [*Exit.*]

FLAGG. Well, keep your head down. I can't waste any grave-diggers on sergeants. [FLAGG *shrugs his shoulders and walks over to above* ALDRICH.] Sorry Moore blew up that way, Aldrich . . . you are a damned sight luckier than he is, but he doesn't know it. I'll have you out to-morrow night with the ration detail, and you'll be parking your body in a big white bed in another two days. Good luck . . . You've been a damned good man. I wish you could get a ribbon for this town.

[*As* FLAGG *leaves*, GOWDY *enters with two lieutenants. They are just like tailor's dummies of a Burberry outfit slicked to the notch and perky and eager. As they enter*, FLAGG *steps on his cigarette and stands facing them. The* LIEUTENANTS *come down and stand side by side.*]

FLAGG [*starts back in mock admiration and salaams deeply as they come forward*]. So *this* is the last of the old guard, eh? In the name of the holy sweet Jumping, are you gentlemen bound for a masked ball, that you come disguised as officers? Or do you wish to save the snipers the trouble of picking you off with a glass, that you wear signboards? [*He goes nearer them, inspecting their clothes.*] Can't you go without those trench coats even to the trenches? How long will you last in those boots? Take 'em off before you even part your hair in the morning. . . . [*He changes to a thundering staccato.*] My name is Flagg, gentlemen, and I'm the sinkhole and cesspool of this regiment, frowned on in the Y.M.C.A. huts and sneered at by the divisional Beau Brummels. I am a lousy, good-for-nothing company commander. I corrupt youth and lead little boys astray into the black shadows between the lines of hell, killing more men than any other company commander in the regiment, and drawing all the dirty jobs in the world. I take chocolate soldiers and make dead heroes out of them. I did not send for you, Mister . . . [*He leans forward, and the first officer salutes and speaks:* "*Cunningham, sir*"] nor for you . . . [*"Lundstrom, sir," also salutes.*]; and I confess I am in a quandary. Four days ago I should have been more hospitable, for I had four gunnery sergeants then. Now I have two, and can't spare them to teach little boys how to adjust their diapers. I've no doubt that one of you was an all-American half-back and the other the editor of the college paper, but we neither follow the ball nor the news here. We are all dirt, and we propose to die in order that corps headquarters may be decorated. I should be happy to receive suggestions as to what should be done with you. Ah, I have it! There are two German gunners over in the enemy railway station. Two bright young men might get them out and cut their throats before dawn; then no more could get in the station all day. Two bright young men, who know very little of anything just yet. I have two bright ones, but they are far too valuable. They are corporals with ten years' experience.

[*The* LIEUTENANTS *are speechless. There is not a smile in the cellar.* CUNNINGHAM, *who is the bigger of the two, finally answers, in a slow southern drawl.*]

CUNNINGHAM. I'll do anything you will. Where is the railway station and the two bucks that have got you buffaloed?

FLAGG. Why, it's Frank Merriwell! All right, Frank. You and me will be playing ball in hell by three o'clock this morning.

LUNDSTROM. Put me in too, sir.

FLAGG. Oh, no, no, no! We must have officers left. Rule of the game. Must have officers. Men would get right up and go home, and then there wouldn't be any war at all. Besides, three would be a crowd, and I hate crowds early in the morning around the railway station. They are so noisy, and they die so fast. [*He turns to* GOWDY.] Gowdy! Take Mr. Lundstrom to the fourth platoon sergeant, and tell him that here's his new officer. [RUNNER *and* LUNDSTROM *move to door.* FLAGG *is all business now.*] And by the way, Mr. Lundstrom, they filter through and bomb twice a week, small parties slipping down that ravine you'll find on your left. Watch it closely, or you'll all have your throats cut before you know it. And let that sergeant sleep for the next two days. Remember, he'll do no details until he's rested. Of course you can wake him for advice. That's all. Shove off. [RUNNER *and* LUNDSTROM *salute, and go out.* CUNNINGHAM *sits down.* QUIRT *enters with his helmet on, limping; steals forward quietly, and sits down on his bunk. There is a nice bloody mess on his right calf.* FLAGG *happens to turn, sees what's going on, sits up, watches* QUIRT. QUIRT *looks back, finally grins, then tries to open a first-aid pack.*]

FLAGG. What's the matter with you?

QUIRT. Got a can opener?

FLAGG. You crook!

QUIRT. I say, Captain, got a can opener?

FLAGG. Those things are supposed to be opened with the teeth.

QUIRT. You don't say! Well, this'n' wasn't. This here can was evidently made for the Red Cross by the Columbia Red Salmon Company. Like as not instead of bandages I'll find the God damnedest mess of goldfish in it.

FLAGG [*rises, crosses to* QUIRT, *takes can away from him*]. Where were you? [*He comes over, strains at the tin. He is looking daggers.*] Where were you?

QUIRT. Just looking around.

FLAGG. Here. [*Hands him tin, opened.*]

QUIRT. Thanks.

FLAGG. Where were you, I said.

QUIRT [*takes out bandage*]. In the vegetable garden, pulling turnips. [*Starts wiping leg.*]

FLAGG. God damn you, Quirt, I believe you stuck your leg out. [*Goes back and sits on bunk.*]

QUIRT. Like hell I did. If I'd wanted to stick my leg out don't you think I've had plenty of chances to do it before? No, sir, I stuck my head out and some bird in the church tower took a shot at me. There she is. In and out without touching the bone. Just let me squeeze the juice out and she'll be all right. Ain't she the prettiest little damn puncture you ever saw, Captain? Ain't she a beauty?

FLAGG. I suppose you think you're going back to Cognac Pete's, huh?

QUIRT. How'd you guess it? Yes, sir, back to my little skookum lady you tried to make me a present of. Am I happy? Am I happy? Oh, boy! Ask me, Captain, am I happy?

FLAGG. You mean to say you aren't cured of Charmaine yet?

QUIRT. Cured of Charmaine? No, sir, I ain't even getting better. Oh, Captain Flagg, ain't you proud of yourself, ain't you a wizard? God, ain't I sorry to leave you all alone here in this mess? Think of her sitting on my lap, lighting my pipe in the kitchen, and you dodging machine guns. I wonder I don't bust out crying. You know, I wouldn't wonder if you got bumped off and never came back. As a matter of fact, I hope you damn well get your head blown off.

FLAGG. Yeah, you always did have a charming disposition.

QUIRT [*squeezing his wound gently*]. Oh, pretty baby, papa doesn't meant to hurt you. Lookit, Captain. By God, I wouldn't take a hundred dollars Mex. for that little bumble-bee that flew in there.

FLAGG. Feel pretty cocky, don't you? Well, you can't go out to-night. I guess you can work all right with that. You'll wait here till Cunningham and I get back with that Alsatian shavetail from the railroad embankment. Then I get leave, the company gets a rest, and we go back together, see?

QUIRT. Not much, I don't see. I've got a very important engagement back to Pete's place. Can't be postponed, not even for the pleasure of your enjoyable company, such as it is. I don't wait for nothing in the world but a medical tag.

[*Enter* PHARMACIST'S MATE; *stands on steps, leans head in door.*]

MATE. Heard your first sergeant was hit in that turnip patch. [FLAGG *indicates* QUIRT. MATE *crosses to* QUIRT; *kneels.*] Let's have a look. Um. Night soil in that patch, and you, like a damned fool, crawl after they hit you, and now you're full of that muck. Can you walk, Sergeant?

QUIRT [*lying back*]. Well, depends on what I see.

MATE [*helps up* QUIRT, *who carries helmet*]. Go to the sick bay at once for a shot of tetanus, and then get out of here. [*Takes his arm, and both cross.*] You can reach a collecting station before you're done.

QUIRT. Ain't this heart-breaking, Flagg? Well, duty calls. But my eyes fill with tears at the thought of leaving my old company commander. I don't know as I can go through with it.

FLAGG. Make it snappy, Quirt, or you'll find the door locked.

QUIRT. Yeah? What door.

FLAGG. Charmaine's.

QUIRT. Are you wounded, too, Mr. Flagg?

FLAGG. No, but inside ten minutes I'm going to be wounded or bumped off or have that God damned prisoner for the Brig.

QUIRT. Try to get killed, will you? To please me—just this once? [QUIRT *and the* MATE *go out.*]

FLAGG. Mr. Cunningham . . . I guess you thought I was joking when I proposed that little expedition to the railroad embankment?

CUNNINGHAM. I did not. When do we start? [*Coming to* FLAGG.]

FLAGG. Well, I was. I was kidding hell out of you. I'd no more let you go in there, boy, than I'd knife you in the back. The air is full of steel this side of that embankment, and a green man has about as much chance as a cootie on Fifth Avenue.

CUNNINGHAM. You going?

FLAGG. I've got official reasons for going, see? The Brig. wants a prisoner, and he also wants that nest wiped out. Also, I got private and personal reasons for wanting to catch up with that baboon that got the little present through his leg.

CUNNINGHAM. If you're going, that suits me. I ain't no green man. I can crawl on my belly.

FLAGG. Yeah?

CUNNINGHAM. I'm a locomotive engineer and I've been crawling under trains for fifteen years. Had several engines shot out from under me likewise. You think you can scare me with this here war? Christ! You ought to see a few railroad wrecks!

FLAGG. Well, Mr. Cunningham, I'm inclined to think you'll do.

CUNNINGHAM. You're God damn right, I'll do.

FLAGG. What do you say we black our faces and give a little party, now the guests will be asleep?

CUNNINGHAM. Sure. I like the cut of your jib, and you can lead me to it. Show me which one is the lootenant, so I won't hurt him.

FLAGG. You from Texas?

CUNNINGHAM. You hit it.

FLAGG. Now I get you. So we've got another damned

Texan in this outfit, wanting to fight anybody that ain't from Texas.

CUNNINGHAM. Yep, and I ain't no God damn college boy, either.

FLAGG. Good stuff! Now throw away them fancy-dress clothes of yours and dip in here. [*He offers a can of lamp-black.*]

CUNNINGHAM. Sure. [*Takes off overcoat.*] I was a loco-motive engineer on the Louisiana Midland. Three wrecks in my division last year. Christ, but this war shore is a great relief to me. [*Both black their faces.*] I'm an engineer officer attached to infantry. My brother's still driving an engine back home. Had a letter last month from him. He says, "You dirty yellow sapsucker, quitting your job on the Louisiana Midland. I knew you always were a yellow dog, but I didn't think you'd go back on the road thataway."

FLAGG. Now if I only had a pretty little engine. [*Suddenly there is a scream upstairs, a shout in a burly strange tongue. "Heraus!" and three bombs explode.* FLAGG, *the* RUNNERS, *and all save* ALDRICH *dash for the door.*] Marines! Marines! Marines! [*The lieutenant who had been put to sleep stirs uneasily. After a brief tumult, the people of the cellar descend stairs,* FLAGG *holding a German officer by the collar. He takes him straight to the candle.*] Let me have a look at you, sweetheart, let me have a look! Boys, he's an Alsatian lieutenant! He couldn't wait for us to go after him, so he came over. [*He embraces his captive.*] Oh, sweetheart—you're the sweetest sight I've seen since Charmaine! Here, Kiper [*Pushes him to* KIPER.]—take care of him for me, and for God's sake don't scare him to death, because he's our ticket of leave!

LEWISOHN [*screams, outside*]. Captain Flagg . . .

FLAGG. Who's that?

LIPINSKY. It's little Lewisohn, sir.

[LEWISOHN *is carried in by* GOWDY *followed by* PHARMA-

CIST'S MATE, *and he is crying monotonously for* CAP-
TAIN FLAGG.]

LEWISOHN. Captain Flagg. Captain Flagg. Stop the
blood. Stop the blood.

FLAGG [*takes him from* GOWDY *and puts him on floor*]. I
can't stop it, Lewisohn, I'm sorry. [*He examines
wound in left side.*]

LEWISOHN. Oh, Captain Flagg, stop the blood.

FLAGG. Fix him with your needle, Mate. [MATE *gives
him needle in arm.*]

LEWISOHN. Oh, Captain Flagg, can't you please, sir, stop
the blood?

FLAGG [*puts hand behind* LEWISOHN'S *head and gently
lowers him to floor*]. You'll be all right, boy. You'll
be all right. You'll be all right.

[LEWISOHN *sighs and relaxes his body.*]

CURTAIN

Act three

*A tavern known colloquially as Cognac Pete's. Evening,
two days later. The outside door is in the rear, small
bar at the right, stairway left, an inside door at right.
Windows rear.* FERGUSON *sits at long table smoking and
playing solitaire, a bottle of Martell and a brandy pony
at his elbow.* CHARMAINE *is in front of the table by the
candles, sewing.* FERGUSON *is enjoying the luxury of
talking to himself, for it is apparent that* CHARMAINE *is
not following all he says.*

FERGUSON. I'm glad they're coming back here. [*He sips,
between sentences.*] It's a good, quiet town . . .
quiet . . . last time we were in a town where the
M.P.'s and the mule skinners fought every night . . .

glad they sent 'em back here. . . . *You* ought to be.
. . . Your father'll do a land office business when the
outfit gets here. He better knock the bung in every
barrel of red ink he's got. God, how they'll eat . . .
what's left of 'em. When two hundred leave me behind with the stuff, I always get ready to mess two
hundred when they return. Of course a hundred
may not return . . . but they'll eat right through to
the bottom of the kettle just the same. Now you
take that big oakum-haired Swede named Swenson.
I never see a Marine eat more than he did . . .
I damn well hope Swenson gets back . . . I like
to see him eat. There was a little Jew named Lewisohn that could out-eat him, weight for weight; but
the Swede weighed twice as much. That Swede could
eat anything but a horse collar. [*He chuckles and*
CHARMAINE *smiles.*] Well, I'll say we've kept each
other company. We sure have, even if you can't speak
a white man's lingo; that is, not to say *speak* it. Now
if you'd been a Spanish girl we could have got together a little better . . . I lived with a Spanish girl
at Cavite back in '99 . . . in those days I was salty as
hell, a sea-going buckaroo.

CHARMAINE. *Est-ce-que* . . . you are lonely?

FERGUSON. It ain't so bad, staying behind this way. It
ain't so bad. Twenty years now I've had 'em leave
me. When I was younger I believed some of the
liars who said they liked to fight . . . liked being
under fire . . . but it always bored me to sit around
and be sniped at. Somehow I never did get angry.
And you've got to get angry when a bird's shooting
at you if you're going to enjoy it. So I didn't have a
good time . . . Now you take Flagg there . . . there's
the sort likes it. Flagg gets mad as hell if you don't
even like him, let alone shoot at him. Flagg and me
are different. Now Flagg—

CHARMAINE. Where is *le capitaine*?

FERGUSON. Pretty near here, I suppose.

CHARMAINE. Near here?

FERGUSON. He'll be here presently, General.

CHARMAINE. *Le Capitaine Flagg*—he has been wounded ever?

FERGUSON. Naw! Flagg ain't never been wounded. Never will, neither, if you ask me. You can't hurt his kind. When you see a man like Flagg, it's curious, but they always have the pleasure of drinking themselves to death . . . funny thing . . . I never knew a man who could float a load of liquor, didn't hold all the cards besides. Now you take Flagg . . . he'll be here in fifteen minutes mebbe—mebbe two hours—but just the same as ever . . . thirsty as hell, wishing he had forty geisha girls to play with.

CHARMAINE. Fifteen minutes. . . .

FERGUSON [*with elaborate gestures*]. Le Capitany . . . ici . . . sank . . . min-use ici, sank min-use . . . Compree?

CHARMAINE. *Oui, oui, oui! Merci bien.* [*She runs upstairs.* FERGUSON *continues smoking, pouring a pony of brandy. Presently the door at rear opens slowly. Enter* SERGEANT QUIRT *in a major's army overcoat, with black braids and a leather-visored garrison cap. He is shaven, crafty-faced. Below the overcoat, which is bursting on his chest, may be seen rough army shoes, gray woolen socks pulled over the bottoms of striped outing-flannel pajamas. He looks exactly what he is, a slightly wounded soldier escaped from hospital in borrowed clothes.* FERGUSON *turns, and seeing him, comes to attention.* QUIRT *also has a bottle with about half a drink in it.*]

FERGUSON [*rising courteously*]. Good evening, Major.

QUIRT [*pours what remains in the bottle he carries into* FERGUSON's *glass; then, taking the full bottle, sets his empty one in its place*]. Sit down, Fergy, and use your eyes. Help me to get out of this rigging.

FERGUSON [*sitting; irritated*]. What are you doing in those gadgets, Quirt? Where's the outfit? Where you been to?

QUIRT. Listen. I ain't writing my memoirs of this war till it's over. All you need to know is, I got two M.P.'s on my trail, and I don't want to meet 'em in these. [*He removes his coat and is found to be in striped pajamas. A small red cross on the jumper pocket.*]

FERGUSON. You come from the lines in that outfit, Quirt? In night-drawers?

QUIRT. I suppose you think I go 'round this way because I like it. [*He stows the overcoat and cap under the bench.*] Major, you're relieved. [*Takes slicker from peg on stair rail.*] Lend me your slicker, Fergy, I'll give it back if it thunders. [*He goes to chair at table, seizes the cognac, pours out two ponies and swallows them, looks at* FERGUSON, *then pours a third drink; drinks it.*]

FERGUSON. Of course you're paying for those, Quirt, even if you have gone cuckoo.

QUIRT. All right, all right! Don't get on your ear about it . . . and now you want to know where I've been.

FERGUSON. Oh, no, if a soldier wants to campaign in a pair of night-drawers, it ain't none of my parade. It takes all kinds of sergeants to make an army.

QUIRT [*drinking his third*]. You're too hard-hearted, Fergy. I ain't in my right mind. I was wounded, and now I've got aspasia. [*Mysteriously.*] My name is Field Marshal von Hindenburg, and I'm looking for a wagonload of pants that got lost in shipment.

FERGUSON. Yeah?

QUIRT. Yeah, sure. I wandered outta a hospital about five miles over at a place called Noisy. It was damned well named too, Fergy. Noisy was no name for it when I came outta the ether after I'd shipped in there with a piece of pants driven through a bullet hole in my leg.

FERGUSON. Have to give you ether to take off your pants?

QUIRT. No. They gave me ether so the stretcher bearers could steal a gold watch and eight hundred bucks off me. I certainly put up a squawk when I woke up and found 'em missing. But a hell of a lot of good it did me. I went looking for the bird that got them and ran into a guy in a bar-tender's coat in the operating room. He tried to pipe me down and I hung a shanty on the bimbo's eye. [*Enjoying the picture himself.*] And when they washed him off he was a captain. So they locked me up, wound and all. And then I got aspasia, and here I am. You ain't seen me.

FERGUSON. No, I ain't seen you. [*Distant voices shouting "Fergy!" "When do we eat?" "Chow," etc. At this sound, very faint,* QUIRT *rises quickly, starting for the stairs with a skip and jump.*] Keep your drawers on, Quirt. They ain't no M.P.'s. That's the outfit. I've got old Pete and his brother down at the bridge, keeping coffee and slum hot for 'em. Better go and give yourself up to Flagg as soon as he drives in. You'll be safe then. I'd like to see a set of doctor's take Flagg's first sergeant off him when he's just out of the lines. It surely would be a pretty sight afterwards, them doctors working on each other like monkeys. [*The voices come nearer. The cry, long drawn out like a wolf's, comes from many throats: "Ch-o-o-o-w-w!"*] That's me. They're calling for me. Well, old Fergy's got their chow, and hot too. [*He goes.* QUIRT *limps quickly to door after* FERGUSON *goes.* CHARMAINE *comes down the stairs at the same time.*]

QUIRT [*turning to find* CHARMAINE]. Hello, Pittsburgh.

CHARMAINE [*with a small cry, comes toward him*]. You are wounded.

QUIRT. Sure I'm wounded. Ain't that enough to put me

nine miles ahead of Flagg with you? I certainly beat
him here.

CHARMAINE [*trying to put arms around his neck*]. Mais,
mais . . . you are . . .

QUIRT [*restraining her*]. Don't embarrass me, darling,
because I ain't clothed and in my right mind. I just
been waiting for Fergy to leave so I could steal a
uniform from him. Where's his room? [CHARMAINE
points to door.] Wait a minute, dearie, until I salvage a pair of breeches. [*He goes out*. CHARMAINE
goes to the outside door, where voices are now heard.
QUIRT *reappears*.] Damn it, he's locked his chest!
Gimme a ice pick.

[QUIRT *takes bottle from bar. There are steps and
voices at the door, and* QUIRT *withdraws hastily to
the right*, CHARMAINE *following. Enter* KIPER, GOWDY,
and LIPINSKY. KIPER *spies the cognac bottle and holds
it over his open gullet. The other two rush him.
There is a tough scuffle*.]

KIPER. Lay off my bottle.

GOWDY. Say, don't drink it all! [*All then sit behind the
table and deliberately begin a tremendous racket*.]

KIPER. Hey! *Vin rouge! Vin blanc!* You, Pete! *Venez
ici*. Toot sweet!

LIPINSKY. Toot sweet—toot sweet—toot God damn sweet
—*jambon? Des oeufs! Fromages! Vin! Vin!*

GOWDY. *Bière, bière, bière!*

[FLAGG *enters. The three jump up and push back their
chairs. When he yells* "*Clear out*," *the tumult instantly ceases*. FLAGG *is cold sober, still in his old
clothes and dusty, but recently shaven, and possessed
of rolled leggings and an old brown shirt*.]

FLAGG. Clear out, you yapping hounds and tell the new
platoon commander to billet every man down the
moment he finishes mess. Tell him I don't want to
see one of 'em around this tavern till that's done.
[*Turns; crosses to bar*.] Tell them not to rag a man
to-night. [*Takes bottle; turns to them*.] As soon as

they know their billets, let 'em out. Let 'em drink.
Let 'em fight. Get out.

THE RUNNERS [*gently; somewhat discouraged*]. Ay, ay,
sir. [*They disappear.* CHARMAINE *enters quietly and
stands leaning in the doorway.* FLAGG *pours a beaker
and drinks it pleasantly, enjoyingly. Then he pours a
second and walks around to chair at table and sits
down.* CHARMAINE *has watched this from the doorway. He sees her at last.*]

FLAGG [*arising and bowing grandiosely, holding aloft
the drink*]. Madame la comtesse de la Cognac!

CHARMAINE [*embarrassed*]. Le grand capitaine de ma
coeur.

FLAGG. Yes, I'm the captain of your heart! Like hell I
am. Why don't you come and kiss me? None but the
brave, you know . . .

CHARMAINE. *Je ne comprends pas.*

FLAGG. Oh, no. You don't understand me. Well, I'm a
weary man, and I don't want any finagling from you.

CHARMAINE [*at door*]. You want me to kiss you?

FLAGG. Sure I want you to kiss me. Even though you
played the dirtiest sort of trick on me. [*The liquor
is beginning to deaden him.*] A dirty trick on your
poor old Captain Flagg. [*Turns to her.*] If I weren't
so kind and gentle I'd go out in the orchard, cut a
cherry switch, and give you a tanning.

[*She crosses over, kisses him quickly, and draws back,
a charmed bird before a snake.*]

CHARMAINE. You're a terrible man, *monsieur.*

FLAGG. I ain't terrible to you, honey. Come sit by your
old man. [*She sits on the table and looks down into
his eyes.*] Ain't I tired? Jeez, but I'm off war for life.
It's all right with thirty or forty men in the hills who
know their business. But there's so many little boys
along with me ain't got any business here at all. [*He
sighs and drinks the rest of the brandy.*] Ah! There
ain't no strength in this stuff any more. [*Hands her
his glass, which she places on table. He gets up un-*

steadily.] Le's go walk by the canal. I wanna get away from these new lieutenants. Le's walk along that bicycle path.

CHARMAINE. *Non, non, non. Demain soir. Demain soir.*

FLAGG. To-morrow? All right. I'm tired anyhow. Never been so tired before. Liquor just takes the pins out of my knees. Gimme a bottle to drink in bed. I don't want to think to-night.

CHARMAINE [*bringing him a bottle from the bar, smiling*]. *Ah, monsieur, vous êtes un grand soldat.*

FLAGG [*wandering to the door, suddenly apathetic.*] Nighty, sweetie. See you to-morrow. [*He goes out at rear.*]

QUIRT [*entering stealthily, in a farmer's smock which comes to his waist*]. So he's gone away.... What's the matter with the old boy? [*He attempts to kiss her. She shudders.*]

CHARMAINE [*drawing away from him*]. *Non, non, non! Merci.*

QUIRT. Why, what's the matter, Pittsburgh? Don't you love me no more?

CHARMAINE. *Oui—mais—*

QUIRT. Of course I understand. Seeing him that way sort of cut you up, especially when I was wearing such a lousy outfit, you liking them all in uniforms. Just wait, baby. When I git that brass lock off Fergie's box and turn out in his blues on sick leave, you'll forget this Flagg person. I understand. Sure. I been with soldiers' girls a lot, myself.

CHARMAINE. When you are beautiful, *mon sergeant,* then I love you— [*She runs up steps.*]

QUIRT. Come back here!

[*She disappears, laughing.* KIPER *and* LIPINSKY *enter.*]

KIPER. Jeez, Sergeant, but you picked a funny outfit to be buried in.

QUIRT [*at foot of stairs—hostile*]. Who's thinking of burying me?

KIPER. I expect Flagg'll make me bury you. But he's

going to lay you out himself.

QUIRT. Is he looking for me? How did he know I'm
here?

LIPINSKY. We just heard Ferguson telling him. I ain't
never heard him swear so much since I been with
him. We came to ask you to run away some more.

QUIRT. You did, eh? Well, you can go down to the
bridge and head him off. You can tell him he passed
up visiting this place just before the outfit shoved
last time. You can tell him if he comes up here I'll
cut his gizzard out for him. You can tell him I'm
engaged to be married, and I ain't got no duty for
him around here.

[FLAGG *enters, drunk and swaggering.*]

FLAGG. Who's the hay-shaker? Well, if it ain't Sergeant
Quirt! A regular family reunion. Quirt, how are you?
When you coming back to the factory?

QUIRT. Flagg, you're out of this here detail. Your hands
off my business after that dirty trick you put over
on me. If I kill you there isn't a court can touch me
for it in this man's army.

FLAGG. Quirt, you're drunk.

QUIRT. Both of us.

FLAGG. Yeah, both of us.

QUIRT. Well, then, Flagg, you're drunk. What are you
going to do about it?

FLAGG. I'm gonna have a drink. [*Turns to bar and takes
bottle; pours two drinks.*]

QUIRT. Both of us.

FLAGG. Yeah, both of us. [*They drink, first bowing to
each other.*] Quirt, I got something I want to tell you.

QUIRT. The hell!

FLAGG. You want to hear it?

QUIRT. I ain't particular.

FLAGG. Well, this is it, Sergeant. You can go jump in
the canal. I knew you'd head for Charmaine as soon
as you got that bullet under your hide. You had half
a day's start of me and you didn't beat me more than

five minutes. You might just as well 'a' stayed on
the bakery route. You ain't no more needed here
than a third leg on a kangaroo. Have one on me.
[FLAGG *pours for both.*]

QUIRT [*they bow*]. Delighted, I'm sure. [*They drink and
replace glasses.*] You're a hell of an officer, Flagg.
[QUIRT *wipes right hand on smock.*] And your views
on me probably ain't worth a damn. On the other
hand, it's only fair to warn you that I'm the sole
survivor of seven catastrophes, any one of which was
calculated to carry off every man-jack in the immediate neighborhood as was adjacent, and if there
was to be a catastrophe of any dimensions in this
here vicinity in the near future, I have expectations
of survival exceeding your own. Have one on me.
[QUIRT *pours drinks.*]

FLAGG. Thank you, Quirt, I will. [*They drink, and
FLAGG drunkenly points finger at* QUIRT *until he can
get his mind to working.*] Your method of expressing
yourself, Quirt, is complicated by your tongue being
as thick as your God damn head. But if you mean
trouble, let me point out to you that among other
things, you forgot to bring your gun along. [QUIRT
feels for his absent weapon; FLAGG *laughs heartily.*]
Ain't you a neat little fool, Hoppergrass, and will
you drink?

QUIRT. I will.

[FLAGG *pours. Both bow, then drink again; but* QUIRT
has taken a sip before he realizes he hasn't bowed.]

FLAGG. Do you give up?

QUIRT. No.

FLAGG [*turns to bar and starts pouring*]. Have another.

[*As* FLAGG *starts to pour,* QUIRT *leaps like a flash on his
back.* KIPER *catches* QUIRT'S *wrists from behind.* LIPIN-
SKY *drags* FLAGG *away. When* QUIRT *jumps* FLAGG, *he
takes the gun out of* FLAGG'S *holster with his right
hand; his left is in stranglehold around* FLAGG'S *neck.*
FLAGG *reaches back and holds* QUIRT *by back of neck.*

They scuffle until separated.]

KIPER [*holding* QUIRT]. What do you want done with him, sir?

FLAGG [*to* LIPINSKY, *who is holding him*]. Let me go or I'll knock you for a row of G.I. cans. Take the gun away from him. [QUIRT *throws the automatic on the floor.* FLAGG *puts his foot on it.*] Let go, all. [QUIRT *is turned loose.*] Well, bo, had enough?

QUIRT. I'll tell you what I'll do with you. I'll go outside with you and try two of them little toys at fifty yards. Come again.

FLAGG. And you, the best pistol shot in the corps, would put one through my carburetor as easy as pitching a penny in a well. Come again.

QUIRT. I'll take you on any way you can think of, you baboon. I can out-shoot you and out-think you and out-drink you. There ain't nothing I can't do better than you.

FLAGG. You're a liar, Quirt, and you know it. I could break you in two. You got my gun because you jumped me without warning. No soldier you ever soldiered with could head me when I got started . . . and by the way, Quirt, if you can out-drink me you ain't leading out very well to-night. You're talking thick and wild, Quirt, thick and wild. You'd better turn in somewhere and sleep it off.

QUIRT. Me? Sleep off a couple of drinks? I was living on cognac when all your buttons was safety pins.

FLAGG. Yeah, well, you can't carry it the way you used to, then. You're getting old, Quirt. Old and feeble. Yeah, you're getting old.

QUIRT. Not me. *You* may be an old man, Flagg. Or an old woman if it suits you better, but not me. Captains and generals, they pass along. I've seen hundreds of 'em. Better men than you, Flagg. They passed along. But top sergeants is eternal. They don't never die.

FLAGG. Well, if you don't want to die, you top sergeant,

don't fool with me. I've seen top sergeants go damn fast— Now, listen, Quirt, are you going to jump in that canal or are you going to need six pall-bearers to take you there?

QUIRT. It'll take more than six pall-bearers to put me in one of these French canals. I don't like the taste of them.

[CHARMAINE *re-enters.*]

FLAGG. Charmaine! Cognac!

[CHARMAINE *crosses behind table; gets bottle; pours drink for* QUIRT, *also for* FLAGG.]

CHARMAINE [*laying a hand on the* CAPTAIN'S *shoulder*]. Is it now—friends again?

FLAGG [*putting an arm about her*]. Best you ever saw, Charmaine. We'll drink to it, Quirt. Flagg and Quirt forever—till you get bumped off. Flagg and Quirt, the tropical twins! There ain't room for both of 'em in the whole world! [FLAGG *pats* CHARMAINE *on hip.*]

QUIRT [*sets down his glass, hard*]. Damn you, Flagg!

FLAGG [*setting down his glass*]. What's the matter, Hoppergrass? Aren't you drinking?

QUIRT. I got here first, Flagg.

FLAGG. I know it. Nobody said you didn't.

QUIRT [*rising*]. You take your hands off Charmaine.

FLAGG. Any time you want my hands off Charmaine, you come and take 'em off.

CHARMAINE. No. No! You must be friends.

FLAGG. With you around!

QUIRT. It strikes me there's only room for one of us in this shanty to-night. Do you plan on going somewhere, or not?

FLAGG. Did you ever see me leaving any place I didn't feel like leaving?

CHARMAINE [*touching the* CAPTAIN'S *sleeve*]. Don't fight —please.

FLAGG [*not looking at her—pushing her back*]. The hell you say! First time in six months I've had a good reason for fighting. The Germans don't want my

woman. I been fighting them for eight dollars a day.
. . . Go on back of the counter.

CHARMAINE. I—I love you both.

QUIRT. You get to hell outta here, Flagg. Dig up a
broad of your own.

FLAGG. Sorry. Rejected.

QUIRT. You ain't man enough to shoot me for her.
Well, here's what I'll do. I'll shoot you dice for her.
[*Tosses out dice on table.*] High dice, aces low.

[KIPER *and* LIPINSKY *take steps forward, interested.*]

FLAGG. Boys, is Quirt crooked with the bones?

[LIPINSKY *goes back to lean on platform.*]

KIPER. He's got a pair ought to be in a circus. [QUIRT
gives KIPER *a bad look.*]

FLAGG. Then we'll deal a hand at blackjack.

QUIRT [*picks up dice; puts them back in pocket, while*
KIPER *goes back with* LIPINSKY]. And the guy that
loses beats it for somewhere else.

FLAGG. What do you mean, beats it? We'll shoot, but
my way. The man that wins gets a gun, and the man
that loses gets a head start. Everybody wins, see?
One gets the girl and the other gets a chance to stay
in bed the rest of this war.

KIPER. Captain Flagg, I don't think you ought to do
this.

FLAGG. Close your hatch. I'll try anything once, soldier. [*Briskly.*] Now for a game of blackjack for one
automatic.

QUIRT. That's all right with me.

FLAGG. And the gun on the table between us. [*He picks
it up.*]

KIPER [*as he and* LIPINSKY *seize* QUIRT'S *arms*]. Come
quiet now, before he notices.

QUIRT [*writhing loose*]. Keep off me, you swine!

[KIPER *and* LIPINSKY *fall back.*]

FLAGG [*having recovered gun, starts to straighten up.*]
March out that door, both of you, and if you stick
a neck in here before the game's over I promise to

wreck you for life. Are you going, or do I demon-
strate? [*They go out quickly.*] Charmaine! Upstairs!
[*She goes.* FLAGG *sits at table;* QUIRT *on table.* FLAGG
shuffles cards, and offering them to QUIRT, *says "Cut."*
QUIRT *fondles cards; says "Be good to me, babies, and
I'll let moonlight into a captain." He cuts.* FLAGG
deals one to QUIRT, *then one to himself; then one to*
QUIRT, *and looks at the next one for himself.*]

QUIRT. What's that, a king?

FLAGG. How many you want? Make it snappy and
knock off that guff. Here's looking down your grave.
May you have many worms, Quirt.

QUIRT. Crawling, right out of your teeth, Flagg. Hit me.

FLAGG [*deals a card face up.*] A two-spot. Well, any
more?

QUIRT. Hit me again.

FLAGG [*dealing one*]. Well, you got a king that time. Remember, if you hold six cards without going bust
you can empty the automatic at me.

QUIRT. Hit me again.

FLAGG. A king, by God! [QUIRT, *with one sweep turns
over the table, with candles and chairs, and dives
through the door; runs off.*] You double-dealing Chinaman! [FLAGG *finds the gun in the darkness and fires
shot just outside the door. He is heard re-entering.*]
Show a light, somebody, Charmaine! [FLAGG *sets up
the table.*]

CHARMAINE [*at the head of the stairs with a lamp*].
What is it? You have killed him? [*Goes up to door.*]

FLAGG. Killed hell! He knocked out the light and ran,
the dirty hound! [CHARMAINE *looks out the door,
shielding the lamp from the wind.*] Oh, he's gone.

CHARMAINE. Maybe you hit him. [*Puts lamp on table;
then crosses to* FLAGG.]

FLAGG. Don't you worry. He was half-way to the river,
the rate he was going, before I found the door. Don't
you weep, sweetheart. [*Puts her on his left knee.*]
You're weeping for a skunk that'd run out on a game

of cards. It's you and me to-night, lady. Listen, Charmaine. [*Putting his arm around her.*] I love you like
the devil. I always did. You love me, Charmaine?

CHARMAINE. Only you.

FLAGG. God, I'm dead—I'm going to sleep for three
days. [FLAGG *rests head on her breast and sighs. Then*
LIPINSKY *and* GOWDY *walk in.*]

LIPINSKY. Sorry to disturb you, sir.

FLAGG. My God, did you hear what I told you?

LIPINSKY. Got bad news, Captain Flagg.

FLAGG. Spit it out.

LIPINSKY. The outfit's going back. Battalion moving
at once.

FLAGG. What? What?

LIPINSKY. We're ordered back. Ordered back in. Everybody's going back in. General movement.

FLAGG. Dammit, I'm on leave.

GOWDY. All leaves revoked, Captain Flagg.

FLAGG. Well, why couldn't you stay away from here?
You knew where I was. Why in hell did you have
to come and tell me?

GOWDY. Well, headquarters sent out, looking for you.

LIPINSKY. Kiper wouldn't come, Captain Flagg. He was
for leaving you alone.

FLAGG. He was, was he? Well, Kiper's got sense. Look
here, you never found me to give me the message,
and I'm not going. Can you remember, or have I
got to bury you to keep your mouth shut? What right
have they got to offer a man leave and then revoke
it? I gave them their prisoner! I've got their damn
papers!

LIPINSKY. Well, you see, the company's going to shove
off. What could we do?

FLAGG. You could have an attack of something, damn
it to hell! You could fall and break your neck on
the way here.

LIPINSKY. I was afraid not to let you know. You always
wanted to know.

FLAGG. Well, you've got to do some tall lying to make up for it, because I'm not going. Tell them any story you think of, only I never got the news. I earned my leave, and it's signed, sealed, and delivered. That crowd at headquarters has got to live up to its end of the bargain. They can't take these men back in. I won't stand for it. [*Turns to* CHARMAINE.] Shall we stay here, Charmaine?

CHARMAINE. *Oui, ici.*

[*They embrace.* FLAGG *rests head on her breast.*]

FLAGG [*after a pause, shakes himself a bit*]. No, I'll go. I may be drunk, but I know I'll go. There's something rotten about this profession of arms, some kind of damned religion connected with it that you can't shake. When they tell you to die, you have to do it, even if you're a better man than they are. Good-bye, Charmaine, put your money in real estate, and marry that cuckoo if you can. You'll never see me again. This town is a jinx for me. [*Again rests head on* CHARMAINE.] God Almighty, but I'm tired. [*He rises and crosses to where* FERGUSON *has entered.* CHARMAINE *sits in chair watching.*] Hello, Fergy. We're shoving off. Follow us, because we don't know where we're going. Nobody knows. [*He goes out, staggering, tired.* FERGUSON *follows him out.* GOWDY *and* LIPINSKY *follow* FERGUSON. CHARMAINE *buries her head in arms on table.*]

QUIRT [*comes in upper floor stairway*]. Hello, Pittsburgh!

CHARMAINE. You are not *killed?*

QUIRT [*coming downstairs to bottom step*]. No, it's me all right. Everybody gone?

CHARMAINE. Everybody.

QUIRT. Outfit's going in again, huh?

CHARMAINE. *Oui.*

QUIRT. Well, well! I been upstairs. Climbed up the kitchen roof. Do you love your papa?

CHARMAINE. *Mais oui.*

QUIRT. Then you better kiss him good-bye. [*Pats her face; then kisses her. Staggers up to door.*] What a lot of God damn fools it takes to make a war! Hey, Flagg, wait for baby!

[CHARMAINE *watches from the table.*]

CURTAIN

THEY KNEW
WHAT THEY WANTED

by Sidney Howard

*First production, November 24, 1924,
at the Garrick Theatre, New York City,
with the following cast:*

JOE, *Glenn Anders*
FATHER MC KEE, Charles Kennedy
AH GEE, *Allen Atwell*
TONY, *Richard Bennett*
THE R.F.D., *Robert Cook*
AMY, *Pauline Lord*
ANGELO, *Hardwick Nevin*
GIORGIO, *Jacob Zollinger*
THE DOCTOR, *Charles Tazewell*
FIRST ITALIAN MOTHER, *Frances Hyde*
HER DAUGHTER, *Antoinette Bizzoco*
SECOND ITALIAN MOTHER, *Peggy Conway*
HER SON, *Edward Rosenfeld*

SCENES

Tony's farmhouse in the Napa Valley, California.
ACT I *Morning, in early summer.*
ACT II *Evening. Same day.*
ACT III *Three months later.*

SCENE—*The scene of the play is the home of an Italian winegrower in the Napa Valley in California. All of the action takes place in the main downstairs room which serves as general living and dining room.*

It is necessary to understand that the house is not in the least Spanish in its architecture. As a matter of fact, it would serve any respectable Middle-Western farmer as a fitting and inconspicuous residence. It was built in the 'nineties of wood, is painted white on its exterior, and has only one story.

A door at the back, the main one to the outer world, gives on the porch. Another door, to the right of the audience, gives on the kitchen. The kitchen is three steps above the level of the room and so placed that the audience can see into it. It is completely furnished. A third door, to the left of the audience, gives on a flight of steps which leads to the cellar of the house. A fourth door, also on the left and farther down stage, gives on the bedroom.

The back wall should also be broken by windows; on the right of the central door, a bay window, on the left, a double flat window.

The view from the house is over a valley and toward brown Californian hills. The landscape is checkered with cultivation. Some of the checkers are orchards. Most of them are vineyards. The foreground is all vines. Vines twine about the pillars of the porch. In the beginning of the play—it begins in summer—the grapes on the porch vines are small and green. In the last act—three months having elapsed—they are large and purple.

The back stage must be so arranged that people who

approach the house from the highroad appear to mount the porch steps from a much lower level. At other times, however, it is required that the characters be able to go and come on the level of the house itself where the farmyard is.

Inside the room the wallpaper and the carpet are new and garish. The cheapest variety of lace curtains hangs in the windows. The furniture is new and includes a golden-oak dining table with chairs to match, a morris chair, another easy chair, a chest of drawers, a sideboard, a hat rack.

On one wall hangs a picture of Garibaldi. A picture of George Washington hangs over the central door. Other mural decorations include a poster of the Navigazione Generale Italiana, a still-life chromo, a religious chromo, and a small mirror.

On the hat rack hangs a double-barrelled shotgun draped with a loaded cartridge belt.

The whole impression must be one of gaiety and simple good living.

Act one

The red, white and green of Italy combine with the red, white and blue of these United States in bunting, garlands of fluted paper, pompons and plumes of shredded tissue, to make up a scheme of decoration which is, to say the least, violent. The picture of Garibaldi is draped with an American flag, the picture of Washington with an Italian flag. The full glare of the early morning sun streams in through door and windows.

The room is fairly littered with boxes. Atop one of these, from which it has just been extracted, stands a handsome wedding cake, surmounted by statuary representing the ideal bride and groom in full regalia under a bell. The boxes are all addressed to

Tony Patucci,
R. F. D. Napa, Calif.

AH GEE *stands on a ladder on the porch outside the open entrance door, hanging Chinese lanterns. He is a silent, spare Chinaman, of age maturely indeterminate. He wears blue overalls and a black chambray shirt.*

JOE—*dark, sloppy, beautiful, and young—is busy opening a packing case in the center of the stage. His back is turned upon the door.*

JOE [*as he works, he half sings, half mutters to himself the words of "Remember," an I. W. W. song, to the tune of "Hold the Fort"*].

"We speak to you from jail to-day,
Two hundred union men,

> We're here because the bosses' laws
>   Bring slavery again."

Through this the curtain rises and FATHER MC KEE *is seen climbing the porch steps. He wears the sober garb of a Catholic priest, not over clean, what with dust, spots, and all. He nods to* AH GEE *and comes into the doorway. He stands a moment to mop his large, pale face with a red bandana. Then he lowers lugubrious disapproval upon everything in sight. Then he yawns.*

He is one of those clerics who can never mention anything except to denounce it. And his technique of denunciation is quite special to himself. It consists in a long, throaty abstention from inflection of any kind which culminates in a vocal explosion when he reaches the accented syllable of a word upon which his emphasis depends. This word always seems to wake him up for an instant. Once it is spoken, however, he relapses into semi-somnolence for the remainder of his remarks. At heart, he is genial and kindly enough, quite the American counterpart of the French village curé.

FATHER MC KEE. Hello, Joe.

JOE. Hello there, Padre. What do you think?

FATHER MC KEE. Looks to me like a bawdy house.

JOE. It's goin' to be *some* festa. . . . Lily Cups! What do you know about that for style?

FATHER MC KEE. Where's Tony?

JOE [*nods toward the door of the bedroom*]. In there gettin' dolled up. . . . Hey, there, bridegroom! The Padre's out here.

FATHER MC KEE. I come up to have a serious talk with Tony.

JOE. Well, for God's sake, don't get him upset no more'n what he is already. He's been stallin' around all mornin', afraid to go down and meet the bride. You better leave him alone.

FATHER MC KEE. I'm always glad to have your advice,

Joe. I didn't look to find you still hangin' 'round.

JOE. Oh, didn't you, Padre?

FATHER MC KEE. Tony told me you'd decided to go away.

JOE. Well, Padre, I'll tell you how it is. [*He grins impudently.*] I don't believe in stayin' any one place too long. 'Tain't fair for me not to give the rest of California a chance at my society. But I ain't goin' before I seen all the fun, got Tony safely married, an' kissed the bride. [*He turns to the door and* AH GEE.] That's fine, Ah Gee. Better take these here Lily Cups in the kitchen when you get through.

[*Magnificently* TONY *enters from the bedroom. He is stout, floridly bronzed, sixty years old, vigorous, jovial, simple, and excitable. His great gift is for gesture. To-day we meet him in his Sunday best, a very brilliant purple suit with a more than oriental waistcoat which serves to display a stupendous gold watch chain. He wears a boiled shirt, an emerald-green tie, and a derby hat. He carries his new patent-leather shoes in his hand. He seems to be perspiring rather freely.*]

TONY. Looka me! I'm da most stylish fella in da world.

FATHER MC KEE. I come up to talk to you, Tony.

TONY. I'm glad you come, Padre. How you like my clothes, eh? Costa playnta good money! [*Attention is called to the shoes.*] For da feet. . . .

JOE [*a motion to the wedding cake*]. How's it strike you, Tony?

TONY. Madonna! [*He throws his shoes into the morris chair. His hat assumes a terrific angle. He cannot keep his hands off that cake.*] Look, Padre! From Frisco! Special! Twelve dollar' an' two bits! Look! [*The miniature bride and groom particularly please him.*] Ees Tony an' his Amy!

JOE. Them lanterns is Ah Gee's personal donation.

TONY. Thank you, Ah Gee! Ees verra fine. Ah Gee, you go an' bring vino, now, for Padre, eh? [AH GEE *obeys the order, taking the Lily Cups with him into his kitchen.*]

JOE. Show some speed now, Tony. It's past nine. 'Tain't hardly pretty to keep the bride waitin'.

TONY [*as he sits down to the struggle with his shoes*]. I'm goin' verra quick.

FATHER MC KEE. I got to have a word with you, Tony, before you go to the station.

JOE. The Padre's been tryin' to tell me you're scared to have me around where I can kiss the bride. [*He picks up a couple of flags and goes outside.*]

TONY [*in undisguised terror*]. You ain't goin' be kissin' no bride, Joe. You hear dat?

JOE [*off stage he is heard singing*].

> "We laugh and sing, we have no fear
>   Our hearts are always light,
> We know that every Wobbly true
>   Will carry on the fight."

TONY. He's too goddam fresh, dat fella, with kissin' my Amy an' all dose goddam Wobbly songs. Don' you think so, Padre?

FATHER MC KEE. I didn't come up here to talk about Joe, Tony. I come up to talk about this here weddin'.

TONY. I'm glad you come, Padre. I'm verra bad scare'.

FATHER MC KEE. You got good reason for bein' scared, if you want to know what *I* think.

TONY. I got verra special reason.

FATHER MC KEE. What reason?

TONY. Don't you never mind! Da's my secret dat I don' tell nobody. You tell Joe he go away quick, Padre. Den, maybe, ees all right.

FATHER MC KEE. So that's it! Well, I don't blame you for that.

TONY [*deeply indignant at the implication*]. Oh! . . . No, by God! You don' ondrastan', Padre. Joe is like my own son to me! Ees som'thing verra different. Madonna mia! Ees som'thing I been doin' myself! Ees som'thing Tony's been doin' w'at's goin mak' verra bad trouble for Tony.

FATHER MC KEE. I'll tell Joe nothin'. You've made your own bed and if you won't get off it while there's time, you got to lie on it. But I want you to understand that I don't like nothin' 'bout this here weddin'. It ain't got my approval.

TONY [*the first shoe slips on and he sits up in amazement*]. You don't like weddin', Padre?

FATHER MC KEE. No, I don't. An' that's just what I come up here to tell you. I don't like nothin' about it, an' if you persist in goin' ahead in spite of my advice, I don't want you sayin' afterwards that you wasn't warned.

TONY. Dio mio! [*He amplifies this with the sign of the cross. Then his confidence rather returns to him.*] Aw . . . tak' a pinch-a snuff! You mak' me tire', Padre! You think festa is no good for people. You padre fellas don' know nothing. Work! Work! Work evra day! Den, by-an'-by, is comin' festa. After festa workin' is more easy. [*He resumes the shoe problem.*]

FATHER MC KEE. Tony, you know perfectly well that I ain't got no more objection to no festa than I have to any other pomp of the flesh. But I'm your spirichool adviser an' I been mullin' this weddin' over in my mind an' I come to the conclusion that I'm agin it. I don't like it at all. I got my reasons for what I say.

TONY [*does the Padre guess his secret?*]. W'at reason you got?

FATHER MC KEE. In the first place, you ain't got no business marryin' no woman who ain't a good Cath'lic.

TONY [*immeasurable relief*]. Ees no matter.

FATHER MC KEE. A mixed marriage ain't no better'n plain livin' in sin.

TONY. Ain' we got you for keep' sin away, Padre?

FATHER MC KEE. Why ain't you marryin' a woman out of your own parish instead of trapesin' all the way to Frisco to pick out a heretic?

TONY. Is no good womans in dees parish.

FATHER MC KEE. What's wrong with 'em?

TONY. Joe is sleepin' with evra one.

FATHER MC KEE. That ain't the point.

TONY [*enlisting the shoe to help his gesticulation*]. Oh, ees point all right, Padre. Joe is told me 'bout evrathing. I been lookin' all 'round here at all da womans in dees parish. I been lookin' evra place for twent' mile. Ees no good womans for wife here. Joe is told me 'bout evra one. Den I'm gone to Napa for look all 'round dere an' in Napa ees no better . . . ees just da same like here. So den I go down all da way to Frisco for look after wife an' I find my Amy. She is like a rose, all wilt'. You puttin' water on her an' she come out most beautiful. I'm goin' marry with my Amy, Padre, an' I don' marry with nobody else. She's been tellin' me she is no Cath'lic. I say, w'at I care? By an' by, maybe, if we bein' patient, we bringin' her in da church, an' showin' her da candles and da Madonna, all fix up good with flowers and da big tin heart, an' evrathing smellin' so prett' an' you preachin' verra loud an' da music an' evrathing, maybe . . . by an' by . . . [*He turns again to his shoe.*] But now ees no matter. W'at I care?

FATHER MC KEE. It don't look good to me.

TONY. Ees all right. . . . If you don't want my Amy an' me gettin' married with good Cath'lic priest like you, den, by God—

FATHER MC KEE. I ain't said I wouldn't marry you.

TONY. Eh bene!

FATHER MC KEE. I'm only tryin' to tell you. . . .

TONY. Ahi! Dio mio. . . . [*The shoe goes on, producing intense pain.*] He look much better as he feel!

FATHER MC KEE. There ain't no good in no old man marryin' with no young woman.

TONY. You think anybody marry with old woman? Tak' a pinch-a snuff!

FATHER MC KEE. I know one old man who married a young woman an' she carried on with a stage driver!

TONY. Dio mio!

FATHER MC KEE. He had knowed her all her life, too, an' you ain't knowed your Amy more'n 'bout five minutes.

TONY. Ees no matter.

FATHER MC KEE. An' I know another fellow who married one of them city girls like your Amy without bein' properly acquainted an' she turned out to be a scarlet woman.

TONY. My Amy don' do dat.

[AH GEE *enters from kitchen with two glasses and a bottle of wine.*]

FATHER MC KEE. Ain't you just now been tellin' me you're scared of her seein' Joe?

TONY. No, by God!

FATHER MC KEE. Joe ain't the only young fellow around, either!

TONY. Young fellas is no matter. Only Joe. An' I ain' scare' over Joe excep' for special reason. You tell Joe, Padre . . . [*He is returning to his old subject, but the wine distracts him.*] Ah-h-h!

FATHER MC KEE. Why didn't you get married forty years ago?

TONY. I think you know verra good w'y. Ees because I'm no dam' fool. . . . W'en I'm young, I got nothing. I'm broke all da time, you remember? I got no money for havin' wife. I don' want no wife for mak' her work all da time. Da's no good, dat. Da's mak' her no more young, no more prett'. Evrabody say Tony is crazy for no' havin' wife. I say Tony is no dam' fool. W'at is happen? Pro'ibish' is com'. Salute! [*A glass of wine.* AH GEE *has returned to his kitchen.*] An' w'at I say? I say, "Ees dam' fool law. Ees dam' fool fellas for bein' scare' an' pullin' up da grape' for tryin' growin' som'thing different." W'at I'm doin'? I'm keep the grape, eh? I say, "I come in dees country for growin' da grape! God mak' dees country for growin' da grape! Ees not for pro'ibish' God mak' dees country. Ees for growin' da grape!" Ees true? Sure ees true! [*Another glass of wine.*] An' w'at happen? Before pro'ibish' I sell my grape' for ten, maybe twelve dollar da ton. Now I sell my grape' sometime one hundra dollar' da ton. Pro'ibish' is mak' me verra rich. [*Another glass of wine.*] I got my fine house. I got Joe for bein' foreman. I got two men for helpin' Joe. I got one Chink for cook. I got one Ford car. I got all I want, evrathing, excep' only wife. Now I'm goin' have wife. Verra nice an' young an' fat. Not for work. No! For sit an' holdin' da hands and havin' kids. Three kids. [*He demonstrates the altitude of each.*] Antonio . . . Giuseppe . . . Anna . . . Da's like trees an' cows an' all good people. Da's fine for God an' evrabody! I tell you, Padre, Tony know w'at he want!

FATHER MC KEE. Whatever made you think a man of your age could have children? [*This staggers* TONY.] I tell you, Tony, it ain't possible.

TONY. Eh? Tony is too old for havin' kids? I tell you, Tony can have twent' kids if he want! I tell you Tony can have kids w'en he is one hundra year' old. Dio mio! From da sole of his feet to da top of his hat, Tony is big, strong man! I think I ondrastan' you verra good, Padre. Tony is not too old for havin' kids. He's too rich, eh? [*This rather strikes home.*] Yah! Tony is rich an', if he don' have no kids, den da church is gettin' all Tony's money an' da Padre is gettin' Tony's fine house all fix' up good for livin' in, eh?

FATHER MC KEE [*a very severe shepherd*]. Tony!

TONY [*the horns of the devil with his fingers*]. Don' you go for puttin' no evil eye on Tony an' his Amy!

FATHER MC KEE. You're givin' way to ignorant superstition, which ain't right in no good Cath'lic.

TONY [*on his feet in a panic*]. Dio mio! My Amy is comin' on dat train an' here you keep me, sittin', talkin'. . . .

FATHER MC KEE. You irreverent old lunatic, you, if you're bent on marryin', I'll marry you. [JOE *reappears in the doorway.*] But I don't want you comin' around afterwards squawkin' about it.

TONY. Eh, Joe! Da Padre don't want me gettin' marry with my Amy because he's scare' da church don' never get my money!

JOE. For cripe's sake, Tony, ain't you heard that whistle?

TONY. I go! I go!

JOE. Train's in now.

TONY. Porco Dio! Ah Gee!

JOE. Fix your tie.

TONY. I fix. . . . [AH GEE *comes from the kitchen for his master's order.*] Un altro fiasco. [AH GEE *returns to the kitchen.*]

JOE. You won't make no hit if you're drunk, Tony.

TONY. Not drunk, Joe. Only scare'. Verra bad scare'.

JOE. Bridegrooms is always scared.

TONY. Jes' Chris', maybe I'm sick!

JOE. No!

TONY. Santa Maria, I *am* sick!

JOE. What's wrong with you?

TONY. I don' know! I'm sick! I'm sick! I'm sick!

[AH GEE *returns with the wine bottle refilled.* TONY *seeks prompt solace.* AH GEE *goes back to his kitchen.*]

JOE. You'll be a helluva sight sicker if you don't lay off that stuff.

TONY. I canno' go for get my Amy, Joe. I canno' go. . . .

JOE. All right. I'll go . . .

TONY. Oh, by God! No! NO!

JOE. Tony, if you drive the Ford down the hill in this state of mind you'll break your dam' neck.

TONY [*more solace*]. I feel good now. I drive fine. I don'

want nobody for go for my Amy but only me. . . .
[*Then he weakens again.*] Joe, I'm scare', I'm scare',
I'm scare'!

JOE. What you scared of, Tony?

TONY. Maybe my Amy . . .

JOE. Come on, beat it!

TONY. I feel good now an' I don' want nobody for go
for my Amy but only me. You bet! [*He starts.*]

JOE. That's the boy!

TONY [*another relapse*]. Joe, you don't get mad if I
ask you som'thing? I got verra good reason, Joe . . .
Joe . . . how soon you goin' away, Joe?

JOE. You don't *want* me to go, do you?

TONY. I think ees much better.

JOE. What's the idea, Tony?

TONY. Joe . . . som'thing is happen', da's all. . . . You
go, Joe. I been tryin' for three days for ask you dees,
Joe, an' I been scare' you get mad. I pay you double
extra for goin' to-day, for goin' now, eh? Joe? Verra
quick?

JOE. An' miss the festa? Like hell!

TONY. Joe, you don' ondrastan'. . . .

JOE. Forget it, Tony.

TONY. Joe . . .

JOE. If you keep her waitin', she'll go back to Frisco.

TONY. Dio mio! [*He goes to the door and turns yet
once again.*] Joe . . . ? [*He catches* FATHER MC KEE'S
eye.] Som'thing verra bad is goin' happen with Tony.
. . . Clean evrathing clean before my Amy come. [*He
is really gone.* JOE *follows him out and stands on
the porch looking after him. A Ford motor roars
and dies away into high speed.*]

FATHER MC KEE [*at the window*]. Look at him!

JOE. He could drive the Ford in his sleep.

FATHER MC KEE. I don't hold with no old man galli-
vantin'.

JOE. Don't you fret, Padre. Didn't I tell you not to get
him all worked up? [*This ruffles the good priest who*

makes to follow TONY. JOE *intercepts him and forces
him back into the room.*]

FATHER MC KEE. Well?

JOE. Sit down a minute. You been tellin' Tony what
you think. Now I got some tellin' to do.

FATHER MC KEE. Have you, indeed? Well, I don't see
no good—

JOE. Maybe *I* don't see much good, but what the hell!

FATHER MC KEE. Young man! That's the pernicious doc-
trine of Lacey Fairey.

JOE. What's that?

FATHER MC KEE. A French expression meanin' "Suffi-
cient unto the day."

JOE. What of it? If folks is bent on makin' mistakes, an'
you can't stop 'em, let 'em go ahead, that's what I
say. I don't want nobody hatin' my guts for bein'
too dam' right all the time, see? Not bein' a priest, I
aim to get along with folks. That way, when they're
in wrong, I can be some use.

FATHER MC KEE. That ain't in accord with the teachin's of Jesus!

JOE. A helluva lot you an' me know about the teachin's
of Jesus.

FATHER MC KEE. Joe, if you ain't goin' to be rev'rent ...

JOE. I'm talkin' now.

FATHER MC KEE. Oh, are you?

JOE. Yeah. I wouldn't have no harm come to Tony,
not for anything in the world, see? An' I been agi-
tatin' against this weddin' a lot longer'n you have an'
I know what it's all about, see? I'm here goin' on five
months, now, an' that's longer'n I ever stayed any
one place.

FATHER MC KEE. Is it?

JOE. Excep' once in jail, it is. An' I been lookin' after
Tony all the time since I come here. I come in to
bum a meal an' I stayed five months. Five months
I been workin' for Tony an' lookin' after him and
he's treated me dam' good an' that's God's truth. I

wouldn't have worked that long for him if he hadn't treated me dam' good, either. I ain't none too strong for stayin' put, you know. I like to move an' now I'm goin' to move. I'm what the papers call a "unskilled migratory" an' I got to migrate, see? Tony wants me to go an' I want to go. But, what I want to know is: who's goin' to look after Tony when I'm gone?

FATHER MC KEE. Ain't that his wife's place?

JOE. Sure it's his wife's place. But suppose this weddin' don't turn out so good? Are you goin' to look out for him?

FATHER MC KEE. Ain't Tony my spirichool charge an' responsibility?

JOE. All *right!* An' I ain't so sure you're goin' to have much trouble, either. Amy looks to me like a fair to middlin' smart kid an' she knows what she's in for, too.

FATHER MC KEE. You seem to be well informed, Joe. Do you happen to know the lady?

JOE. I ain't never laid eyes on her. [*Then the implication percolates.*] Oh, I may go chasin' women plenty, but I don't chase Tony's wife, see? An' I ain't fixin' to, neither. Just get that straight.

FATHER MC KEE. I'm glad to hear it, Joe.

JOE. But I happen to know about her. Didn't I have to write all Tony's letters for him? You wouldn't expect Tony to be writin' to no lady with *his* education, would you?

FATHER MC KEE. No, I can't say that I would.

JOE. Why, I even had to read him the letters she wrote back. That's how I got my dope. An' what I say is: she's got plenty of sense. Don't you fool yourself she hasn't. I'll show you. [*He goes to the chest of drawers for some letters and photographs. He brings them back to the* PADRE.] You can see for yourself. [*And he submits Exhibit A—a letter.*] Tony goes to Frisco lookin' for a wife, see? The nut! An' he finds

Amy waitin' on table in a spaghetti joint. Joint's called "Il Trovatore." Can you beat it? He ain't even got the nerve to speak to her. He don't even go back to see her again. He just falls for her, gets her name from the boss an' comes home an' makes me write her a letter proposin' marriage. That's her answer.

FATHER MC KEE. It's good clear writin'. It's a good letter. It looks like she's got more character'n what I thought. But, just the same, it ain't no way to conduct a courtship.

JOE. There's worse ways.

FATHER MC KEE. She says she likes the letter you wrote.

JOE. The second time I wrote, I told her all about the farm an' just how she was goin' to be fixed. Oh, I was careful not to say nothin' about Tony's money. Only the Ford. I thought she ought to know about the Ford. [*He hands the second letter over.*] An' she wrote this one back.

FATHER MC KEE. She likes the country, does she? She wants Tony's photo.

JOE. Say, you ought to have seen Tony gettin' his face shot! By God! It took me a whole week to talk him into it. An' when I did get him down there—you know that place across from the depot?—dam' if he wasn' scared right out of his pants!

FATHER MC KEE. By what?

JOE. By the camera! Would you believe it? We had to clamp him into the chair, both of us, the photographer an' me! You ought to have seen the wop sweat! And when we try to point the machine at him, he gives a yell you could hear a block an' runs right out in the street!

FATHER MC KEE. No!

JOE. I couldn't get him back, only I promised to let the guy shoot me first. They was some pictures! Tony's [*He hands a specimen to the* PADRE.] sure looks like him, but she must have seen somethin' in it, because she sent hers right back. [*He studies* AMY's *photograph for a moment before submitting it.*] Here. Not bad, huh?

FATHER MC KEE [*a long and very pleased contemplation*]. There ain't no explainin' women! [*He returns the photograph.*] Do you think she's straight, Joe?

JOE. What the hell! If she ain't, she wants to be. That's the main thing.

FATHER MC KEE. Maybe it won't turn out so bad, after all. There's always this about life: no man don't never get everything he sets out to get, but half the time he don't never find out he ain't got it.

JOE. Oh, if you're goin' off on that tack!

FATHER MC KEE. It's the tack life travels on, with the help of Almighty God.

JOE. What the hell! Life ain't so bad.

FATHER MC KEE. I'm delighted to hear you say so!

JOE [*he has returned the exhibits to the drawer*]. I never put over anything half so good myself!

FATHER MC KEE. Do you think Tony's goin' to put it over?

JOE. Wait and see.

FATHER MC KEE. Well, I don't know how I can approve of this weddin', but I'm willin' to give it the benefit of my sanction an' do all I can to help it along an' look out for Tony. Does that satisfy you? . . . Just the same, I don't believe in unnecessary chances, Joe. Pull along out of here like Tony asked you to.

JOE. Say, you make me sore! Why, anybody 'ud think, to hear you talk, that I'm all set to . . .

[*The* R. F. D. *has appeared on the porch. He carries a dusty coat on his arm, and wipes the sweat from his brow with his blue handkerchief. He wears a gray flannel shirt, old trousers hitched to suspenders that are none too secure. His badge is his only sign of office. He is an eager, tobacco-chewing old countryman.*]

THE R. F. D. Hey, Tony! Tony! [*As he reaches the door.*]

Where's Tony? 'Mornin', Padre.

JOE. Tony's gone to town. You're early.

THE R. F. D. That's more'n Tony is. I got to get his signature on a piece of registered mail.

JOE. What is it?

THE R. F. D. It's his wife. [JOE *and the* PRIEST *rise astonished.*] Sure! I got her outside in the buckboard an' she's madder'n hell because Tony didn't meet her. She's some girl, too. I never heard the beat! Lands a girl like that an' don't even take the trouble to— [*The other two are already at the windows.*]

JOE. Where'd *you* find her?

THE R. F. D. I finds her pacin' up and down the platform and I gives her a lift. I sure do hate to see a good-lookin' girl cry—an' she sure was cryin.' I reckoned Tony couldn't get the Ford started so—

FATHER MC KEE. He went down all right. I wonder what happened to him?

JOE. He must have took the short cut.

FATHER MC KEE. Didn't you pass him?

JOE. I knew I ought to have went instead.

FATHER MC KEE. He wasn't in no condition.

THE R. F. D. I'll have a look on my way back.

JOE. What are *we* goin' do to with her?

THE R. F. D. Ask her in.

JOE. Ah Gee! [*He goes out, calling.*] Giorgio! Angelo! [THE R. F. D. *follows him.* AH GEE *comes from his kitchen and evinces some confusion, but does not hold back from the summons.* FATHER MC KEE *arranges his costume and goes out last. The stage remains empty for a moment. A babble of voices is heard, voices that speak both English and Italian.* JOE *is heard shouting.*] Lend a hand with that trunk!

AMY'S VOICE. How do you do? I'm pleased to meet you. I certainly had some time getting here. I certainly expected somebody would meet me at the station.

FATHER MC KEE'S VOICE. The old man left all right.

JOE'S VOICE. He started a little too late.

THE R. F. D.'S VOICE. I'll have a look for him. [*The rest is lost in a babble of Italian as* AMY *comes on to the porch and the others follow her, not the least among them being the two Italian hands,* GIORGIO *and* AN-GELO *whose volubility subsides only as* AMY *enters the room. As for* AMY, *she is all that* TONY *said of her and much more. She wears a pretty dress, new, ready-made, and inexpensive, and a charming and equally cheap hat. Her shoes are bright coloured and her handbag matches them. But her own love-liness is quite beyond belief. She is small and plump and vivid and her golden hair shimmers about her face like morning sunshine. She herself shines with and inner, constitutional energy. Her look is, to be sure, just a little tired. She probably is not more than twenty-two or -three, but she seems older. Her great quality is definiteness. It lends pathos to her whole personality. At the moment, her vanity is piqued by* TONY'S *remissness and she carries matters with a hand a little too high to be entirely convinc-ing. She is embarrassed, of course, but she won't ad-mit it.*]

AMY [*as she enters*]. I must say it ain't my idea of the way a gentleman ought to welcome his blooming bride. I don't get it. I don't get it at all. What was the matter?

JOE. Why, nothin'.

FATHER MC KEE. He was scared.

AMY. Scared of me? Why didn't you come yourself?

JOE. I wanted to, but . . .

AMY [*the decorations have caught her eye*]. Say, did you folks go and do all this for the wedding?

JOE. Sure we did.

AMY. Well, if that ain't the cutest ever! A regular wop wedding! Excuse me. I meant Italian. [*The "I" is long.*]

JOE. That's all right.

AMY. And here's the priest, too, all set and ready. Say! I can see right now I'm going to like it here.

JOE. I don't guess nobody's goin' to kick at that.

AMY. All right, then, I'll forgive you. That's the way I am. Forgive and forget! I always believe in letting bygones be bygones. And down at the station I was thinking: Well, if they ain't got enough sense of politeness to come after the bride, I'm going to hop the next train back to Frisco. I'd have done it, too, only—would you believe it?—I didn't have the price of a ticket! I spent the last cent I had on this hat. Say, when I remembered that, maybe I didn't cry! That's what I was crying over when you come up. [*This to the* R. F. D.; *otherwise her eyes have scarcely left* JOE'S *face.*]

THE R. F. D. Pleased to have been of service, ma'am.

AMY. Well, you certainly was of service. But here I am alive and well, as they say, so I guess we don't need to fuss about that any more. I guess I'll sit down. [*She does so.*]

JOE. Here's the cook an' the hands to pay their respects.

ANGELO [*a deep obeisance to* AMY]. Eh, la nostra padrona! Tanti auguri, cara Signora, e buona festa! Come sta? Ha fatto buon viaggio? [*Here* GIORGIO *adds his voice.*]

ANGELO [*together*] GIORGIO

Siamo tanto contenti di vedevla. Speriamo che si troverà sempre bene e felice nella casa ospitale del nostro generoso padrone.

Sia la benvenuta, egregia Signora. Auguriamo la buona fortuna a lei, e al suo stimatissimo sposo. Che la Santa Madonna le dia la sua benedizione e che tutti i santi l'accompagnino nel matrimonio!

JOE. Hey, that's enough!

AMY. Now, that was very nice of them. I liked every word they said. I guess I better study up on the

lingo. All I know is words like spaghetti and ravi-
oli. . . .

ANGELO *and* GIORGIO [*sotto voce*]. Ah! La Signora parla
Italiano!

AMY. . . . I guess you got plenty of that around. Well,
you can't make me mad. I just love it. [*Then she
sees* AH GEE's *ceremonious obeisance.*] How do you
do? Are you the cook?

AH GEE. Yes, missy. Velly good cook.

AMY. Say, I didn't know I drew a chef. You didn't tell
me. [AH GEE *takes himself off.*] Say, my baggage is
out there.

JOE. All right, boys, lend a hand.

[ANGELO *and* GIORGIO *go down the steps.*]

AMY. If you don't mind I'll just keep an eye on them.
My wedding dress is in that trunk. I bet you didn't
expect me to bring a wedding dress. Well, I didn't
expect to, myself. And I don't know why I did. But
I did! I just blew myself. I said: "You only get married once" and—I got a veil, too. I got the whole
works. [*She hears her trunk en route.*] Go easy there!
[*She is out on the porch.*]

THE R. F. D. Well, that's her.

JOE [*as he goes to help*]. She ain't bad.

FATHER MC KEE. No, she ain't half bad.

AMY [*calling down*]. Not upside down! Be careful, can't
you?

THE R. F. D. I don't hold much with city girls myself,
but—

JOE [*calling down*]. Careful, boys! Look out for that
vine! Gimme the grip.

FATHER MC KEE. Oh, she's above the average.

THE R. F. D. [*nudging him*]. Do you think she . . . ?

FATHER MC KEE. I wouldn't hardly like to say off-hand,
but . . .

THE R. F. D. I wouldn't think so.

FATHER MC KEE. Joe, do you think she . . . ?

JOE. No. Not her. Not on your life. [*He puts grip down*

inside the bedroom door. At the same time ANGELO
and GIORGIO *carry in* AMY'S *pathetic little trunk,
which they take into the bedroom.*]

THE R. F. D. Well, I got my deliveries.

FATHER MC KEE. I'll come along with you. You stay here
an' keep things conversational, Joe.

JOE. No! I'll come, too.

THE R. F. D. Till the groom turns up, Joe. You don't
want her to get all upset again, do you?

FATHER MC KEE [*as* AMY *comes along the porch to the
door*]. Shh! Don't get her worryin'.

AMY [*in the doorway, finishing the feminine touch of
powder to the nose*]. I thought a little of this
wouldn't make me any harder to look at.

THE R. F. D. We'll have to be movin' on, ma'am.

FATHER MC KEE. Yes.

AMY [*shaking hands with him*]. I'm pleased to have
made your acquaintance.

THE R. F. D. I hope to have the pleasure soon again.

AMY. Why, ain't you coming to the wedding?

THE R. F. D. Sure I am, if I'm invited.

AMY. I'll never forgive you, if you don't. And I certainly want to thank you for the lift. [*A handshake
to him.*] Thank you. . . . Good-bye. . . . Good-bye. . . .

THE R. F. D. Good-bye, ma'am. [*He shuffles out.* JOE
starts to follow.]

AMY. You ain't going, too?

JOE. Well, I—

THE R. F. D. [*through the window*]. Just the Padre an'
me.

FATHER MC KEE [*as he goes, to* JOE]. We'll send him
right up.

THE R. F. D. [*as they disappear*]. Good-bye, ma'am.

AMY. Good-bye. See you later. [*Awkward silence.*]
I ain't sorry they went. I think they ought to have
done it sooner and left us to get acquainted. They
got me all fussed up staring that way. I just couldn't
think of what to say next. A girl gets kind of fussed,

coming off like this to marry a man she ain't never seen. I was a mile up in the air. I—I guess I must have sounded kind of fresh. I wouldn't want you to think I was fresh.

JOE. I didn't.

AMY. I'm glad you didn't. You know, I like it up here already. You got it fixed up so cute and—[*She discovers the cake.*] and that. . . . It was awful nice of you to think of that. And the view! Is them all vines?

JOE. Yeah. . . . [*An awkward pause.*]

AMY. It certainly is a pretty sight. Coming up I could taste the wind way down inside me. It made me think of where I used to live.

JOE. Where was that?

AMY. In the Santa Clara. You know, I wrote you.

JOE. Oh, yeah. In the Santa Clara. I forgot.

AMY. We had a big place in the Santa Clara. Prunes and apricots. Ninety acres in prunes and fifty in apricots. . . . [*Again an awkward silence.*] I guess I'll sit down. [*She does so.*] There ought to have been good money in prunes and apricots. But the prunes didn't do so good and the apricots got the leaf curl.

JOE. You're quite a farmer.

AMY. My old man was, but he got to drinking.

JOE. That's bad.

AMY. So we lost it after my mother died. But I used to love it there. In the spring, when the blossoms was out, I used to climb up on the windmill at night, when there was a moon. You never saw such a pretty sight as them blossoms in the moonlight. You could see for miles and miles all round—for miles and miles.

JOE. It must have been pretty. [*Awkward pause.*]

AMY. Ever been in the Santa Clara?

JOE. Sure. I worked there before I come here.

AMY. Where did you work?

JOE. Near Mountain View. I forget the guy's name.

AMY. I went to school in Mountain View. Our place

was near there. Ever know Father O'Donnell?

JOE. No.

AMY. Thought you might have, being a Catholic and all.

JOE. I was organizer for the Wobblies.

AMY. The Wobblies?

JOE. I. W. W.

AMY. Say! You ain't one of them?

JOE. I used to be.

AMY. I sure am glad you gave that up. You don't talk one bit like an Italian.

JOE. I ain't. Only by descent. I was born in Frisco.

AMY. Oh, in Frisco? I see. . . . I'm Swiss by descent myself. My father was born in Switzerland and my grandfather, on my mother's side, he was born there, too. I don't know what that makes me—Swiss cheese, I guess. . . . [*She laughs.* JOE *does not. This crushes her and there is another awkward gap.*] Our old house in the Santa Clara was bigger than this one, but it wasn't near so pretty. I must say you keep this house nice and clean for having no woman around. Our house got awful dirty toward the end. You see, my mother got to drinking, too. Hard stuff, you know. I got nothing against beer or vino, but the hard stuff don't do nobody any good. . . . That how you stand on prohibition?

JOE. Sure, I guess so.

AMY. I'm glad to hear that. I sure am. I don't want no more experience with the hard stuff. . . . That certainly is some view. Got the Santa Clara beat a mile. The Santa Clara's so flat. You couldn't get no view at all unless you climbed up on that windmill like I told you about. . . . Our old house had a cellar. Has this house got a cellar?

JOE. Sure, it has. Underneath the whole house. [*She goes to the cellar door to see.*]

AMY. I used to hide in our cellar when things got too rough upstairs. You could hear the feet running around over your head, but they never come down in the cellar after me because there was a ladder, and when you're that way you don't care much for ladders. . . . They always took it out on me.

JOE. Did they?

AMY. Yeah. I always had the cellar though. I used to play down there hot days. It smelt like apricots.

JOE. Our cellar smells like hell. It's full of vino.

AMY. That's a nice clean smell. It's sour, but it's healthy.

JOE. You're a regular wop, ain't you?

AMY. Well, after two years in a spaghetti joint! I like Italians. They always left me alone. Guess it wouldn't have done 'em much good getting fresh with me, at that. . . . Say, I'm getting pretty confidential.

JOE. Go right ahead.

AMY. All right. . . . I guess I ain't got much reason for being shy with you, at that. I wouldn't never have said I was going to marry an Italian, though. But I guess I just jumped at the chance. I got so tired of things. Oh, everything! I used to think I just couldn't keep on any longer.

JOE. Poor kid!

AMY. Oh, I usually know which side my bread's buttered on. I just said to myself: "He looks all right and I like the country and anyway it can't be no worse than this." And I said: "Why shouldn't I take a chance? He's taking just as much of a chance on me as I am on him."

JOE. That's fair enough.

AMY. Sure it is. And—maybe I hadn't ought to say it—but when I come in here and seen all you done, fixing things up for the wedding and all, and looked out the window, and smelt that wind, I said to myself, I said: "Amy, old kid, you're in gravy." Now, what do you think of that for an admission?

JOE. You're dead right. That's just what I said when I

come here. I only intended to stay a few days. I'm that way, see? I been here goin' on five months now.

AMY. Is *that* all?

JOE. That's the longest I ever stayed any one place since I was old enough to dress myself.

AMY. You *have* been a rover!

JOE. I been all over—with the Wobblies, you see. Before I come here, that is.

AMY. What did you used to do?

JOE. Cherries an' hops—melons down in the Imperial an' oranges down South an' the railroad an' the oilfields. . . . Before I come here. When I come here I just stayed. Maybe I was gettin' tired of bummin'. Now I'm tired of this. But I don't mind.

AMY. Well, don't get too tired of it. I'm not a bit strong for moving myself. I had all I want of that in my time.

JOE. I guess you have.

AMY. I wonder what you think of me coming all the way up here like I did, all by myself, to marry a man I ain't never seen, only his photograph.

JOE. You couldn't have picked a better man.

AMY. Say! Don't get a swelled head, will you?

JOE. Who, me?

AMY. Oh, no, nobody! [AH GEE *passes along the porch.*] I hope you're right, that's all. And I guess you are, at that. And believe me, if I thought this wasn't a permanent offer, I wouldn't be here. I mean business. I hope you do.

JOE. Me?

AMY. Well, I certainly ain't referring to the Chink.

JOE. Say, who do you think . . . ?

AMY [*touching his sleeve with a kind of gentle diffidence which is her first attempt at intimacy*]. Don't get sore. The minute I came in I knew I was all right. I am. Why, I feel just as comfortable as if we was old friends. There don't seem to be anything strange in me being here like I am. Not now, anyhow. It just goes to show you: you never can tell how things is going to turn out. Why, if a fortune-teller had told me that I would come up here like I did, do you know what I would have said to her? I'd have said, "You're no fortune-teller." Life sure is funny, though. It's lucky for me I can say that now and laugh when I say it. I ain't always been so good at laughing. I guess we'll get used to each other in time. Don't you think we will, Tony?

JOE. Tony? Say, I ain't . . . ! Oh, Jesus! [*His words are lost in the roar of a Ford motor as it approaches, and the motor, in turn, is drowned in wild cries of dismay from* GIORGIO *and* ANGELO.]

[*The tension between the two in the room is broken by the excited entrance of* AH GEE, *who has evidently seen, from his kitchen window, the cause of disturbance.*]

FATHER MC KEE [*calling from off stage*]. Joe! Joe!

JOE [*following* AH GEE *toward the door*]. What is it? [*From the porch he sees what it is.*] What— Is he dead? . . . Take that bench! [*He disappears in the direction of the disturbance which continues in both English and Italian.*]

AMY. What's the matter? Is somebody hurt?

[*The* DOCTOR, *with his fedora hat and his little black satchel, appears. He is the perfect young rural medico, just out of medical school and full of learned importance.*]

THE DOCTOR. I'll get the ambulance.

JOE [*following him in*]. Is he bad, Doc?

THE DOCTOR [*as he goes into the bedroom*]. Both legs above the knee—compound fractures.

JOE. Why didn't you take him to the hospital?

THE R. F. D. [*as he enters*]. The Ford went right off the bridge.

FATHER MC KEE [*as he enters*]. Not two hundred yards from here, Joe.

THE R. F. D. Must have fell twenty feet!

FATHER MC KEE. Never seen such a wreck! [*To* AMY.] We found him lyin' in two feet of water. The car was turned right upside down.

AMY. But who is it? I don't get it. I don't know what's happened.

FATHER MC KEE. Two broken legs, that's what's happened.

THE DOCTOR [*he reappears in his shirt sleeves*]. Better lend a hand, Joe!

[*He vanishes again.* GIORGIO *and* ANGELO *appear, carrying the bench and apostrophizing the deity in Italian.* TONY *is recumbent and unconscious on this improvised stretcher. Much "Steady" from* JOE. *Much "There now, Tony" from the* R. F. D. *Much and prolonged groaning from* TONY.]

JOE [*as the bench is set down*]. All right now, Tony.

TONY [*reviving*]. AH-h-h! . . . Ees you, Joe?

JOE. Yeah. It's me. Amy's here.

TONY. Amy? Ees all right, Joe? You been makin' evrathing all right?

JOE. Sure. Everything's fine.

TONY. Where is my Amy? [*He sees her where she stands dumbfounded against the wall.*] Ah-h-h, Amy! . . . Amy, don' be standin' way off dere! Come over here for shake hands. [AMY *shakes her head.*] You ain' mad with me, Amy? . . . [AMY *shakes her head again.*] Amy ain' mad with me, Joe?

JOE. Nobody's mad. . . . Don't you worry.

TONY. Den we have da weddin' just da same? We have da weddin' just da same? [*The* DOCTOR *appears in the bedroom doorway, holding a hypodermic.*]

JOE. Sure, we will.

THE DOCTOR. All right, boys, bring him in. I want to give him another one of these and clean up his cuts.

JOE. Come on now, boys! Avanti! Careful there!

TONY. Amy! . . . Amy! . . . [*The jar of movement hurts*

*him. He breaks down into groans and is carried into
the bedroom. All others go with him except* JOE *and*
AMY.]

JOE [*as he starts to go, a strangled sound from* AMY *arrests him. He turns and meets her gaze. He closes the
door*]. This is tough on you.

AMY [*almost voiceless with her terrible surmise*]. Who—
who is that old guy?

JOE. That? That's Tony. . . .

AMY. Tony?

JOE. It's too bad he never got to meet you. It's too bad
he wasn't here when you come. [AMY *sways desperately a moment, then, with a choked cry, makes for
the bedroom.*] You can't go in there.

AMY. I want my trunk.

JOE. Now, listen! It ain't Tony's fault he's had an accident. . . .

AMY. Of all the dirty, low-down tricks that was ever
played on a girl!

JOE. An' it ain't his fault you made a little mistake.

AMY. What do you think you are—a bunch of Houdinis? [*She tears open her handbag which she put
down on the table at her first entrance and produces
a photograph.*] Is this your photo or isn't it?

JOE [*in amazement*]. Where did you get it?

AMY. Where do you think I got it?

JOE. Good God, Tony didn't send you this, did he? For
God's sake, tell me! Did Tony send you this?

AMY. Ain't I just told you?

JOE. By God, he must have been plumb crazy! By God,
he was so dead gone on you he was afraid you
wouldn't have nothin' to do with an old man like
him. . . . He didn't have the nerve. . . . An' he just
went an' sent you my photo instead of his. . . . Tony's
like that, Amy. He ain't nothing but a kid. He's like
a puppy, Tony is. Honest, Amy, it's God's truth I'm
telling you. . . . I wouldn't have had nothin' to do
with no such thing. Honest I wouldn't. I did write

the letters for him, but that was only because he don't write good English like I do.

AMY. That ain't no excuse.

JOE. But there wasn't one word in them letters that wasn't God's own truth. I never knew nothin' about this photo, though. Honest to God, I never! An' Tony never meant no harm neither, Amy. Honest he never. An' he's been after me to beat it, too. Every day he has. . . . Sure it was a dirty trick an' he was crazy to think he could get away with it. I ain't denyin' it's the dirtiest trick I ever heard of. . . . Only he didn't mean no harm.

AMY. Oh, didn't he? Well, how about *my* feelings? How about *me?*

JOE. I'll do everything I can to square it. I'll drive you right down to the station now, and you can hop the first train back.

AMY. Oh, *can* I? And what do you expect me to do when I get there? Ain't I thrown up my job there? Do you think jobs is easy for a girl to get? And ain't I spent every cent I had on my trousseau?

JOE. I'll make Tony square it.

AMY. Oh, my God! Oh, my God! I got to go back and wait on table! What'll all those girls say when they see me? And I ain't even got the price of my ticket!

JOE. We can fix that.

AMY. I'll get a lawyer, I will! I wish to God I hadn't never heard of no wops!

JOE. Don't start cryin'. [*He tries to comfort her.*]

AMY. You take your hands off me and get my things.

JOE. All right. . . . [*He looks at her a moment, his distress quite evident. Then he gives it up and goes into the bedroom. As he opens the door, the* DOCTOR *and* TONY *are audible. He closes the door after him.*]

[AMY *picks up the few belongings she has left about the room. She stands a moment holding them, looking about her, at the four walls, at the country outside. Then her eye falls upon* JOE'S *photograph*

*which still lies, face-up, on the table. She takes it in
her hand and looks at it. Mechanically she makes as
though to put it into the bosom of her dress. She
changes her mind, drops it on the table and looks
around her again. She seems to reach a decision. Her
face sets and she pushes the photograph vigorously
away from her.* JOE *returns with her satchel.*]

JOE. The doc's give him something to make him sleep.
They're goin' to get an ambulance an' take him to
the hospital. We can take the doc's Ford an' . . . It's
a shame, but . . .

AMY. I ain't going.

JOE. What?

AMY. No. I ain't going. Why should I go? I like the
country. This place suits me all right. It's just what
I was looking for. I'm here and I might as well stick.
I guess he ain't so bad, at that. I guess I could have
done a lot worse. If he wants to marry me, I'm game.
I'm game to see it through. It's nice up here. [*She
pulls off her hat and sits, exhausted.* JOE *stares in
mute admiration as the curtain falls.*]

Act two

*The scene remains unchanged. It is late evening of the
same day. The lanterns out-of-doors have been burning so long that some of them have already guttered
out. The room is lighted by two oil lamps.*

TONY *lies groaning faintly on a cot, his legs encased
in a plaster cast, his eternal wine bottle by his side. The
*DOCTOR *sits beside him.*

*Outside, the festa is in full swing. A desperate Italian
tenor is singing "La Donna è Mobile" from "Rigoletto" as the curtain rises. His tones ring frantically
out.*

A short pause follows the song. The hiss of a sky-rocket is audible. The light from the rocket flares through the windows and a long "Ah" rises from the crowd out-of-doors.

TONY. Fireworks!

THE DOCTOR. Lie quiet.

TONY. Someone verra sick in bed. Povereto! Povereto! Tony miss festa. [*Gay voices outside call to children and children answer. The* DOCTOR *rises impatiently and goes to the door.* TONY *turns his head ever so slightly.*] Eh, Doc! W'ere you go?

THE DOCTOR. It's high time those coyotes went home.

[*Applause rings from the crowd. The tenor is again vigorously repeating the last phrase and cadenza of "La Donna è Mobile."*]

TONY. Dat fella is no coyot'! He is music artiste.

THE DOCTOR. It's a marvel to me the man has any lungs left. He's been howling for five hours.

TONY. You don't ondrastan' such music. Come è bella! Ees "Rigoletto"!

THE DOCTOR. Look here now, Tony! I let you out of the hospital to get married.

TONY. You bet your life! You think any goddam doc is stoppin' me from gettin' married?

THE DOCTOR. I'm talking medicine, not love.

TONY. You talkin' too goddam much. You been spoil evrathing.

THE DOCTOR. Now, be reasonable, Tony. I let them bring you in here where you could see your friends.

TONY. An' den you mak' all my friends go outside.

THE DOCTOR. You're a sick man.

TONY. Ahi! Tony is verra sick . . . verra sick!

THE DOCTOR. Enough's enough. Why, half of what you have been through to-day would have killed a white man! You wops are crazy.

TONY. I don't let nobody stop no festa in my house. You go outside an' have a good time.

THE DOCTOR. I don't sing and I don't dance and I don't talk Italian and I don't drink.

TONY. I'm surprise' how much you don' know, Doc. [*He laughs. The jar is painful. He groans. The* DOCTOR *comes over to his bedside.*] W'ere is my Amy?

THE DOCTOR. She's all right. Keep quiet.

TONY. You goin' look for my Amy, Doc? You goin' see if she is havin' fine time?

[*Mandolins, a guitar, and an accordion strike up a sentimental waltz outside.*]

THE DOCTOR. If you'll be quiet. [*Humoring him, he goes to the door.*] I can see her from here and she's having a splendid time. Does that satisfy you?

TONY. Now evrabody goin' for dance!

[*A brief silence filled by the dance music to which* TONY, *the incorrigible, beats time. Then* JOE *and* AH GEE *come along the porch pushing a wheelbarrow, a little flurry of the crowd in their wake. The* DOCTOR *shoos out the crowd.* JOE *and* AH GEE *come in.*]

JOE. How you makin' out, Tony?

TONY. Verra sick, Joe. Is festa goin' good?

JOE. Festa's goin' fine, Tony. Me and Ah Gee's after more vino.

TONY. Da's good! Da's good!

JOE. Sure it's good. But it's a wonder everybody ain't drownded already.

TONY. Italian fellas don't get drownded in vino. Is my Amy havin' good fun, Joe?

JOE. Sure, she is! She's playin' with the kids.

TONY. Ah! . . . You go in da cellar with Ah Gee, Joe, and bring back playnta vino. Den you come back here and mak' little talk with Tony.

JOE. That's the idea. . . . [*He goes into the cellar, followed by* AH GEE.]

THE DOCTOR [*in the door, a fractious eye on the festa*]. Those mothers ought to be reported for keeping youngsters up this time of night. [*A pause filled with voices and laughter.*]

TONY [*crescendo*]. Doc! Doc! Doc! [*The* DOCTOR *turns.*] You think I am well next week, Doc?

THE DOCTOR. I sincerely hope, Tony, that you may be well in six months.

TONY. Six month'?

THE DOCTOR. You don't seem to realize what a bad smash you had. [*As he sits down to his professional manner.*] Both tibia and fibula are fractured in the right leg. The femur is crushed in the left, and the ischium damaged as well. Now, if no systemic complications develop . . .

TONY. Oh, my God!

THE DOCTOR. . . . six months. . . .

TONY [*crescendo again*]. Six month'! Six month'! Six month'!

THE DOCTOR. You won't make it any shorter by exciting yourself.

TONY. Da's right, Doc. Ees no good get excit'. I ondrastan'. But six month' . . . [*A pause.*] Doc, I'm goin' ask you som'thing an' you goin' tell me just da truth, eh?

THE DOCTOR. I know what's on your mind, Tony. If you keep quiet and take care of yourself, you'll have all the kids you want.

TONY. How many?

THE DOCTOR. Ten, anyway!

TONY. Three is playnta.

[*The music is loud again as* JOE *and* AH GEE *come back from the cellar with the new barrel of wine. They load it on the wheelbarrow and* AH GEE *takes it off to the thirsty populace,* JOE *remains behind.*]

THE DOCTOR. In the meanwhile Amy's going to have her hands full, taking care of you.

TONY [*violently*]. I don' marry with no woman for mak' her work. I don't want my Amy do nothing but only be happy an' fat.

JOE. There ain't nothin' too good for Tony. He marries a fine wife to play the piano for him an' he's goin' to rent a trained nurse to take care of him.

[AH GEE *is greeted with shouts of "Vino! Vino!" from the men and "Viva Antonio" from the girls.*]

TONY. You bet your life!

THE DOCTOR. Renting trained nurses is expensive, Tony.

TONY. I got playnta money.

[*The concertina and the mandolin begin playing the chorus of "Funiculi, Funicula!" The music is continued throughout the following scene.*]

JOE [*cigarette business*]. You old son of a gun! Give us a light, Doc.

THE DOCTOR. Not in here, Joe!

[JOE *takes his cigarette outside. He sits with a wave to the crowd, who answer, "Joe! Joe!"*]

TONY. Is my Amy havin' good fun, Joe?

JOE. Sure. She's dancin' with the postman.

TONY. Da's good! Ees verra funny weddin' for me, Joe, but my Amy must have good time.

THE DOCTOR. Tony's got it bad.

JOE. Don't blame him. She's some girl.

TONY. I got to talk verra secret with Joe, Doc. You go outside for talk with my Amy. You better get good acquaint' with my Amy, Doc.

[*Applause outside for the dancers.*]

JOE. You could do worse, an' that's a fact.

THE DOCTOR. Tony's got to go to sleep.

[*The crowd outside shouts vociferously.*]

JOE. I won't keep him up.

TONY. Just a little w'ile, Doc? Fifteen minute'?

THE DOCTOR. Well, don't make it any longer. I want some sleep myself. Anybody would think I haven't a thing to do but take care of Tony.

JOE. We know you're a busy baby, Doc.

THE DOCTOR. Busy is right. [*Very expansive.*] To-morrow, now, I've got two confinements I'm watching and an appendicitis, all up on the St. Helena road. Then, just the other side of town, I've got the most beautiful tumor you could hope to see. And the sheriff's wife! Operated her yesterday. Gallstones. Gallstones? They were cobblestones. I never saw such a case! And then, with my regular practice and my own scientific researches to keep up with things.

TONY. Corpo Dio, goddam, Doc; don' be tellin' me no more 'bout who is sick and w'at he's sick for! I'm sick playnta myself, an' I got playnta trouble here. You go outside an' leave me for talk with Joe.

THE DOCTOR. All right, but I won't have any more nonsense when I come back. [*He goes; to* JOE *on the porch.*] I cannot be responsible unless the patient enjoys complete quiet, after a shock like this to his nervous system.

JOE. Has Tony got a nervous system?

THE DOCTOR. Of course he has! [*He disappears. A shout welcomes him.*]

TONY. W'at is nervous system, Joe?

JOE. It's what makes things hurt, Tony.

TONY. I got playnta.

[JOE *comes in and stands over* TONY *for a moment with a look of half-tender amusement on his face.* TONY *hums, distractedly keeping time with one hand to the music of "Funiculi, Funicula." With the end of the music he drops his hands with a sigh.*]

JOE. What's on your mind, Tony?

TONY. Oh, Joe! . . . Joe!! . . . Joe!!

JOE. What's the matter, Tony. Ain't you feelin' good?

TONY. Ees Amy! . . .

[JOE *sits in the* DOCTOR'S *chair, hitching it closer to the bed.*]

JOE. What do you want for a nickel? She married you, didn't she?

TONY. I'm scare', Joe. I'm scare' verra bad. I love my Amy, but my Amy don' love me.

JOE. Give her time, can't you? She wouldn't have married you if she wasn't all set to go through on the level.

TONY. You think?

JOE. Hell, I *know*.

TONY. W'at Amy say w'en she see me dees morning?

JOE. Oh, forget it, I tell you.

TONY. I got to know, Joe. You got to tell me. She's pretty goddam mad, eh?

JOE. Well, if she was, she got over it.

TONY. W'at I'm goin' to do for mak' evrathing all right, Joe? Da's w'at I want to know.

JOE. I tell you everythin' *is* all right, Tony. Oh, I ain't sayin' you ain't got to keep things movin' along easy an' friendly an' all. But that ain't goin' to be so hard. Just be good to her and take care of her. That's what Amy needs. She's tired, poor kid!

TONY. I'm all ready for tak' care like hell.

JOE. From what Amy was tellin' me this mornin', she's been a-havin' a helluva hard life for a girl, an' if she come through straight like she did, well, there ain't no credit due nobody but just only herself, and that's a fact.

TONY. You're a goddam smart fella, Joe.

JOE. I dunno how smart I am, Tony, but you can't tell me much. Not about women, you can't. Believe me, a girl gets a lousy deal any way you look at it. [*He reflects upon this for an instant before he illustrates.*] Take a fella, now, a young fella like me, see? It's goin' to do him good to knock around an' have his troubles an' all. [*A solemn shake of the head.*] But knockin' around just raises hell with a girl. She can't stand it. She can't stand it, because it ain't in her nature to get away with the whole show like a fella can. [TONY *is much impressed and signifies approval with a grunt.*] If a fella wants a meal, he swipes it, don't he? A girl can't be swipin' things. It 'ud make her feel bad. She'd think she was doin' somethin' wrong. [*This surprises* TONY, *but he is willing to take* JOE's *word for it.*] Gee, I sure would hate to be a woman!

TONY [*nodding agreement*]. Nobody is wantin' to be

woman, Joe . . . But ees playnta good womans like my Amy!

JOE. Sure, there's good ones an' bad ones. But that ain't exactly what I mean, Tony. What I mean is, as far as I can see, it don't make a helluva lot of difference what a woman is: good or bad, young or old . . .

TONY. I lik' best fat!

JOE. . . . all women is up against it, and it's a dirty shame, too, because women ain't so bad. They ain't much use, maybe, but they ain't so bad.

TONY. My Amy is goin' have evrathing she want.

JOE. Ever heard anythin' about this dam' women's rights stuff? You know. Equality of the sexes. Woman doin' a man's work an' all that bunk?

TONY. Da's crazy idea!

JOE. The idea ain't so bad.

TONY. Ees crazy idea! Looka me! You think any woman is goin' be doin' my work? No, by God! I tell you, Joe, woman is best for sit in da house an' love da husband.

JOE. The trouble with women is, there's too goddam many of 'em. Why, I was readin' in the paper only the other day about England havin' three and a half women to every man.

TONY. W'at you mean?—half a womans!

JOE. I'm only tellin' you what the paper said.

TONY. Ees crazy idea! Half a womans! I tell you, Joe . . .

JOE. I been lookin' women over from San Diego to Seattle an' what most of 'em is after is a home. A good safe home, whether they get any rights with it or not. You take my advice an' make everythin' nice an' comfortable for Amy an' you won't have no trouble. Amy's satisfied here. Don't you kid yourself she ain't.

[*Outside the crowd is off again, the tenors leading them in "Maria Mari."*]

TONY. You're a good boy, Joe, you're pretty smart.

JOE. I'm just tellin' you the truth. You're dam' lucky you picked a girl like Amy.

TONY [*a moment of comfort; then despair again*]. Ees no good, Joe—ees no good.

JOE. Oh, for cripe's sake, Tony!

TONY. I'm tellin' you, Joe, ees no good. I'm the most unhappy fella in the world. W'y? Because I been verra bad sinner an' God is goin' get me for sure! He's broke both my legs already an' he's not finish' with me yet! God is no cheap fella, Joe. God is lookin' out at Tony right now, and you know what he's sayin'? He's sayin': "Tony, you been one goddam sonuvabitch for playin' goddam dirty trick on Amy!" Da's w'at God is sayin', Joe, an' I know verra good w'at God is goin' do more. Just for playin' goddam dirty trick like dat on Amy, Tony don' never have no kids, never! W'at you think is mak' me do such a thing, Joe?

JOE. Oh, hell, you always was crazy.

TONY. Ees no good, for such a bad fella like me gettin' married. God is goin' fix me playnta, all right.

JOE. I seen God let worse guys'n you get by.

TONY. You think?

JOE. If you want to square things, you better make Amy glad you done what you done.

TONY. You think? . . . Yes. . . . [*Pause.*] Look, Joe. . . . [*He draws a plush box from under his blanket.*] Ees present for Amy. You open him.

JOE [*obeying*]. Say! Them's what I call regular earrings!

TONY. You bet your life! He's cost four hundra dollar'!

JOE. Are them real diamonds?

TONY [*nodding*]. I guess Amy like 'em pretty good, eh?

JOE. She'll be crazy about 'em. You're a pretty wise old wop, Tony, ain't you? [*He hands the box back to* TONY, *who laughs delightedly.* JOE *looks at him for a moment then goes to door and calls out.*] Amy!

TONY. Eh, Joe!

JOE. You're goin' to make the presentation right away now. That'll settle your worries for you. . . . Amy, come here! Tony wants to see you!

TONY. You think is good time now?

JOE. *I know. . . .* Amy?

[AMY *appears in doorway. She wears her wedding dress and veil. The dress is undeniably pretty and only wrong in one or two places. The veil has been pulled rather askew. The whole picture is at once charming and pathetic.*]

AMY. What's the idea? [*Her voice is a little tired. She does not look at* JOE.]

JOE. Tony wants you.

AMY [*she comes in stolidly and takes the chair farthest from* TONY's *cot. She sits there stiffly*]. Well, here I am.

TONY [*ultra-tenderly*]. My Amy is tire'!

AMY. You don't blame me, do you? I've had quite a day. Gee, them kids out there have been climbing all over me.

TONY. Da's good.

AMY. Oh, I don't mind kids if they go to bed when they ought to and know how to behave. Believe me, if I ever have any kids, they're going to behave.

TONY. You hear dat, Joe?

AMY. I said "if." [*A silence.*] I wouldn't object.

TONY [*amorously*]. Amy . . . Come over here.

AMY [*rising quickly*]. I guess I ain't so tired. I guess I better go back or they'll be wondering what's become of the blooming bride. Some bloom, huh? [*The fireworks hiss and flare again and* AMY, *very like a little girl, is out on the porch for the delight of seeing them. The enthusiasm of the crowd fairly rattles the windows.*] They sure do yell out there! When you get enough wops together and put enough vino in 'em, they sure can speak up! . . . I think I'll take off my veil. [*She does.*] Phew! That thing don't look like no weight at all, but it feels like a ton of bricks.

TONY. Amy, come over here.

AMY. I'm all right where I am.

TONY. Amy!

AMY. What?

TONY. You like earrings, Amy?

AMY. Earrings? I'm human, ain't I?

JOE. That's the idea.

AMY [*a real snarl*]. I didn't speak to you. I was addressing Tony.

TONY. Ah, you call me Tony for da first time!

AMY. Expect me to call my husband mister? That'd
sound swell, wouldn't it? Tony. Short for Antonio.
Antonio and Cleopatra, huh? Can you beat it? You'll
have to call me Cleo.

TONY. I like better Amy.

AMY. There ain't no short for Amy. It's French and it
means beloved. Beloved! Can you beat it? The boss
in the spaghetti palace told me that the night he
tried to give me a twelve-dollar pearl necklace.
Twelve dollars! He was some sport. When he seen I
couldn't see it that way, he give it to Blanche. She
was the other girl that worked there. He had a wife
and three kids too. [TONY *beckons again and* AMY
takes further refuge in conversation.] I like that
name Blanche. I used to wish my name was Blanche
instead of Amy. Blanche got in trouble. Poor
Blanche! Gee, I was sorry for that girl!

TONY. Come over here, Amy. [*He holds out the box.*]

AMY. What's that?

TONY. Ees my present for my Amy.

AMY. What you got there, Tony?

TONY. For you.

AMY. Something for me? [*By this time, she has got over
to the cot. She takes the box.*] Honest? Well, now, if
that isn't sweet of you, Tony. [*She opens it.*] Oh! . . .
Oh!! . . . Oh!!!

TONY. Ees for mak' Amy happy.

JOE. They're real! Real diamonds!

TONY. You bet our life! Four hundra dollar'.

AMY. I . . . I . . . [*Tears come.*] Real diamonds. . . .

[*She sits in the* DOCTOR'S *chair and cries and cries.*]

TONY. Don' cry, Amy! Don' cry! Ees no' for cry, earrings! Ees for festa! Ees for marryin' with Tony!

AMY. I don't know what to say! I don't know what to do!

JOE. Put 'em on. [*He gets the mirror, brings it over to where* AMY *sits, and holds it for her while she begins to put the earrings on. Her sobs gradually subside.*]

AMY. I had another pair once, so I got my ears pierced already. Ma pierced my ears herself with a needle and thread. Only these kind screw on! Say, ain't they beautiful! My others were turquoises and gold. Real turquoises and real gold. But these here cost four hundred dollars! Oh, I never dreamed of anything so gorgeous! [*She takes the mirror from* JOE.]

TONY. Amy . . . Amy . . .

AMY. Can I wear 'em whenever I want?

TONY. You can wear 'em in da bed if you want!

AMY. Oh, thank you, Tony! [*She is just about to kiss him.*]

JOE. Now, everything's fine!

AMY [*furiously*]. Say what's the idea? What have you got to do with this? You're always buttin' in. Say . . . [*Suddenly she remembers the momentous photograph which still lies on the table.*] Wait a minute. [*She picks it up and hands it quite violently to* JOE.] Here's your picture.

TONY [*watching in terror*]. Santa Maria!

AMY. *Here!* You better take it! Take it, I tell you! I don't want it.

[JOE *looks first at the photograph, then at the lady.*]

JOE. I guess you ain't far wrong, Amy. I hope there ain't no hard feelin's.

AMY. Why should there be any hard feelings?

TONY. Benissimo!

JOE. All right. Only I didn't want you to think. . . . [*A long pause.*]

AMY [*very steadily*]. You ain't got much of a swelled head, have you, Mr. Joe?

[JOE'S *face falls. The tension is snapped by a gesture from* TONY.]

TONY. Tear him up, Joe! Tear him up! [JOE *obeys.*]

AMY. Now we don't ever have to think of that again.

TONY. Madonna! . . . Da's verra good.

AMY. You see, that's the only way to do. There ain't no use of keeping things around to remind you of what you want to forget. Start in all over again new and fresh. That's my way. Burn up everything you want to put behind you. No reminders and no souvenirs. I been doing that regular about once a month ever since I was a kid. No memories for me. No hard feelings. It's a great life, if you don't weaken. I guess, if I keep at it long enough, I may get somewhere, some day. [*She turns and deliberately kisses* TONY *on the brow.*]

JOE [*to* TONY]. Will that hold you? I guess you don't need to worry no more after that. I guess that fixes your troubles for good. I guess you better admit I was pretty near right.

TONY. Now you know for w'y I been wantin' you go away, Joe. Dat goddam picture photograph! But evrathing is fix' now. Evrathing is fine. You don' need go away now, Joe.

JOE. You don't need me now. I guess I can migrate now. You got Amy to take care of you.

TONY. No! No! I need you here for tak' care of my vineyard. I don't let you go away now. Amy don' let you go away now.

AMY. Is he thinking of going away, Tony?

TONY. He don't go now, Dio mio! Ees no good Joe goin' away and leavin' Tony sick in da bed with nobody for runnin' vineyard!

JOE. You'll get somebody.

AMY. When's he going?

TONY. He say to-morrow. You don't let him go, Amy?

AMY. I got nothing to say about it.

TONY. You hear dat, Joe. Amy is askin' you for stay here.

AMY [*scorn*]. *Yes,* I am!

JOE. I got to go, Tony. I just plain got to go.

AMY. If he won't stay for you, Tony, he won't stay for me. It ain't the place of a lady to be coaxing him, anyhow. . . . [*She again turns malevolent attention upon* JOE.] Where you headed for?

JOE. The next place.

AMY. What's the idea?

JOE. I just got to be on my way, an' that's all there is to it.

TONY. Ees all dose goddam Wobblies, Amy. You tell him stay here w'ile Tony is so sick in da bed like dees. You don' go to-morrow, Joe. You and me is talkin' more by-an-by, in da mornin'.

JOE. Oh, what's the use? I'm goin', I tell you.

AMY [*smiling darkly*]. It must be pretty swell, being free and independent and beating it around the country just however you feel like, sleeping any place the notion hits you, no ties, work a day and bum a week, here and there, you and the—what do you call 'em? Wobblies? Huh! I never could see much in it myself. Calling in at farmhouses for a plate of cold stew and a slab of last Sunday's pie. Down in the Santa Clara we used to keep a dog for those boys. I guess it's a fine life if you like it. Only I never had much use for hoboes myself.

TONY. Joe ain' no hobo, Amy!

AMY. Ain't he?

JOE [*completely discomfited*]. I guess I'll say good-night.

FATHER MC KEE [*furiously shouting off stage*]. You got no business callin' it sacramental, because it ain't got no sanction from the Church!

[TONY *looks at the pair of them in unbelieving horror.* JOE *starts to go.* AMY *smiles triumphantly. Then the situation is saved by a tumult of voices and the porch is suddenly packed with the guests of the festa: men, women, and children, old and young, fat and lean. They follow* THE DOCTOR *and* FATHER MC KEE, *who are engaged in a furious argument.*]

THE DOCTOR. Is the Church opposed to the law or is it not?

FATHER MC KEE. The Church is opposed to interfering with the divine gifts of Providence.

THE DOCTOR [*as he enters*]. It's the greatest reform since the abolition of slavery.

FATHER MC KEE [*as he enters*]. "The ruler of the feast calleth the bridegroom and sayeth unto him: 'Every man setteth on first the good wine'."

THE DOCTOR. Oh, hell!

FATHER MC KEE. You're a godless heretic, young man, or you wouldn't be talkin' such blasphemy! I ain't got no sympathy with drunkenness, but there's plenty of worse things. How about chamberin'? Ain't chamberin' a worse sin than drunkenness? You think you can put a stop to drunkenness by pullin' up all the grapes. I suppose you can put a stop to chamberin' by pulling up all the women!

JOE. There's an argument for you, Doc.

THE DOCTOR. Alcohol is a poison to the entire alimentary system whether you make it in a still or in a wine barrel. It's poison, and poison's no good for any man. As for the Church . . .

FATHER MC KEE [*beside himself*]. It ain't poison if you don't get drunk on it, an' you don't get drunk if you're a good Cath'lic!

THE DOCTOR. I suppose that drunkenness is confined to such scientific heretics as myself?

AMY. You certainly was lappin' it up outside, Doc.

TONY. Don' fight!

FATHER MC KEE. You'll have to pardon me, Tony, but when I hear these heretics gettin' full on bootleg liquor and callin' it sacramental!

[*The rest of the argument is drowned in the pande-monium of the crowd. At first* THE DOCTOR *tries to keep them out.*]

THE GUESTS. Buona notte! Buon riposo! Evviva Antonio! Tanti auguri! Felice notte! Tante grazie!

JOE. Festa's over.

THE GUESTS. Come sta Antonio? Come vas Voglio veder la padrona! Grazie, Antonio! Buona notte! Tanti auguri! A rivederci!

THE DOCTOR [*to* JOE]. Tell them to cut the row!

THE GUESTS. Grazie, Antonio! Mille grazie, Antonio! Buona notte, Antonio! Tanti auguri! A rivederci!

THE DOCTOR. Keep those wops out of here! There's been enough noise already with this bigoted old soak.

FATHER MC KEE. You heretical, blasphemin' . . .

TONY. Padre, Madonna mia, don' fight no more! [*To the crowd.*] Eh!

THE DOCTOR [*still holding the crowd back in the door-way*]. No, you can't come in here!

THE GUESTS. Si, si, dottore! Si, si, dottore! Prego, dottore!

THE DOCTOR. No! Tony's too sick!

TONY. Tak' a pinch-a snuff, Doc, an sit down. [*The guests surge in as* TONY *calls to them.*] Vieni! Vieni qui! Venite tutti! Venite tutti!

THE GUESTS. Come va? Sta bene? Sta meglio, Antonio? Ha tanto sofferto, poveretto! Poveretto!

TONY [*picking out a small boy*]. Ecco il mio Giovan-nino! Ah, com' è grande e bello e forte! Quanto pesa?

GIOVANNINO'S MOTHER. Ah, si, è grande, non è vero? Pesa sessanta cinque libbre.

TONY. Sessanta cinque! [*To* AMY.] Amy, looka him! He weigh' sixty-five pound', an' he's only . . . [*To the mother.*] Quant' anni?

GIOVANNINO'S MOTHER. Soltanto nove.

TONY. He's only nine year' old an' he weigh sixty-five pound'!

ANOTHER MOTHER. Antonio, ecco la mia.

[*A little girl runs to throw her arms around* TONY'S *neck and kiss him. Exclamations of delight.*]

TONY [*to the mother.*]. Ah! Come so chiama?

THE SECOND MOTHER. Maria Maddalena Rosina Vittoria Emanuela.

TONY. Maria Maddalena Rosina Vit— [*To* AMY.] Looka Maria Maddalena! Ah, Maria Maddalena is goin' grow up an' be a fine, beautiful lady like my Amy.

GIOVANNINO'S MOTHER. E il mio Giovannino! [*To* MARIA'S MOTHER.] Santa Madonna! Ella non è più bella che il mio Giovannino!

MARIA'S MOTHER [*furious*]. Si è più bella! E molto più bella che un ragazzone come questo.

GIOVANNINO'S MOTHER. Non è ragazzone, senti!

MARIA'S MOTHER. Si! Ma, la mia carina.

THE MEN [*hilariously*]. Giovannino! Giovannino!

THE WOMEN [*at the same time*]. Maria Maddalena! Maria Maddalena!

THE DOCTOR. Come on, now, get out! We've had enough of this!

ANGELO *and* GIORGIO [*facing the howling mob*]. Basta! Basta! Via! Via! Fuori! Avanti! Al diavolo!

[*Uproar and retreat.*]

AMY [*on the porch, she stops them*]. No, wait a minute! I want to tell 'em all good-night. Good-night! Good-night! Thank you. I've had the very best wedding that ever was and I'm the happiest girl in the world because you've been so good to me. Come back to-morrow and see Tony and tell him all the news. Good-night and God bless you.

VOICES. Siamo molto contenti! Com' è gentile! Com' è bella! Com' è simpatica! Grazie tanto, Amy!

JOE. They say thank you and God bless you. . . . Beat it, now. Buona notte! Run along. Come back to-morrow.

[*As they go down the hill, tenor, concertina, and chorus strike into song.*]

TONY. Oh, Amy, I w'isper in your ear, Amy. You ain'

goin' be mad with Tony for bein' so crazy-wild with love? You come in da house like da spring come in da winter. You come in da house like da pink flower dat sit on da window sill. W'en you come da whole world is like da inside da wine cup. You ondrastan', Amy? I canno' help talkin' dees way. I got for tell you, Amy, an' I ain't got no English language for tell you. My Amy is so good, so prett'! My Amy.... [*He fairly breaks down.* AMY *pats his hand.*]

JOE [*to* FATHER MC KEE]. Look at the poor wop. [*He is just going.*]

THE DOCTOR. Don't go, Joe. I want a hand with Tony.

FATHER MC KEE. Listen.... [*He holds up his hand for them to attend to the music. He pours wine into a cup.*] Here's to the bridal couple!

JOE [*same business*]. Doc?

THE DOCTOR. No, thanks.

AMY. Oh, Doctor!

TONY. Doc, you no drink Tony's health?

THE DOCTOR. Oh, all right! [*He drinks with the others.*] Nasty stuff. [*He drains his glass. They laugh, all of them.*] Off to bed with you now, Tony!

TONY. My leg is hurt too much. I canno' sleep.

THE DOCTOR. I've got something that'll make you sleep. [*He mixes a powder in water and presents it to* TONY *for consumption.*]

TONY. Jes' Chris'! I canno' drink water, Doc! [*With the* DOCTOR's *consent he adds wine to the draught.*]

THE DOCTOR. That's right. Drink up.... [*The potion is downed.*]

TONY. Amy, you lookin' sad!

JOE. Do you blame her? She's had some day. [*A pat on her shoulder. She shrinks angrily.*]

AMY. I ain't sad.... It was a swell wedding and everybody had a swell time. Hear that? They're still singing. Ain't it pretty? And I don't want to hear no more of what the Doc was telling me outside about bringing a trained nurse up here from Napa. I'm all the nurse Tony needs, and don't nobody be afraid of my working, because there's nothing I like better. And when Tony's good and strong and don't have to be in bed all the time, we'll have Giorgio and Angelo carry him out in the sun and I'll sit beside him and read the paper out loud and we'll look at the view and feel that nice wind and we'll just enjoy ourselves. And the doc'll come up and see us. And the Padre, too, if they can keep from fighting. And if Joe goes away—why—he goes away, that's all. Don't nobody fret about little Amy. She's going to be all right.

[*The* DOCTOR *and the* PRIEST *exchange approving glances.*]

FATHER MC KEE. Amy, you're a credit to the parish.

THE DOCTOR [*at the head of the cot*]. Joe, take that end!

TONY [*still spellbound*]. My Amy. . . .

AMY. Yes, Tony?

TONY. I'm sleepy.

THE DOCTOR [*as* JOE *and he lift the cot*]. Not too high.

TONY [*groaning, he can still reach to take his bottle along*]. Wait!

JOE. Steady! You hold the door, Padre.

THE DOCTOR. Easy now! Not too fast.

AMY. Watch out for his hand!

THE DOCTOR. Take shorter steps, Joe. Every man ought to be taught how to carry a stretcher. Why, when I was in France . . . [*He backs through the door.*] Lower your end, Joe! You'll give him apoplexy.

TONY. Oh! . . .

JOE. I got him. . . . [*He follows through the door with the foot of the cot. Another groan from* TONY. AMY *takes a step toward door.*]

FATHER MC KEE. Better give 'em a minute. [*He goes into the bedroom.* AMY *is left alone. She stands quite still for a moment; then, giddily, drops into a chair.* FATHER MC KEE *returns.*]

FATHER MC KEE. You're a fine brave girl.

AMY. Thanks.

FATHER MC KEE. We have our trials, all of us.

AMY. Sure, I know that.

FATHER MC KEE. If ever you need a word of comfort, call on me, my daughter.

AMY. Thanks.

FATHER MC KEE. You may not be a Cath'lic, but I'll do my best by you. [AMY *smiles wanly.*] I had my doubts of this here marriage, but God knows who's meant for who in this world. He ain't done a bad turn by either you or Tony.

AMY. I got no kick.

[*The* DOCTOR *enters, quietly closing the bedroom door after him.*]

FATHER MC KEE. Be patient with him. He's old enough to be your father, and no man ain't got no business marryin' at his age, but he's a good fella.

AMY. I guess I better go in there now.

THE DOCTOR [*wiping his hands medically on his spotless handkerchief*]. He's asleep. I've never known the like. Never in all my years of practice. It's a case that ought to be written up for the whole, entire medical profession. Both legs broken in the morning. Tibia, fibula, femur, and ischium. X-rayed and set inside of an hour after the accident. Patient married at noon and survives ten hours of whooping Dago celebration with no apparent ill effects.

AMY [*grim*]. Yeah! What do you want me to do, Doctor?

THE DOCTOR. Let me send up a nurse in the morning.

AMY. No.

THE DOCTOR. A man in a cast's a handful. It's going to be a long siege.

AMY. I can manage. [*Suddenly desperate.*] God! I got to have something to do!

THE DOCTOR. Well. . . . [*He shrugs his shoulders.*] If he wakes up to-night, give him another one of those powders in a little wine. Wine won't harm the drug and the water might kill the patient. Eh, Padre?

AMY. Is that all, Doctor?

THE DOCTOR. That's all. I'll come up early in the morning.

AMY. Thanks.

THE DOCTOR. Sure about the nurse? [*She nods.*] You take it pretty calmly.

AMY. Ain't much else I can do, is there?

THE DOCTOR. Good-night. Joe's fixing you up a bed. He'll be here if you want him.

FATHER MC KEE [*going with the* DOCTOR]. I ain't kissed the bride.

THE DOCTOR. Come on! [*He pushes* FATHER MC KEE *in front of him and they go off. Their voices die away.*] [AMY *goes to the table and mechanically removes her earrings.* AH GEE *enters by the outer door with a tray of glasses.* JOE *enters from the bedroom, closing the door carefully after him.*]

JOE. You turn in, Ah Gee. I'm going to sleep in here. [AH GEE *goes to his kitchen.* JOE *watches* AMY *with the same puzzled frown he has worn since she first turned upon him.*] Amy . . . [*She stiffens.*] I got you fixed up in Tony's big bed. I'm goin' to sleep in here in case you want any help.

AMY. All right.

JOE. Well, good-night. [*He goes about making himself comfortable for the night.*]

AMY. Good-night, Joe.

JOE. Keep a stiff upper lip. Everything's going to turn out O. K. Good-night.

AMY. You certainly do think you're God Almighty, don't you?

JOE. I don't get you.

AMY. Oh, well, let it go. I guess I don't feel so good.

JOE [*still busy with his bed*]. Maybe it's the vino. It don't agree with some folks.

[*A slight pause.*]

AMY. I guess I'm just nervous.

JOE. I'd be nervous myself if I'd just been married.

AMY. Would you?

JOE. If I was a girl, I would.

AMY. Maybe that's why I'm nervous.

JOE. Sure it is. I often think how it must be for a girl takin' a big, important step like gettin' married. Everything new an' diff'rent an' all that.

AMY. Yeah.

JOE. But I wouldn't let it worry me if I was you.

AMY. I won't, Mister Joe. [*She takes up one of the lamps*].

JOE. That's the idea. Good-night.

AMY. Good-night. [*She turns and looks desperately at him.*]

JOE. Say, look here, Amy . . .

AMY. I don't remember of giving you leave to use my Christian name.

JOE. Excuse me . . . only . . . there's something I just got to say to you before I go away. Because I am going. I'm going in the morning just as soon as Tony wakes up so's I can tell him good-bye. But there's something I just got to ask you.

AMY. What is it?

JOE. You like Tony all right, don't you?

AMY. I married him, didn't I? And I let him give me jewelry, too, didn't I? A nice, self-respecting girl don't accept jewelry from a man she don't like. Not real jewelry.

JOE. I know that . . . only . . . it ain't just what I mean. Because, Tony—oh, he's a nut an' a wop an' all that, but he's just the best old fella I ever knew. Regular salt of the earth, Tony is. I wouldn't like to see Tony in trouble or unhappy or gettin' his feelings hurt or anything in that line. . . .

AMY [*dangerously*]. Oh, wouldn't you?

JOE. No. An' it's all up to you now. . . . An' . . . well, you see what a fine old fella he is, don't you?

AMY. I ain't been complaining about him that I remember. When I start in complaining there'll be plenty of time then for outsiders to butt in and make remarks.

JOE. Don't get sore.

AMY [*fury again*]. Who's sore? Say, listen to me. I know what I'm about, see? I married for a home, see? Well, I got a home, ain't I? I wanted to get away from working in the city. Well, I got away, didn't I? I'm in the country, ain't I? And I ain't working so very hard, either, that I can notice. Oh, I know what's expected of me and I ain't going to lay down on my job. Don't you fret. You be on your way, and mind your own business.

JOE. Oh, all right!

AMY. I got all I bargained for and then some. I'm fixed. I'm satisfied. I didn't come up here . . . like I did . . . looking for love . . . or . . . or . . . anything like that.

JOE. All I got to say is it's a good thing you got so dam' much sense.

AMY. I'll thank you not to swear about me, too. . . .

JOE. You got me wrong, Amy. I apologize. Maybe I was only seein' Tony's side of the question. Some girls would have been sore'n you was over what old Tony done to get you here. But you're a real sport, that's what you are. You're a great girl an' I'm all for you. [*He emphasizes his approval with another patronizing pat on her shoulder.*]

AMY. Oh, for God's sake, leave me alone, can't you?

JOE [*who can grow angry himself*]. Sure, I can! Good-night!

AMY. Good-night! [*She stands quite still, so does he. Far, far away the irrepressible tenor resumes "Maria Mari."*]

JOE. I'm sleeping in here in case . . .

AMY. There won't be any need of you putting yourself out.

JOE. How do you know but what Tony. . . .

AMY. I can take care of Tony and the further off *you*

keep yourself the better I'll be pleased. [*Their eyes blaze.*]

JOE. Well, if you feel that way, I'll go back to my own shack. [*He grabs his coat and makes for the door.*] That wop'll be singing all night. [*He is out on the porch.*]

AMY. Joe!

JOE. What? [*He returns.*]

AMY. Would you mind waiting just a minute? There's something I got to ask *you.*

JOE. Shoot. . . .

AMY. You got to tell *me* the truth this time. You just got to tell me the truth. . . . You really and honestly didn't know nothing about his sending me that photo of you instead of his own, did you? You didn't know nothing at all about that?

JOE. Honest to God, I didn't. . . . Honest to God. . . .

AMY. On your sacred word of honor?

JOE. Honest.

AMY. I'm glad. And I want to apologize to you for what I said just now . . . and for that other thing I said about your being a common hobo and all. . . . I'm sorry, Joe. Will you forgive me?

JOE. Oh, that's all right.

AMY. I wouldn't want to have you go away to-morrow thinking what a mean character I got.

JOE. Nothing like that.

AMY. You mean it?

JOE. Shake. [*They shake hands, standing in the doorway.*] You're cryin'! . . . What's the matter, kid?

AMY. Oh, I don't know. . . . Nothing. . . . I'm all right. . . .

JOE. Come on! Don't get upset. Just make the best of things.

AMY. It ain't that.

JOE. Well, just make the best of things, anyway.

AMY. I'm trying to! I'm trying to!

JOE [*his hands on her shoulders*]. You're married to a

good man. I know the weddin' was kind of funny
with Tony all smashed up an' all. But you just hold
on a while an' everythin'll be O. K. You'll see!

AMY. I bet all those people are laughing at me.

JOE. No, they ain't.

AMY. I bet you're laughing at me.

JOE. I ain't, Amy. I'm sorry. . . .

AMY [*moving back from him*]. Leave me alone, can't
you?

JOE [*his voice very low*]. Say, you're all right, Amy. . . .
You're plumb all right.

AMY. I always was all right till I come up here. Now I
wish I was dead! I wish I was dead!

JOE. Don' talk that way. You're all right. . . . [*Clumsily,
he takes her arm. She stumbles. He catches her.
There is a moment of silence broken only by their
deep breathing as the physical being of one is com-
municated to the physical being of the other. Suddenly and irresistibly he clutches her to his breast
and kisses her. She struggles a moment, then aban-
dons herself.*]

TONY [*calling out in the bedroom*]. Amy! [*She breaks
loose, sobbing hysterically.*]

JOE [*a whisper*]. Jesus! [*She stifles a little cry and turns
for the bedroom door.*] No, you don't. . . . [*He
catches her.*]

AMY [*struggling*]. Let me go!

TONY. Amy!

[*She breaks free, terrified, and runs out of the house.
JOE stands listening a moment, then runs after her as
the curtains falls.*]

Act three

The scene is unchanged, but the woman's presence has made itself felt. Handsome, though inexpensive, cretonne curtains grace the windows. A garish jardinière of porcelain holds a geranium plant and stands upon a colored oriental tabouret. The lamps have acquired art shades: one of some light-colored silk on a wire form and adorned with roses of the same material in a lighter shade, the other of parchment painted with windmills and Dutch kiddies. New pictures selected from the stock-in-trade of almost any provincial "art department" hang upon the walls; one of them, perhaps, a portrait of a well-known lady screen star. These have replaced Washington and Garibaldi and the Italian Steamship Company's poster. Painted and elaborately befringed leather sofa cushions fill the large chairs. It is hoped that one of the variety showing the head of Hiawatha can be secured for this, as they say, "touch." A brilliantly embroidered centerpiece covers the dining-room table and the flowers in the middle are palpably artificial. A white waste-paper basket is girt by a cerise ribbon which makes some corner of the room splendid. A victrola graces another corner.

Three months have passed. It is midafternoon.

An invalid chair has been made by laying a board between the seat of the morris chair and the top of a box. In this TONY *reclines, his crutches lying on the floor by his side.* FATHER MC KEE *nods drowsily in another chair.* JOE *sits on the porch rail outside the window perusing the scareheads of an I. W. W. paper.*

FATHER MC KEE [*continuing the discussion*]. Now, Joe, don't be tryin' to tell me that things is goin' to be any

better for havin' a revolution, because they ain't.
Gover'ment's always gover'ment no matter what you
call it, an' no particular kind of gover'ment ain't no
more'n a label anyway. You don't change nothin' by
givin' it a new name. Stick a "peppermint" label on
a bottle of castor oil an' then drink it an' see what
happens to you. Castor oil happens!

TONY. I am work' just as much like Joe an' I don' want
changin' nothing.

JOE. I suppose you both come over here in the first
place because you was satisfied with everythin' just
like it was in the old country?

FATHER MC KEE. Human nature ain't nothin' but human nature an' the only way you ever could make a
gover'ment is by obedience. Scalliwaggin' around
about grievances an' labels don't accomplish nothin'.
An' the only way you can make a revolution anythin'
but a mess to no purpose is to change the people's
ideas an' thank goodness there ain't nobody can accomplish that. It can't be done.

JOE. They're changin' already, Padre.

FATHER MC KEE. I'm talkin' to you with the cassock off,
Joe. I'm lettin' you in on the secrets of the Mother
Church. She knows the stock of ideas the world over
an' she knows they don't never change. The Mother
Church just keeps hammerin' an' hammerin' the
same old nails because she knows there ain't no new
ones worth hammerin'.

TONY. People come in da Unita State' because ees good
place. I been comin' for mak' money.

JOE. You certainly succeeded.

TONY. You don't ondrastan', Joe. You got crazy idea.
I'm comin' here for mak' money an' you want tak'
my money all away.

JOE. What's your idea of progress, Padre?

FATHER MC KEE. Improvin' yourself! Now, Joe, it comes
to my notice that you been 'round here talkin' pretty
uppity 'bout the U. S. gover'ment. 'Tain't no good

just makin' slurrin' remarks 'bout the gover'ment when you ain't got the ability nor the power to do nothin' toward improvin' it. You have got the power to do somethin' toward improvin' yourself, but I don't see you doin' it.

TONY. W'at I care for gover'ment? People is tellin' me king is no good an' freedom is verra fine. W'at I care for king? W'at I care for freedom? Evrabody say dees gover'ment is bad for havin' pro'ibish'. I say pro'i-bish' mak' me dam' rich. Evra man got his own idea w'at is good for evrabody else.

JOE. You're a bloomin' capitalist, that's what you are!

TONY. You mak' me tire', Joe. Evra minute talkin' 'bout Russia. . . . Russia. . . . Tak' a pinch-a snuff an' shut up!

JOE. Russia's got the right idea.

FATHER MC KEE. Now, listen to me, young man. If you had the energy an' the reverence for authority and the continence that Tony has, you wouldn't be car-ryin' on 'bout no revolutions in Russia. 'Tain't sense. I've read a-plenty of your radical literature an' if you ask me, it's just plain stupid. I may be a priest an' I may be a celibate, but that don't make me no less of a man. An' no real man ain't never got no use for carryin's on. You radicals, Joe, you're always an' forever hollerin' an' carryin' on 'bout your rights. How 'bout your duties? There ain't no one to pre-vent your doin' your duties but you ain't never done 'em in your life.

JOE. I'm savin' my duties for the brotherhood of man.

TONY. Dio mio!

FATHER MC KEE. You're talkin' a lot of balderdash. Mind your own business an' leave the brotherhood of man to me. Brothers is *my* job.

TONY. You think evrabody's goin' be brother like dat an' don' scrap no more? Ees crazy idea! You ain' got no good sense, Joe, you an' dos goddam Wobblies.

FATHER MC KEE. I been mullin' this over in my mind,

Joe, ever since Tony asked me to come up an' talk to you. An' I come to the conclusion that capital an' labor'll go on scrappin' to the end of time and they'll always be a certain number of people that'll stand up for the underdog. I been standin' up for the underdog all my life . . .

JOE [*indignant, he comes into the room*]. Yes, you have! A helluva lot of standin' up you ever done for anybody but yourself!

TONY [*talking at the same time*]. Now, Joe, don't you be getting fresh! You listen to w'at da Padre's sayin'!

FATHER MC KEE [*talking at the same time*]. . . . but I learned a long time ago that the dog on top needs just as much standin' up for as the other kind and I ain't got much use for either of 'em because both of 'em's always complainin' an' carryin' on.

TONY. I been 'Merican citizen for twent' year'. I been vote evra year—some times two times. Ees fine thing, vote! I like. He mak' me feel like I am good man an' patriotic fella. But w'at I know 'bout vote? I don't know nothing. I don' care nothing. You think you know so much, eh? You want for change evrathing an' w'en you got evrathing change' like you want, some other fella is comin' for changin' you. Ees no good. [*A defiant look about him.*] You look-a me an' do like I done. You marry with good wife like my Amy an' live quiet in a fine house an' gettin' rich like me an' . . . an' . . . an' raisin' playnta kids like I am goin' do. Da's w'at is for life. Not for runnin' evra place, goddam to hell gover'ment with goddam Wobblies!

JOE. Now you got Tony goin' on kids again. I sure am catchin' all that's comin' my way. But, just the same, I'm goin' to take my trip to Frisco an' see what's what.

FATHER MC KEE. Well, Joe, I can understand your wantin' to shake the dust of this place off'n your feet. But I got to tell you that the adventures of the spirit is a great deal more interestin' than the adventures of the flesh. No man can't do no more'n 'bout six things with his flesh. But he can have a heap of fun with his immortal soul.

TONY. Joe is dam' lucky havin' good job here. Last time he talk 'bout goin' away, he tak' my advice an' stay here for runnin' da vineyard. Dees time he better tak' my advice some more.

[FATHER MC KEE *is fingering* JOE's *papers ominously.*]

JOE. I'll just trouble you for them papers, Padre.

FATHER MC KEE. If you take my advice you'll burn 'em.

TONY. Joe don't mean no harm.

JOE. Maybe I don't mean nothin' at all. Maybe I'm just restless an' rarin' to go. I read these things an' they make me think. A man ought to think if he can. Oh, not tall talk. Just what he could be doin' himself. I think how I could get into the scrap. I ought to have been in on the dock strike at San Pedro, but I wasn't. I don't want to miss another big fight like that, do I? You fellows don't understand, but that's the way it is. An' maybe you're right an' I'm wrong. I can't help that. Maybe when I get down to Frisco I'll hear the same old bull from the same old loud-mouths, just like it used to be. Maybe I'll get disgusted and beat it south for the orange pickin's, or maybe go back on the railroad, or maybe in the oil fields. But, what the hell! I been hangin' around here on the point of goin' for three months now. I might just as well pick up and clear out to-morrow or the day after. I'll come back some day, Tony. Anyway, there ain't no use of expectin' anythin' out of a guy like me. Don't get sore. What the hell!

TONY. You goin' in da jail, sure!

JOE. I could go worse places. A guy went to jail up in Quincy, in Plumas County, awhile back, for carryin' a Wobbly card—like this one, see? [*He displays the famous bit of red cardboard.*] His lawyer pleads with the judge to go easy on the sentence. "Your honor," he says, "this chap served in France an' won the Croy de Gaire an' the Distinguished Service Cross." An' right there the guy jumps up an' says: "Don't pay no attention to that stuff," he says. "I don't want no credit for no services I ever performed for no gover'-ment that tells me I got to go to jail to stand up for my rights."

FATHER MC KEE. Do you want to go to jail?

JOE. There's worse places, I tell you. I been there be-fore, too. That guy in Quincy got the limit an' I'd like to shake hands with him, I would. Tony says this is a free country. Well, Tony ought to know. He's a bootlegger.

TONY [*indignantly*]. Hah!

JOE. What I say is: about the only freedom we got left is the freedom to choose which one of our rights we'll go to jail for.

FATHER MC KEE [*super-sententiously*]. Joe.

TONY. Shhh! Here's Amy!

AMY [*off stage*]. Ah Gee!

[JOE *rises;* FATHER MC KEE *pauses in his harangue;* TONY *beams;* AMY *enters. She wears a bright dress and a red straw hat which pushes her hair down about her face. A duster swings dashingly from her shoulders. Her market basket hangs from her arm. She has stuffed some late lupin in the top of it.*]

AMY. Scrapping again, are you? What's the matter, this time? Has Joe got another attack of the foot-itch? [*She sets the basket down on the table, doffs hat and duster, and, as she does so, sees* JOE's *papers.*] Oho! So that's it. [*Patiently* JOE *folds the papers up.*] See them, Tony? [*She exhibits the lupin and begins to stuff it into the vase with the artificial flowers.*] Ain't they sweet? They're so pretty they might be artificial.

FATHER MC KEE. We been talkin' about reformin' the social system.

AMY. Well, you got a fine day for it. [*She hugs* TONY's

head and lets him pat her hand.] Ain't the doctor come yet?

TONY. Doc don' come to-day.

AMY. Sure he does.

JOE. He comes on Thursday.

FATHER MC KEE. To-day's Wednesday.

AMY. Well, I never! Here they are reforming the world and they don't even know what day of the week it is. Ain't men the limit?

TONY. Nobody is so smart like my Amy.

[*With a toss of her head she swirls off into the kitchen.*]

AMY. Don't let me stop you! Go right ahead. [*In the kitchen.*] Ah Gee . . . Oh, there you are. . . .

FATHER MC KEE. Thursday! It's my day to talk to the boys down at the parish school.

JOE. Hand 'em what you just been handin' me, Padre.

FATHER MC KEE. What I told you was confidential, Joe. I'm sorry you won't listen to it.

AMY [*she returns, carrying a dish with apples and a knife*]. See them, Tony?

TONY. Apples!

AMY. Guess what for?

TONY. Apples pie?

AMY [*she sits beside* TONY *and falls to on the apples*]. Well, the world may need reforming but I got no kick. The grapes is near ripe and ready for picking. The nights is getting longer, the mornings is getting colder, and Tony's getting better. Down town they're putting up the posters for the circus and I hear the show's going into winter quarters just the other side of Napa. I guess that's all the remarks I got to make now.

JOE. Here's the doc, now. . . .

[*A Ford motor.*]

THE DOCTOR [*off stage*]. Hello!

AMY. Yoo hoo!

[*The* DOCTOR *appears, shakes hands with* AMY, *nods to*

JOE *and the* PADRE, *and then he comes in to* TONY.]

THE DOCTOR. Well, how do the crutches go?

AMY. Just fine.

TONY. You want see me walkin', Doc?

THE DOCTOR. Perhaps, I do. Let's see . . . [*He feels the injured legs.*] Tibia . . . Fibula . . . Feels all right.

TONY [*with a proud, anatomical gesture*]. Ischium?

THE DOCTOR [*he rises and nods approvingly*]. All right, Tony, show us what you can do. No jumping, mind! Lend him a hand, Joe.

[*He stands aside to watch.* JOE *assists* TONY. *Grunting,* TONY *stands on his crutches and grins proudly.*]

TONY. Ees hurtin' here. [*Indicating arm pits.*] But ees goin' fine! [*A few tottering steps.*]

THE DOCTOR. Steady! Whoa! [*Laughter as* TONY *barely makes a chair.*] You ought to be put on exhibition. If anyone had told me that day when I had you on the table that I should see you on crutches in three months! Well, all I can say is, it pays to know how to set a fracture.

AMY. I guess it makes you realize what a good doctor you are.

THE DOCTOR. He owes something to your nursing, ma'am.

FATHER MC KEE. It's like the layin' on of hands, her nursin' is.

AMY. Funny you're saying that, Padre. I once had my fortune told down in Frisco. Out of a palmistry book one of my friends had. Everything in your hand means something, you know. See those bumps? Ain't they funny? Well, the book said that those bumps mean you're a good nurse and can take care of anybody no matter how sick he is. That's why I wouldn't let you send for no trained nurse, Doc. I was afraid she wouldn't have my bumps. . . . Gee, I got funny hands! . . .

THE DOCTOR. I'm not sure that medical science pays much attention to the nursing bump, ma'am, but you have certainly got it. I'll admit that.

TONY. My Amy is da best nurse I ever see.

AMY. Oh, Tony!

THE DOCTOR. I'm going to put your patient outside in the sun. Is there a good level place?

AMY. Under the arbor! . . . Oh, Tony!

TONY. After three month' in dees goddam house!

THE DOCTOR. Fix him up right with a big easy chair.

AMY. And plenty of pillows.

TONY. Amy, you ain' forgot how you promise' 'bout readin' da paper outside in da sun?

AMY. You bet I ain't forgot.

THE DOCTOR. Go on, now. I want to see you fixed.

TONY [*hobbles to the door and calls out*]. Giorgio . . . Angelo . . . Eccomi!

[GIORGIO *and* ANGELO *arrive in a whirlwind of Italian.* TONY *hobbles out of sight.* AMY *follows with two pillows, looking back at the* DOCTOR *and laughing.* FATHER MC KEE *carries the board and box. The* DOCTOR *goes to the door as though he intended following them. He stands looking out and speaks without turning.*]

THE DOCTOR. Joe . . .

JOE. What is it?

THE DOCTOR. I hear you're going away.

JOE. Yeah. I'm really goin' this time.

THE DOCTOR. Where to?

JOE. Search me. Frisco first.

THE DOCTOR. Hadn't you better take Amy with you? [*He turns then and looks sternly into* JOE's *startled eyes.*]

JOE. What?

THE DOCTOR. You heard me.

JOE. I don't get you.

THE DOCTOR. Amy came to see me last week. I didn't tell her what the trouble was. I didn't have the heart. I put her off. . . . Oh, it's easy to fool a woman. But you can't fool a doctor, Joe. [*A step nearer* JOE *and eyes hard on his face.*] Tony isn't the father. . . . He couldn't be. [*A long pause.*]

JOE [*under his breath*]. Oh, Christ!

THE DOCTOR. I thought so. [*Another long pause.*] I've been trying to figure out how to make things easiest for Tony. It upset me a good deal. Doctors get shocked more often than you'd think. . . . And a girl like Amy, too. . . . I didn't know what to do. I guess it's up to you.

JOE. Poor old Tony!

THE DOCTOR. You might have thought of him sooner— and of Amy, too, for that matter.

JOE. It wasn't on purpose. It was only once! But—honest to God, we wouldn't either of us have put anything like that over on old Tony. Not for a million dollars!

THE DOCTOR. You couldn't have wasted much time about it.

JOE. It was the first night.

THE DOCTOR. Good Lord!

JOE. It just happened. There was a reason you don't know about. I'm a swell guy, ain't I? To do a thing like that to a fellow like Tony.

THE DOCTOR. Shall I tell Tony? Or Amy?

JOE. No. . . . Gimme time to think.

THE DOCTOR. There's no concealing this. Don't try anything of that sort. I won't have it.

JOE. No.

THE DOCTOR. This is going to come near killing him.

[JOE *nods fearsomely. The* DOCTOR *turns and is going when* AMY *appears, marshalling* ANGELO *and* GIORGIO.]

AMY. Just cut out the welcome to our city stuff and carry this chair down there under the arbor where the boss is. [*As they pick it up, she turns to the* DOCTOR.] Say! You'd think to hear 'em that Tony'd just been raised from the dead. [*She turns back to the two Italians.*] Put it in the shade. . . . Mind that varnish, you clubfooted wops. . . . There. . . . [*She has seen the chair safely along the porch. She returns and makes for the bedroom, saying, as she goes.*] He wants a cover and everything you can think of. . . .

THE DOCTOR [*to* JOE]. Let me know if I can do anything.

[AMY *returns carrying a great, thick quilt. She cuts for the door, muttering happily to herself. On the porch she stops to call through the window to the stricken* JOE.]

AMY. Joe—just hand me them newspapers, will you?

JOE [*obeying*]. Here.

AMY [*in the doorway, her arms filled with papers and comforter, she sees his face*]. Gee—you look something fierce.

JOE [*in a strangled voice*]. Amy . . .

AMY. What is it?

JOE. I got to see you by an' by. . . . I got to see you alone . . . [*She starts to speak. He sees that he has frightened her.*] God damn . . . oh, God damn. . . .

AMY. What's the matter with you? What are you scaring me this way for?

JOE. Amy. . . . Just a minute ago . . .

AMY. Make it snappy. . . . I don't like this being alone with you. . . . It makes me think . . . I want to forget all that.

JOE. Yeah . . . An' me . . . that's what I mean.

AMY. What?

JOE [*after an awful pause*]. You're goin' to have a kid. [*She stares incredulously at him without making a sound.*] Yeah. . . . It's so, Amy. . . . I'm awfully sorry. . . . The doc just told me. . . . He found out when you was sick last week. . . . He knows all about it . . .

AMY [*she stands a moment without moving at all. Suddenly she lets quilt and papers slip to the floor and her hands clasp themselves over her abdomen*]. Oh, my God! [*She picks the quilt and papers up very carefully and puts them on the table. She drops weakly into one of the chairs as though her knees had failed her, her face rigid with terror.*]

AMY. What am I going to do?

JOE. I got to think. . . .

AMY. If you go wrong, you're sure to get it sooner or later. I got it sooner.

JOE. That kind of talk won't help any.

AMY. I'm glad of it. It serves me right. . . .

JOE. There's ways, you know . . . there's doctors . . .

AMY [*shakes her head vigorously*]. Them kind of doctors is no good.

JOE. But maybe . . .

AMY. They're no good. I'm too far gone anyway . . . I know . . . and anyway . . . doing that . . . It's worse than the other.

JOE. I'm sorry, Amy. . . .

AMY. You being sorry ain't got nothing to do with it, either. I'm thinking of Tony.

JOE. So'm I.

AMY. Tony's a white guy if he *is* a wop.

JOE. Yeah. . . .

AMY [*desperately loud*]. What am I going to do? What am I going to do?

JOE. Hey! . . . Not so loud!

AMY. But I ain't got no money . . . only my earrings. . . .

JOE. I got money enough.

AMY. You?

JOE. Tony made me save it. It's in the bank. More'n two hundred bucks. That'll see you through.

AMY. Tony'll be crazy. . . . Tony'll be just crazy.

JOE. The doc said for me to take you away with me.

AMY. You?

JOE. Yeah. . . . An' believe me, Amy, I'll do anything . . .

AMY. Going away with you won't help things any.

JOE. I'll treat you right, Amy.

AMY. Poor Tony!

JOE. I'll do the right thing if it kills me.

AMY. I must have been crazy that night.

JOE. We both was . . . but there's no use sayin' that now.

AMY. No. . . . Tony'll be crazy. [*She lifts her head, recognizing the inevitable.*] I guess the doc's right. I guess I'll have to go with you. . . . Somebody's got to help me out. . . . There ain't nobody but you.

JOE. That's all right. . . . I'm willing. . . .

AMY. And afterwards . . . Oh, my God! . . . And Tony'll be thinking that all the time . . . you and me . . . Oh! [*This is an exclamation of unutterable disgust.*] Poor Tony! You don't know how good he's been to me. And all the time he was so crazy for a kid. . . . Oh, I can't stick around here now! I got to go. I got to go quick.

JOE. I'm ready, if you are.

AMY. I'll just pack my grip.

JOE. Don't take it too hard, Amy. [*He tries to take her hand.*]

AMY [*shaking him off*]. None of that! I don't want no sympathy.

JOE. Excuse me.

AMY. You better get your own things.

JOE. All right. . . . I'll be back in a minute.

AMY. I'll get a move on, too.

[AH GEE *comes in with the dishes for dinner and begins to lay the table. Apparently* JOE *thinks of something more to say, but is deterred by* AH GEE'S *presence. He goes quickly.* AMY *hears* AH GEE *and watches him for a moment as though she were unable to understand what he is doing.*]

AH GEE [*as he puts down dishes*]. Velly good dinner tonight, Missy. Beans an' roas' veal an' apple pie!

TONY [*calling from off stage*]. Eh, Joe! Eh, JOE! W'ere you go like dat? Amy! W'ere are you, Amy? [*He comes up on the porch.*] Ah! Here you are!

AH GEE. Oh, Bossy! Velly good dinner tonight. Apple pie!

TONY [*pleased*]. Ah! Apples pie! [AH GEE *goes into his kitchen*. TONY *leans against door*.] Amy! W'y you no' come back?

AMY [*who has been clinging desperately to the back of a chair*]. I don't know!

TONY. You leave me alone so long.

AMY. I just come in for the papers and . . .

TONY. . . . An' Joe is runnin' crazy wild an' don' say nothing w'en I'm askin' him, "Joe, w'ere you goin' like dat?"

AMY. Joe's going away.

TONY. He's no' goin' without sayin' goo'-by?

AMY. I dunno. . . . Maybe he is. . . .

TONY. That boy mak' me verra unhappy. I been lovin' Joe like he was my own son an' he's goin' away like dat. He's no good.

AMY. People who ain't no good ain't worth worrying about. The thing to do is let 'em go and forget 'em.

TONY. Da's no' so easy like you think, Amy. I been lovin' Joe like my own son.

AMY. Joe ain't no worse than other people I could mention.

TONY. I love Joe but he don' love me.

AMY. I love you, Tony! I love you!

TONY. I know, Amy, I know.

AMY. And you ain't never going to believe that I do again.

TONY. W'at you talkin' 'bout, Amy?

AMY. Something's happened, Tony!

TONY. Eh?

AMY. It's going to make you terrible mad.

TONY. Amy!

AMY [*nerving herself*]. It's going to make you just crazy, but I'm going to tell you just exactly what it is, Tony, because I ain't going to have you thinking afterwards that I wasn't grateful or that I ain't been happy here . . . happier than I ever been in my whole life. . . .

TONY. Amy!

AMY. Wait a minute. . . . I got to confess, Tony. I got to tell you the whole business so's you won't be thinking I'd been any worse than just what I have. . . .

TONY. Amy!

AMY. Yeah. . . . And I don't want you blaming Joe no more'n what you blame me and anyway you're a-bound to find out sooner or later, an' it'll hurt you a lot less in the long run if I tell you the truth right now, and I got to tell you the truth anyway. I simply got to. Wait a minute, Tony! I'm going to tell you the truth and after I go away and you don't see me no more you can say: "Well, she wasn't no good but it wasn't my fault." Because it wasn't your fault, Tony. Not one bit, it wasn't. You didn't have nothing to do with it. And I wouldn't be going away, neither, not for a million dollars I wouldn't, only for what's happened. . . .

TONY. Amy, w'at you talkin' 'bout goin' away?

AMY. That's what I'm trying to tell you, Tony, only you got to give me a chance because it ain't easy to tell you no more'n it's easy to go away. And I got to go. But it ain't because I don't love you. I do. And it ain't because I don't appreciate all you done for me. I ain't never going to forget none of it, nor you, nor this place. . . .

TONY. Amy!

AMY. Listen to me, Tony! You're going to kick me out when you hear what I got to say, but I don't care if you do. I'm going to have a baby, Tony . . . and it's . . . God help me! . . . it's Joe's baby.

TONY [*raising his crutch with a great cry of anger*]. Ah!

AMY. Didn't I tell you you'd kick me out?

TONY [*faltering*]. Dio mio! Dio mio! No! Amy, you fool with me? Eh?

AMY. No, I'm not fooling. It's so. And that's why I'm going away, Tony.

TONY [*pursuing her as she retreats*]. You been Joe's woman!

AMY. I was crazy!

TONY. You been Joe's woman!

AMY. I was crazy!

TONY. You been lovin' Joe!

AMY. No . . . I ain't . . . I ain't . . . I never loved Joe. Honest, I never. I was crazy.

TONY. You been just like da Padre say you was. . . . You been a whore. . . .

AMY. I ain't! . . . I ain't! I been straight all my life! Only that one night. . . .

TONY. W'at night?

AMY. The first night I come here.

TONY. Da night you marry with me!

AMY. I ain't even spoke to Joe alone since that night.

TONY. You lyin'!

AMY. I swear to God I ain't! Not once! Not till to-day after the doc told him what was going to happen.

TONY. You lyin' to me! You been Joe's woman!

AMY. I ain't, Tony! That's what I'm trying to tell you. It's the truth I'm trying to tell you and now I'm going away.

TONY. You goin' away with Joe?

AMY. My God, what else can I do?

TONY [*furiously he forces her back into the corner where the shotgun is hanging, spluttering all the time with slobbering, half-intelligible rage*]. I don' let you go! I don' let you go! By God, I'm goin' kill dat Joe! Questo bastardo, Joe! I'm goin' kill him an' keep you here for see me kill him! Goddam you! You goddam dirty . . . [*He has got the gun down, broken it, and is loading it.*]

AMY [*speaking at the same time*]. No, you won't, Tony! Don't do anything like that, now, Tony! You'll be sorry if you do! You know what'll happen to you if you do that! You know what'll happen to you, Tony!

That ain't no way to act! You'll see what you get! You'll see!

TONY. Goddam! . . . You wait, you dirty . . . [*He flourishes the broken gun. She covers her eyes with her hands.* JOE *arrives, sees what* TONY *is doing, gives a cry, springs on him, wrenches the gun away. The struggle upsets* TONY's *balance and he topples headlong off his crutches.* AMY *screams.*]

AMY. Oh, his leg! [JOE *drops the gun and bends over him.*]

JOE. I tried to catch him. . . . [TONY's *bellows are terrifying to hear.*] Did you hurt yourself, Tony? [TONY's *answer is untranslatable into speech.*]

AMY [*as she pulls a chair over*]. For God's sake, pick him up, can't you?

JOE [TONY *fights him, trying to choke him, and sinks into the chair, howling with pain and fury*]. All right now, Tony! Steady!

AMY. Tony. . . . Tony. . . . [*She kneels down by him.* TONY's *roars subside into moans.*] I had to tell him! Oh, my God! I just had to tell him!

JOE. He didn't hurt himself much. [TONY's *moans break into sobs.*]

AMY. This is awful.

JOE. Get your things. Let's pull out of here. We can send the Padre up to look after him.

AMY. I'm only taking my little grip, Tony. I'm leaving the earrings on the dresser. [*She goes quickly into the bedroom.* TONY's *sobs keep up wretchedly and terribly.*]

JOE. Tony, I . . . [*Again* TONY *springs madly at* JOE's *throat.* JOE *wrenches away and runs quickly to the table where he gets a glass of wine which he brings back to* TONY. TONY *pushes it away, spilling the wine over his shirt.* JOE *drops the glass.*]

TONY. Amy! Amy! Amy! Amy!

AMY [*she comes back, with her hat on and her coat over*

her arm. She has her yellow grip half open with clothes sticking out. JOE *takes it from her*]. Here I am, Tony. Here I am.

TONY. W'ere you goin', Amy? W'ere you goin' away from here?

AMY. I dunno . . . Frisco, I guess. . . .

TONY [*bitter sobs*]. You goin' be livin' with Joe?

AMY [*vague misery*]. I dunno. . . . No, I ain't going to live with Joe. . . . No matter what happens, I ain't.

TONY. Who is goin' be lookin' after you, Amy?

JOE. I am, Tony. I'll do the right thing if it kills me.

TONY. You? . . . You? . . . Oh, Dio mio! Dio mio! No! No!

JOE. Come on, Amy, for the love of Pete!

AMY. I'm coming.

TONY [*a hand out to stop her*]. You ain't got no money, Amy.

AMY. It don't matter.

TONY. Yes!

JOE. I got plenty.

TONY. No! . . . No! . . . No! . . . Joe is no good for lookin' after womans an' baby!

AMY. Don't take on, Tony. . . . Please don't take on! Let me go, and forget all about me. There ain't no use in talking any more.

TONY. You goin' have baby!

AMY. God, I know I am!

TONY. How you goin' mak' money for keep him? Before you go, you tell me dat!

AMY. God knows. . . . I don't.

TONY. Pretty quick Joe is leavin' you desert, and den w'at is goin' happen?

JOE. I swear I'll stick, Tony!

TONY. No! *No!* NO!! Ees no good! My Amy havin' baby in da street. Ees no good.

AMY. Don't say that for God's sake, Tony, don't say that . . .

TONY. W'at is goin' happen, Amy? W'at's goin' happen with you?

AMY. Joe . . . I can't stand no more of this.

TONY [*frenzied*]. No! *No!* NO!! NO!!!

AMY. Let go, Tony! Let go of my skirt!

TONY. You ain' goin', Amy! I don't let you go! You stayin' here with Tony!

AMY. Don't talk that way, Tony! It ain't no good.

TONY. No! No! You goin' listen to w'at Tony say now. You goin' listen, Amy. You don' love Joe. You love Tony. You been good wife, Amy. . . .

AMY. Good wife!

TONY. W'at is Tony goin' do without you?

JOE. Come on!

TONY. Amy, I get excite' just now, Amy. Excuse! Excuse! I think verra good once more. You ain' goin' with Joe. You stayin' here with Tony just like nothin' is happen', an' by an' by da little fella is come. . . .

AMY. Don't talk that way, Tony!

TONY. W'y not?

AMY. Because it ain't no way to talk!

TONY. Yes . . . yes . . . ees good sense! Ees w'at is evrabody wantin' here! You an' Joe an' me! . . . Looka Joe. Joe is wantin' go with Wobblies, eh? With goddam Wobblies. All right . . . Looka Amy . . . Amy is wantin' stay here nice an' safe in dees fine house with Tony. Is not true, eh? [AMY *nods through her tears.*] Sure is true. Look Tony, Dio mio, an' ask him w'at he want? Don' he want baby?

AMY. But not this baby, Tony?

TONY. W'at I care?

AMY. But, think of what people would say!

TONY. W'at I care w'at evrabody say? We tellin' evrabody he's Tony's baby. Den evrabody say Tony is so goddam young an' strong he's break both his leg' an' havin' baby just da same! . . . Ees good, eh? You don' go with Joe now, Amy? . . . Oh, Amy! . . .

AMY [*he has swayed her, but she looks at him as at a madman*]. No. . . . It wouldn't work, Tony. . . . You wouldn't mean it afterward. . . . You're crazy. . . .

TONY [*a last frantic appeal*]. No! No! No! [*Leaning back in his chair and looking around the room.*] W'at's good for me havin' dees fine house? W'at's good for me havin' all dis money w'at I got? I got nobody for give my house an' my money w'en I die. Ees for dat I want dis baby, Amy. Joe don' want him. Ees Tony want him. Amy, . . . Amy, . . . for God's sake don' go away an' leave Tony!

AMY. But, Tony! Think of what I done?

TONY. What you done was mistake in da head, not in da heart. . . . Mistake in da head is no matter.

AMY. You—you ain't kiddin' me, are you? . . . You're serious, ain't you—Tony? You'll stick to this afterwards, won't you, Tony? [*She walks slowly over to him. She throws her arms around his neck and presses his head against her breast. A prolonged pause.*] Well, Joe, I guess you better be going.

JOE. You mean?

AMY. I guess you'd better be going. [JOE *straightens in great relief.*]

JOE. All right. [*He picks up his knapsack which he dropped when he came in.*] I guess you're right. [*He pulls on his cap and stands a moment in the doorway, a broad grin spreading over his face.*] I guess there ain't none of us got any kick comin', at that. No real kick. [*He goes out slowly.*]

AMY [*lifting her face*]. No.

[TONY *clutches her even closer as the curtain falls.*]

PORGY

by DuBose and Dorothy Heyward

First production, October 10, 1927,
at the Guild Theatre, New York City,
with the following cast:

MARIA, *Georgette Harvey*
JAKE, *Wesley Hill*
LILY, *Dorothy Paul*
MINGO, *Richard Huey*
ANNIE, *Ella Madison*
SPORTING LIFE, *Percy Verwayne*
SERENA, *Rose MacClendon*
ROBBINS, *Lloyd Gray*
JIM, *Peter Clark*
CLARA, *Marie Young.*
PETER, *Hayes Pryor*
PORGY, *Frank Wilson*
CROWN, *Jack Carter*
CROWN'S BESS, *Evelyn Ellis*
A DETECTIVE, *Stanley de Wolfe*
TWO POLICEMEN, *Hugh Rennie, Maurice McRae*
UNDERTAKER, *Leigh Whipper*
SCIPIO, *Melville Greene*
SINN FRAZIER, *A. B. Comathiere*
NELSON, *G. Edward Brown*
ALAN ARCHDALE, *Edward Fielding*
THE CRAB MAN, *Leigh Whipper*
THE CORONER, *Garrett Minturn*

The action takes place in a Charleston,
South Carolina tenement neighborhood known as
Catfish Row, and in a palmetto jungle near by.

Act one

Before the rise of each curtain, the bells of St. Michael's, adjacent to the Negro quarter of old Charleston, chime the hour. The chimes are heard occasionally throughout the play.

Before the rise of first curtain, St. Michael's chimes the quarters and strikes eight.

The curtain rises on the court of Catfish Row, now a Negro tenement in a fallen quarter of Charleston, but in Colonial days one of the finest buildings of the aristocracy. The walls rise around a court, except a part of the rear wall of the old house, which breaks to leave a section of lower wall pierced at its center by a massive wrought-iron gate of great beauty which hangs unsteadily between brick pillars surmounted by pineapples carved of Italian marble.

By day, the walls of the entire structure present a mottled color effect of varying pastel shades, caused by the atmospheric action of many layers of color wash. A brilliant note is added by rows of blooming flame-colored geraniums in old vegetable tins on narrow shelves attached to each window sill. All of the windows are equipped with dilapidated slat shutters, some of which are open, others closed, but with the slats turned so that any one inside could look out without being seen. The floor of the spacious court is paved with large flagstones, and these gleam in faintly varying colors under their accumulated grime.

*Beyond the gate and above the wall, one sees a lit-
tered cobbled street, an old gas street lamp, and, beyond that again, the blue expanse of the bay, with Fort
Sumter showing on the horizon. Over the wall can be
seen masts and spars of fishing boats lying on the beach.*

*By night, the court depends for its illumination
upon the wheezing gas lamp, and the kerosene lamps
and lanterns that come and go in the hands of the occupants of the Row.*

At left front is PORGY'S *room (door and window), and
beyond it, an arch letting on an inside yard. The pump
stands against the wall right back; then, on around
right wall,* SERENA'S *doorway, with her window above
it, two more doors, then the door to* MARIA'S *cookshop.
Center right is seen* SERENA'S *wash bench, and near
right wall, well down front, is table on which* MARIA
serves her meals during the warm weather.

*As the curtain rises, revealing Catfish Row on a sum-
mer evening, the court reëchoes with African laughter
and friendly banter in "Gullah," the language of the
Charleston Negro, which still retains many African
words. The audience understands none of it. Like the
laughter and movement, the twanging of a guitar from
an upper window, the dancing of an urchin with a
loose, shuffling step, it is a part of the picture of Catfish
Row as it really is—an alien scene, a people as little
known to most Americans as the people of the Congo.*

*Gradually, it seems to the audience that they are be-
ginning to understand this foreign language. In reality,
the "Gullah" is being tempered to their ears, spoken
more distinctly with the African words omitted.*

*It is Saturday night, and most of the residents of Cat-
fish Row are out in the court, sitting watching the crap
shooters or moving to and fro to visit with one neighbor, then another. Among those present are:*

MARIA, matriarch of the court, massive in proportions
and decisive in action.

ANNIE, middle-aged, quiet, and sedate.

LILY, loud, good-natured, the court hoyden.

CLARA, who has her baby in her arms. She is scarcely more than a girl and has a sweet, wistful face.

JAKE, CLARA's husband. A successful captain of the fishing fleet; good-looking, good-natured.

"SPORTING LIFE," bootlegger to Catfish Row; a slender, overdressed, high-yellow Negro.

MINGO, young and lazy.

JIM and NELSON, fishermen.

SCIPIO, a boy of twelve, one of the numerous offspring of ROBBINS and SERENA.

ROBBINS *and* SERENA *are still in their room on the second floor,* SERENA *is seen occasionally as she moves back and forth past her lighted window. She is a self-respecting "white folks" Negress, of about thirty.*

The men are gathering for their Saturday-night crap game. They are grouped between gate and PORGY's *room.* JAKE *is squatting right,* MINGO *center rear, and* SPORTING LIFE *is left, forming triangle. A smoking kerosene lamp is in center of group, and the men are tossing and retrieving their dice in the circle of light.*

JAKE [*rolling*]. Seems like dese bones don't gib me nuttin' but box cars tonight. It was de same two weeks ago, an' de game broke me. I ain't likes dat luck.

[SPORTING LIFE *produces his own dice, and throws with a loud grunt and snap of his fingers.* MINGO *snatches the dice and balances them in his hand.*]

SPORTING LIFE. Damn yo', gib me dem bones.

[MINGO *holds him off with one hand while he hands the dice to* JAKE.]

MINGO. Whut yo' say to dese, Jake?

JAKE [*examining them*]. Dem's de same cock-eye bones whut clean de gang out las' week. Ef dey rolls in dis game, I rolls out. [*Hands the dice back to* SPORTING LIFE.] Eberybody rolls de same bones in dis game,

Sportin' Life—take 'em or leabe 'em.

[ROBBINS *comes from door, rear right. He is a well-set-up Negro of about thirty. The window above him opens, and* SERENA *leans from sill.*]

SERENA [*pleadingly*]. Honey-boy!

ROBBINS. Now, fuh Gawd's sake, don't start dat again. I goin' play—git dat.

SERENA. Ef yo' didn't hab licker in yo' right now, yo' wouldn't talk like dat. Yo' know whut yo' done promise me las' week.

ROBBINS. All right, den, I wouldn't shoot no more dan fifty cents. [*Joins the group.*] [CLARA *paces up and down the court, singing softly to her baby.*] Dat ole lady ob mine hell on joinin' de buryin' lodge. I says, spen' um while yo' is still alibe an' kickin'. [*Picks up dice. Throws them with a loud grunt.*] I ain't see no buzzards 'round her yit.

[JIM, *a big, strong-looking fellow, saunters over to the group of crap players. A cotton hook swings from his belt.*]

JIM. Lor', I is tire' dis night. I'm t'inkin' ob gettin' out ob de cotton business. Mebby it all right fo' a nigger like Crown dat Gawd start to make into a bull, den change He min'. But it ain't no work fo' a man.

JAKE. Better come 'long on de *Sea Gull.* I gots place fo' nudder fishermans.

JIM. Dat suit me. Dis cotton hook hab swung he las' bale ob cotton. Here, Scipio, yo' wants a cotton hook?

[*Throws the hook to* SCIPIO, *who takes it eagerly, fastens it at his waist, and goes about court playing that he is a stevedore, lifting objects with the hook and pretending that they are of tremendous weight.* CLARA *passes the group, crooning softly.*]

CLARA.

"Hush, li'l baby, don' yo' cry.
Fadder an' mudder born to die."

JAKE [*standing up*]. Whut! dat chile ain't 'sleep yit.

Gib 'um to me. I'll fix um fo' yo'. [*Takes baby from* CLARA, *rocks it in his arms, sings.*]

"My mammy tells me, long time ago,
Son, don' yo' marry no gal yo' know.
Spen' all yo' money—eat all yo' bread,
Gone to Savannah, lef' yo' fo' dead."

[*Several of the men join in on the last line.* JAKE *rocks the baby more violently and begins to shuffle.* CLARA *watches anxiously.*] "Spen all yo' money. Steal all yo' clothes. Whut will become of yo', Gawd only knows." [*The light leaves* SERENA'S *window.* JAKE *swings the baby back to* CLARA.] Dere now! Whut I tells yo'. He 'sleep already. [*The baby wails. The men laugh.* CLARA *carries baby to her room. Closes door.* SERENA *comes from her door with a lamp which she sets on her wash bench. She sits beside it and looks anxiously toward crap players.*]

MARIA [*to* SERENA]. Whut worryin' yo', Serena? Yo' gots one ob de bes' mens in Catfish Row. Why yo' ain't let um play widout pickin' on um?

SERENA. He gots licker in um tonight, an' Robbins ain't de same man wid licker.

[MINGO *is rolling and retrieving the dice. While he does so, he looks and laughs at* ROBBINS, *then sings at him.*]

MINGO [*singing*].

"My mammy tell me, long time ago,
Son don't yo' marry no gal yo' know."

[*Speaking to* ROBBINS]. Ought to be single like Porgy an' me. Den yo' kin shoot bones without git pick on.

ROBBINS. Oh, my lady all right; only 'cep' she don' like craps. She born a w'ite folks nigger. She people b'long to Gob'nor Rutledge. Ain't yo' see Miss Rutledge come to see she when she sick?

MARIA [*overhearing, to* SERENA]. Oh, dat Miss Rutledge come to see yuh?

SERENA. Sho! yo' ain' know dat?

MARIA. She eber sell any ob she ole clothes?

SERENA. Not she. But sometime she gib 'em away to de nigger'.

MARIA [*sighing*]. I wish I could git a dress off she. She de firs' pusson I ever see whut hipped an' busted 'zac'ly like me.

ROBBINS [*boasting*]. Yes, suh! my lady—Yo' bes' sabe yo' talk fo' dem dice. Bones ain't got no patience wid 'omen.

MINGO. Dat's de trut'. Course dey can't git along togedder. Dey is all two atter de same nigger money.

JAKE. Annie dere likes de single life, ain't it, Annie? Whut become ob dat ole fisherman used to come fo' see yo'?

ANNIE. He ain't fisherman.

JAKE. Whut he do?

ANNIE. Him ain't do nuttin' mos' all de time. Odder time, him is a shoe carpenter.

[*The voice of* PETER, *the old "honey man," is heard in the street, drawing nearer and nearer.*]

PETER. Here comes de honey man. Yo' gots honey?—Yes, ma'am, I gots honey.—Yo' gots honey in de comb?— Yes, ma'am, I gots honey in de comb.—Yo' gots honey cheap?—Yes, ma'am, my honey cheap.

[PETER *enters gate and closes it behind him. He is a gentle, kindly Negro, verging on senility. A large wooden tray covered with a white cloth is balanced on his head.*]

LILY [*going to meet him*]. Well, here come my ole man. [*Takes tray from his head and shouts in his ear.*] Now gimme de money. [*He hands her some coins. She points to bench.*] Now go sit an' res'. [*He does as he is told. She places tray in her room and returns to circle.*]

MARIA. Yo', Scipio! Here come Porgy! Open de gate fo' uh!

[PORGY *drives up to the gate in his soap-box chariot. He is a crippled beggar of the Charleston streets, who*

*has done much to overcome his handicap of almost
powerless legs by supplying himself with a patri-
archal and very dirty goat, which draws a cart made
of an upturned soap box, on two lopsided wheels,
which bears the inscription, "*WILD ROSE SOAP, PURE
AND FRAGRANT.*"*

PORGY *is no longer young, and yet not old. There is a
suggestion of the mystic in his thoughtful, sensitive
face. He is black, with the almost purple blackness of
unadulterated Congo blood.*

SCIPIO *reluctantly interrupts his performance on a
mouth organ, shuffles across court, and opens one
side of the ponderous gate.*

PORGY *drives through and pulls up beside the crap
ring.*]

JAKE. Here de ole crap shark.

PORGY. All right, Mingo! Jake! Gib' me a han' out dis
wagon. I gots a pocket full ob de buckra money, an'
he goin' to any man whut gots de guts fo' shoot 'em
off me!

[MINGO *and* JAKE *help* PORGY *from wagon to a seat on
ground at left front of circle.* SCIPIO *leads goat away
through arch at rear left.*]

[JIM *saunters to gate and looks out.*]

ROBBINS. All right, mens! Roll 'em! We done wait long
'nough.

JIM [*returning to group*]. Yo' bes' wait for Crown. I
seen um comin', takin' de whole sidewalk, an' he
look like he ain't goin' stan' no foolin'.

PORGY. Is Bess wid um?

JAKE. Listen to Porgy! I t'ink he sof' on Crown's Bess!
[*All the men laugh.*]

PORGY. Gawd make cripple to be lonely. 'Tain't no use
for um to be sof' on a 'oman.

MARIA. Porgy gots too good sense to look twice at dat
licker-guzzlin' slut.

LILY. Licker-guzzlin'! It takes more'n licker fo' sati'fy
Crown's Bess.

SERENA. Happy dus'! Dat's what it take! Dat gal Bess ain't fit for Gawd-fearin' ladies to 'sociate wid!

SPORTING LIFE. Sistuhs! You needn't worry! Gawd-fearin' ladies is de las' t'ing on eart' Bess is a-wantin' for 'sociate wid.

PORGY. Can't yo' keep yo' mout' off Bess! Between de Gawd-fearin' ladies an' de Gawd-damnin' men, dat gal ain't gots no chance.

JAKE. Ain't I tells yo' Porgy sof' on um? [*More laughter.*]

PORGY. I ain't neber swap one word wid she.

[CROWN *and* BESS *appear at gate.* CROWN *is lurching slightly and* BESS *is piloting him through the entrance.*

CROWN *is a huge Negro of magnificent physique, a stevedore on the cotton wharfs. He is wearing blue denim pants and tan shirt with a bright bandanna about his neck. From his belt hangs a long gleaming cotton hook.*

BESS *is slender, but sinewy; very black, wide nostrils, and large, but well-formed mouth. She flaunts a typical, but debased, Negro beauty.*

From the occupants of Catfish Row there are cries of, "Here comes Big Boy!" " 'Low, Crown!" " 'Low, Bess," *etc.*]

CROWN [*to* SPORTING LIFE]. All right, high stepper. Gib us a pint, an' make it damn' quick. [SPORTING LIFE *pulls a flask from his hip pocket and hands it to* CROWN. CROWN *jerks out cork and takes a long pull.*] [*To* BESS.] Pay um, Bess!

[BESS *settles for the bottle, then takes her seat by* CROWN, *ignoring the women of the court.*

CROWN *hands her the flask, from which she takes a long pull. She meets* SERENA'S *eyes, laughs at their hostility, and at once extends the bottle to* ROBBINS.]

BESS. Hab one to de Gawd-fearin' ladies. Dere's nuttin' else like 'em—t'ank Gawd!

[ROBBINS *tries to resist, but the fumes of raw liquor are*

too much for him. He takes a deep drink.

CROWN *snatches the bottle from him, gulps the entire remaining contents, and shatters it on the flags behind him.*

The crap circle is now complete. The positions are as follows:

Rear

X BESS   X CROWN
                     X DADDY
                       PETER

      X MINGO   X SPORTING LIFE
   X JAKE
X ROBBINS   X PORGY

Footlights

[CROWN *throws coin down before him.*]

CROWN. I'm talkin' to yo' mans. Anybody answerin' me?

[*They all throw down money.*]

ROBBINS [*to* JAKE]. An' dem fine chillen ob mine!

CROWN. Shet yo' damn mout' an' t'row.

ROBBINS [*taken aback and rolling hastily*]. Box cars again! [*They all roar with laughter.*]

MINGO. Cover 'em, brudder, cover 'em.

ROBBINS. Cover hell! I goin' pass 'em along an' see ef I kin break my luck.

MINGO. He lady ain't 'low um but fifty cent, an' he can't take no chance wid bad luck.

[*All laugh at* ROBBINS.]

BESS [*with a provocative look at* SERENA]. Dat all right, Honey-boy, I'll stake yo' when yo' four bits done gone.

SERENA [*to* ROBBINS]. Go ahead an' play, yo' ain't need no charity off no she-devils.

BESS [*to* ROBBINS]. See whut I git fuh yo'. De she-gawds is easy when yo' knows de way.

[CROWN *claps his hand over* BESS'S *mouth.*]

CROWN. Shet yo' damn mout'. Yo' don' gib Mingo no chance to talk to de bones.

[JAKE *has cast and lost, and the dice are now with* MINGO, *who is swinging them back and forth in his hand. Sings.*]

MINGO. "Ole snake-eye, go off an' die. Ole man seben, come down from Heaben." [*Grunts, throws, and snaps fingers.*] Seben! [*Scoops up dice.*]

CROWN. I ain't see dat seben yit. [*Snatches* MINGO's *hand and open fingers. Looks at dice.*] Yo' done tu'n um ober.

MINGO [*to Circle*]. Whut I t'row?

[*Cries of* "Seben," "Jus' as he says," *etc.* MINGO *pulls in pot.*]

CROWN. Well, dere's more'n one nigger done meet he Gawd fuh pullin' 'em in 'fore I reads 'em. See? An' I'm a-sayin' it over tonight. [*All ante again.*]

MINGO. Come home again to yo' pappy. [*Shoots.*] Four to make! Come four! [*Shoots.*]

[*Cries of* "Seben," "Crapped out," *etc.* MINGO *passes dice to* CROWN.]

CROWN. Come clean, yo' little black-eyed bitches! [*Shoots. Cries of* "Six," "Six to make," *etc.* CROWN *takes up bones and produces rabbit foot from pocket. He touches dice with it.*] Kiss rabbit foot. [*Shoots.*]

SPORTING LIFE [*reaching for dice*]. Crapped out! Come to your pappy.

[CROWN *extends a huge arm and brushes him back. He tries to focus his eyes on dice.*]

ROBBINS. Crown too cock-eyed drunk to read um. What he is say, Bess?

BESS. Seben.

CROWN [*scowls at* ROBBINS, *then turns to* SPORTING LIFE]. I ain't drunk 'nough to read 'em, dat's de trouble. Licker ain't strong 'nough. Gimme a pinch ob happy dus', Sportin' Life.

[SPORTING LIFE *takes from his pocket a small folded paper.*]

BESS. Don' gib' um dat stuff, Sportin' Life. He's ugly drunk already.

CROWN. Yo' is a good one to talk! Pay um and shut up. [*Takes the paper from* SPORTING LIFE, *unfolds it, and inhales the powder.*

BESS *pays* SPORTING LIFE. DADDY PETER *takes his pipe from his mouth and crowds in between* CROWN *and* SPORTING LIFE, *putting a hand on the arm of each.*]

PETER. Frien' an' dice an' happy dus' ain't meant to 'sociate. Yo' mens bes' go slow.

[CROWN *draws back his fist. Cries of* "*Leabe Uncle Peter be!*" "*He ain't mean no harm!*" *etc.* CROWN *relaxes.* SPORTING LIFE *picks up the dice.*]

SPORTING LIFE. Huh, seben! Huh, seben! Huh, seben! [*Shoots.*] 'Leben! Come home, Fido! [*Whistles, snaps fingers, and pulls in pot.*]

[*All ante.*]

CROWN. Gawd damn it. I ain't read um yet.

[*All laugh at him. Cries of* "*Crown cock-eye drunk.*" "*Can't tell dice from watermillion,*" *etc.*]

CROWN [*growling*]. All right. I'm tellin' yo'.

SPORTING LIFE [*shooting*]. Six to make! Get um again! [*Shoots.*] [*Cries of* "*Seben,*" "*Crapped out,*" *etc.* PORGY *takes up dice and commences to sway, with his eyes half closed. He apostrophizes dice in a sort of sing-song chant.*]

PORGY. Oh, little stars, roll me some light. [*Shoots.*] 'Leben little stars, come home. [*Pulls in pot.*] [*All ante.*] Roll dis poor beggar a sun an' moon! [*Shoots.*]

MINGO. Snake eyes!

PORGY. Dem ain't no snake eyes. Dey is a flock ob mornin' an' ebenin' stars. An' jus' yo' watch um rise for dis po' beggar. [*Shoots.*]

[*Cries of* "*Made um,*" "*Dat's he point,*" *etc.* PORGY *pulls in pot.*]

CROWN. Roll up dat nigger sleeve. [PORGY *rolls up his sleeves.*] Well, yo' gots dem damn dice conjer den.

[*All ante.* PORGY *rolls. Cries of* "*Snake eyes,*" "*Crapped out!" All ante.* ROBBINS *takes up bones, whistles, shoots, snaps them back up very rapidly.*]

ROBBINS. Nine to make! [*Whistles, shoots, snaps fingers.*] Read um! Nine spot! [*Sweeps them up, and reaches for money.* CROWN *seizes his wrist.*]

CROWN. Tech dat money an' meet yo' Gawd.

ROBBINS. Take yo' han' off me, yo' lousy houn'! [*Turns to* JAKE.] Han' me dat brick behin' you'.

[JAKE *reaches brickbat and puts it in his free hand.* CROWN *jerks his cotton hook out of his belt and lunges forward, bowling* ROBBINS *over, and knocking brick from his hand.* CROWN *then steps back and kicks over lamp, extinguishing it.*

The stage is now dark except for the small lamp at SERENA'S *wash bench. This lights up the woman's terrified face as she strains her gaze into the darkness.* MARIA, CLARA *and the others of her group stand behind her.*

From the crap ring come cries and curses. Suddenly, shutters are thrown open in right and left walls of building, and forms strain from the sills. As the shutters are banged open, shafts of light from them flash across the court, latticing it with a cross-play of light. CROWN *and* ROBBINS *are revealed facing each other:* CROWN *crouched for a spring with gleaming cotton hook extended;* ROBBINS *defenceless, his back to the wall. Then* ROBBINS *lunges under the hook and they clinch. The fight proceeds with no distinguishable words from the combatants, but with bestial growls and breath that sobs and catches in their throats. In and out of the cross-play of light they sway—now revealed, now in darkness. The watchers move back and stand around the wall. They commence a weird, high-keyed moaning that rises as the figures take the light, and subsides almost to silence when they are obscured. Suddenly, out of the dark,* CROWN *swings* ROBBINS *into a shaft of light.* CROWN *is facing the audience and is holding* ROBBINS *at arms' length.*

*With a triumphant snarl, he swings the hook down-
ward.* ROBBINS *drops back toward audience into darkness, and* CROWN *stands in high light. There is dead
silence now. In it* CROWN *looks down at his hands,
opening and closing them. Then he draws his arm
across his eyes.*

The silence is shattered by a piercing scream, and
SERENA *runs across the court and throws herself on
the body.*

BESS *appears in the light beside* CROWN. *She shakes him
violently by the arm.*]

BESS. Wake up an' hit it out. Yo' ain't got no time to
lose.

CROWN [*looking stupidly into the gloom at* SERENA *and
the body of her man.*] Whut de matter?

BESS [*hysterically*]. Yo' done kill Robbins, an' de police'll be comin'. [*She starts to pull him toward the
gate.*]

CROWN. Whar yo' goin' hide? Dey knows you an' me
pulls togedder.

[*In the half light, it can now be seen that the court has
been deserted, except for* SERENA, *who sits beside the
body with her head bowed, and sways from side to
side with a low, steady moaning.*

A match is scratched and held in PORGY'S *hand. He is
crouched on his doorstep. He looks toward* ROBBINS'S
*body, and his face shows horror and fear. He gives a
whimpering moan, and as the match burns out, he
drags himself over his threshold and closes the door.*]

BESS. Dey wouldn't look fuh me here. I'll stay here an'
hide. Somebody always willin' to take care ob Bess.

CROWN [*now at gate*]. Well, git dis: he's temporary. I'se
comin' back when de hell dies down.

BESS. All right. Only git out now. Here, take dis.
[*Thrusts the money into his hand. She pushes him
out of gate. He disappears into the shadows. She
turns around and faces the court. It is silent and
empty except for the body and* SERENA. SPORTING LIFE

steps out of the shadows under SERENA'S *steps, startling her.*] Dat yo', Sportin' Life? Fo' Gawd's sake, gib' me a little touch happy dus'. I shakin' so I can hardly stan'. [*Suddenly remembering.*] Oh, I done gib' all de money to Crown. I can't pay fo' um. But, for Gawd's sake, gib me jus' a touch!

SPORTING LIFE. Yo' ain't needs to pay fo' um, Bess. [*Pours powder into her hand.*] Sportin' Life ain't go back on a frien' in trouble like dese odder low-life nigger'. [BESS *quickly inhales the powder. Sighs with relief.*] Listen! I'll be goin' back up to Noo Yo'k soon. All yo' gots to do is to come wid me now. I'll hide yo' out an' take yo' on wid me when I go. Why, yo' an' me'll be a swell team! Wid yo' looks an' all de frien's I gots dere, it'll be ebery night an' all night —licker, dus', bright lights, an' de sky de limit! [*He looks apprehensively toward gate. Takes her arm.*] Come 'long! We gots to beat it while de beatin's good. [BESS *draws away sharply from his grasp.*] Nobody 'round here's goin' to take in Crown's Bess. Yo' bes' go wid yo' only frien'.

BESS. I ain't come to dat yet.

SPORTING LIFE. Well, de cops ain't goin' find me here fo' no 'oman! [*Slinks out gate.*]

[BESS *looks desperately about for shelter. She advances timidly and takes up lamp from the wash bench. She starts at rear left, and tries all of the doors as she goes. They are either locked, or slammed in her face as she reaches out to them. She comes to* MARIA'S *shop door, and as she reaches it, it is jerked open and* MARIA *confronts her.*]

MARIA [*in a tense voice*]. Yo' done bring trouble 'nough. Git out 'fore de police comes.

BESS. Yo' wouldn't hab' a heart, an' let me in?

MARIA. Not till hell freeze!

[*A light is lit in* PORGY'S *room, showing at window and crack in door.*]

BESS [*indicating* PORGY'S *room*]. Who lib ober dere?

MARIA. He ain't no use to yo' kin'. Dat's Porgy. He a cripple an' a beggar.

[BESS *seems to agree with* MARIA *that* PORGY *is of no use to her. Crosses to gate, hesitates. Then she turns slowly toward* PORGY'S *room and crosses, shuddering away from* SERENA *and the body, which she must pass on the way. She reaches the door, puts her hand on the knob, hesitates, then slowly she opens it, enters, and closes it behind her.*]

CURTAIN

SCENE II

St. Michael's chimes the quarters and strikes seven.

The curtain rises on SERENA'S *room, a second story room in Catfish Row, which still bears traces of its ancient beauty in its high panelled walls and tall, slender mantel with Grecian frieze and intricate scroll work. The door is in left wall at back. Near the center of back wall a window looks toward the sea. The fireplace is in right wall. Over the mantel is a gaudy lithograph of Lincoln striking chains from the slaves.*

The room is vaguely lighted by several kerosene lamps, and is scantily furnished: a bed against the back wall at left, and a few chairs.*

ROBBINS'S *body lies upon the bed, completely covered by a white sheet. On its chest is a large blue saucer. Standing about the bed or seated on the floor are Negroes, all singing and swaying and patting with their large feet.*

SERENA *sits at the foot of the bed swaying dismally to the rhythm.*

They have been singing for hours. The monotony of the dirge and the steady beat of the patting has lulled several into a state of coma.

"Deat', ain't yuh gots no shame, shame?
Deat', ain't yuh gots no shame, shame?
Deat', ain't yuh gots no shame, shame?
Deat', ain't yuh gots no shame?

"Teck dis man an' gone, gone,
Teck dis man an' gone, gone,
Teck dis man an' gone, gone,
Deat', ain't yuh gots no shame?

"Leabe dis 'oman lone, lone,
Leabe dis 'oman lone, lone,
Leabe dis 'oman lone, lone,
Deat', ain't yuh gots no shame?"

[*The door opens and* PETER *comes in. Doffs his old hat, crosses, and puts coins in saucer. The singing and swaying continue. He finds a seat at right front and begins to sway and pat with the others.*

SERENA *reaches over, gets saucer, and counts coins. Replaces saucer with a hopeless expression.*]

JAKE. How de saucer stan', Sistuh?

[*The singing dies gradually as, one by one, the Negroes stop to listen, but the rhythm continues.*]

SERENA [*dully*]. Fourteen dolluh and thirty-six cent.

MARIA [*encouragingly*]. Dat's a-comin' on, Sistuh. Yo' can bury him soon.

SERENA. De Boa'd ob Healt' say he gots to git buried tomorruh.

CLARA. It cost thirty-four dolluh for bury my grandmudder, but she gots de three carriage'.

SERENA. What I goin' to do ef I ain't gots de money?

PETER [*understanding that they refer to saucer*]. Gawd gots plenty coin' fo' de saucer.

SERENA. Bless de Lo'd.

PETER. An' He goin' soften dese nigger heart' fo' fill de saucer till he spill ober.

SERENA. Amen, my Jedus!

PETER. De Lord will provide a grabe fo' His chillun.

CLARA. Bless de Lo'd!

[*The swaying gradually changes to the rhythm of* PETER's *prayer.*]

PETER. An' he gots comfort fo' de widder.

SERENA. Oh, my Jedus!

PETER. An' food fo' de fadderless.

SERENA. Yes, Lo'd!

PETER. An' he goin' raise dis poor nigger out de grabe.

JAKE. Allelujah!

PETER. An' set him in de seat of de righteous, Amen.

SERENA. Amen, my brudder.

[*They all sway in silence.*]

ANNIE [*looking toward the door*]. What dat?

CLARA. I hear somebody comin' up de steps now bringing much penny fo' de saucer.

[MARIA *opens the door and looks out.*]

SERENA. Who dat?

MARIA. It's Porgy comin' up de steps.

JAKE [*starting to rise*]. Somebody bes' go help um.

MARIA. He got help. Crown's Bess is a-helpin' um.

SERENA [*springs to her feet*]. What's she a-comin' here fo'? [*They are all silent, looking toward door.* PORGY *and* BESS *enter.* PORGY *looks about; makes a movement toward corpse.* BESS *starts to lead him across room.* SERENA *stands defiant, silent, till they have gone half the way.*] What yo' bring dat 'oman here fo'?

PORGY. She want to come help sing. She's a good shouter.

[BESS, *self-possessed, leads* PORGY *on toward saucer. He deposits his coins. Then* BESS *stretches her hand toward saucer.*]

SERENA. I don' need yo' money fo' bury my man. [BESS *hesitates.*] I ain't takin' money off he murderer.

PORGY. Dat ain't Crown's money. I gib um to Bess fo' put in de saucer.

SERENA. All right. Yo' can put um in. [BESS *drops the*

money in saucer and leads PORGY *to a place at left front. They sit side by side on the floor.* SERENA *stands glaring after them.*]

PETER [*trying to make peace*]. Sing, Sistuh, sing! Time is passin', an' de saucer ain't full.

SERENA [*to* PORGY]. She can sit ober dere in de corner, ef she want to. But she can't sing!

[BESS *sits with quiet dignity; seeming scarcely to notice* SERENA'S *tone and words.*]

PORGY. Dat all right. Bess don' want fo' sing, anyway.

[*The spiritual begins again.*]

"Leabe dese chillun starve, starve,
Leabe dese chillun starve, starve,
Leabe dese chillun starve, starve,
Deat', ain't yuh gots no shame?"

MINGO [*looking upward*]. Dat rain on de roof?

JAKE. Yes, rainin' hard out.

PORGY. Dat's all right now fo' Robbins. Gawd done send He rain already fo' wash he feetsteps offen dis eart'.

LILY. Oh, yes, Brudder!

SERENA. Amen, my Jedus!

[*The spiritual continues. The swaying and patting begin gradually and grow. Slowly* BESS *begins to sway with the others, but she makes no sound.*

The door is burst suddenly open and the DETECTIVE *enters.* TWO POLICEMEN *wait in the doorway.*

The spiritual ceases abruptly. All the Negroes' eyes are riveted on the white man and filled with fear. He strides over to the corpse, looks down at it.]

DETECTIVE. Um! A saucer-buried nigger, I see! [*To* SERENA.] You're his widow?

SERENA. Yes, suh.

DETECTIVE. He didn't leave any burial insurance?

SERENA. No, boss. He didn't leabe nuttin'.

DETECTIVE. Well, see to it that he's buried to-morrow. [*Turns away from her. Slowly circles room, looking fixedly at each Negro in turn. Each quails under his gaze. He pauses abruptly before* PETER. *Suddenly shouts at him.*] You killed Robbins, and I'm going to hang you for it!

[PETER *is almost paralyzed by terror, his panic heightened by the fact that he cannot hear what the* DETECTIVE *says. His mouth opens and he cannot find his voice.*]

LILY [*to* DETECTIVE]. He ain't done um.

PETER [*helplessly*]. What he say?

LILY [*shouting in* PETER'S *ear*]. He say yo' kill Robbins.

DETECTIVE [*laying his hand on* PETER'S *shoulder*]. Come along now!

PETER. 'Fore Gawd, boss, I ain't neber done um!

[*The* DETECTIVE *whips out his revolver and points it between* PETER'S *eyes.*]

DETECTIVE. Who did it, then? [*Shouting.*] You heard me! Who did it?

PETER [*wildly*]. Crown done um, boss. I done see him do um.

DETECTIVE [*shouting*]. You're sure you saw him?

PETER. I swear to Gawd, boss. I was right dere, close beside um.

DETECTIVE [*with satisfied grunt*]. Umph! I thought as much. [*Swings suddenly on* PORGY *and points the pistol in his face.*] You saw it, too! [PORGY *trembles but does not speak. He lowers his eyes.*] Come! Out with it! I don't want to have to put the law on you! [PORGY *sits silent. The* DETECTIVE *shouts with fury.*] Look at me, you damned nigger!

[PORGY *slowly raises his eyes to the* DETECTIVE'S *face.*]

PORGY. I ain't know nuttin' 'bout um, boss.

DETECTIVE [*angrily*]. That's your room in the corner, isn't it? [*Points downward toward left.*]

PORGY. Yes, boss. Dat's my room.

DETECTIVE. The door opens on the court, don't it?

PORGY. Yes, boss, my door open on de cou't.

DETECTIVE. And yet you didn't see or hear anything?

PORGY. I ain't know nuttin' 'bout um. I been inside asleep on my bed wid de door closed.

DETECTIVE [*exasperated*]. You're a damned liar. [*Turns away disgusted. Saunters toward door. To* POLICE-MEN, *indicating* PETER.] He saw the killing. Take him along and lock him up as a material witness.

[FIRST POLICEMAN *crosses to* PETER.]

FIRST POLICEMAN [*helping* PETER *to his feet*]. Come along, Uncle.

PETER [*shaking with terror*]. I ain't neber done um, boss.

POLICEMAN. Nobody says you did it. We're just taking you along as a witness. [*But* PETER *does not understand.*]

SERENA. What yo' goin' to do wid um?

POLICEMAN. Lock him up. Come along. It ain't going to be so bad for you as for Crown, anyway.

SECOND POLICEMAN [*to* DETECTIVE]. How about the cripple?

DETECTIVE [*sourly*]. He couldn't have helped seeing it, but I can't make him come through. But it don't matter. One's enough to hang Crown—[*With a short laugh.*]—If we ever get him.

MARIA [*to* FIRST POLICEMAN]. How long yo' goin' lock um up fo'?

FIRST POLICEMAN. Till we catch Crown.

PORGY [*sadly*]. I reckon Crown done loose now in de palmetto thickets, an' de rope ain't neber made fo' hang um.

DETECTIVE. Then the old man's out of luck. [*To* SE-RENA.] Remember! You've got to bury that nigger tomorrow or the Board of Health will take him and turn him over to the medical students.

PETER. I ain't neber done um, boss.

DETECTIVE [*to* FIRST POLICEMAN]. Come on! Get the old man in the wagon.

[PETER, *shaking in every limb, is led out. The* DETECTIVE

and SECOND POLICEMAN *follow. A moment of desolated silence.*]

MARIA. It sho' pay nigger to go blin' in dis world.

JAKE. Porgy ain't got much leg, but he sho' got sense in dealin' wid de w'ite folks.

PORGY [*slowly, as though half to himself*]. I can't puzzle dis t'ing out. Peter war a good man. An' dat nigger Crown war a killer an' fo'eber gettin' into trouble. But dere go Peter fo' be lock up like t'ief, and he're lie Robbins wid he wife and fadderless chillun. An Crown done gone he was fo' do de same t'ing ober again somewheres else.

[*The Negroes begin to sway and moan.*]

CLARA. Gone fo' true! Yes, Jedus!

[*A voice raises the spiritual, "What de Matter, Chillun?" It swells slowly. One voice joins in after another. The swaying and patting begin and grow slowly in tempo and emphasis. As before,* BESS *sways in silence.*]

> "What' de mattuh, chillun?
> What' de mattuh, chillun?
> What' de mattuh, chillun?
> Yuh can't stan' still.
> Pain gots de body.
> Pain gots de body.
> Pain gots de body.
> An' I can't stan' still.
>
> "What de mattuh, Sistuh?
> What de mattuh, Sistuh?
> What de mattuh, Sistuh?
> Yuh can't stan' still.
> Jedus gots our brudder,
> Jedus gots our brudder,
> Jedus gots our brudder,
> An' I can't stan' still."

[*The door opens and the* UNDERTAKER *bustles into the room with an air of great importance. He is a short, yellow Negro with a low, oily voice. He is dressed entirely in black. He crosses to* SERENA. *The song dies away, but the swaying continues to its rhythm.*]

UNDERTAKER. How de saucer stan' now, my sistuh? [*Glances appraisingly at saucer.*]

SERENA [*in a flat, despairing voice*]. Dere ain't but fifteen dollah.

UNDERTAKER. Umph! Can't bury um fo' fifteen dollah.

JAKE. He gots to git buried tomorruh or de Boa'd ob Healt' 'll take um an' gib um to de students.

SERENA [*wildly*]. Oh, fo' Gawd's sake bury um in de grabeyahd. [*She rises to her knees and seizes the* UNDERTAKER'S *hand in both hers. Imploringly.*] Don' let de students hab um. I goin' to work Monday, an' I swear to Gawd I gon' to pay yo' ebery cent.

[*Even the swaying ceases now. The Negroes all wait tensely, their eyes riveted on the* UNDERTAKER'S *face, pleading silently. After a moment's hesitation, the* UNDERTAKER'S *professional manner slips from him.*]

UNDERTAKER [*simply*]. All right, Sistuh. Wid de box an' one carriage, it's cost me more'n twenty-five. But I'll see yo' t'rough. [*An expression of vast relief sweeps into every face.* SERENA *silently relaxes across the foot of the bed, her head between her outstretched arms.*] Yo' can all be ready at eight tomorruh. It's a long trip to de cemetery.

[*The* UNDERTAKER *goes out door. The Negroes gaze silently after him with eyes filled with gratitude. There is a moment of silence after his departure. Then, carried out of herself by sympathy and gratitude,* BESS, *forgetful of the ban laid upon her, lifts her strong, beautiful voice triumphantly.*]

BESS. "Oh, I gots a little brudder in de new grabeyahd
   What outshine de sun,
   Outshine de sun,"

[PORGY'S *voice joins hers.*]

"Outshine de sun."

[*By the fourth line, many of the Negro voices have joined in, and the song grows steadily in volume and fervor.*]

"Oh, I gots a little brudder in de new grabeyahd
What outshine de sun,
An' I'll meet um in de Primus Lan'."

[BESS's *voice is heard again for one brief moment alone as it rises high and clear on the first line of the chorus.*]

"I will meet um in de Primus Lan'!"

[*Then a full chorus, with deep basses predominating, crashes in on the second line of the refrain.* SERENA, *last of all, joins enthusiastically in the chorus.*]

"Oh, I'll meet um in de Primus Lan'!
I will meet um, meet um, meet um,
I will meet um, meet um, meet um,
I will meet um in de Primus Lan'!

"Oh, I gots a mansion up on high
What ain't make wid' han',
Ain't make wid han',
Ain't make wid han',
Oh, I gots a mansion up on high
What ain't make wid' han',
An' I'll meet um in de Primus Lan'!"

[*The beautiful old spiritual beats triumphantly through the narrow room, steadily gaining in speed.* SERENA *is the first to leap to her feet and begin to "shout." * One by one, as the spirit moves them, the Negroes follow her example till they are all on their feet, swaying, shuffling, clapping their hands.* BESS *leads the "shouting" as she has the singing, throw-*

* "Shouting" is the term given by the Carolina Negroes to the body rhythms and steps with which they accompany their emotional songs.

ing her whole soul into an intricate shuffle and complete turn. Each Negro "shouts" in his own individual way, some dancing in place, others merely swaying and patting their hands.
"*Allelujahs*" *and cries of* "*Yes, Lord*" *are interjected into the singing. And the rhythm swells till the old walls seem to rock and surge with the sweep of it.*]

CURTAIN

Act two

SCENE I

St. Michael's chimes the quarters and strikes one. Morning.

The court is full of movement, the Negroes going about their tasks. At right front a group of fishermen are rigging their lines. They are working leisurely with much noisy laughter and banter. Occasionally, a snatch of song is heard.

PORGY *is sitting at his window. The soap-box car stands by his door, the goat is inside the room. Occasionally looks out door.*

JAKE. Fish runnin' well outside de bar dese days.

MINGO [*an onlooker*]. Hear tell de Bufort mens bring in such a catch yesterday dat de boat look like he gots floor ob silber.

JIM. I hears dey gots to t'row away half de catch so as not glut de market.

JAKE. Yes, suh! Fish runnin' well, an' we mens bes' make de mores ob it.

JIM. Dats de trut'. Dem Septembuh storm due soon, an' fish don' like eas' win' an' muddy watuh.

ANNIE [*calling across court*]. Mus' be you mens forget 'bout picnic. Ain't yo' know de parade start up de block at ten o'clock?

MINGO. Dat's de trut', Sistuh.

[*The men begin to gather up their fishing gear.*]

PORGY [*at window. Solicitously*]. Bess, ain't you wants to go to de picnic after all? Yo' know I is membuh in good standin' ob "De Sons and Daughters ob Repent Ye Saith de Lord."

BESS [*unseen within room*]. I radder stay home wid yo'.

PORGY. Yo' gots jus' as much right to go as any 'oman in Catfish Row.

BESS [*in unconvincing voice*]. I ain't care much 'bout picnic.

[PORGY *is troubled. Sits in silence.*]

SPORTING LIFE [*who has sauntered over to group of fishermen*]. All yo' mens goin' to de picnic?

JAKE. Goin' fo' sho'. How come yo' t'ink we ain't goin'?

SPORTING LIFE. I jus' ask. Don' hab no picnic in Noo Yo'k. Yo' folks still hab yo' picnic on Kittiwah Island?

JIM. Listen to Sporting Life. He been six mont' in Noo Yo'k, an' he want to know ef we still hab we picnic on Kittiwah! [*They laugh.*]

[SPORTING LIFE *moves off. Sits at* MARIA'S *table.* LILY *joins the group of men.*]

JAKE. All right, mens. I'm all fuh ridin' luck fur as he will tote me. Turn out at four to-morruh mornin', an' we'll push de *Sea Gull* clean to de Blackfish Banks 'fore we wets de anchor. I gots a feelin' we goin' be gunnels under wid de pure fish when we comes in at night.

LILY. Yuh goin' fuh take de *Sea Gull* out beyond bah? [*She laughs. Calls out to* NELSON, *who is on far side of court.*] Heah dis, Nelson. Dese mens aimin' fuh take de *Sea Gull* to de Blackfish Banks! [NELSON *joins the group.* CLARA, *overhearing, slowly approaches, her baby in her arms.* LILY *turns to the others.*] Yo'

mens bes' keep yo' ol washtub close to home. Wait
till yo' gets a good boat like de *Mosquito* 'fore yo'
trabble. [*All the men and* LILY *laugh delightedly.*]

JAKE. Mosquito born in de water, but he can drown
jus' de same.

[*All laugh,* LILY *slapping* NELSON's *shoulder in her ap-
preciation.* CLARA *has stood silently beside them with
anxious eyes.*]

CLARA. Jake! Yo' ain't plannin' to take de *Sea Gull* to
de Blackfish Banks? It's time fuh de Septembuh
storms.

JAKE [*laughing reassuringly*]. Ain't yo' know we had
one stiff gale las' yeah, an' he nebber come two yeah
han' runnin'.

CLARA. Jake, I don' want yo' fuh go outside de bah!

JAKE. How yo' t'ink we goin' gib dat man child college
edication?

[*They all laugh, except* CLARA.]

CLARA. Deys odder way fuh make money 'sides fish.

JAKE. Hear de 'oman! Mebbe yo' like me to be a cotton
nigger! Huh? [*The men laugh.* SCIPIO *is playing
about the court with a broad red sash pinned across
his breast from shoulder to waist. It bears the legend,
"Repent Ye Saith the Lord." From the boy's breast
flutters a yellow ribbon with the word "Marshal." He
struts about court leading an imaginary parade.*
JAKE, *looking about for change of subject, sees* SCIPIO
and starts to his feet.] Heah, Scipio! Who sash dat yo'
gots? [SCIPIO *backs away.* JAKE *pursues.*] Come heah,
yo'l Jus' as I t'ought. Dat's my sash!

[*Not watching where he is going,* SCIPIO, *in his flight
from* JAKE, *runs straight into* MARIA, *who delivers
him to* JAKE.]

MARIA. Heah yo' is, Jake.

JAKE. T'ank yo' kindly, Sistuh. [*To* SCIPIO, *while he
rescues his sash and badge.*] How yo' t'ink I goin'

lead dis picnic parade atter yo' been ruin my sash?
[*Pins ribbons on his own breast. Sits on washing
bench. Lights pipe.*]

[*The crowd begins to break up with noisy laughter and
joking.* SERENA *comes in at gate, wearing a neat white
apron and a hat. Crosses to* PORGY'S *door, greeting
her friends as she passes them.*]

SERENA [*to the men*]. Fine day fuh de picnic.

JIM. Fine fuh true, Sistuh.

[SERENA *knocks at* PORGY'S *door.* BESS *opens it.* SERENA
pays no attention to her.]

SERENA [*looking through* BESS]. Porgy! [*Sees him at window. Crosses to him.*] Oh, dere yo' is. I gots news. I
done been to see my white folks 'bout Peter.

PORGY. What dey say?

SERENA. Dey say dey gots a white gentleman frien',
name ob Mistah Archdale, who is lawyer an' he can
get um out. I tells um yo' is de pusson fo' um to talk
to 'cause yo' gots so much sense when yo' talks to
w'ite folks. An' dey say he'll come fo' see yo' cause he
pass right by here ebery day, an' yo' is cripple.
[*Turns away, ignoring* BESS. *Crosses, sits beside* JAKE,
takes out and lights her pipe. MARIA *is serving a late
breakfast to* SPORTING LIFE. JIM *and* MINGO *have
joined him at table. St. Michael's chimes the quarter
hour.* MARIA *crosses to pump to fill kettle. After a few
puffs,* SERENA *whispers loudly to* JAKE.] It's a shame
when good Christian 'omans got to lib under de same
roof wid a murderin' she-debil like dat Crown's Bess.

JAKE. She don' seem to harm nobody, an' Porgy seem
to like to hab she 'roun'.

MARIA. Porgy change since dat 'oman go to lib' wid he.

SERENA. How he change?

MARIA. I tell yo' dat nigger happy now.

SERENA. Go 'long wid yo'. Dat 'oman ain't de kin' fo'
make cripple happy. It take a killer like Crown to
hol' she down.

MARIA. Dat may be so, but Porgy don't know dat yet. An', sides, ef a man is de kin' what need a 'oman, he goin' be happy regahdless.

JAKE. Dat's de trut', Sistuh. Him dress she up in he own eye, till she stan' like de Queen ob Sheba to he.

MARIA. Porgy t'ink right now dat he gots a she-gawd in he room.

SERENA. Well, dere is gawds and gawds, an' Porgy sho' got de kin' what goin' gib um hell. Much as I likes Porgy, I wouldn't swap a word wid she.

MARIA. Dat all so, Sistuh. But yo' keep yo' eye on Porgy. He use to hate all dese chillen, but now he nebber come home widout candy ball fuh de crowd.

JAKE. I tells yo' dat 'oman—

[BESS *crosses to pump with bucket.*]

SERENA. Sh!

[*The three are silent watching* BESS. *She is neatly dressed, walks with queenly dignity, passes them as though they did not exist, fills her bucket, swings it easily to her head, turns from them with an air of cool scorn, and recrosses to her own door. The three look after her with varying expressions:* MARIA *interested,* SERENA *indignant,* JAKE *admiring.*]

JAKE. Dat's de t'ing. She sho' ain't askin' no visit ofen none ob she neighbors.

SERENA. Yo' poor sof'-headed nigger! Ain't yo' shame to set dere 'fore me an' talk sweet-mout' 'bout dat murderin' Crown's Bess? [*Making eyes at him.*] Now, ef I was a man, I'd sabe my sof' wo'd fuh de God-fearin' 'omans.

JAKE. Ef yo' was a man— [*Pauses, looking thoughtfully at her, then shakes his head.*] No, it ain't no use. Yo' wouldn't understan'. Dat's somethin' shemale sense ain't goin' help yo' none wid. [*Knocks ashes from his pipe.*]

[MARIA *has turned toward her table. She suddenly puts down her kettle, strides to the table, seizes* SPORTING LIFE'S *hand, opens the fingers before he has time to resist, and blows a white powder from his palm.*]

SPORTING LIFE [*furiously*]. What yo' t'ink yo' doin'! Dat stuff cos' money.

[MARIA *stands back, arms akimbo, staring down at him for a moment in silence.* SPORTING LIFE *shifts uneasily in his chair.*]

MARIA [*in stentorian tones*]. Nigger! I jus' tryin' to figger out wedder I better kill yuh decent now, wid yo' frien' about yo'—or leabe yo' fuh de white folks to hang atter a while. I ain't say nuttin' no matter how drunk yo' gets dese boys on you' rot-gut whisky. But nobody ain't goin' peddle happy dus' roun' my shop. Yo' heah what I say?

SPORTING LIFE. Come now, ole lady, don't talk like dese ole-fashioned, lamp-oil niggers. Why, up in Noo Yo'k, where I been waitin'—in a—hotel—

MARIA. Hotel, eh? I suppose dese gal' yo' tryin' to get to go back to Noo Yo'k wid yo' is goin' to be bordahs! [*Shouting.*] Don' yo' try any ob yo' Noo Yo'kin' roun' dis town. Ef I had my way, I'd go down to dat Noo Yo'k boat an' take ebery Gawd's nigger what come up de gangplank wid a Joseph coat on he back an' a glass headlight on he buzzum an' drap um to de catfish 'fore he foot hit decent groun'. Yes! my belly fair ache wid dis Noo Yo'k talk.

[*Bangs table so violently with her fist that* SPORTING LIFE *leaps from his chair and extends a propitiating hand toward her.*]

SPORTING LIFE. Dat's all right, Auntie. Le's you an' me be frien'.

MARIA. Frien' wid you! One ob dese day I might lie down wid rattlesnake, an' when dat time come, yo' kin come right 'long an' git in de bed. But till den, keep yo' shiny carcass in Noo Yo'k till de debil ready to take cha'ge ob um.

[SIMON FRAZIER, *an elderly Negro dressed in black frock coat, comes in at the gate, looks about, crosses to* MARIA's *table.* MARIA *is still glaring at* SPORTING LIFE *so ferociously that* FRAZIER *hesitates.* MARIA *looks up and sees him. She is suddenly all smiles.*]

MARIA. Mornin', lawyer. Lookin' fuh somebody?

FRAZIER. Porgy live here, don't he?

MARIA. Sho' he do. Right ober dere he room.

FRAZIER. T'ank yo', Sistuh. [*Crosses towards* PORGY'S *door.*]

LILY [*who is near* PORGY'S *door*]. Porgy! Lawyer Frazier to see yo'.

[MARIA *gives* SPORTING LIFE *final glare and enters shop.* BESS *helps* PORGY *on to doorstep and returns to room.*]

FRAZIER. Mornin', Porgy.

PORGY. Mornin', lawyer.

FRAZIER. I come to see yo' on business fo' one ob my w'ite client'.

PORGY. Huh?

FRAZIER. I been in to see Mistah Alan Archdale yesterday an' he gib' me message fo' yo'.

PORGY. Who he?

FRAZIER [*in disgust*]. Who he? Yo' ain't know who is Mistah Alan Archdale? He lawyer, same as me.

PORGY [*uneasily*]. Whut he wants wid me?

FRAZIER. I been in to see um on private business like we lawyers always has togedder. An' he say to me, "Mistah Frazier, do yo' know dat black scoundrel dat hitches his goat outside my window ebery mornin'?" I sez: "Yes, Mistah Archdale, I knows um." An' he say: "Well, when yo' goes out, tell um to mobe on." When I comes out, yo' is gone, so I come heah fo' tell yo. *Mobe on.*

PORGY. Why he don't tell me heself?

FRAZIER. Yo' t'ink Mistah Alan Archdale gots time fo' tell nigger to mobe on? No, suh! He put he case in my han', an' I is authorize fo' tell yo' yo' gots to fin' nudder hitchin' place.

PORGY [*unhappily*]. I been hitch on dat corner mos' a mont' now. Why he don't want me 'roun'?

FRAZIER [*scratching his head*]. I ain't quite make dat out. He say sompen 'bout de goat an' de commodity advertise on de chariot. [*Pointing to cart.*] "Pure an' fragrant." Dat's soap, ain't it? I gather dat he t'ink yo' goat need soap.

PORGY [*astonished*]. Whut a goat want wid soap?

FRAZIER [*also puzzled*]. I ain't know ezac'ly. [BESS *comes to doorway and stands behind* PORGY. FRAZIER *resumes his authoritative tone.*] All I knows is yuh gots to *mobe on!* [FRAZIER *looks up and sees* BESS.] How yo' do? [*Looks at her, scrutinizing.*] Ain't yo' Crown's Bess?

PORGY. No, suh, she ain't. She's Porgy's Bess.

FRAZIER [*sensing business*]. Oh! I guess den yo' goin' be wantin' divorce.

PORGY. Huh?

FRAZIER. Ef de 'oman goin' stay wid yo', she gots to hab divorce from Crown or else it ain't legal. [*Takes legal-looking document from pocket. Shows it to* PORGY. PORGY *looks at it, much impressed. Passes it to* BESS.]

PORGY. How much it cos'?

FRAZIER. One dollah, ef dere ain't no complications. [PORGY *looks dubious.* FRAZIER *quickly takes huge seal from his coat-tail pocket. Shows it to* PORGY.]

FRAZIER. When yo' gits divorce, I puts dis seal on de paper to show you has paid cash.

PORGY. Bess, yo' likes to hab divorce?

BESS [*with longing*]. Whut yo' t'ink, Porgy?

[*The other Negroes are gradually edging nearer to listen.*]

PORGY. I goin' buy yo' divorce. Bring me my pocket-book.

[BESS *goes into room and returns immediately with a number of small coins tied up in a rag, hands it to* PORGY. *He laboriously counts out a dollar in nickels and pennies. In the meantime,* FRAZIER *is filling in document with fountain pen. Group of Negroes now listening frankly.* FRAZIER *takes coins from* PORGY. *Counts them.* BESS *holds out her hand for document.*]

FRAZIER [*pocketing coins*]. Wait a minute. 'Tain't legal yet. [*Holding paper in hands, lowers glasses on his nose. Begins in solemn tones.*] Yo' name?

BESS. Bess.

[FRAZIER *makes note.*]

FRAZIER. Yo' age?

BESS. Twenty-six yeah.

FRAZIER. Yo' desire to be divorce from dis man Crown?

BESS. Yas, boss.

FRAZIER. Address de co't as Yo' Honor.

BESS. Yas, Yo' Honor.

FRAZIER. When was yo' an Crown marry?

[BESS *hesitates.*]

BESS. I don' rightly 'member, boss—Yo' Honor.

FRAZIER. One yeah? Ten yeah?

BESS. Ain't I done tell yo' I don' remember?

LILY. She ain't neber been marry.

FRAZIER [*to* BESS]. Dat de trut'?

BESS. Yas, Yo' Honor.

FRAZIER [*triumphantly*]. Ah, dat's a complication.

BESS. I ain't know dat mattered.

PORGY. Yo' can't gib she divorce? Gib me back my dol-lah.

FRAZIER. Who say I can't gib she divorce? But, under circumstances, dis divorce cos' two dollah. It take ex-pert fuh divorce 'oman whut ain't marry.

BESS. Don't yuh pay um no two dollah, Porgy. It ain't wuth it.

FRAZIER. Berry well, den, ef yo' wants to go on libin' in sin. [*Takes coins from pocket and begins to count. Seeing that they do not weaken, he pauses abruptly in his counting.*] Seein' that we is ole frien', I goin' make dis divo'ce dollah an' er half.

[*Again takes out impressive seal.* PORGY *eyes seal, greatly impressed. Begins counting out more pen-*

nies. FRAZIER *affixes seal. Hands it to* PORGY. *Pockets extra money.*]

FRAZIER. Dat ain't much money considerin' whut yo' gets. One dollah an' er half to change from a 'oman to a lady.

BESS [*happily*]. T'ank yo' kindly, Yo' Honor.

FRAZIER. Glad to serbe yo'. When yo' ready to buy license, come to me.

PORGY. Whut she want wid license? She gots divorce, ain't she?

FRAZIER. Well, yo' ought to be stylish like de white folks, an' follow up divorce wid marriage license. [PORGY *and* BESS *look quite depressed at prospect of further complications.*] Well, good mornin', Missus Porgy. [*Turns to go. To* MARIA.] Yo' gots de cup coffee fo' sweeten my mout'?

MARIA. Sho' I is. Step right ober.

[*She and* FRAZIER *enter cookshop. The court is alive with noisy laughter and action. A fish vendor is calling his wares. St. Michael's is chiming the half hour.* MARIA *is bustling back and forth serving the men at her table.* SERENA *is pumping water and calling to her friends.* ANNIE *is holding* CLARA'S *baby, rocking and tossing it.* CLARA *is rearranging sash with motto "Repent Ye Saith the Lord" across* JAKE'S *breast, and consulting the others as to the proper angle. The sash adjusted,* JAKE *bursts into song. "Brer Rabbit, whut yo' da do dey!"* LILY *answers with second line of song. The duet continues.* SCIPIO *runs in at gate. Runs to* SERENA.]

SCIPIO. Dey's a buckra comin'. I heah um axin' outside ef dis Catfish Row.

[*The Negroes suddenly break off in their tasks.* JAKE *ceases to sing.*]

NELSON [*calling to* SERENA]. Whut he say?

SERENA [*in guarded voice, but addressing the court in general*]. W'ite gen'man. [*There is a sudden deep*

*silence, contrasting strangely with noise and move-
ment that preceded it.* ANNIE *gives* CLARA *her baby,
goes quickly inside her own door.* JAKE *removes sash,
puts it in pocket.* SERENA *retreats behind her tubs.
The men at table give absorbed attention to their
food.* MARIA *serves them in silence without looking
up.* SCIPIO *becomes engrossed in tinkering with an
old barrel hoop.* BESS *goes inside.* PORGY *feigns sleep.*

ALAN ARCHDALE, *a tall, kindly man in early middle age,
whose bearing at once stamps him the aristocrat, enters the court, looks about at the Negroes, all ostensi-
bly oblivious of his presence.*]

ARCHDALE [*calling to* SCIPIO]. Boy! [SCIPIO *approaches,
reluctant, shuffling.*] I'm looking for a man by the
name of Porgy. Which is his room? [SCIPIO *shuffles
and is silent.*] Don't you know Porgy?

SCIPIO [*his eyes on the ground*]. No, suh.

ARCHDALE. He lives here, doesn't he?

SCIPIO. I ain't know, boss.

[CLARA *is nearest.* ARCHDALE *crosses to her. She listens
submissively, her eyes lowered.*]

ARCHDALE. I'm looking for a man named Porgy. Can
you direct me to his room?

CLARA [*polite, but utterly negative*]. Porgy? [*Repeats
the name slowly as though trying to remember.*] No,
boss, I ain't nebber heah ob nobody 'roun' dese parts
name Porgy.

ARCHDALE. Come, you must know him. I am sure he
lives in Catfish Row.

CLARA [*raising her voice*]. Anybody heah know a man
by de name Porgy?

[*Several of the Negroes repeat the name to one another,
with shakes of their heads.*]

ARCHDALE [*laughing reassuringly*]. I'm a friend of his,
Mr. Alan Archdale, and I want to help him.

[SERENA *approaches. Looks keenly at* ARCHDALE.]

SERENA. Go 'long an' wake Porgy. Can't yo' tell *folks*
when yo' see um?

[*A light of understanding breaks over* CLARA's *face.*]

CLARA. Oh, you means *Porgy!* I ain't understan' whut name yo' say, boss. [VOICES *all about the court:* "Oh, de gen'man mean Porgy. How come we ain't onderstan'!" CLARA *crosses to* PORGY's *door, all smiles.*] A gen'man come fuh see Porgy. [PORGY *appears to awake.* ARCHDALE *crosses to him.*]

PORGY. How yo' does, boss?

ARCHDALE. You're Porgy? Oh, you're the fellow who rides in the goat cart. [*Sits on step.*]

PORGY. Yes, boss, I gots goat.

ARCHDALE. Tell me about your friend who got locked up on account of the Robbins murder.

PORGY [*his face inscrutable*]. How come yo' to care, boss?

ARCHDALE. Why, I'm the Rutledges' lawyer, and I look after their colored folks for them. Serena Robbins is the daughter of their old coachman, and she asked them to help out her friend.

PORGY [*a shade of suspicion still in his voice*]. Peter ain't gots no money, yo' know, boss; an' I jus' begs from do' to do'!

ARCHDALE [*reassuringly*]. It will not take any money. At least, not much. And I am sure that Mrs. Rutledge will take care of that. So you can go right ahead and tell me all about it.

[PORGY's *suspicions vanish.*]

PORGY. It like dis, boss. Crown kill Robbins, an' Peter see um do it. Now Crown gone he ways, an' dey done gots ole Peter lock up.

ARCHDALE. I see, as a witness.

PORGY. Till dey catch Crown, dey say, but ef dey keep um lock up till den, dat ole man gots er life sentence.

ARCHDALE [*under his breath*]. The dirty hounds! [*He is silent for a moment, his face set and stern.* PORGY *waits.* ARCHDALE *turns wearily to him.*] Of course, we can go to law about this, but it will take no end of time. There is an easier way.

[*Across the sunlit walls of Catfish Row falls the shadow
of a great bird flying low, evidently just out of range
of vision of audience. There is a sudden great commotion in the court. Cries of "Drive um away,"
"Don't let um light," "T'row dis brick." Brooms are
waved at the bird overhead. Bricks thrown.* PORGY
looks up in anxiety. BESS *comes to door with broom.*
ARCHDALE *rises in perplexity.*]

PORGY. Dribe um off, Bess! Don't let um light.

ARCHDALE. What is it? What's the matter?

[*The shadow rises high. The commotion dies down.*]

PORGY. Dat's a buzzard. Yo' don' know dat bird like fo'
eat dead folks?

ARCHDALE. But there's no one dead here, is there?

PORGY. Boss, dat bird mean trouble. Once de buzzard
fold he wing an' light ober yo' do, yo' know all yo'
happiness done dead.

[*With relief, the Negroes stand watching the bird disappear in the distance.* ARCHDALE *also looks after it.*]

SERENA [*leaning from her window and surveying court*].
It sho' make me 'shamed to see all dese superstitious
nigger' makin' spectacle ob demself befo' de w'ite
gentlemans. Ain't we all see dat buzzard sit smack
on Maria's table day fo' yesterday? An' whut happen? Nuttin'! No bad luck 'tall.

MARIA [*indignantly*]. Bad luck! Whut dat 'oman call
bad luck? Ain't I had more drunk customer' yesterday dan any day dis mont'? Dey fair bus' up my shop.
[*Goes into shop muttering indignantly.*]

ARCHDALE [*turning back to* PORGY]. Now listen. Peter
must have someone to go his bond. Do you know a
man by the name of Huysenberg who keeps a corner
shop over by the East End wharf?

PORGY [*his face darkening*]. Yes, boss, I knows um. He
rob ebery nigger he git he han' on.

ARCHDALE. I see you know him. Well, take him this ten
dollars and tell him that you want him to go Peter's
bond. He hasn't any money of his own, and his shop

is in his wife's name, but he has an arrangement with the magistrate that makes him entirely satisfactory. [*Hands* PORGY *a ten-dollar bill.*] Do you understand?

PORGY. Yes, boss. T'ank yo', boss.

[ARCHDALE, *about to go, hesitates, looks at goat-cart.*]

ARCHDALE. Porgy, there's another little matter I want to speak to you about. The last few weeks you've been begging right under my office window. I wish you'd find another place. [*Noticing* PORGY'S *troubled expression.*] There are lots of other street corners.

PORGY [*sadly*]. I done try all de oder corner, boss. Ebery time I stop fo' beg, somebody tell' me to keep mobin'. But I been beggin' under yo' window fo' t'ree week' now, an' I beginnin' to say to myself, "Porgy, yo' is fix fo' life. Mus' be yo' is found a gentlemans whut got place in de heart fo' de poor cripple."

ARCHDALE. I have a place in my heart for the cripple but not for the goat.

PORGY. Dis bery nice goat, boss. Lawyer Frazier say yo' t'ink he need soap. But I don't see how dat can be, boss. Two week han' runnin' now dat goat eat up Serena's washin' soap.

ARCHDALE. He doesn't need it inside.

PORGY [*mystified*]. Whut goat want wid soap outside? [*Suddenly enlightened.*] Oh, yo' don' like to smell um? [FRAZIER *comes from shop. Sees* ARCHDALE. *Approaches. Stands waiting, hat in hand.* PORGY *is now all smiles.*] Dat all right, boss. By tumorroh I goin' hab' dis goat wash till yo' can't tell um from one ob dose rose bush in de park.

ARCHDALE. I'm sorry, Porgy. But you must find another place.

FRAZIER. Good-mornin', Mistah Archdale. I done gib' dis nigger yo' message. [*Sternly to* PORGY.] 'Membuh what I tell yo'—*Mobe on!*

ARCHDALE. All right, Frazier. [*To* PORGY.] If Peter isn't out in a week, let me know. [*Turning to take leave.*]

I suppose you're all going to the picnic today. [*The Negroes nod and smile.* PORGY *looks wistfully at* BESS, *who stands behind him in the doorway.* ARCHDALE *is crossing toward gate.*]

JAKE. Yas, boss. We goin'.

PORGY. Bess, ain't yo' change yo' mind 'bout picnic now yo' gots divo'ce?

[ARCHDALE *catches word "divorce," turns.*]

ARCHDALE. Divorce?

PORGY [*proudly*]. Yas, boss, Mistah Frazier jus' sell my 'oman a divo'ce. She an honest 'oman now.

ARCHDALE [*sternly, to* FRAZIER, *who is looking guilty*]. Didn't the judge tell you that if you sold any more divorces he'd put you in jail? I've a good mind to report you.

FRAZIER. Mus' be dat judge fergit dat I votes de Democratic ticket.

ARCHDALE. That won't help you now. The gentleman from the North, who has come down to better moral conditions among the Negroes, says you are a menace to morals. He's going to have you indicted if you don't quit.

PORGY [*suspiciously; handing paper to* ARCHDALE]. Ain't dis no good as he stan', boss? 'Cause I ain't goin' pay um fo' no more complications. [*As* ARCHDALE *glances over the paper,* PORGY *glares vindictively at* FRAZIER.] Dat nigger come 'round heah in he By-God coat, an' fo' yo' can crack yo' teet', he gone wid yo' las' cent.

ARCHDALE [*reading*]. "I, Simon Frazier, hereby divorce Bess and Crown for a charge of one dollar and fifty cents cash. Signed, SIMON FRAZIER." Well, that's simple enough. [*Examines seal.*] "Sealed—Charleston Steamboat Company." Where did you get this seal?

FRAZIER. I done buy um from de junkshop Jew, boss.

ARCHDALE. Don't you know that there is no such thing as divorce in this state?

FRAZIER. I heah tell dere ain't no such er t'ing fuh de w'ite folks; but de nigger need um so bad, I ain't see

no reason why I can't make one up whut sattify de
nigger. [*His voice breaks.*] Dem divo'ce is keepin' me
alibe, boss, an' whut mo', he is keepin' de nigger
straight.

ARCHDALE. How's that?

FRAZIER. Dat jedge say dey gots to lib togedder anyhow
till dey done dead. Dat's de law, he say. But nigger
ain't make dat way. I done get my black folks all
properly moralize, an' now he say he goin' jail me.
Ef I stops now de nigger leabe each odder anyway.
Ef it don't cos' de nigger nuttin' to leabe he wife, he
ain't goin' keep she er mont'. But when he gots fuh
pay dolluh to get way, he goin' t'ink twice 'fore he
trabble.

[ARCHDALE *keeps from laughing with difficulty.*]

BESS. Ain't mah divo'ce no good, boss? Porgy done pay
one dolluh an' er half fuh it.

ARCHDALE [*looking at paper*]. I could hardly say that it
is legal.

BESS. Legal! Dat wo'd mean good?

ARCHDALE. Well, sometimes.

PORGY. Plenty ob our frien' is divo'ce', boss.

ARCHDALE [*with accusing look at* FRAZIER, *who cringes*].
So I hear. [*Again consults paper.*] You've left this
man, Crown, and intend to stay with Porgy?

BESS. Yes, suh.

ARCHDALE. I suppose this makes a respectable woman
of you. Um—on the whole—I'd keep it. I imagine
that respectability at one-fifty would be a bargain
anywhere. [*Hands paper to* BESS. *Turns back to* FRA-
ZIER.] But remember, Frazier: *No more divorces!* Or
to jail you go. I won't report you this time. [*The goat
sticks its head out door.* PORGY *throws his arm
around its neck.* ARCHDALE *turns to go.*] Good morning. [*Crosses toward gate.*]

FRAZIER [*close by* PORGY'S *door. Recovering from his
emotion enough to speak*]. Gawd bless yo', boss.
Good mornin', boss.

PORGY [*imitating* FRAZIER's *professional manner*]. Mobe on, please. Mobe on! I gots er bery polite goat heah whut object to de smell ob de jail bird. [ARCHDALE, *overhearing, laughs suddenly. Goes out gate, his shoulders shaking with laughter.* FRAZIER *moves off, talks to Negroes in background, and soon leaves the court.* BESS *sits by* PORGY *on step.*] Ain't yo' hear de boss laugh?

BESS. Fo' sho' I heah um laugh.

PORGY [*hugging goat*]. No, no, bruddah, we ain't goin' mobe on. When de nigger make de buckra laugh, he done win. We goin' spend we life under Mistah Archdale's window. Yo' watch!

[*Draws himself up by door frame, goes inside.* BESS *remains on step. St. Michael's chimes the three-quarter hour. Preparations for the picnic are now at their height. One by one the women, when not on stage, have changed to their most gorgeously colored dresses. Men and women are now wearing sashes all bearing the legend: "Repent Ye Saith the Lord." The leaders have also badges denoting their various ranks: "Marshal," etc. Baskets are being assembled in the court. The court is full of bustle and confusion.* SPORTING LIFE *saunters over to* BESS, *who is sitting on step wistfully watching the picnic preparations.*]

SPORTING LIFE. 'Lo, Bess! Goin' to picnic?

BESS. No, guess I'll stay home.

SPORTING LIFE. Picnics all right fo' dese small-town nigger', but we is used to de high life. Yo' an' me onderstan' each odder. I can't see fo' de life ob me what yo' hangin' round dis place for! Wid yo' looks, Bess, an' yo' way wid de boys, dere's big money fo' you' an' me in Noo Yo'k.

BESS [*quietly*]. I can't remembuh eber meet a nigger I likes less dan I does yo'.

SPORTING LIFE [*laughingly*]. Oh, come on, now! How 'bout a little touch happy dus' fo' de ole time' sake?

BESS. I t'rough wid dat stuff.

SPORTING LIFE. Come on! Gib me yo' hand.

[*Reaches out and takes her hand, draws it toward him, and with other hand unfolds paper ready to pour powder.*]

BESS [*wavering*]. I tells yo' I t'rough!

SPORTING LIFE. Jus' a pinch. Not 'nough to hurt a flea. [BESS *snatches her hand away.*]

BESS. I done gib' up happy dus'.

SPORTING LIFE. Tell dat to somebody else! Nobody *eber* gib' up happy dus'. [*Again he takes her hand and she does not resist. Gazes fascinated at the powder.* PORGY'S *hand reaches suddenly into the open space of the door; seizes* SPORTING LIFE'S *wrist in an iron grip.* SPORTING LIFE *looks at the hand in astonishment mixed with a sort of horror.*] Leggo, yo' damn cripple! [*The hand twists* SPORTING LIFE'S *wrist till he relinquishes* BESS'S *hand and grunts with pain. Then* PORGY'S *hand is silently withdrawn.*] Gawd, what a grip fo' a piece ob a man!

BESS [*rising*]. Go 'long now.

SPORTING LIFE [*regaining his swagger*]. All right! Yo' men friend' come an' dey go. But 'membuh, ole Sportin' Life an' de happy dus' here all along. [*Saunters along—goes out gate.*]

[*From the distance is heard the blare of a discordant band. It is playing "Ain't It Hard to Be a Nigger," though the tune is scarcely recognizable to the audience. The Negroes, however, are untroubled by the discords. One or another sings a line or two of the song. A jumble of voices rises above the music: "Here come de orphans!" "Dere de orphan band down de block!" "Le's we go!" etc.*

A man passes outside the gate, stopping long enough to call in to the occupants of Catfish Row: "Eberybody gettin' in line up de block. You nigger' bes' hurry."

PORGY *comes out on doorstep to watch. Sits.* BESS *stands beside him absorbed in the gay scene.* PORGY *looks at her keenly, troubled.*]

JAKE [*in the midst of his preparations*]. Come 'long to de picnic, Bess! [*Does not wait for reply.*]

PORGY [*triumphantly*]. Dere! Don' yo' hear Jake ask yo' to go? Go 'long!

BESS. Plenty ob de mens ask me. Yo' ain't hear none ob de ladies sayin' nuttin'.

PORGY. Bess, yo' can put on my lodge sash an' be just as good as any 'oman in dat crowd.

BESS [*with a little laugh*]. Yo' an' me know it takes more'n sash.

[*The confusion grows. Picnickers once started on their way come scurrying back for forgotten bundles.* SCIPIO *runs in at gate in high excitement.*]

SCIPIO [*breathless; to* SERENA]. Ma, I gots good news fo' yo'.

SERENA. What dat?

SCIPIO. De bandmaster say I can be a orphan! [*The song breaks out in greater volume.*]

> "Ain't it hahd to be a nigger!
> Ain't it hahd to be a nigger!
> Ain't it hahd to be a nigger!
> Cause yo' can't git yo' rights when yo' do.
> I was sleepin' on a pile ob lumbah
> Jus' as happy as a man could be
> When a w'ite man woke me from my slumbah
> An' he say, 'Yo' gots fo' work now cause yo' free'."

[*Other voices are calling back and forth:* "How dem little nigger' can play!" "Ain't yo' ready! Time fo' go!" "We off fo' Kittiwah!"
The band plays with more abandon. BESS *wears the expression of a dreamer who sees herself in the midst*

*of the merrymakers. Her feet begin to shuffle in time
to the music.* PORGY *does not look up, but his eyes
watch the shuffling feet.*]

PORGY [*mournfully*]. Yo' can't tell me yo' ain't wants to
go.

[*The Negroes troop across the court all carrying their
baskets. In twos and threes they go out at the gate.
Among the last to go,* MARIA *comes hurrying from
her shop carrying a gigantic basket. Turns to follow
the others. Sees* PORGY *and* BESS. *Hesitates. As though
afraid of being left behind, turns again toward gate.
Then resolutely sets down her basket.*]

MARIA. What de mattuh wid you', Sistuh? Ain't yo'
know yo' late fo' de picnic?

[*A sudden wave of happiness breaks over* BESS's *face.
She is too surprised to answer.*]

PORGY. Bess says she ain't figgerin' to go.

MARIA [*crosses rapidly to them*]. Sho' she goin'! Ever-
body goin'. She gots to help me wid my basket. I gots
'nough fo' six. Where yo' hat? [*Reaches hat just inside door and puts it on* BESS's *head*].

PORGY [*taking sash from pocket and holding it out to*
BESS]. Here my sash, Bess.

[MARIA *unties* BESS's *apron. Throws it through door.
Takes sash from* PORGY, *pins it across* BESS's *breast,
jerking her peremptorily about to save time. Then
starts for her basket.*]

MARIA. Come 'long now!

BESS [*hesitating*]. I hate fo' leabe yo', Porgy.

PORGY [*happily*]. I too happy fo' hab' yo' go.

MARIA. Ain't yo' goin' help me wid dis basket? [BESS
hurries to her and takes one handle of basket.] See
yo' some mo', Porgy! [MARIA *crosses rapidly to gate.
To keep her hold on the basket,* BESS *is forced to
hurry.*]

BESS [*looking back*]. Good-bye, Porgy!

[MARIA, *apparently seeing the others far ahead and anxious not to be left behind, breaks into a lumbering run, dragging* BESS *after her.* BESS *is waving to* PORGY *as she goes.*

The voices of the Negroes grow fainter. Then the last distant crashes of the band are heard, and the court is quiet.

PORGY *sits on his doorstep dreaming, gazing happily into space, rocking a little. Takes pipe from his pocket, knocks out ashes; lights it.*

Across the sunlit walls falls the shadow of the buzzard flying lazily over the court. PORGY *remains in happy abstraction, oblivious of the bird. Puffs leisurely at his pipe.*

The shadow hovers over his door; then falls across his face. He looks up suddenly and sees the bird. Swift terror sweeps into his face.]

PORGY [*frantically*]. Get out ob here! Don' yo' light! Lef' it! Yo' hear me! Lef' it! [*He waves futile arms at it. The bird continues to hover above him.*] Get out! Somebody bring broom! Don' yo' light on my door, yo' debil! Help! Somebody help me! Oh, Gawd! [*He struggles down the steps and at last reaches the brick. The shadow wings of the bird close as it comes to rest directly over* PORGY'S *door. Grasping the brick, he again looks up to take aim. His fingers slowly relax, and the brick falls to the ground.*] 'Tain't no use now. 'Tain't no use. He done lit.

[PORGY *regains his seat on step and sits looking up at the bird with an expression of hopelessness as the curtain falls.*]

CURTAIN

*Kittiwah Island. Moonlight revealing a narrow strip
of sand backed by a tangled palmetto thicket. In the
distance (right) the band is playing "Ain't It Hard to
Be a Nigger."* JAKE, MINGO, *and several others troop
across stage from left to right, swinging apparently
empty baskets.*

MINGO. Dis been some picnic, but, Lor', I tired!

JAKE [*swinging his basket in a circle*]. Dis basket some
lighter fo' carry dan when we come out.

[*Breaks into song: "Ain't It Hard," etc. The others join
in. They go off right, their song growing fainter in
distance.* SERENA *and* LILY *enter, followed a moment
later by* BESS *and* MARIA. MARIA *is puffing, out of
breath.*]

MARIA. I ain't no han' fo' walk so fas' on a full stomach.
[*Stops abruptly. Looks about her on ground.*]

SERENA. Yo' goin' miss de boat ef yo' ain't hurry, Sistuh.

MARIA. It was jus' about heah I los' my pipe. I 'membuh
dere was palmetto sort ob twisted like dat.

LILY. How come yo' lose yo' pipe?

MARIA [*searching ground. The others help her*]. I was
sittin' under de tree a-smokin', an' I see a Plat-eye
ha'nt a-lookin' at me t'rough de palmetto leaf. An',
'fo yo' can crack yo' teet', I is gone from heah, but
my pipe ain't gone wid me.

LILY. Plat-eye ha'nt! What was he like?

MARIA. Two big eye' like fireball a-watchin' me.

SERENA [*scornfully*]. Plat-eye ha'nt! Yo' ain't read nuttin' in de Bible 'bout Plat-eye is yo'?

MARIA. I ain't needs to read 'bout 'em. I sees 'em lookin'
at me t'rough de palmetto leaf.

SERENA. Jus' like yo' hab' buzzard set on yo' table two

day ago, an' yo' hab' mighty ha'd time a-thinkin' up some bad luck to lay to um.

MARIA. Bad luck! Ain't I lose my pipe dat I smoke dese twenty yeah', an' my mudder smoke um befo' me?

LILY. I ain't partial to sleepin' out wid de rattlesnake'. Le's we go or de boat go widout us.

MARIA. Ef dat boat go without me, dey's goin' to be some sick nigger' in Catfish Row when I gets back. [*Steamboat whistles off right.* MARIA *answers it.*] Hold yo' halt! I ain't goin' till I gets my pipe.

BESS. Yo' bes' go along, Maria, and le's we whut is de fas' walker' look fo' um a bit.

MARIA [*pointing left*]. It might hab' been a little farder back dat way I lose um. [BESS *begins to search at left and wanders off left, her eyes combing the ground.*] An' it might hab' been a little farder dese way. [*Goes off right searching.* LILY *follows.* SERENA *continues her search on stage.*]

LILY [*off right*]. I ain't see um nowheres. Le's we go.

MARIA [*farther in distance*]. I goin' fine um.

[*From the blackness of the thicket two eyes can be seen watching* SERENA. *As she turns in her quest, she sees them. For a moment, she is motionless; then her breath catches in a shuddering gasp of horror, and she flees swiftly off right. A snatch of the song rises suddenly in distance and quickly dies down again.* BESS *comes on from left, her head bent, still searching. A great black hand creeps slowly out among the palmetto branches and draws them aside.* BESS *hears the sound. Straightens, stands rigid, listening.*]

BESS [*in a low, breathless voice*]. Crown?

CROWN. Yo' know bery well dis Crown. [*She turns and looks at him. He partly emerges from the thicket, naked to the waist, his cotton trousers frayed away to the knees.*] I seen yo' land, an' I been waitin' all day fo' yo'. I mos' dead on dis damn islan'!

BESS [*looks at him slowly*]. Yo' ain't look mos' dead. Yo' bigger'n eber.

CROWN. Oh, plenty bird' egg, oyster, an' t'ing. But I
mos' dead ob lonesome wid not a Gawd's person fo'
swap a word wid. Lor' I'se glad yo' come!

BESS. I can't stay, Crown, or de boat go widout me.

CROWN. Got any happy dus' wid you?

BESS. No.

CROWN. Come on! Ain't yo' gots jus' a little?

BESS. No, I ain't. I done gib up dope.

[CROWN *laughs loudly*.]

CROWN. It sho' do a lonesome man good to hab' he
'oman come an' swap a couple joke wid um.

BESS. Dat's de Gawd's trut'. An' 'sides—I gots sompen
fo' tell yo'.

CROWN. Yo' bes' listen to whut I gots fo' tell yo'. I
waitin' here til de cotton begin comin' in. Den libin'
'll be easy. Davy 'll hide yo' an' me on de ribber boat
fur as Savannah. Who yo' libin' wid now?

BESS. I libin' wid de cripple Porgy.

CROWN [*laughing*]. Yo' gots de funny tas' in men. But
dats yo' business. I ain't care who yo' takes up wid
while I'm away. But 'membuh whut I tol' yo'! He's
temporary! I guess it be jus' couple ob weeks now fo'
I comes fo' yo'!

BESS [*with an effort*]. Crown, I got sompen fo' tell yo'.

CROWN. What dat?

BESS. I—I sort ob change' my way'.

CROWN. How yo' change'?

BESS. I—I libin' wid Porgy now—an' I libin' decent.

CROWN. Yo' heah whut I tol' yo'? I say in couple week I
comin' for yo', an' yo' goin' tote fair 'less yo' wants
to meet yo' Gawd. Yo' gits dat?

BESS. Crown, I tells yo' I change'. I stayin' wid Porgy
fo' good. [*He seizes her by the arm and draws her
savagely toward him. The steamboat whistles.*] Take
yo' han' off me. I goin' miss dat boat!

CROWN. Dere's anudder boat day atter tomorruh.

BESS. I tells yo' I means what I says. Porgy my man now.

CROWN [*jeering at her*]. I ain't had a laugh in weeks.

BESS. Take yo' hot han' off me. I tells yo' I stayin' wid Porgy for keeps.

CROWN. Yo' is tellin' me yo' radder hab' dat crawlin' cripple dan Crown?

BESS [*taking a propitiatory tone*]. It like dis, Crown—I de only 'oman Porgy eber hab'. An' I thinkin' how it goin' be if all dese odder nigger' goes back to Catfish Row tonight, an' I ain't come home to um. He be like a little chil' dat los' its ma. [CROWN, *still holding her, throws back his head and laughs.* BESS *begins to be frightened.*] Yo' can laugh, but I tells yo' I change'l

CROWN. Yo' change' all right. Yo' ain't neber been so funny.

[*The boat whistles. She tries to pull away. He stops laughing and holds her tighter with lowering look. Draws her nearer.*]

BESS. Lemme go, Crown! Yo' can get plenty odder women.

CROWN. What I wants wid odder women? I gots a 'oman. An' dat's yo'. See?

BESS [*trying flattery*]. Yo' know how it always been wid yo', Crown—yo' ain't neber want for a 'oman. Look at dis chest, an' look at dese arm' yo' got! Dere's plenty better-lookin' gal dan me. Yo' know how it always been wid yo'. Dese five year 'now I been yo' 'oman—yo' could kick me in de street, an' den, when yo' ready fo' me back, yo' could whistle fo' me, an' dere I was again a-lickin' yo' han'. What yo' wants wid Bess? She gettin' ole now. [*She sees that her flattery has failed and is terrified.*] Dat boat goin' widout me! Lemme go! Crown, I'll come back fo' see yo'. I swear to Gawd I'll come on de Friday boat. Jus' lemme go *now!* I can't stop out here all night. I 'fraid! Dere's t'ings movin' in de t'icket—rattlesnake, an' such! Lemme go, I tells yo'. Take yo' han' off me!

CROWN [*holding her and looking steadily at her*]. No man ever take my 'oman from me. It goin' to be good

joke on Crown ef he lose um to one wid no leg' an'
no gizzard. [*Draws her closer.*] So yo' is change, is yo'?
[*Grips her more tightly. Looks straight into her eyes.*]
Whut yo' say now?

BESS [*summoning the last of her resolution*]. I stayin'
wid Porgy fo' good.

[*His jaw shoots forward, and his huge shoulder muscles
bulge and set. Slowly his giant hands close round her
throat. He brings his eyes still closer to hers. The
boat whistles long and loud, but neither gives sign
of hearing it. After a moment,* CROWN *laughs with
satisfaction at what he sees in* BESS'S *eyes.*
*His hands leave her throat and clasp her savagely by
the shoulders.* BESS *throws back her head with a wild
hysterical laugh.*]

CROWN. I knows yo' ain't change'! Wid yo' an' me, it always goin' be de same. See?

[*He swings her about and hurls her face forward
through an opening in the thicket. Then, with a low
laugh, he follows her. She regains her balance and
goes on ahead of him. The band is still playing, but
growing faint in the distance.*]

CURTAIN

Act three

SCENE I

*St. Michael's chimes the half hour. Curtain. The court
before dawn. Lights in a few windows:* MARIA'S, JAKE'S,
PORGY'S.
The fishermen are preparing for an early departure.

JAKE [*coming from his door*]. Dat all de breakfas' I got

time fo'. [*Calls to men in* MARIA's *shop.*] Come on, yo'
mens! It almost light. [CLARA *comes from their room,
the baby in her arms. Her eyes are anxious and re-
proachful, but she says nothing.*]

JIM [*coming from* MARIA's *shop, wiping his mouth*]. Yo'
ready, Jake? We bes' be off.

JAKE. Let's we go!

[MARIA *appears in her doorway, wiping hands on her
apron.*]

MARIA. Good-bye, boys! Hope yo' has de same good luck
today!

[JAKE *quickly takes baby from* CLARA's *arms, kisses it
hurriedly, and returns it to* CLARA.]

JAKE. 'Bye, big boy!

[BESS's *voice is heard from her room, droning in delirium. All the Negroes stop suddenly to listen.*]

BESS. Eighteen mile to Kittiwah—eighteen mile—palmetto bush by de sho'—rattlesnake an' such.

[JAKE *crosses to* PORGY's *window.*]

JAKE. How Bess dis mornin'?

[PORGY *appears at window.*]

PORGY. She no better.

JAKE. She still out she head?

[PORGY *nods.*]

BESS. Bess goin' fin' um fo' yo'. Dat all right, Maria,
Bess goin' fin' um . . .

[JAKE *shakes his head sadly. Hurriedly recrosses to the
other men. They go toward gate together,* CLARA *following.*]

JIM. I bet dat catch we made yesterday de bigges' catch
eber made 'round dese parts.

NELSON. We bes' make de mores ob today. Look to me
like de las' good day we goin' hab'. Gots a wet tas' to
um.

JAKE. Don' yo' know dat ain't de kin' ob talk to talk
'fore my 'oman? Ain't yo' hears de raggin' I gits ebery
day? [*Laughs.*] But, see! I gots 'er trained now. She
ain't sayin' a word. So long, Clara!

[JAKE *gives* CLARA *a hurried, affectionate pat and follows the other men as they troop out the gate, talking and laughing. The gate clangs shut behind them.* CLARA *goes silently into her room, closes door.*]

BESS. Mus' be right heah on de groun'. Bess goin' fin' um . . . [BESS'S *voice drones on.*]

[MARIA, *in her doorway, listens a moment. Then crosses to* PORGY'S *door; hesitates, awed by the mystery of delirium.* SERENA *silently crosses the court and joins* MARIA. *They listen a moment longer.*]

SERENA [*in a low voice*]. She still out she head? [MARIA *nods. They stand silent.*]

BESS [*from the room*]. Eighteen mile to Kittiwah—Palmetto bush by de sho'. Eighteen mile to Kittiwah . . .

[PETER *appears outside the gate. He seems older and feebler, but his face is joyful. Pushes gate open, comes into court, looking eagerly about. Sees the two women and crosses toward them.*]

PETER. How eberybody?

[*They turn and see him.*]

MARIA [*joyfully*]. Ef it ain't ole Peter!

SERENA. Heah Daddy Peter home again. Hey, yo' Lily! Heah yo' ole man. Lordy, we is glad fo' see yo'!

[LILY *comes running from her door. Hurries to* PETER *and greets him joyfully.*]

LILY. Ef it ain't my ole gran'daddy!

PETER. I begin fo' t'ink mebby I ain't eber see Catfish Row—

[BESS'S *voice rises in a sudden wail. The women turn awestricken faces toward* PORGY'S *door.* PETER, *who has not heard, is mystified by their expressions. His words die away. He looks questioningly from one to another.* BESS *again takes up her monotonous refrain.*]

BESS. Palmetto bush sort ob twisted like—rattlesnake an' t'ing . . .

PETER. Whut de mattuh?

MARIA [*shouting into his ear*]. Porgy's 'oman bery sick.

LILY [*shouting*]. She out she head.

PETER. How long she been like dat?

MARIA. More'n a week now. Eber since we hab de picnic on Kittiwah.

SERENA. She wander off by sheself an' git lost in de palmetto t'icket. She ain't come home fo' two day.

BESS. Dat's right, Maria, I goin' fin' um—eighteen mile to Kittiwah—eighteen mile . . .

PORGY [*within room, soothingly*]. Da's all right, Bess. Yo' here wid Porgy now.

BESS [*monotonously*]. Palmetto bush by de sho' . . .

[MARIA, SERENA, *and* PETER *stand wide-eyed, looking in at the door. They do not go too near.*]

PORGY. Yo' right here wid Porgy an' nuttin' can't hurt yo'. Soon de cool wedder comin' an' chill off dese febers.

PETER [*shaking his head*]. Dat 'oman bery sick. [*The women nod.*]

PORGY. Ain't yo' remembuh how de cool win' come to town wid de smell ob pine tree, an' how de stars is all polishin' up like w'ite folks silber? Den eberybody git well. Ain't yo' know? Yo' jus' keep still an' watch what Porgy say.

[*Silence in the room.* CLARA *comes from her door carrying her baby, crosses to the gate and stands looking out toward the sea.*

After a moment, PORGY *comes from his door, softly closes it behind him.*]

PORGY. I t'ink mebby she goin' sleep now. [*Sinks wearily on to step.*] [*Dully.*] Dat yo' Peter? A whole week gone, now, an' she ain't no better! What I goin' do? [*A moment of silence.*]

PETER. Ef yo' wants to listen to me, I advise yo' to send she to de w'ite folks' hospital.

[*Blank consternation.* MARIA *is first to find her voice.*]

MARIA [*speaking into his ears*]. Fo' Gawd's sake, Peter! Ain't yo' know dey lets nigger' die dere so dey can gib um to de student'? I say dey gib um to de student'.

PETER. De student' ain't gits um till he done dead. Ain't dat so? Den he can't hurt um none. Ain't dat so too? An' I gots dis to say. One ob my w'ite folks is a nurse to de hospital. An' dat lady is a pure angel wid de sick nigger. Ef I sick to-morruh I goin' to she, an' what she say is good wid me. I wants dis carcass took care ob w'ile he is alibe. When he done dead, I ain't keer.

LILY [*shouting*]. Yo' ain't keer wedder yo' is cut up an' scatter, 'stead ob bein' bury in Gawd's own grabe-yahd!

PETER. Well, mebby I ain't say I jus' as lief. But I t'ink Gawd onderstan' de succumstance an' make allowance.

PORGY [*moaning*]. Oh, Gawd! Don't let um take Bess to de hospital!

SERENA [*in injured tone*]. Mus' be yo' is all fergit how I pray Clara's baby out ob de convulsion. Dey ain't nebber been a sick pusson or corpse in Catfish Row dat I has refuse' my prayers. Dey is fo' de righteous an' fo' de sinner all two.

PORGY. Dat's right, Sistuh. Yo' pray ober um. Dat can't hurt um none.

[SERENA *closes her eyes and begins to sway.*]

SERENA. Oh, Jedus who done trouble de watuh in de Sea ob Gallerie—

PORGY. Amen!

SERENA. —an' likewise who done cas' de debil out ob de afflicted time an' time again—

PETER. Oh, Jedus! [*Begins to sway.*]

SERENA. —what make yo' ain't lay yo' han' on dis sistuh' head—

LILY. Oh, my Fadder!

SERENA. —an' sen' de debil out ob she, down a steep place into de sea, like yo' used to do, time an' time again.

PORGY. Time an' time again.

SERENA. Lif' dis poor cripple up out ob de dus'—

PETER. Allelujah!

SERENA. —an' lif' up he 'oman an' make she well, time an' time again.

[*They sway a moment in silence. Then* SERENA *silently rises and departs. After a moment,* PETER *and* LILY *follow her.*]

MARIA [*in a low voice*]. Listen to me. Yo' wants dat 'oman cure up, ain't yo'?

PORGY. Yo' knows I does.

MARIA. Bery well, den. Why ain't yo' sen' to Lody?

PORGY. Fo' make conjur'?

MARIA. Yo' gots two dollah? [PORGY *nods.*] Den yo' bes' waste no time. Yo' go quick to Lody an' gib she de two dollah an' tell she to make conjur' fo' cas' de debil out ob Bess.

[MINGO *has sauntered in and taken a seat at the table by* MARIA'S *door.*]

PORGY. How I goin' leabe Bess?

MINGO. Hey, Marie! How 'bout a little serbice?

MARIA. Here, yo' Mingo, come here! [*He crosses to them.*] Yo' do little job fo' Porgy an' I gib yo' de free breakfas' when yo' gits back. Yo' know Lody, de conjur' 'oman?

MINGO. Who don't know Lody!

MARIA. Yo' go to Lody an' tell she fo' make conjur' fo' cas' de debil out ob Porgy's Bess. He goin' gib' yo' two dollah fo' she.

[PORGY *has taken out his money bag and is counting out pennies.*]

MINGO. Dat long way to Lody's 'fore breakfus'.

MARIA. Listen to de nigger! Ef yo' wa'n't dead on yo' feet, yo' could get dere an' back in ten minute'.

MINGO. Whut yo' gots fo' breakfus'?

MARIA. I gots de butts meat fo' grease yo' mout', an' de corn bread an' 'lasses fo' sweet yo' mout'.

MINGO. How 'bout er little shark steak?

MARIA. Listen to me, nigger! I ain't serbe no free breakfus' alley cat.

MINGO [*belligerently*]. Who you callin' alley cat?

MARIA [*despairingly*]. Dis nigger ain't know nuttin'! Get dis! I decides fo' my customer' whut dey goin' hab', but ain't yo' neber been in one ob dem stylish rest'rant where de name ob all de victual' is writ up on de wall, an' you can pick an' choose 'mong um? Dat's alley cat.

PORGY. I goin' gib yo' quarter fo' goin'.

MINGO. Ah! He ain't so far now!

PORGY [*handing him money*]. Here de two dollah fo' Lody an' de quarter fo' yo'self.

[MINGO *starts for gate.*]

MARIA. Dat breakfas' I promise yo' goin' be on de table in ten minute'. Ef yo' ain't hurry, he'll be cold.

MINGO. I be back fo' yo' can crack yo' teet'.

[*Goes out gate and off to left. St. Michael's chimes the three-quarter hour.*]

MARIA. Quarter till five. Eben dat lazy nigger can't spend more'n ten minute' *gittin'* to Lody's. By fib o'clock sure, she goin' hab she conjur' make.

PORGY [*eagerly*]. Yo' t'ink dat cure she?

MARIA. I ain't t'ink. I know. Yo' watch what I say, my brudder. Bess good as cure right now. Yo' gots jus' a quartuh hour to wait. Come five o'clock, dat 'oman well. [*Crosses to her shop. Goes about her work.*]

[SERENA *has gone to work at her tubs. She now calls to* CLARA, *who still stands gazing out through gate.*]

SERENA. What yo' stan' dere fo', Clara? Boats must be out ob sight by now.

CLARA. Dey been out ob sight fo' long time now.

MARIA [*working at her table*]. Yo' ain't gots no call fo' worry 'bout yo' man. Dis goin' be a fine day.

CLARA. I neber see de watuh look so black.

MARIA. Well, has yo' eber see it look so still?

CLARA. No. He too still. An' somet'ing in my head keep a-listenin' fo' dat hurricane bell. [*Crosses to* SERENA.

Sits on bench.] Let me sit here wid yo', an' yo' talk a lot.

MARIA [*who has crossed to pump with kettle*]. I got a feelin'—

SERENA. What yo' gots a feelin' 'bout?

MARIA. I got a feelin' when dat 'oman of Porgy's got lost on Kittiwah Islan' she done been wid Crown.

SERENA [*her face darkening*]. Yo' t'ink dat nigger on Kittiwah?

MARIA. I always figger he been dere in dem deep palmettuhs, an' when I hear de t'ings dat 'oman keep sayin' in she sickness, I sure ob two t'ing'—one, dat he is dere, and two, dat she been wid um.

CLARA. Yo' beliebe she still run wid dat nigger!

MARIA. Dem sort ob mens ain't need to worry 'bout habin' women.

SERENA. Bess goin' stay wid Porgy ef she know what good fo' she!

MARIA. She know all right, an' she lobe Porgy. But, ef dat nigger come after she, dey ain't goin' be nobody 'round here but Porgy an' de goat.

[*As* MARIA *speaks,* PORGY *comes from his door. The other women sign to* MARIA *to be careful. Seeing* PORGY, *she drops the subject and returns to her shop.*]

SERENA [*piling clothes in basket*]. Come on, Clara, lend me a han' wid dese clothes.

[CLARA, *holding baby on one arm, takes one handle of basket.* SERENA *lifts the other. They carry it through* SERENA'S *door.* PORGY *sits on his doorstep, his face tense, waiting.* DADDY PETER *comes from his door followed by* LILY, *who carries the honey tray. She places it on his head and returns to room, closing the door.* PETER *crosses toward gate, beginning instantly to chant.*]

PETER. I gots honey.—Has yo' gots honey.—Yes, ma'am, I gots honey.—You gots honey cheap?

[*A woman leans from an upper window and calls.*]

THE WOMAN. Oh, honey man! Honey man!

PETER [*going on*]. Yes, ma'am, my honey cheap.

THE WOMAN. Hey, dere! I wants some honey!

[PETER *goes out gate and off to the right.*]

PETER. You gots honey in de comb?—Yes, ma'am, I gots honey in de comb.—Heah comes de honey man!—I gots honey.

[PORGY *sits waiting. St. Michael's begins to chime the hour.* PORGY *grows suddenly rigid. As the chimes continue,* MARIA *comes to her doorway and stands motionless, also listening. She and* PORGY *gaze at each other across court with tense, expectant faces. The chimes cease.*]

PORGY [*in a low, vibrant voice*]. Now de time! Oh, Gawd!

[*St. Michael's strikes five. As* PORGY *and* MARIA *still wait motionless,* BESS'S *voice is heard, weakly.*]

BESS. Porgy! [PORGY *and* MARIA *are both electrified by the sound. They gaze at each other with joyful faces, but for a second neither moves.*] Porgy! Dat yo' dere, ain't it? Why yo' ain't talk to me?

PORGY [*with a half-laugh that breaks in a sob*]. T'ank Gawd! T'ank Gawd!

[BESS *appears in the doorway in her white nightgown. She is very weak.*]

BESS. I lonesome here all by myself.

[MARIA *crosses to her quickly. Gently assists her as she lowers herself to seat beside* PORGY.]

BESS. It hot in dere. Let me sit here a while in de cool.

MARIA. I'll get yo' blanket.

PORGY. Maria, ain't she ought to go back to bed?

MARIA [*going past them into room*]. Let she be. What I done tell yo'? Ain't dat conjur' cured she?

BESS. I been sick, ain't it?

PORGY. Oh, Bess! Bess!

BESS. What de mattuh?

PORGY [*almost sobbing with relief*]. Yo' been bery sick! T'ank Gawd de conjur' cure yo'! [MARIA *reappears with blanket, which she wraps about* BESS.]

MARIA. I ain't goin' let yo' set here bery long. [*Returns to her shop.*]

PORGY. I got yo' back, Bess!

BESS. How long I been sick, Porgy?

PORGY. Jus' a week. Yo' come back from Kittiwah wid yo' eye like fireball, an' Maria git yo' in de bed. An' yo' ain't know me! [BESS *suddenly catches her breath in a stifled sob.*] What de mattuh, Bess?

BESS. I guess I ain't know nuttin' wid de feber—or I ain't come back at all!

PORGY. Yo' ain't come back to Porgy?

[*She begins to moan hysterically.*]

BESS. No, I ain't ought to come back!

PORGY [*soothingly*]. Dat all right. Don' yo' worry none, Bess. I knows yo' been wid Crown. [BESS *draws in her breath sharply, then speaks in a whisper.*]

BESS. How yo' know?

PORGY. Yo' been talk 'bout um while yo' out ob yo' head.

BESS. What I say?

PORGY. Yo' ain't say nuttin' 'cept crazy stuff, but Gawd gib cripple to know many t'ing' he ain't gib strong men.

BESS. Yo' ain't want me to go away?

PORGY. No, I ain't want yo' go, Bess. [*Looks at her keenly.*] [*A moment of silence.*] Yo' neber lie to me, Bess.

BESS. No, I neber lie to yo'. Yo' gots to gib me dat. [*Another silence.*]

PORGY. How t'ings stan' 'tween yo' an' Crown?

BESS [*after a pause*]. He comin' for' me when de cotton come to town.

PORGY. Yo' goin'?

BESS. I tell um—yes. [PORGY *turns his head from her and sits looking straight before him. After a moment,* BESS *reaches out timidly and lays her hand on his arm. Then she tries to encircle it with her fingers.*]

Porgy! Gawd! Yo' gots de arm like stebedore! Why
yo' muscle pulls up like dat? [*He looks at her, his
face set and stern. She cowers, her hand still on his
arm.*] It makes me 'fraid!

[*A pause.*]

PORGY. Yo' ain't gots nuttin' fo' be 'fraid of. I ain't try
to keep no 'oman what don' want to stay. Ef yo'
wants to go wid Crown, dat fo' yo' to say.

BESS. I ain't wants to go, Porgy.

[PORGY *looks at her with hope.*]

BESS. But I ain't yo' kin'. When Crown put he hand on
me dat day, I run to he like watuh. Some day again
he goin' put he han' on my throat. It goin' be like
dyin', den. But I gots to talk de trut' to yo'. When
dem time come, I goin' to go. [*Silence.*]

PORGY [*in a whisper*]. Ef dey wa'n't no Crown, Bess! Ef
dey was only jus' yo' an' Porgy, what den?

[*She looks into his face with an expression of yearning.
Then, suddenly, the weakness of her illness sweeps
down upon her and she breaks out hysterically, trembling with fear.*]

BESS. Oh, fo' Gawd's sake, Porgy! Don' let dat man
come an' handle me! Ef yo' is willin' to keep me, den
lemme stay! [*Her voice rises hysterically, broken by
sobs.*] Ef he jus' don' put dem hot han' on me, I can
be good! I can 'membuh! I can be happy! [*The sobs
overcome her.*]

PORGY. Dere, dere, Bess. [*Pats her arm soothingly, waiting for the storm to spend itself. She grows suddenly
quiet, except for occasional silent, rending sighs.*]
Yo' ain't need to be afraid. Ain't yo' gots yo' man?
Ain't yo' gots Porgy fo' take care ob yo'? What kin'
ob nigger yo' t'inks yo' gots anyway, fo' let anudder
nigger carry he 'oman? No, suh! Yo' gots yo' man
now! Yo' gots Porgy! [BESS *has become quiet. A
pause.*] Dere, now. Yo' been set up too long. Let
Porgy help yo' back to bed.

[*He draws himself up by the door frame.* BESS *rises un-*

steadily and, with a hand on his arm, they make their way into the room. PORGY *closes the door behind them.* MINGO *appears outside the gate, steadies himself against it, then staggers through and crosses to* MARIA'S *table. Slumps into chair. Pounds on table, then buries head in his hands.* MARIA *comes to doorway.]*

MARIA. Oh, dat yo', Mingo! Gawd A'mighty, how yo' gits drunk so fas'! [*Goes into shop and immediately returns with breakfast things on a tray. Begins putting them before him.*] I bet yo' drink dat rot-gut stuff straight! Ain't yo' know nuff to pollute yo' whisky wid watuh?

MINGO [*pushing dishes away*]. Don' want dat stuff. Wants de shark steak.

MARIA [*hands on hips*]. So yo' don' want dat stuff! Bery well! Yo' wants de shark steak. Yo' t'ink I gibin' shark steak wid de free breakfas'?

MINGO. I tells yo' I wants de shark steak. [*With uncertain movements, draws a handful of change from pocket.*]

MARIA [*mollified*]. Ob course, ef yo' goin' pay fo' um! [MINGO *spills the money in a pile on table. It is all pennies.* MARIA *stares at it, then at him. Her eyes are suddenly filled with suspicion.*] Where yo' gits dat money? [MINGO *looks up at her stupidly. She speaks in a ferocious whisper.*] Where yo' gits dat money? [MINGO *seems to try to recollect.*] He all pennies—jus' like Porgy gits fo' beggin'! [*She suddenly seizes him, jerks him to his feet.*] Dat's Porgy's money, I tells yo', what he gibe yo' fo' Lody! [MINGO *opens his mouth to protest, searching wildly for words.*]

MARIA. Don' yo' lie to me, nigger!

MINGO. I jus take 'nough fo' li'l' drink. [MARIA *gives him a savage shake which seems to spill out further words.*] I t'ink Lody must hab move'. I can't find she. [*With weak bravado.*] Leggo me, ole lady! [*Tries to shake off her grip.*]

[MARIA *holds him tighter and brings her face close to his. His eyes suddenly meet hers, and he sees a look of such cold ferocity that he quails and sobs with terror.*]

MINGO. Oh, Jedus.

MARIA. Yo' low, crawlin' houn'! Yo' drink up de conjur' money ob a poor dyin' 'oman, an' ain't leabe she nuttin' but de Christian prayers! You listen to me, nigger! [*Slowly and impressively.*] Fo' yo' own good, I goin' lock yo' up in my closet till yo' sober nuff to keep yo' mout' shut. Den mebby I lets yo' loose. But I goin' to where I can git my han' on yo' again! Ef yo' eber tell Porgy—or any libin' pusson—dat yo' ain't deliber dat message to Lody, I goin' hab nigger blood on my soul when I stan' at de Jedgment. Now, yo', gots dat straight in yo' head? [MINGO, *unable to speak, nods. She swings him suddenly about, hurls him into her room, and closes the door on him. Wipes her face on apron, looks with mystified expression toward* PORGY's *closed door. Baffled.*] Mus' hab been Jedus done cure Bess after all. [*Considers a moment. Takes a few steps toward* PORGY's *door. Then stops, with decision.*] No, I be damn ef He did. He ain't gots it in um. [*Goes into her room. Bangs door behind her.*]

[*For a moment, the court is empty and silent. Suddenly, the silence is broken by the deep, ominous clang of a bell, very different from the silver tone of St. Michael's.*

Instantly, every resident of Catfish Row, excepting MINGO *and* BESS, *is in the court or leaning from his window. Having come, they now stand motionless, scarcely breathing, listening to the bell.*

CLARA, *with her baby, has come from* SERENA's *door, her eyes bright with terror.*]

MARIA. Mus' be de bell fo a hot wave. Yo' see! He ain't goin' ring more'n twelbe.

LILY [*who has been counting half audibly*]. —ten—

eleben—twelbe—

[*For a moment no one breathes. Then the bell rings on. Every face is suddenly rigid with horror.*]

CLARA [*wildly*]. Twenty! [*She runs to the gate and looks off left.*]

SERENA [*following and seeking to comfort her*]. Dat bell mus' be mistake! Ain't yo' membuh de las' hurricane? How he take two day' fo' blow up?

ANNIE. Now eberyt'ing quiet. Not a breaf ob air.

[*All the Negroes have gone to the gate and are gazing off to left.*]

PORGY [*from his window*]. How de Custom House flag?

SERENA. He right dere on de pole, jus' like always.

MARIA [*seeing it too, relieved*]. Don' yo' see dat flag dere, Clara?

SERENA [*reassuringly to* CLARA]. Dat ain't no hurricane signal, is it?

MARIA. Ain't yo' know long as de American flag wabin' ober de Custom House dat mean eberyt'ing all right, jus' like—

[*They are all gazing off left at the distant flag. Suddenly, a new wave of horror sweeps simultaneously over every face.* MARIA'S *speech breaks off with her lips still parted.*]

LILY [*in a low, awed voice*]. Gawd! Dey take um down! [*They continue to gaze, fascinated, but* CLARA *turns away, back into the court. Her terror has given way to dull hopelessness.*]

CLARA. Dey don' hab to run up no hurricane signal to tell me nuttin'. My head stop listenin' fo' um now.

PORGY. De mens goin' see de signal an' come home quick.

CLARA. Dey can't see dat signal from de Blackfish Banks, an' dey dere by dis time.

ANNIE [*hysterically*]. How dey goin' come back wid no win' fo' de sail?

MARIA [*sternly silencing her*]. Dey can row in 'fo' dis storm come. He ain't here yet, is he?

PORGY. No, he ain't here yet.

LILY. I ain't fo' worryin' 'bout t'ing dat mightn't happen 'tall.

[*There is a general babble of voices:* "Time 'nough fo' worry when de storm come!" "Mebby by to-morruh we habe li'l' storm!" *etc.*

While they reassure themselves, the sea is darkening. The shutters of Catfish Row begin to flap back and forth in a sudden wind. CLARA *stands watching the swinging shutters.*]

CURTAIN

SCENE II

Before the rise of the curtain the sound of wind and water begins and swiftly swells and rises. Through the wind the chimes and bell of St. Michael's are heard, sometimes rising clear and strong as the wind lulls, then lost completely in a sudden gust.

The curtain rises on SERENA'S *room, dim and shadowy in the light of guttering kerosene lamps. The Negroes are huddled together in groups. A few have found seats on the chairs and bed. Others sit on the floor. A small group at right, including* SERENA *and* PETER, *are on their knees, swaying and singing the monotonous chant of "The Judgment Day Spiritual."*

PORGY *and* BESS *sit together on the floor at left front.* CLARA *stands motionless at window, her baby in her arms. Every face is filled with fear. They shudder and draw closer together as the wind rises.*

THE SINGERS.

"We will all sing togedduh on dat day,
We will all sing togedduh on dat day,

An' I'll fall upon my knees an' face de risin'
sun,
Oh, Lord, hab' mercy on me!"

MARIA [*speaking above the monotonous chant*]. What
yo' stand ere all de time a-lookin' out fo', Clara? Yo'
can't see nuttin' in de dark.

CLARA [*gazing out between slats of closed shutters; in a
flat, dull voice*]. I t'ink I see a little light now 'round
de edge ob dis storm. He mus' be mos' daytime.

[*In a sudden silence of the wind, a faint, distant sound
is heard.*]

ANNIE. What dat? Sound like a whinny.

CLARA. Somebody's poor horse in de watuh.

PORGY [*moaning*]. My poor li'l' goat. He goin' to dead.
Dat goat's my leg, I can't neber walk again!

MARIA. Dat's right sma't goat, Porgy. He going to climb
on yo' bed an' keep he head out ob de watuh. Yo'
watch whut I say!

PETER. Yo' bes' come sing wid me, Clara. Dat make yo'
feel better.

CLARA [*suddenly hysterical*]. I mos' lose my min' wid
yo' singin'. Yo' been singin' de same speritual since
daylight yesterday!

SERENA [*severely*]. Ain't we want to be ready when de
grabe gib up de dead an' Gabriel sound he trumpet?

SPORTING LIFE. I ain't so sure dis de Jedgment Day. We
hab bad storm 'fore.

SERENA. Not like dis.

MINGO. I 'membuh my ma tell me, when dey hab' de
earthquake here, all day de nigger' sing dat Jedgment Day speritual, waiting fo' de sound ob de
trumpet. But he ain't de Jedgment Day den, an'
mebby he ain't now.

SERENA. Dat may be so, but dis ain't no time fo' takin'
chances. [*Bursts again into song. Her group joins
her.*]

[*The shutters suddenly fly apart and flap violently in the wind, drowning out the singing. The Negroes cower and draw closer together. Some of the men struggle to capture the flying shutters.* BESS *sits calm, gazing straight ahead of her.* PORGY *is watching her thoughtfully.*]

PORGY [*in a brief moment of quiet*]. Yo' ain't 'fraid, Bess? [BESS *shakes her head. A pause.*] What make yo' ain't say nuttin'?

BESS. I jus' t'inkin. [*The men finally lash the shutters together with rope.*] Yo' know whut I t'inkin' 'bout, Porgy?

PORGY. Yo' t'inkin' whut storm like dis mus' be like out on de sea islands.

[BESS *nods.*]

BESS. Wabe' like dese mus' wash clean across Kittiwah.

[*After a moment, she lays her hand on his arm.* PORGY *looks keenly into her eyes.*]

PORGY. Yo' sorry?

BESS. I sorry fo' any man lef' out in storm like dis. But I can stop a-listenin' now fo' his step a-comin'. [*Puts her hand in his.*] I guess yo' gots me fo' keeps, Porgy.

PORGY. Ain't I tells yo' dat all 'long.

[*A distant roar is heard, coming steadily nearer.*]

LILY [*terror-stricken*]. Here he come now!

SERENA. Oh, Masteh! I is ready!

[*The crash and roar sweep by.*]

MARIA. Yo' can see um, Clara?

CLARA. He somebody's roof goin' by.

ANNIE. Gawd A'mighty!

PETER. Oh, Jedus, hab' a little pity!

SERENA. Le's we sing!

[SERENA'S *group begins to sing, but before they have completed a single line* CLARA *cries out loudly.*]

CLARA. Fo' Gawd's sake, sing somet'ing else!

[*The singers are startled into silence. A blank pause. Then* BESS *begins to sing, "Somebody's Knockin' at de Door," and one by one the others join her till the whole room is singing.*]

ALL.

"Dere's somebody knockin' at de do'.
Dere's somebody knockin' at de do'.
Oh, Mary, oh, Mart'a,
Somebody knockin' at de do'.
It's a-moaner, Lord,
Somebody knockin' at de do'.

"It's a moaner, Lord,
Somebody knockin' at de do'.
Oh, Mary, oh, Mart'a,
Somebody knockin' at de do'.

"It's a sinnuh, Lord," etc.
"It's my preachuh, Lord," etc.
"It's my Jedus, Lord," etc.

[*The spiritual swells and gains in tempo; the rhythm of the patting and swaying grows. A few begin to shout.*]

PETER. I hear death knockin' at de door. [*Looks fearfully at door.*]

[*His haunted expression draws the attention of the others. One by one, they stop singing.*]

ANNIE. What yo' say, Daddy Peter?

[*The singing stops, but the rhythm continues.*]

PETER. I hear death knockin' at de do'.

[*A horrified silence. All eyes turn to door.*]

LILY [*in an awed whisper*]. It mus' be death, or Peter can't hear um.

MINGO. He ain't hear nuttin'. Nobody knock.

LILY. Yes, dey is! Somebody dere!

PETER. Death is knockin' at de do'.

MARIA. Open de do' an' show um nobody ain't dere.

MINGO. Open um yo'self.

[MARIA *rises and starts toward door.*]

LILY [*wildly*]. I tells yo' dere is somebody dere! An'
Peter can't hear no libbin' person!

[MARIA *hesitates. A loud knock is heard. The Negroes
immediately burst into a pandemonium of terror.
There are cries of "Oh, Gawd, hab' me'cy!" "Don't
let um come in!"*

*The knock is repeated, louder. Some begin to pray, but
the more energetic begin piling furniture in front of
door. "Bring dat dresser!" "Wedge um under de
knob," etc. The door is shaken violently.*]

BESS. Dat ain't no use. Ef he death, he comes in, anyway.

MARIA. [*now the most terrified of all*]. Oh, Gawd!
Gawd! Don't let um in!

[*With a sucking sound of the wind, the door slowly
opens, pushing away the flimsy furniture. Shrieks of
terror and prayers fill the room.*

CROWN, *bent double against the wind, enters. As one by
one they gain courage to look toward the door, the
prayers die away. For a moment, the Negroes stare at
him in silence. Then there are cries of "Crown!"
"Gawd, it's Crown!"* BESS *sits silent, rigid.* PORGY
gazes at her searchingly.]

CROWN. Yo' is a nice pa'cel ob nigger! Shut a frien' out
in a storm like dis!

SERENA. Who' frien' is yo'?

CROWN. I yo' frien', Sistuh. Glad fo' see yo'! Still mopin'
or has yo' got anudder man?

SERENA. I prayin' Gawd to hold back my han'.

CROWN [*laughing*]. Well, he'll hold it, all right. Better
try de police.

MARIA. Yo' know bery well Serena too decent to gib' a
nigger away to de w'ite folks.

CROWN [*to* SERENA]. Well, between yo' Gawd an' yo'
manners, yo' sho' makes t'ings soft fo' a hard nigger!
[*Sees* BESS.] Oh, dere's who I'm lookin' fo'! Why ain't
yo' come say hello to yo' man?

BESS. Yo' ain't my man.

CROWN. It's sho' time I was comin' back! Dere jus' ain't no 'oman a man can leabe! [*Looking at* PORGY.] Yo' ain't done much fo' yo'self while I been gone. Ain't dere no whole ones left?

BESS [*rising and facing him*]. Keep yo' mout' off Porgy!

CROWN. Well, fo' Gawd's sake! Dem humn-whiners got yo' too?

BESS. I tol' yo' I ain't goin' wid yo' no more. I stayin' wid Porgy fo' good.

CROWN. 'Oman! Do yo' want to meet yo' Gawd? Come here!

BESS [*holding her ground*]. Porgy my man now.

CROWN [*laughing*]. Yo' call dat a man! Don' yo' min'. I gots de forgivin' nature, an' I goin' take yo' back. [*Reaches for her.* BESS *violently repulses him.*]

BESS. Keep yo' han' off me!

SERENA [*to* CROWN]. Ef yo' stick 'round here, yo' sure to get killed sooner or later. Den de w'ite folks goin' figger I done um. Dey gots it in de writin' now dat I been Robbins' wife. An' dey goin' lock me up fo' um anyway. So I might as well do um.

[BESS *returns to her seat by* PORGY.]

CROWN [*laughing*]. What makes yo' t'ink I goin' get killed? Ef Gawd want to kill me, he got plenty ob chance 'tween here an' Kittiwah Islan'. Me an' Him been havin' it out all de way from Kittiwah; first Him on top, den me. Dere ain't nuttin' He likes bet-ter'n scrap wid a man! Gawd an' me frien'!

[*A terrific roar of wind.*]

SERENA [*terror-stricken*]. Yo' fool! Ain't yo' gots more sense dan talk 'bout Gawd like dat in a storm like dis! [*Another sudden gust.*]

CROWN. Gawd's laughin' at yo'!

PETER. It bery dangerous fo' we all to hab' dat blas-phemin' nigger 'mong us. Le's we sing unto de Lord!

[*A woman's voice leads the spiritual,* "Got to Meet de Jedgment."]

THE WOMEN. "All I know—

SEVERAL MEN. I got to meet de Jedgment.

THE WOMEN. "All I know—

THE MEN. Got to meet de Jedgment.

THE WOMEN. "All I know—

THE MEN. Got to meet de Jedgment.

TOGETHER. All I know, All I know, All I know—

THE WOMEN. "All I moan—

THE MEN. I got to meet de Jedgment. . . ."

[*As the wind subsides, the spiritual rises strong and clear. The Negroes sing and sway for a moment uninterrupted.*]

CROWN [*his voice rising above the singing*]. Yo' folk mus' t'ink de Lord bery easy pleased ef yo' t'ink he like to listen to dat. [*They sing on.*] Ef it affec' Him de way it do me, yo' is gibin' um de lonesome blues. [*They continue to sing.* CROWN *shouts above singing.*]

CROWN. Here, here! Cut dat! I didn't come all de way from Kittiwah to sit up wid no corpses! Dem as is in such a hurry fo' de Jedgment, all dey gots fo' do is to kiss demselves good-bye an' step out dat door. Yo', Uncle Peter, here's yo' chance. The Jim Crow's leabin' an' yo' don' need no ticket! [*Turning to* SERENA.] How 'bout yo', Sistuh? All abo'd! What, dey ain't no trabbelers?

[*A roar of wind.*]

CROWN. Dere go de train! An' yo' miss yo' chance! [*The wind rises above the singing.* CROWN *shouts up at ceiling.*] Dat's right, drown um out! Don' yo' listen to um sing! Dey don' gib' yo' credit fo' no taste in music. How 'bout dis one, Big Frien'? [*Sings.*]

"Rock in de mountain,
    Fish in de sea,
    Dere neber was a nigger
    Take an 'oman from me."

LILY. Jedus! He goin' call down Gawd' wrath on we

all! [*The wind rises to its highest pitch. The Negroes huddle together in terror. They begin to sway and moan.* CROWN *stands in middle of room, his arms thrown wide. His voice rises above the wind.*]

CROWN. Don' yo' hear Gawd A'mighty—laughing up dere? Dat's right, Ole Frien'! Gawd laugh, an' Crown laugh! [*Throws back his head and laughs. The wind shrieks above his laugh.*] Dat's right! Yo' like um, Gawd? I'll gib yo' anudder verse! [*Sings.*]

> "I ain't no doctor,
>   No doctor' son,
>   But I can cool yo' feber
>   Till de doctor come."

[*While he is singing, the wind suddenly ceases. The Negroes look at one another, appalled by the suddenness of the change.*]

BESS. Mus' be de storm ober.

PORGY. He jus' takin' a res. When de wind lull like dis, he come back soon, worse'n eber.

CROWN. Ain't I tell yo' Gawd like um? He quiet now fo' listen. [*He bursts again into song.*]

> "I laugh in de country,
>   I laugh in de town,
>   'Cause a cripple t'ink he goin'
>   Take an 'oman from Crown."

[*Then begins to shuffle.*] Come on, Bess! Yo' ain't one ob dese spiritual-whimperin' niggers. What, ain't yo' got no guts! Come 'long! Yo' used to be de bes' dancer in Charleston. Ef yo' don' want to dance wid Crown, mebby yo' new man'll dance wid yo'! [*Roars with laughter.* BESS *is silent. He dances a few more steps.*] Come 'long, Maria! Yo' can't tell me dese Gawd-f'arin' whiners has got yo'! [MARIA *hesitates,*

CROWN *dances on. Laughs.*] Dis ole lady too fat fo' dance!

MARIA [*indignantly*]. Who say I'm too fat!

[*Gets lumberingly to her feet and begins to shuffle.* MINGO *begins to clap for them.*]

CROWN [*dancing*]. How 'bout ole Sportin' Life? [SPORTING LIFE *joins in the dancing.* PETER *begins to clap.*]

LILY. Stop dat, yo' ole fool!

CROWN [*dancing near* PETER *and shouting in his ear*]. Dis nigger too ole fo' dance!

PETER [*indignant, puffing out his chest*]. Who say I too ole! [*Gets laboriously to his feet and begins a feeble shuffle.*]

[*A group are now forgetting their terror in song and dance in the middle of the room. Another group, including* SERENA, *are looking on disapprovingly and with fear in their faces.* CLARA *pays no attention to it all, gazes steadily from window.* PORGY *and* BESS *sit together, absorbed in each other. Every now and then* CROWN *cuts a pigeon wing before* BESS. *She ignores him. He laughs and dances away. A wild crescendo shriek cuts across the sound of merriment. The dancers stop in their places. Everyone turns to* CLARA, *who is pointing from the window, her eyes wild and horror-stricken. They all rush to the window.* SERENA *and* ANNIE *are already trying to comfort* CLARA.]

ANNIE. Course it's a boat upside down, but 'tain't de *Sea Gull*.

CLARA. It got red gunnels same as *Sea Gull*.

SERENA. Don' yo' know *Sea Gull* gots bird wid spread wing on he bow.

MINGO [*pointing*]. He goin' come up ober dere now.

SERENA. You'll see! He gots no bird! Dere! Watch um! See he—

[*She breaks off suddenly with widening eyes.* CLARA *cries out.*]

MINGO. Gawd! It de *Sea Gull* fo' true!

CLARA [*shaking off* SERENA's *arm*]. Lemme go!

PETER. What yo' goin' do?

SERENA [*holding her*]. Yo' wait now, Clara!

CLARA. Lemme go! [*Breaks from* SERENA's *hold. Runs frantically to the door. Then turns back suddenly to* BESS.] Bess, yo' keep my baby till I come back. [*Thrusts the baby into* BESS's *arms. Wrests the door open while the Negroes call protests after her.*]

BESS. Clara! Don' go!

[CLARA *rushes out. The door bangs shut behind her. A startled moment of silence. They all stand looking at closed door.*]

MINGO. Dat 'oman t'ink she goin' find Jake *alibe!*

BESS. Clara oughtn't to be out dere by sheself.

SPORTING LIFE. Eberyt'ing quiet now.

PORGY. Dat storm comin' back any minute.

BESS. Somebody go fo' Clara. Don' leabe she out dere alone! [*No one moves.*]

SPORTING LIFE. What de fool 'oman go fo'!

MARIA. Dey ain't nobody in here got de guts ob a chicken.

MINGO. Go long yo'self, Auntie. Dere ain't no wabe big nough fo' drown yo'.

PETER [*starting for door*]. Who goin' wid me?

BESS [*holding him back*]. Yo' ain't goin', Daddy Peter! Yo' too ole. [*Looking scornfully over the room.*] Ain't dere no *man* 'round here?

CROWN. Yes! Where all dem nigger been wantin' to meet de Jedgment? Go 'long! Yo' been askin' fo' somet'ing, an' yo' ain't got de gizzards to go an' get um. Now's yo' chance. [*Laughs. Goes and stands before* BESS, *looking sideways to see effect on her.*] Porgy, what yo' sittin' dere fo'? Ain't yo' hear yo' 'oman calling fo' a *man?* Yes, looks to me like only *one* man 'round here! [*Again glances toward* BESS; *then runs to door, throwing up his arms and calling.*

Calls the men by name: "Go 'long, Sam!" etc.] All right, Ole Frien' up dere! We's on fo' anudder bout! [*Jerks door open and runs out.*] [*A moment of silence. The stage has grown perceptibly lighter. All the Negroes crowd to the window, looking over each other's shoulders through slats of the closed shutters.*]

PETER. Dere Clara almost to de wharf already.

BESS. De watuh deep?

SERENA. Almost to she waist.

SPORTING LIFE. Gawd! How Crown splash t'rough dat watuh!

[*They watch a moment in silence. A roar of wind and water. The stage darkens suddenly. With a swift, sucking sound, the shutters fly apart. Confused cries of "Oh, Jedus! Hab' a little me'cy!" "Gawd A'might'! De storm come back!" "Ain't I tell yo' he comin' worser'n eber."*]

SERENA [*kneeling center*]. Gawd answerin' Crown!

[*Others kneel with her, shrinking close together, moaning with terror.*]

MINGO [*at window, his voice rising high in horror*]. De wharf goin'! Gawd A'mighty!

BESS [*screaming futilely against the wind*]. Clara! Clara!

[*Wild shrieks of horror from all the Negroes at window. Then a terrific roar, accompanied by the splintering of timber. Then a sudden awed silence in the room.* PETER *turns the women from the window, blocking further view. They huddle together in the center of the room around* SERENA'S *group.* BESS *crosses to* PORGY. *Sits beside him, the baby in her arms. All the others fall upon their knees as with one accord they begin to sing the "Jedgment Day Spiritual."*

BESS *does not sing, but sits holding the baby close, with a rapt look in her eyes.*]

"We will all pray togedduh on dat day,
We will all pray togedduh on dat day,
An' I'll fall upon my knees an' face de risin'
sun.
Oh, Lord, hab' mercy on me!
"We will drink wine togedduh on dat day.
We will drink wine togedduh on dat day,"
etc.
"We will eat bread togedduh on dat day,
We will eat bread togedduh on dat day,
An' I'll fall upon my knees an' face de risin'
sun.
Oh, Lord, hab' mercy on me!"

DADDY PETER [*in the midst of the singing*]. Allelujah!
Gawd hab' mercy on de souls ob Clara an' Crown!
[BESS *turns and looks directly at* PORGY. *With an expression of awe in his face, he reaches out a timid hand and touches the baby's cheek.*
The roar increases. The shutters fly back and forth. With fear-stricken eyes, the Negroes sway and pat and sing, their voices sometimes rising above the roar of the wind and sometimes drowned by it.
BESS *continues silent, looking straight ahead of her, tenderness, yearning, and awe in her face.* PORGY *sits watching her. The shutters crash more violently. The roar of wind and water increases. The Negroes huddle closer and sing on.*]

CURTAIN

Act four

Chimes, St. Michael's strikes one. Curtain. The court, dark except for lights around the closed shutters of a second-story room at back left and the glow from MA-RIA'S open door.

PORGY is at his window but is only vaguely seen in the darkness. He holds the shutters partly closed so as to screen himself, while he is able to look out.

From the second-story room comes the sound of a spiritual muffled by the closed shutters.

Door to stairway at back left open and SERENA comes out. Through the open door the spiritual is heard more plainly. It is sung by women's voices—a slow, mournful dirge.

> "Nelson, Nelson, don' let yo' brudder con-
> demn yo'.
> Nelson, Nelson, don' let yo' brudder con-
> demn yo'.
> Nelson, Nelson, don' let yo' brudder con-
> demn yo'.
> Way down in dat lonesome grabeyahd."

[SERENA *closes door, muffling the chant. She crosses toward her room; sees the light from MARIA'S door and pauses.*]

SERENA. Yo' still up, Maria? How come yo' ain't sing wid we women fo' de dead in de storm?

MARIA [*coming to her doorway*]. Some ob dose nigger' liable to sing all night, I too tired clearin' t'ing up. My stove been wash' clean 'cross de street. An' 'sides, it break my heart to hear dese 'omans mourning fo' de mens dat provide um wid bread and what was dey lover' too. All dem fine, strong mens, dead in de storm! [*In lower voice.*] It gib' me de creeps, Serena, to t'ink how many ghost must be listenin' round dis court to-night.

SERENA [*nervously*]. I ain't no patience wid yo' talk 'bout ghost'.

[PORGY *softly moves his shutter.* SERENA *starts.*] What's dat?

MARIA. Jus' Porgy watchin' at he window. [*Draws* SERENA *farther from* PORGY'S *window and lowers her voice ominously.*] What's he watchin' for?

SERENA [*impatiently*]. How I know?

MARIA. He been dere all day. He ain't gone out on de street to beg like he always does. An' he ain't gone up wid Bess to sing for de dead in de storm.

SERENA. What ob dat?

MARIA. Crown dead, ain't he? [*Lowers voice still further.*] Mus' be he t'ink Crown' ghost is a-comin' for trouble Bess. [SERENA *gives a scornful grunt.*] Bery well, Sistuh. But I knows dis— Gawd gib' dat cripple to see many t'ing yo' an' me can't see—an' if he is watch for sompen, den dere is sompen for watch for.

[BESS, *the baby in her arms, opens door at left back. The spiritual is again heard clearly.* BESS *does not close door, but stands listening, holding baby close.* MARIA *and* SERENA *move over to listen.*]

WOMEN'S VOICES.
"Jake, Jake, don' let yo' brudder condemn yo'
Jake, Jake, don' let yo' brudder condemn yo' . . ."

BESS. Dey singin' for Jake an' Clara now. I couldn't stay. [*The three women listen a moment in silence.*]

VOICES. "Clara, Clara, don' let yo' sistuh condemn yo'
Way down in dat lonesome grabeyahd . . ."

[BESS *softly closes door, muffling the singing. Turns toward her own door.*]

SERENA. What we all goin' to do wid dat poor mudderless baby?

BESS [*stopping short. Turns slowly back*]. Mus' be Clara has come back already.

SERENA [*looks fearfully about her*]. What yo' means?

BESS. Mus' be Clara has come back an' say sompen to yo' I ain't hear. I ain't hear her say nuttin' 'bout "we." She say, "Bess, yo' keep dis baby for me till I comes for um."

SERENA. Somebody oughts to make sure de poor chile gets a proper Christian raisin'.

BESS. Clara ain't say nuttin' to me 'bout dat, an', until she do, I goin' stan' on she las' libin' word an' keep she baby for she till she do come back. [*Again starts toward her door. Again turns back impulsively.*] Oh, let me be, Serena. Can't yo' see I ain't de same 'oman what used to run wid Crown? Gawd wouldn't ha' let Clara gib' me dis baby if He hadn't seen I was different inside. He wouldn't ha' gib me Porgy if he didn't want to gib me my chance. [*Looking down at baby.*] See! He t'ink already dat I he ma. I gots de big brightness all inside me to-day. I can't stan' not to hab' eberybody kind to me to-day! [*Holds baby out to* SERENA.] Look at um now, Serena—hold um a minute. Tell um he gots a good ma what goin' stan' by um!

[SERENA *takes the baby reluctantly, but responds when it touches her bosom. She rocks it in her arms.*]

SERENA. Yes—I reckon yo' gots a good ma now. She gots Gawd in she heart at las'. Yo' ain't gots no cause for fret. [*Hands baby back to* BESS, *who draws it close.*]

BESS. Ain't yo' see, Serena, how he scroogin' down? Dis baby know already dat he done git back home. [*Turns to go.*]

SERENA. Good-night, Sistuh.

[BESS *pauses slightly, as though taken by surprise.*]

BESS. Good-night—Sistuh.

[*Goes into her room. A dim light appears in the room. The shutters are closed from within.*

SERENA *goes to her room.* MARIA *begins to shut up her shop for the night. Several women carrying lanterns come from the funeral room, leaving the door open. They go out of the gate.*

The spiritual is again heard.]

THE SINGERS. "Ummmmm, Ummmmm, yeddy ole Egypt duh yowlin'

Way down in dat lonesome grabeyahd.

"Crown, Crown, don't let yo' brudder condemn yo',

Crown, Crown, don't let yo' brudder condemn yo' . . ."

[*There is a sudden raucous laugh in the darkness.* MARIA *starts; then turns and peers into the shadows under* SERENA'S *stairs.*]

MARIA. Yo' low-live skunk! What yo' hidin' 'round here fo'?

SPORTING LIFE [*sauntering into the light from* MARIA'S *window*]. Jus' listenin' to de singin'. Nice happy little tune dat. Now dey's stowin' my ole frien' Crown. [*Laughs again.*]

[MARIA *crosses quickly; closes the door, muffling the singing.*]

MARIA [*returning to* SPORTING LIFE]. Yo' ain't gots no shame—laughin' at dem poor 'omans singin' for dere dead mens!

SPORTING LIFE. I ain't see no sense makin' such a fuss ober a man when he dead. When a gal's man done gone, dere's plenty mens still libin' what likes good-lookin' gals.

MARIA. I know it ain't dem gals yo' is atter. Ain't yo' see Bess gots no use for yo'? Ain't yo' see she gots a man?

SPORTING LIFE. I see more'n dat, Auntie. [*Laughs as though at a joke all his own.*]

MARIA. What yo' means?

SPORTING LIFE. I see she gots two mens—an' when a

'oman gots two mens—pretty soon she ain't got none
at all!

MARIA [*threateningly*]. What yo' means by dat—Bess
gots two mens?

SPORTING LIFE. What make yo' all so sure Crown dead?

MARIA. Ain't we see de wharf wash' away under um?

SPORTING LIFE. Ain't he tell yo' Gawd an' he frien'?

MARIA [*alarmed*]. Yo' is tellin' me Crown ain't dead?

SPORTING LIFE [*nonchalantly*]. I ain't tellin' yo' nuttin',
Auntie.

MARIA [*advancing on him threateningly*]. Yes, yo' is. Yo'
tellin' me eberyt'ing yo' knows, an' damn quick!
[*Corners him.*]

SPORTING LIFE. Ob course he dead! Ain't we hear um
singin' he funeral song?

MARIA [*grabbing his arm and bringing her face close to
his*]. Yo' has seen um?

SPORTING LIFE. How can I seen um if he dead? Mus' be
he ghos' I seen hangin' 'round here.

MARIA [*meditatively*]. So yo' has seen um. [*Menacingly.*]
Well, if Bess gots two men, dat sho' count yo' out.

[SPORTING LIFE *laughs at her. While they talk,* PORGY'S
shutter opens inch by inch.]

SPORTING LIFE. Dat jus' where I comes in. When a
'oman got jus' one man, mebby she gots um for keep.
But when she gots two mens—dere's mighty apt to
be carvin'!—An' de cops takes de leabin's.

MARIA [*warningly*]. Dere ain't nobody in dis court
would gib' a nigger 'way to de cops.

SPORTING LIFE. *Oh, no,* Auntie! But dem cops is bery
smart, an' dey gots it in fo' Crown, remembuh! An',
when dat time comes, yo' can tell Bess for me dat
little ole Sportin' Life is still on de premises.

MARIA [*starting for him*]. Well, he ain't goin' stay bery
long on my premises!

SPORTING LIFE [*hurriedly withdrawing, but not forgetting his swagger.*] Dat's all right, ole lady! I was jus'
leabin'. [*Saunters toward gate.*]

[MARIA *turns back to the closing of her shop.* SPORTING LIFE *glances at her over his shoulder. Sees her engaged in barring her windows. Steps swiftly into the darkness under* SERENA'S *stairs.* MARIA *finishes her work. Looks about court. Sees it's apparently empty. Goes into her shop. Locks door. A child's whimper is heard from* BESS'S *room, then* BESS'S *voice singing in the darkness.*]

> "Hush, little baby, don' yo' cry,
> Hush, little baby, don' yo' cry,
> Hush, little baby, don' yo' cry,
> Mother an' fadder born to die.
>
> "Heard a thunder in de sky,
> Heard a thunder in de sky,
> Heard a thunder in de sky,
> Mus' be Jedus passin' by.
>
> "Heard a rumblin' in de groun',
> Heard a rumblin' in de groun',
> Heard a rumblin' in de groun',
> Mus' be Satan turnin' 'roun'.
>
> "Hush, little baby, don' yo' cry,
> Mother an' fadder born to die."

[*Her voice trails off sleepily and is silent. During her lullaby, the last singers have come from the funeral room and crossed to their own rooms or gone out at gate. The light in the funeral room goes out.* MARIA'S *light goes out.*

A moment of complete darkness and silence in Catfish Row; then the sudden flash of a match in the darkness reveals SPORTING LIFE *about to light a cigarette. He hears something at gate and hurriedly extinguishes match, with cigarette unlit. Against the gray*

*background beyond the gate a gigantic figure can be
seen. The gate opens very slowly and noiselessly.*
CROWN *comes stealthily into court; very gently closes
gate behind him. Picks his way slowly and silently
across court. Stops to listen. Silence. Goes on to*
PORGY'S *door. Again listens. Puts his hand on knob
and softly tries door. Opens it very cautiously, inch
by inch. When it is wide enough, he stealthily slips
through. Inch by inch the door closes. A full minute
of absolute silence.* MARIA *is in her wrapper; opens
her door and stands listening. Satisfied, she is turning back.*

A muffled thud sounds from PORGY'S *room,* MARIA *stops
short. Stands motionless. Suddenly* PORGY'S *laugh is
heard, deep, swelling, lustful. The baby cries out.*]

BESS [*within room. Horror in her voice*]. Fo' Gawd's
sake, Porgy! What yo' laughin' 'bout?

PORGY [*triumphantly*]. Dat all right, honey. Don' yo' be
worryin'. Yo' gots Porgy now, an' he look atter he
'oman. Ain't I don' tell yo'? Yo' gots a *man* now!

[MARIA *crosses the court swiftly. Opens* PORGY'S *door,
goes in, and closes it behind her.*

Again the flash of a match in the shadows. SPORTING
LIFE *lights his cigarette and continues his vigil.*]

CURTAIN

SCENE II

*St. Michael's chimes and strikes six. The curtain rises
on the court, silent and apparently deserted.*

*After a moment, three white men appear outside the
gate. One is the* DETECTIVE *who arrested* PETER. *The second is the* CORONER, *a fat, easy-going, florid man. The
third is a* POLICEMAN.

DETECTIVE [*to* POLICEMAN, *pointing off right*]. Bring the wagon 'round to the corner, Al, and wait for us there. [*The* POLICEMAN *goes off right. The* DETECTIVE *and* CORONER *come in at gate.*] This is the joint. I'd like to get something on it this time that would justify closing it up as a public nuisance and turning the lot of 'em into the street. It's alive with crooked niggers.

CORONER [*looking around him*]. Looks pretty dead to me.

DETECTIVE. Dead, hell! If you was on the force, 'stead of sitting down in the coroner's office, you'd know we don't make a move that isn't watched by a hundred pair of eyes. [*The* CORONER *looks exceedingly uncomfortable. Glances apprehensively about him.*] There! did you catch that? [*Points at a window.* CORONER *starts.*] They're gone now.

CORONER. Don't know as I have much business, after all. Just to get a witness to identify the body at the inquest. Maybe you'll bring one along for me when you come.

DETECTIVE. Like hell I will! You stay and get your own witness, and I'll learn you something about handling niggers, too. Now, let's see—got several leads here! The widow of Robbins, the fellow Crown killed. That's her room there. And then there's the corpse's woman. She's living with the cripple in there now.

CORONER. What makes you think the buck was killed here?

DETECTIVE [*pointing toward sea*]. Found right out there.

CORONER. Found at flood tide. Might have been washed in from miles out.

DETECTIVE. A hell of a lot you know about niggers. Come on! I'll show you. [CORONER *nods and follows* DETECTIVE. *They stop at door leading to* SERENA'S *room.* DETECTIVE *kicks it open, and shouts up the stairs.*]

DETECTIVE. Come on down, Serena Robbins, and make it damn quick!

[*There is silence for a moment, then the shutters of* SERENA'S *window are slowly opened, and* ANNIE *looks out.*]

ANNIE. Serena been sick in she bed three day, an' I been here wid she all dat time.

DETECTIVE. The hell she has! Tell her, if she don't come down, I'll get the wagon and run her in.

ANNIE. She bery sick, boss. She can't leabe she bed.

DETECTIVE. She'll leave it damn quick if she knows what's good for her. [ANNIE *disappears. A loud moaning is heard. Then* ANNIE *reappears accompanied by another woman. Between them they support* SERENA. *She wears a voluminous white nightgown, and her face and head are bound in a towel. She collapses across the window sill with a loud groan.*] Drop that racket. [SERENA *is silent.*] Where were you last night?

SERENA [*slowly and as though in great pain*]. I been sick in dis bed now three day an' night.

ANNIE. We been sittin' wid she an' nursin' she all dat time.

THE OTHER WOMAN. Dat's de Gawd's trut'.

CORONER. Would you swear to that?

SERENA, ANNIE, *and* OTHER WOMAN [*in unison, as though the answer had been learned by rote*]. Yes, boss, we swear to dat.

CORONER [*to* DETECTIVE]. There you are—an airtight alibi. [DETECTIVE *regards* CORONER *with scorn.*]

DETECTIVF [*to* SERENA]. You know damn well you were out yesterday. I've a good mind to send for the wagon and carry you in. [*The women are silent.* DETECTIVE *waits, then shouts abruptly.*] Well?

THE THREE WOMEN [*again in unison*]. We swear to Gawd we been in dis room three day'.

DETECTIVE [*bluffing*]. Ah-hh, that's what I wanted! So you were in last night, eh? [*The women are fright-*

ened and silent.] And just two months ago—right here—Crown killed your husband, didn't he? [*No answer.*] Answer me! [DETECTIVE *runs halfway upstairs.*] You'll either talk here or in jail. Get that! Did Crown kill Robbins? Yes or no! [SERENA *nods her head.*] Exactly. And last night Crown got his right here—didn't he? [*Women are silent except* SERENA, *who groans as though in pain.* DETECTIVE *pretends to construe groan as assent—triumphantly.*] Yes, and how do you know he was killed if you didn't see it?

WOMEN [*in unison*]. We ain't see nuttin', boss. We been in here t'ree day an' night, an' de window been closed.

DETECTIVE [*shouting*]. Look at me, Robbins! Do you mean to tell me that the man who killed your husband was bumped off right here, under your window, and you didn't know?

WOMEN [*in unison*]. We ain't see nuttin', boss. We been in here—

DETECTIVE [*interrupting*]. —three days and nights with the window closed. You needn't do that one again. [*Turning away disgustedly.*] Oh, hell! You might as well argue with a parrot cage, but you'll never break them without your own witnesses, and you'll never get 'em. [*The three women leave the window, closing shutters.*] Well, come along. Let's see what's here. [*Goes to* LILY's *and* PETER's *door. Throws it open.*] Come on out here, you! [LILY *comes to door.*] What's your name?

LILY [*seeing* CORONER]. Do, Lord! Ef it ain't Mr. Jennings!

CORONER. Well, Lily! So you live here? [*To* DETECTIVE.] I'll answer for this woman. She worked for us for years.

DETECTIVE. That don't prove she don't know anything about this murder, does it? [*To* LILY.] What's your name?

LILY [*stubbornly*]. I don't know nuttin' 'bout um.

DETECTIVE [*shouting at her*]. I didn't ask you whether—

CORONER. Let me question her. [*Kindly to* LILY.] What's your name?

LILY. Do, Mr. Jennings! You ain't 'membuh my name is Lily Holmes?

CORONER. I know your name was Lily Holmes, but you left us to get married. What's your name now?

LILY. Lord, Mr. Jennings! I de same Lily Holmes. You ain't t'ink I goin' be responsible for no ole nigger' name? No, suh! An' I ain't gib' um my name, nedder!

DETECTIVE [*looking through door*]. That your husband? [*Calling into room.*] Come on out here, you!

LILY. I'll fetch um. [*Goes into room. Returns with* PETER.]

CORONER. Why, it's the old honey man! [PETER *is terror-stricken at sight of* DETECTIVE.]

DETECTIVE [*recognizing him*]. Oh, so it's you, is it? Well, Uncle, do you want to go back to jail or are you going to come clean?

LILY [*appealing to* CORONER]. Ain't no use to ask him nuttin'. He deaf, an' 'sides, he ain't got good sense nohow.

CORONER. But, Lily, you didn't marry the old honey man?

LILY [*surveying* PETER]. Whut wrong wid um?

CORONER. He's not a suitable age.

LILY [*puzzled*]. Whut he ain't?

CORONER. Do you think he's the right age?

LILY. Sho he de right age. He eighty-two.

CORONER. An old man like that's apt to linger on your hands.

[DADDY PETER, *hearing nothing of conversation, but feeling that he is its subject, is nodding and smiling with self-appreciation.*]

LILY. No, boss. Ef I is marry to young man an' he took sick, mebbe he linger on my hand. But—[*Points to* PETER, *who smiles more amiably*.] He ain't linger on my han'. He took sick—he gone.

CORONER. What did you marry him for?

LILY. Why, yo' see, boss, he like dis. Ain't yo' 'membuh how I used to hab' dem crazy fits ob misery in my stomach? I wake up in de night wid 'em. De doctor say to me, "Lily Holmes, one ob dese nights yo' goin' dead in yo' bed all by yo'self." So I t'ink I bes' marry dat nigger so as I won't go dead all by myself. But since I marry um, I gets well ob my misery, an' I ain't got no furder use for um.

DETECTIVE [*to* CORONER]. Say, are you investigating a murder or just paying social calls? [*To* LILY *and* PETER.] That'll do for you two. Get inside.

[LILY *and* PETER *hurriedly return to their room.*]

CORONER. Well, seems to me I get as much out of them as you do.

DETECTIVE. Come on, let's put the cripple and his woman through. I have a hunch that's where we'll find our bacon. [*Crosses toward* PORGY'S *door.* CORONER *follows.*]

CORONER. All right. Go ahead. I'm watching you handle them.

DETECTIVE. You won't find the cripple much of a witness. I tried to break him in the Robbins case but he wouldn't come through. [*Kicks the door open with a bang.*] Come on out, both you niggers. Step lively now!

[BESS *helps* PORGY *to seat on doorstep. Then she stands by him, the baby in her arms.* DETECTIVE *enters room.*]

CORONER [*to* PORGY]. What is your name?

[PORGY *looks at him keenly, then, reassured, smiles.*]

PORGY. Jus' Porgy. You knows me, boss. Yo' done gib' me plenty ob pennies on Meetin' Street.

CORONER. Of course! You're the goat man. I didn't know you without your wagon. Now, this nigger Crown—you knew him by sight, didn't you?

PORGY [*as though remembering with difficulty*]. Yes,

boss—I 'membuh um when he used to come here,
long ago.

CORONER. You could identify him, I suppose. [PORGY
looks blank.] You'd know him if you saw him again,
I mean.

PORGY [*slowly*]. Yes, boss, I'd know um. [*With dawning
apprehension.*] But I ain't care none 'bout see um.

[CORONER *laughs. Makes note in notebook. Puts it in
pocket. Calls to* DETECTIVE.]

CORONER. Well, I'm through. Let's pull freight.

DETECTIVE [*appears in doorway; looks knowingly at
PORGY and BESS*]. Mighty clean floor in there. Funny
it got its first scrubbing in twenty years this morning.

BESS. I scrubs my floor ebery week. You can ask these
people here 'bout um.

DETECTIVE [*sneering*]. Oh, yes! More witnesses! [*Then
triumphantly.*] But you missed the blood under the
bed this time. [*Jerks out his gun, covers* PORGY,
shouts.] Come, out with it! You killed Crown, didn't
you? Speak up, or I'll hang you sure as hell! [PORGY
and BESS *sit silent, with eyes lowered.*] Well?

BESS. I ain't understan', boss. Dere ain't no blood dere,
an' nobody ain't kill Crown in our room.

CORONER [*drawing* DETECTIVE *aside*]. For God's sake,
Duggan, let's call it a day. The cripple couldn't kill
a two-hundred-pound buck and tote him a hundred
yards.

DETECTIVE. You don't know much about niggers, do
you?

CORONER [*turning toward gate*]. Anyway, *I'm* through,
and I've got to get along. It's 'most time for my inquest.

[BESS *and* PORGY *go swiftly inside. Close door.*]

DETECTIVE [*following* CORONER *reluctantly*]. Got your
witness?

CORONER. Yeh.

[*They go out gate and off to left.*

Again the court is deserted and silent. For a moment,
there is no sound or movement. Then, in one of the
rooms, a voice is raised singing.]

VOICE.
> "Ain't it hard to be a nigger!
> Ain't it hard to be a nigger!"

[*Another voice joins, then another. In a moment, the*
empty court is ringing with the song, sung mock-
ingly, triumphantly. Another moment, and doors
and shutters begin to fly open. The Negroes come
from their doors or lean from their windows, and
the court is quickly filled with life and movement.
They are all singing.

SERENA'S *door flies open, and she comes out singing. She*
is fully dressed and carries a great basket of clothes,
which she begins to hang on line while she sings.

BESS *helps* PORGY *on to the doorstep and sits beside him,*
the baby in her arms. Both are singing. LILY *comes*
out carrying the honey tray. PETER *follows. She bal-*
ances it on his head. SCIPIO *drives* PORGY'S *goat cart*
in through archway.

Then someone breaks into a wilder tune, and all the
others instantly change to the new song.]

> "Sit down! I can't sit down!
> Sit down! I can't sit down!
> My soul's so happy dat I can't sit down!"

[*A Negro near the gate looks out, suddenly gives a loud*
hiss and waves his arms—in a warning gesture.

The song ceases abruptly. SERENA *grabs her wash from*
the line. The Negroes return swiftly and silently to
their rooms. Doors and shutters close stealthily.

BESS *attempts to help* PORGY *to his feet, but, seeing that*
they have no time, he sinks down again on his door-
step and pretends to doze. BESS *goes inside, closes*

door. SCIPIO *drives the goat back through archway.*
The court is again silent, and deserted by all but PORGY.
A POLICEMAN *enters from left. Comes in at gate. Looks
about court. Sees* PORGY, *who is apparently oblivious
of him. Crosses to* PORGY.]

POLICEMAN. Hey, you! [PORGY *opens his eyes.*] You're
Porgy, aren't you? I've got something for you. [*Holds
out paper.* PORGY *looks at it in alarm.* POLICEMAN
speaks kindly.] You needn't be afraid to take it. It's
just a summons as a witness at the coroner's inquest.
All you've got to do is view the body and tell the
coroner who it is.

[PORGY *is suddenly terror-stricken. His voice shakes.*]

PORGY. I gots to go an' look on Crown's face?

POLICEMAN. Yes, that's all.

PORGY. Wid all dem w'ite folks lookin' at me?

POLICEMAN. Oh, cheer up! I reckon you've see a dead
nigger before. It'll be all over in a few minutes.

[BESS *appears in doorway, listening, her eyes wide with
horror.*]

PORGY. Dere ain't goin' to be no nigger in dat room
'cept me?

POLICEMAN. Just you and Crown—if you still call him
one. [*Turns away.*]

PORGY [*scarcely able to speak for terror*]. Boss—I
couldn' jus' bring a 'oman wid me? I couldn't eben
carry my—my 'oman?

POLICEMAN [*slightly impatient*]. No, you can't bring
anyone. Say, you're the cripple, aren't you? I'll get
the wagon and carry you down. And as soon as
you've seen Crown, you can come home. [*Starts for
gate.*]

PORGY [*desperately*]. Boss—

POLICEMAN. Now, listen, I've summoned you, and
you've got to go, or it's contempt of court. I'll call
the wagon for you. [*Goes out gate and off to left.*]

[*As soon as he has gone, doors open stealthily. The Ne-*

groes come out and gather about PORGY, *speaking in low, frightened tones.*]

PORGY. Oh, Gawd! Whut I goin' to do?

BESS. Yo' got to go, Porgy. Mebby yo' can jus' make like to look at um an' keep yo' eye shut.

MARIA. Yo' goin' be all right, Porgy. Yo' jus' goin' to be a witness.

SPORTING LIFE. I ain't so sure ob dat. [*They all look at him in alarm.*] I don' know who done de killin'. All I knows is, when de man what done um goes in dat room, Crown' wounds begin to bleed.

PORGY [*terror-stricken*]. Oh, Jedus!

SPORTING LIFE. Dat's one way de cops got ob tellin' who done um.

PORGY [*in a panic, moaning*]. I can't look on he face! Oh, Gawd! Whut I goin' to do!

SPORTING LIFE [*taking command of the situation*]. Listen to me! Yo' do jus' as I say an' yo' won't hab to look on he face.

PORGY. What I do, Sporting Life?

SPORTING LIFE. Get busy, yo' niggers. We gots to get Porgy out ob here! Get de goat, Scipio. Here, Mingo! Yo' stan' by to gib' me a han' wid Porgy.

BESS. Don' yo' go, Porgy! He can't get away!

SPORTING LIFE. He gots to get away or dey'll hang um sure.

PORGY. Oh, Gawd!

[SCIPIO *has brought the goat cart.* SPORTING LIFE *and* MINGO *are lifting* PORGY *in while he moans with terror and mutters unintelligibly.*]

SPORTING LIFE. Now listen! Make straight for Bedens Alley. When yo' gets dere, turn in an' lie low.

MINGO. Bedens Alley too far. He'll neber make it.

SPORTING LIFE. Shut up, Mingo. I'm runnin' dis. All right, Porgy, light out!

MARIA. Quick! Start um!

BESS. Make um run!

[*The clang of the patrol wagon bell is heard approaching rapidly. The Negroes stand as though paralyzed with terror.*]

MINGO. Here dey is!

BESS. Oh, Gawd! It's too late now!

SPORTING LIFE. No, it ain't. Here, yo' niggers, get um in dere!

[*Directs them to the archway. They drive the goat through, then mass in front of archway, hiding* PORGY *from view.*

SPORTING LIFE *saunters across the court as though he had nothing to do with the affair, and awaits developments.*

The patrol bell rings more slowly as the wagon slows down, then comes to a stop at left of gate just out of view.

The POLICEMAN *again comes in at gate. Looks toward* PORGY'S *door. Crosses to it abruptly. Throws it open.*]

POLICEMAN. Hey, you there! [*Runs to gate. Calls.*] Jim! The fool's trying to make a get-away! Come on! [*Turns to the Negroes.*] Where did he go? [*They look at him with blank faces.*] All right! [*Starts for* PORGY'S *door.*] [*The* SECOND POLICEMAN *enters from left.*] You take that side, Jim. I'll take this. [*Goes into* PORGY'S *room.*]

[SECOND POLICEMAN *goes through* SERENA'S *door. As soon as both* POLICEMEN *are out of sight, the Negroes beckon to* PORGY, *who drives from archway and quickly toward gate.*

The shutters of an upper window are thrown open, and the FIRST POLICEMAN *looks out.*]

POLICEMAN. Hey, you! What d'you think you're doing? [PORGY *leans forward and wrings the goat's tail. The astonished animal leaps forward and goes out gate at a run.*] Jim! [*The* SECOND POLICEMAN *throws open shutters of room opposite and leans from window.*] Look there! [*Points to* PORGY *as he disappears off left.*] [*Both* POLICEMEN *burst into peals of laughter. The Negroes follow to gate, pushing it shut, looking out through bars.*]

SECOND POLICEMAN. He must want to have a race.

[*The two* POLICEMEN *leave the windows and a minute later come running from doors.*]

FIRST POLICEMAN. Racing the wagon! That's good!

[*They start toward gate.*]

SECOND POLICEMAN [*laying a hand on the other's arm*]. Say, let him get a start. [*They double up with laughter.*] This is going to be good!

FIRST POLICEMAN. Here, you niggers! Get away from the gate. [*The Negroes stand back. He opens gate.*] Come on now! We're off!

[*They run out gate, still shouting with laughter. They run off right. The Negroes press close about gate to watch.*

The clang of the patrol wagon bell is heard as the vehicle sets off at top speed.]

ANNIE. Oh, Gawd! Dey'll get um!

MARIA. Ef he can jus' git 'round de corner!—

LILY. —Mebby dey won't fin' um.

BESS [*turning hopelessly away*]. 'Tain't no use. [*The tension in the crowd of watchers suddenly relaxes, and their faces assume hopeless expressions.*] Dey got um?

LILY. Yeh. Dey got um.

SERENA. Dey putting him an' de goat all two in de wagon.

[BESS *sits hopelessly on her doorstep. The other Negroes return to their various rooms and tasks.* SPORTING LIFE *saunters across court and sits down on step by* BESS.

The stage is darkening. A light appears in a window.]

BESS. Oh, Gawd! Dey goin' carry um to look on Crown' face!

SPORTING LIFE [*laughing*]. Don' yo' worry none 'bout

dat, Sistuh. Dat nigger ain't a witness now. Dey goin' lock um up in de jail.

MINGO [*at gate*]. Dat's de trut'. Dey done turn de wagon 'round toward de jail.

BESS. Well, dat better'n makin' um look on Crown. [*Fearfully*.] Not for long, Sportin' Life?

SPORTING LIFE [*sympathetically*]. No, not for long. Jus' a yeah, mebbe.

BESS. A yeah.

SPORTING LIFE. Contempt ob court—dat's a serious offence. [BESS *drops her face into her hands*.] Jus' like I tol' yo'. Nobody home now but Bess an' ole Sportin' Life.

BESS. I ain't gots no time fo' yo'.

SPORTING LIFE [*laughing*]. Fo' sho' yo' has. Yo' jus' gots nice little vacation now fo' play 'round wid yo' ole frien'. Contempt ob court—dat serious offence. Dat nigger ain't be back heah fo' a yeah.

BESS [*alarmed*]. Sportin' Life, yo' ain't t'ink dey puts Porgy up fo' a yeah?

SPORTING LIFE. A yeah for sho'. Cheer up, Sistuh! Gib' me yo' han'. [*He takes her hand. She is too preoccupied to resist.*] Ole Sportin' Life got de stuff fo' scare away de lonesome blues.

[*Pours powder into her hand.* BESS *looks down at it.*]

BESS. Happy dus'! [*Gazes at the powder with fascinated horror.*] I ain't want none ob dat stuff, I tells yo'.

SPORTING LIFE. Ain't nuff ter hurt er flea.

BESS. Take dat stuff away, nigger! [*But she continues to hold it in her hand.*]

SPORTING LIFE. Jus' a little touch fo' ole time' sake. [BESS *suddenly claps her hand over her face. When she takes it away, it is empty.* SPORTING LIFE *smiles with satisfaction.*] Dat de t'ing, ain't it? An' 'membuh, dere's plenty more where dat come from. Dere's a boat to Noo Yo'k to-morruh an' I'm goin'. [*Pauses significantly.* BESS *says nothing.*] Why yo' such a fool,

Bess? What yo' goin' to do a whole yeah here by yo'self? Now's yo' chance.

[BESS *leaps to her feet, her eyes blazing. She glares at* SPORTING LIFE *with contempt and hatred.*]

BESS. Yo' low, crawlin' houn'! Git 'way from my door, I tell you'! Lef it, yo'! Rattlesnake! Dat's whut yo' is! Rattlesnake! [*While she berates him,* SPORTING LIFE *lights a cigarette, continues to sit on step.*]

SPORTING LIFE. Rave on, Sistuh! But I'll be right heah when yo' is wantin' dat second shot.

[BESS *runs suddenly past him into her room. Slams door behind her.* SPORTING LIFE *sits smiling to himself and leisurely blowing smoke rings.*]

[MARIA *comes to her doorway. Sees him. Crosses to him.*]

MARIA [*contemptuously*]. What yo' waitin' 'round here for?

SPORTING LIFE. Jus' waitin'. [*Smokes contentedly.*]

MARIA. What yo' t'ink yo' goin' to get?

SPORTING LIFE [*with shrug of shoulders*]. Uummmmmm —jus' waitin'.

MARIA [*turning scornfully away*]. Yo' don' know Bess. [*Recrosses to her shop.*]

[SPORTING LIFE *watches her till she has reached her doorstep.*]

SPORTING LIFE [*in a low voice, not intended for* MARIA *to hear*]. You don' know happy dus'.

[MARIA *does not hear. Goes into shop; closes door.* SPORTING LIFE *continues to wait. St. Michael's chimes the half hour.*]

CURTAIN

SCENE III

Chimes. Two o'clock. The court is as usual, except that PORGY'S *door and shutters are closed. Negroes are coming and going about their tasks.*

PETER, LILY, *and* MINGO *sit at* MARIA'S *table. She is busy serving them.* SCIPIO *is playing near the gate.* SERENA *sits near her door rocking a baby in her arms and singing,* "Hush little baby, don't you cry." MARIA *goes into her shop.*

PORGY *drives up outside the gate and calls softly to* SCIPIO. *His air is one of mystery.*

PORGY. Here, Scipio! Here Porgy back from jail. Open de gate an' don't make no noise.

[SCIPIO *goes reluctantly to gate, opens it, and leads the goat inside.* SERENA *looks up, sees* PORGY, *stops singing in the middle of a bar, and hunches over the baby as though to hide it. Various Negroes about the court look up, see him, and go silently into their rooms.*

PORGY *is too preoccupied with his secret to notice anything. He drives over and stops beside* MARIA'S *table.* LILY, PETER, *and* MINGO *half rise, then see that it is too late to escape, and resume their seats.*]

PORGY [*in a joyous but guarded voice*]. Shhh, don't nobody let on yet dat I is home again. I gots a surprise for Bess, an' I ain't want she to know till I gots eberyt'ing ready. [*He does not notice that the others are silent and embarrassed, and, reaching into the wagon, commences to remove packages, talking volubly all the time. He unwraps a harmonica and hands it to* SCIPIO.] Here, boy. T'row away dat ole mout' organ you gots an' start in on dis one. See, he gots picture ob brass band on um. Work on dat, an' fus'

t'ing dat yo' know, yo'll be playin' wid de orphans.
[*He turns to* LILY.] Here, gal, hol' up yo' head. Dat's
right. I nebber did like dem ole funeral bonnet Peter
buy fo' yo'. [*Unwraps a gorgeous, feather-trimmed
hat, and hands it to her.*] Now get underneat' dat,
an' make all de red bird and de blue jay jealous.

[LILY *takes hat, but is unable to speak her thanks.*
PORGY *is hurrying on, and does not notice this. He
opens a package and shakes out a gay dress, then lays
it on the table.*]

Now, dat's de style for Bess. She is one gal what always
look good in red. [*He opens a hat and places it beside the dress.*] I reckon I is de fus' nigger anybody
roun' here ebber see what go to jail po', an' leabe
dere rich. But Porgy' luck ridin' high now. Ain't nuttin' can stop um. When de buckra search me in de
jail, I all de time gots my lucky bones in my mout'
—see! an time I get settle' in my new boardin' house,
I start to go right t'rough dem odder crap-shootin'
nigger' like Glory Hallelujah. [*He takes a package
from the cart, opens it, and holds up a baby dress.*]

Now, ain't dis de t'ing! Course, de baby ain't really big
'nough for wear dress yet, but he goin' grow fas'. You
watch, he goin' be in dat dress by de fus' frost. [*Continues his story.*] Yes, suh! dere warn't no stoppin'
dem bones. Dey jus' gone whoopin' right t'rough dat
jail, a-pullin' me after 'em. And den, on de las' day,
de big buckra guard hear 'bout it, an' he come an'
say I gots to gib up de bones. But I been seein' um
roll wid de jailer in de watch house, an' I know he
weakness. I ask dat buckra if he ain't likes me to
teach um how to sing lucky to de bones 'fore I gib'
dem up, an' 'fore he git 'way I done gone t'rough um
for t'ree dollar an' seben cent an' dis shirt. [*He
proudly exhibits shirt that he is wearing. His pur-
chases are now all spread out on the table, and he
looks from them to the faces of the Negroes.*]

Now it time to call Bess. Oh, Bess. Here Porgy come home.

[*There is a moment of absolute silence.* LILY *gets to her feet, buries her face in her hands, and runs to her room.* PETER *starts to follow.* MINGO *rises and goes toward* MARIA'S *door.*]

Here, Lily, Peter, Mingo, where you all goin'? What de hell kin' ob a welcome dis for a man what been in jail for a week, an' for de contemp' ob court at dat. Oh, now I see. Well, yo' ain't gots to min' Bess an' me. All de time we wants to hab we frien' wid us. Eben now, we ain't wants to be jus' by weself.

[*They continue to withdraw. He looks about him in growing surprise, and discovers* SERENA *hunched up silently over the baby.*]

Why, hello! Dere's Serena. Yo' sho' work fas', Sistuh. I ain't been gone a week, an' yo' done gots a new baby.

[SERENA *rises hurriedly, exposing baby for first time.*] Here, hold on. Let me see dat chile. Dat's Bess's baby, ain't it? Where yo' get um? Where Bess, anyhow? She ain't answer me.

SERENA [*calling*]. Maria, come out dat cookshop. Here Porgy come home. *You* gots to talk wid um.

[PORGY *drives to his own door.*]

PORGY. Bess! Ain't yo' dere, Bess? [MARIA *comes to her doorway.* PORGY *turns to her, his eyes wide with alarm.*] Where's Bess? [MARIA *sits on her doorstep.* PORGY *turns his goat and drives over to her.*] Tell me quick. Where's Bess? [MARIA *does not answer.*] Where? Where?

MARIA [*trying to put on a bold face*]. Ain't we tell yo' all along, Porgy, dat 'oman ain't fit for yo'?

PORGY [*frantically*]. I ain't ask yo' opinion. Where's Bess? [*They all shrink from telling him. Each evades, trying to leave it to the others.*]

MARIA. Dat dirty dog Sportin' Life make us all t'ink yo' is lock up for a yeah.

PORGY. Won't somebody tell me, where Bess?

SERENA. Bess very low in she min' 'cause she t'ink yo' is gone for a yeah. [*Pauses, unable to come to the point.*]

PORGY. But I home *now*. I want to tell she I is here.

SERENA. She gone back to de happy dus' an' de red eye. She been very drunk two day'.

PORGY. But where she now? I ain't care if she was drunk. I want she now.

LILY. Dat houn' Sportin' Life was foreber hangin' 'round and gettin' she to take more dope.

PORGY [*driving again to his own door. Calls*]. Bess! Bess! Won't nobody tell me—

MARIA [*following him*]. Ain't we tellin' yo'? Dat houn' Sportin' Life—

PORGY [*desperately*]. I ain't ask 'bout Sportin' Life. Where Bess?

SERENA. She gone, Porgy. An' I done take dis chile to gib um a Christian raisin'—

PORGY. *Where* she gone?

SERENA. Dat gal ain't neber had Gawd in she heart, an' de debil get um at last.

MARIA. 'Tain't de debil. De happy dus' done for um.

PORGY [*wildly*]. You—Bess?—Yo' ain't means Bess dead?

SERENA. She worse dan dead.

LILY. Sportin' Life carry she away on de Noo Yo'k boat. [*They are all silent, gazing at* PORGY. *He, too, is silent for a moment.*]

PORGY. Where dat dey take she?

MINGO. Noo Yo'k.

MARIA. Dat's way up Nort'.

PORGY [*pointing*]. It dat way?

MARIA. It take two days by de boat. Yo' can't find um.

PORGY. I ain't say I can find um. I say, where it is?

MARIA. Yo' can't go after she. Ain't yo' hear we say yo' can't find um.

ANNIE. Ain't yo' know Noo Yo'k mos' a t'ousand mile' from here?

PORGY. Which way dat?

LILY [*pointing*]. Up Nort'—past de Custom House.

[PORGY *turns his goat and drives slowly with bowed head toward the gate.*]

MARIA. Porgy, I tells yo' it ain't no use!

LILY. Dat great big city. Yo' can't find um dere!

SERENA. Ain't we tells yo'—

[*But* PORGY *is going on toward gate as if he did not hear, and they cease to protest and stand motionless watching him. As* PORGY *reaches the gate,* SCIPIO *silently opens it.* PORGY *drives through and turns to left, as* LILY *pointed. St. Michael's chimes the quarter hour. The gate clangs shut.*]

CURTAIN

STREET SCENE

by *Elmer Rice*

First production, January 10, 1929,
at the Playhouse, New York City, with the following cast:

ABRAHAM KAPLAN, *Leo Bulgakov*
GRETA FIORENTINO, *Eleanor Wesselhoeft*
EMMA JONES, *Beulah Bondi*
OLGA OLSEN, *Hilda Bruce*
WILLIE MAURRANT, *Russell Griffin*
ANNA MAURRANT, *Mary Servoss*
DANIEL BUCHANAN, *Conway Washburne*
FRANK MAURRANT, *Robert Kelly*
GEORGE JONES, *T. H. Manning*
STEVE SANKEY, *Joseph Baird*
AGNES CUSHING, *Jane Corcoran*
CARL OLSEN, *John M. Qualen*
SHIRLEY KAPLAN, *Anna Kostant*
FILIPPO FIORENTINO, *George Humbert*
ALICE SIMPSON, *Emily Hamill*
LAURA HILDEBRAND, *Frederica Going*
MARY HILDEBRAND, *Eileen Smith*
CHARLIE HILDEBRAND, *Alexander Lewis*
SAMUEL KAPLAN, *Horace Braham*
ROSE MAURRANT, *Erin O'Brien-Moore*
HARRY EASTER, *Glenn Coulter*
MAE JONES, *Millicent Green*
DICK MCGANN, *Joseph Lee*
VINCENT JONES, *Matthew McHugh*
DR. JOHN WILSON, *John Crump*
OFFICER HARRY MURPHY, *Edward Downes*
MARSHAL JAMES HENRY, *Ellsworth Jones*
FRED CULLEN, *Jean Sidney*

Act one

SCENE—*The exterior of a "walk-up" apartment house, in a mean quarter of New York. It is of ugly brownstone and was built in the '90's. Between the pavement of large, gray flagstones and the front of the house, is a deep and narrow "areaway," guarded by a rusted, ornamental iron railing. At the right, a steep flight of rotting wooden steps leads down to the cellar and to the janitor's apartment, the windows of which are just visible above the street level. Spanning the areaway is a "stoop" of four shallow, stone steps, flanked on either side by a curved stone balustrade. Beyond the broad fourth step, another step leads to the double wooden outer doors of the house; and as these are open, the vestibule, and the wide, heavy glass-panelled entrance door beyond are visible. Above the outer doors, is a glass fanlight, upon which appears the half-obliterated house number. At the left side of the doorway is a sign which reads: "Flat To-Let. 6 Rooms. Steam Heat."*

On either side of the stoop are the two narrow windows of the ground-floor apartments. In one of the windows, at the left, is a sign bearing the legend: "Prof. Filippo Fiorentino. Music for all occasions. Also instruction." Above, are the six narrow windows of the first-floor apartments, and above that, the stone sills of the second-floor windows can just be seen.

To the left of the house, part of the adjoining building is visible: the motor entrance to a storage warehouse. Crude boarding across the large driveway and rough planks across the sidewalk and curb indicate that an excavation is in progress. On the boarding is painted in rude lettering: "Keep Out"; and at the curb is a small barrel bearing a sign with the words: "Street Closed." To the wall of the warehouse is affixed a brass plate, bearing the name: "Patrick Mulcahy Storage Warehouse Co. Inc."

To the right of the house, scaffolding and a wooden sidewalk indicate that the house next door is being demolished. On the scaffolding is a large wooden sign reading: "Manhattan House-Wrecking Corp." In the close foreground, below the level of the curb, is a mere suggestion of the street.

At rise, the house is seen in the white glare of an arc-light, which is just off-stage to the right. The windows in the janitor's apartment are lighted, as are also those of the ground-floor apartment, at the right, and the two windows at the extreme left of the first-floor. A dim, red light is affixed to the boarding of the excavation at the left.

In the lighted ground-floor window, at the right of the doorway, ABRAHAM KAPLAN *is seated in a rocking-chair, reading a Yiddish newspaper. He is a Russian Jew, well past sixty: clean-shaven, thick gray hair, hooked nose, horn-rimmed spectacles. To the left of the doorway,* GRETA FIORENTINO *is leaning out of the window. She is forty, blonde, ruddy-faced, and stout. She wears a wrapper of light, flowered material and a large pillow supports her left arm and her ample, un-corseted bosom. In her right hand is a folding paper fan, which she waves languidly.*

Throughout the act and, indeed, throughout the play, there is constant noise. The noises of the city rise, fall, intermingle: the distant roar of "L" trains, auto-mobile sirens, and the whistles of boats on the river; the rattle of trucks and the indeterminate clanking of metals; fire-engines, ambulances, musical instruments, a radio, dogs barking and human voices calling, quar-

relling, and screaming with laughter. The noises are subdued and in the background, but they never wholly cease.

A moment after the rise of the curtain, an elderly man enters at the right and walks into the house, exchanging a nod with MRS. FIORENTINO. A MAN, *munching peanuts, crosses the stage from left to right.*

A VOICE [*off-stage*]. Char-lie!

[EMMA JONES *appears at the left. She is middle-aged, tall, and rather bony. She carries a small parcel.*]

MRS. FIORENTINO [*she speaks with a faint German accent*]. Good evening, Mrs. Jones.

MRS. JONES [*stopping beneath Mrs. Fiorentino's window*]. Good evenin', Mrs. F. Well, I hope it's hot enough for you.

MRS. FIORENTINO. Ain't it joost awful? When I was through with the dishes, you could take my clothes and joost wring them out.

MRS. JONES. Me, too. I ain't got a dry stitch on me.

MRS. FIORENTINO. I took off my shoes and my corset and made myself nice and comfortable, and tonight before I go to bed, I take a nice bath.

MRS. JONES. The trouble with a bath is, by the time you're all through, you're as hot as when you started. [*As* OLGA OLSEN, *a thin, anemic Scandinavian, with untidy fair hair, comes up the cellar steps and onto the sidewalk.*] Good evenin', Mrs. Olsen. Awful hot, ain't it?

MRS. OLSEN [*coming over to the front of the stoop*]. Yust awful. Mrs. Forentiner, my hoosban' say vill you put de garbage on de doom-vaider?

MRS. FIORENTINO. Oh, sure, sure! I didn't hear him vistle. [*As* MRS. JONES *starts to cross to the stoop.*] Don't go 'vay, Mrs. Jones. [*She disappears from the window.*]

MRS. OLSEN [*pushing back some wisps of hair*]. I tank is more cooler in de cellar.

MRS. JONES [*sitting on the stoop and fanning herself with her parcel*]. Phew! I'm just about ready to pass out.

MRS. OLSEN. My baby is crying, crying all day.

MRS. JONES. Yeah, I often say they mind the heat more'n we do. It's the same with dogs. My Queenie has jes' been layin' aroun' all day.

MRS. OLSEN. The baby get new teet'. It hurt her.

MRS. JONES. Don't tell me! If you was to know what I went t'roo with my Vincent. Half the time, he used to have convulsions.

[WILLIE MAURRANT, *a disorderly boy of twelve, appears at the left, on roller skates. He stops at the left of the stoop and takes hold of the railing with both hands.*]

WILLIE [*raising his head and bawling*]. Hey, ma!

MRS. JONES [*disapprovingly*]. If you want your mother, why don't you go upstairs, instead o' yellin' like that?

WILLIE [*without paying the slightest attention to her, bawls louder*]. Hey, ma!

MRS. MAURRANT [*appearing at one of the lighted first-floor windows*]. What do you want, Willie?

[*She is a fair woman of forty, who looks her age, but is by no means unattractive.*]

WILLIE. Gimme a dime, will ya? I wanna git a cone.

MRS. MAURRANT [*to* MRS. OLSEN *and* MRS. JONES]. Good evening.

MRS. OLSEN *and* MRS. JONES. Good evenin', Mrs. Maurrant.

MRS. MAURRANT [*to* WILLIE]. How many cones did you have today, already?

WILLIE [*belligerently*]. I'm hot! All de other guys is havin' cones. Come on, gimme a dime.

MRS. MAURRANT. Well, it's the last one. [*She disappears.*]

MRS. JONES. You certainly don't talk very nice to your mother. [*To* MRS. OLSEN.] I'd like to hear one o' mine talkin' that way to me!

MRS. MAURRANT [*appearing at the window*]. Remember, this is the last one.

WILLIE. Aw right. T'row it down.

[MRS. FIORENTINO *reappears and leans out of the window again.*]

MRS. MAURRANT. Catch it!

[*She throws out a twist of newspaper.* WILLIE *scrambles for it, hastily extracts the dime, drops the newspaper on the pavement and skates off, at the left.*]

MRS. FIORENTINO [*twisting her neck upwards*]. Good evening, Mrs. Maurrant.

MRS. MAURRANT. Good evening, Mrs. Fiorentino. [*Calling after* WILLIE.] And don't come home too late, Willie!

[*But* WILLIE *is already out of earshot.*]

MRS. FIORENTINO. Why don't you come down and be sociable?

MRS. MAURRANT. I'm keeping some supper warm for my husband. [*A slight pause.*] Well, maybe I will for just a minute. [*She leaves the window. The lights in her apartment go out.*]

MRS. FIORENTINO. She has her troubles with dot Willie.

MRS. JONES. I guess it don't bother her much. [*Significantly.*] She's got her mind on other things.

MRS. OLSEN [*looking about cautiously and coming over to the left of the stoop between the two women*]. He vas comin' again today to see her.

MRS. JONES [*rising excitedly, and leaning over the balustrade*]. Who—Sankey?

MRS. OLSEN [*nodding*]. Yes.

MRS. FIORENTINO. Are you sure, Mrs. Olsen?

MRS. OLSEN. I seen him. I was doostin' de halls.

MRS. FIORENTINO. Dot's terrible!

MRS. JONES. Wouldn't you think a woman her age, with a grown-up daughter—!

MRS. OLSEN. Two times already dis veek, I seen him here.

MRS. JONES. I seen him, meself, one day last week. He was comin' out o' the house, jest as I was comin' in wit' de dog. "Good mornin', Mrs. Jones," he says to me, as if butter wouldn't melt in his mouth. "Good mornin'," says I, lookin' him straight in the eye— [*Breaking off suddenly, as the vestibule door opens.*] Be careful, she's comin'.

[MRS. MAURRANT *comes out of the house and stops, for a moment, on the top step.*]

MRS. MAURRANT. Goodness, ain't it hot! I think it's really cooler upstairs. [*She comes down the steps to the sidewalk.*]

MRS. JONES. Yeah, jes' what I was sayin', meself. I feel like a wet dish-rag.

MRS. MAURRANT. I would have liked to go to the Park concert tonight, if Rose had got home in time. I don't get much chance to go to concerts. My husband don't care for music. But Rose is more like me—just crazy about it.

MRS. JONES. Ain't she home yet?

MRS. MAURRANT. No. I think maybe she had to work overtime.

MRS. JONES. Well, all mine ever comes home for is to sleep.

MRS. FIORENTINO. The young girls nowadays—!

MRS. OLSEN. My sister was writin' me in Schweden is same t'ing—

MRS. JONES. It ain't only the young ones, either.

[*A baby is heard crying in the cellar.*]

OLSEN'S VOICE [*from the cellar*]. Ol-ga! [*A* MAN, *in a dinner jacket and straw hat, appears at the left, whistling a jazz tune. He crosses the stage and goes off at the right.*]

MRS. OLSEN [*hurrying to the right*]. I betcha the baby, she's cryin' again.

OLSEN'S VOICE. Ol-ga!

MRS. OLSEN. Yes. I come right away. [*She goes down the cellar steps.*]

MRS. JONES. What them foreigners don't know about bringin' up babies would fill a book.

MRS. FIORENTINO [*a little huffily*]. Foreigners know joost

as much as other people, Mrs. Jones. My mother had eight children and she brought up seven.

MRS. JONES [*tactfully*]. Well, I'm not sayin' anythin' about the Joimans. The Joimans is different—more like the Irish. What I'm talkin' about is all them squareheads an' Polacks—[*with a glance in* KAPLAN'S *direction*]—an' Jews.

BUCHANAN'S VOICE [*from a third story window*]. Good evening, ladies.

THE WOMEN [*in unison, looking upward*]. Oh, good evening, Mr. Buchanan.

BUCHANAN'S VOICE. Well, is it hot enough for you?

MRS. JONES. I'll say!

BUCHANAN'S VOICE. I was just saying to my wife, it's not the heat I mind as much as it is the humidity.

MRS. JONES. Yeah, that's it! Makes everything stick to you.

MRS. MAURRANT. How's your wife feeling in this weather?

BUCHANAN'S VOICE. She don't complain about the weather. But she's afraid to go out of the house. Thinks maybe she couldn't get back in time, in case —you know.

MRS. JONES [*to the other women*]. I was the same way with my Vincent—afraid to take a step. But with Mae, I was up an' out till the very last minute.

MRS. FIORENTINO [*craning her neck upward*]. Mr. Buchanan, do you think she would eat some nice mine-strone—good Italian vegetable-soup?

BUCHANAN'S VOICE. Why, much obliged, Mrs. F., but I really can't get her to eat a thing.

MRS. JONES [*rising and looking upward*]. Tell her she ought to keep up her strength. She's got two to feed, you know.

BUCHANAN'S VOICE. Excuse me, she's calling.

MRS. JONES [*crossing to the railing, at the left of* MRS. FIORENTINO]. You'd think it was him that was havin' the baby.

MRS. MAURRANT. She's such a puny little thing.

MRS. FIORENTINO [*with a sigh*]. Well, that's the way it goes. The little skinny ones have them and the big strong ones don't.

MRS. MAURRANT. Don't take it that way, Mrs. Fiorentino. You're a young woman, yet.

MRS. FIORENTINO [*shaking her head*]. Oh, well!

MRS. JONES. My aunt, Mrs. Barclay, was forty-two— [*Breaking off.*] Oh, good evenin', Mr. Maurrant!

[FRANK MAURRANT *appears, at the left, with his coat on his arm. He is a tall, powerfully-built man of forty-five, with a rugged, grim face.*]

MRS. FIORENTINO. Good evening, Mr. Maurrant.

MAURRANT. 'Evenin'. [*He goes to the stoop and seats himself, mopping his face.*] Some baby of a day!

MRS. MAURRANT. Have you been working all this while, Frank?

MAURRANT. I'll say I've been workin'. Dress-rehearsin' since twelve o'clock, with lights—in this weather. An' to-morra I gotta go to Stamford for the try-out.

MRS. MAURRANT. Oh, you're going to Stamford to-morrow?

MAURRANT. Yeah, the whole crew's goin'. [*Looking at her.*] What about it?

MRS. MAURRANT. Why, nothing. Oh, I've got some cabbage and potatoes on the stove for you.

MAURRANT. I just had a plate o' beans at the Coffee Pot. All I want is a good wash. I been sweatin' like a horse all day. [*He rises and goes up the steps.*]

MRS. FIORENTINO. My husband, too; he's sweating terrible.

MRS. JONES. Mine don't. There's some people that just naturally do, and then there's others that don't.

MAURRANT [*to* MRS. MAURRANT]. Is anybody upstairs?

MRS. MAURRANT. No. Willie's off playing with the boys. I can't keep him home.

MAURRANT. What about Rose?

MRS. MAURRANT. I think maybe she's working overtime.

MAURRANT. I never heard o' nobody workin' nights in a real-estate office.

MRS. MAURRANT. I thought maybe on account of the office being closed to-morrow— [*To the others.*] Mr. Jacobson, the head of the firm, died Tuesday, and tomorrow's the funeral, so I thought maybe—

MRS. JONES. Yeah. Leave it to the Jews not to lose a workin' day, without makin' up for it.

MAURRANT [*to* MRS MAURRANT]. She shouldn't be stayin' out nights without us knowin' where she is.

MRS. MAURRANT. She didn't say a word about not coming home.

MAURRANT. That's what I'm sayin', ain't it? It's a mother's place to know what her daughter's doin'.

MRS. FIORENTINO [*soothingly*]. Things are different nowadays, Mr. Maurrant, from what they used to be.

MAURRANT. Not in my family, they're not goin' to be no different. Not so long as I got somethin' to say.

A GIRL'S VOICE [*off-stage*]. Red Rover! Red Rover! Let Freddie come over!

[GEORGE JONES, *a short, rather plump, red-faced man, cigar in mouth, comes out of the house, as* MAURRANT *enters the vestibule.*]

JONES. Hello, Mr. Maurrant.

MAURRANT [*curtly*]. 'Evenin'. [*He enters the house.* JONES *looks after him in surprise for a moment.* MRS. MAURRANT *seats herself on the stoop.*]

JONES. Good evenin', ladies.

MRS. FIORENTINO *and* MRS. MAURRANT. Good evening, Mr. Jones.

JONES [*seating himself on the left balustrade*]. What's the matter with your hubby, Mrs. Maurrant? Guess he's feelin' the heat, huh?

MRS. MAURRANT. He's been working till just now and I guess he's a little tired.

MRS. JONES. Men are all alike. They're all easy to get along with, so long as everythin's goin' the way they want it to. But once it don't—good night!

MRS. FIORENTINO. Yes, dot's true, Mrs. Jones.

JONES. Yeah, an' what about the women?

MRS. MAURRANT. I guess it's just the same with the women. I often think it's a shame that people don't get along better together. People ought to be able to live together in peace and quiet, without making each other miserable.

MRS. JONES. The way I look at it, you get married for better or worse, an' if it turns out to be worse, why all you can do is make the best of it.

MRS. MAURRANT. I think the trouble is people don't make allowances. They don't realize that everybody wants a kind word now and then. After all, we're all human, and we can't just go along by ourselves, all the time, without ever getting a kind word.

[*While she is speaking,* STEVE SANKEY *appears at the right. He is in the early thirties, and is prematurely bald. He is rather flashily dressed, in a patently cheap, light-gray suit and a straw hat with a plaid band. As he appears,* MRS. JONES *and* MRS. FIORENTINO *exchange a swift, significant look.*]

SANKEY [*stopping at the right of the stoop and removing his hat*]. Good evening, folks! Is it hot enough for you?

THE OTHERS. Good evening.

MRS. MAURRANT [*self-consciously*]. Good evening, Mr. Sankey.

[*Throughout the scene,* MRS. MAURRANT *and* SANKEY *try vainly to avoid looking at each other.*]

SANKEY. I don't know when we've had a day like this. Hottest June fifteenth in forty-one years. It was up to ninety-four at three P.M.

JONES. Six dead in Chicago. An' no relief in sight, the evenin' paper says.

[MAURRANT *appears at the window of his apartment and stands there, looking out.*]

MRS. FIORENTINO. It's joost awful!

SANKEY. Well, it's good for the milk business. You

know the old saying, it's an ill wind that blows nobody any good.

MRS. MAURRANT. Yes. You hardly get the milk in the
morning, before it turns sour.

MRS. JONES. I'm just after pourin' half-a-bottle down
the sink.

[MAURRANT *leaves the window.*]

MRS. FIORENTINO. You shouldn't throw it away. You
should make—what do you call it?—schmier-käs'.

SANKEY. Oh, I know what you mean—pot-cheese. My
wife makes it, too, once in a while.

MRS. MAURRANT. Is your wife all right again, Mr. Sankey? You were telling me last time, she had a cold.

[MRS. JONES *and* MRS. FIORENTINO *exchange another
look.*]

SANKEY. Was I? Oh, sure, sure. That was a couple weeks
ago. Yes, sure, she's all right again. That didn't
amount to anything much.

MRS. JONES. You got a family, too, ain't you?

SANKEY. Yes. Yes, I have. Two little girls. Well, I got to
be going along. [*He goes to the left of the stoop and
stops again.*] I told my wife I'd go down to the drug-
store and get her some nice cold ginger-ale. You want
something to cool you off in this kind of weather.

MRS. JONES [*as* SANKEY *passes her*]. If you ask me, all
that gassy stuff don't do you a bit of good.

SANKEY. I guess you're right, at that. Still it cools you
off. Well, good-night, folks. See you all again. [*He
strolls off, at the left, with affected nonchalance; but
when he is almost out of sight, he casts a swift look
back at* MRS. MAURRANT. *A dowdy* WOMAN, *wheeling
a dilapidated baby carriage, appears at the left, and
crosses the stage.*]

JONES. What's his name—Sankey?

MRS. JONES. Yeah—Mr. Sankey.

MRS. MAURRANT. He's the collector for the milk company.

[AGNES CUSHING *comes out of the house. She is a thin,*

dried-up woman, past fifty.]

MISS CUSHING [*coming down the steps*]. Good evening.

THE OTHERS. Good evening, Miss Cushing.

MRS. MAURRANT. How is your mother today, Miss Cushing?

MISS CUSHING [*pausing at the left of the stoop*]. Why, she complains of the heat. But I'm afraid it's really her heart. She's seventy-two, you know. I'm just going down to the corner to get her a little ice-cream.

[*As she goes off at the left,* OLSEN, *the janitor, a lanky Swede, struggles up the cellar steps with a large, covered, tin garbage barrel. The others look around in annoyance as he bangs the garbage barrel upon the pavement.*]

OLSEN. Phew! Hot! [*He mops his face and neck with a dingy handkerchief, then lights his pipe and leans against the railing.*]

MRS. JONES [*significantly, as she crosses to the center of the stoop and sits*]. Between you and I, I don't think her mother's got long for this world. Once the heart starts goin' back on you—!

MRS. FIORENTINO. It's too bad.

MRS. MAURRANT. Poor soul! She'll have nothing at all when her mother dies. She's just spent her whole life looking after her mother.

MRS. JONES. It's not more than her duty, is it?

MRS. FIORENTINO. You could not expect that she should neglect her mother.

A VOICE [*off-stage*]. Char-lie!

MRS. MAURRANT. It's not a matter of neglecting. Only— it seems as if a person should get more out of life than just looking after somebody else.

MRS. JONES. Well, I hope to tell you, after all I've done for mine, I expect 'em to look after me in my old age.

MRS. MAURRANT. I don't know. It seems to me you might just as well not live at all, as the way she does. [*Rising, with affected casualness.*] I don't know what's become of Willie. I think I'd better walk down to

the corner and look for him. My husband don't like
it if he stays out late.

[*She goes off at the left. They all watch her, in dead silence, until she is out of earshot. Then the storm breaks.*]

MRS. JONES [*rising excitedly*]. Didja get that? Goin' to
look for Willie! Can ya beat it?

MRS. FIORENTINO. It's joost terrible!

JONES. You think she's just goin' out lookin' for this
guy Sankey?

MRS. JONES [*scornfully*]. Ain't men the limit? What do
you think he come walkin' by here for? [*Mincingly.*]
Just strolled by to get the wife a little ginger-ale. A
fat lot he cares whether his wife has ginger-ale!

MRS. FIORENTINO. Two little girls he's got, too!

JONES. Yeah, that ain't right—a bird like that, wit' a
wife an' two kids of his own.

MRS. FIORENTINO. The way he stands there and looks
and looks at her!

MRS. JONES. An' what about the looks she was givin'
him! [*Seating herself again.*] You'd think he was the
Prince of Wales, instead of a milk-collector. And
didja get the crack about not seein' him for two
weeks?

MRS. FIORENTINO. And joost today he was upstairs, Mrs.
Olsen says.

[OLSEN *approaches the stoop and removes his pipe from
his mouth.*]

OLSEN [*pointing upwards*]. Some day, her hoosban' is
killing him. [*He replaces his pipe and goes back to
his former position.*]

MRS. FIORENTINO. Dot would be terrible!

JONES. He's li'ble to, at that. You know he's got a
wicked look in his eye, dat baby has.

MRS. JONES. Well, it's no more than he deserves, the
little rabbit—goin' around breakin' up people's
homes. [*Mockingly.*] Good evenin', folks! Jes' like
Whozis on the radio.

JONES. D'ya think Maurrant is wise to what's goin' on?

MRS. JONES. Well, if he ain't, there must be somethin' the matter with him. But you never can tell about men. They're as blind as bats. An' what I always say is, in a case like that, the husband or the wife is always the last one to find out.

[MISS CUSHING, *carrying a small paper bag, hurries on, at the left, in a state of great excitement.*]

MISS CUSHING [*breathlessly, as she comes up the left of the stoop*]. Say, what do you think! I just saw them together—the two of them!

MRS. JONES [*rising excitedly*]. What did I tell you?

MRS. FIORENTINO. Where did you see them, Miss Cushing?

MISS CUSHING. Why, right next door, in the entrance to the warehouse. They were standing right close together. And he had his hands up on her shoulders. It's awful, isn't it?

JONES. Looks to me like this thing is gettin' pretty serious.

MRS. JONES. You didn't notice if they was kissin' or anythin', did you?

MISS CUSHING. Well, to tell you the truth, Mrs. Jones, I was so ashamed for her that I hardly looked at all.

JONES [*sotto voce, as the house door opens*]. Look out! Maurrant's comin'.

[*A conspirators' silence falls upon them as* MAURRANT, *pipe in mouth, comes out of the house.*]

MISS CUSHING [*tremulously*]. Good evening, Mr. Maurrant.

MAURRANT [*on the top step*]. 'Evenin'. [*To the others.*] What's become of me wife?

MRS. JONES. Why, she said she was goin' around the corner to look for Willie.

MAURRANT [*grunts*]. Oh.

MRS. JONES. They need a lot of lookin' after when they're that age.

[*A momentary silence.*]

MISS CUSHING. Well, I think I'd better get back to my mother. [*She goes up the steps.*]

MRS. JONES, MRS. FIORENTINO, *and* JONES. Good night, Miss Cushing.

MISS CUSHING. Good night. [*As she passes* MAURRANT.] Good night, Mr. Maurrant.

MAURRANT. 'Night.

[*She looks at him swiftly, and goes into the vestibule.*]

A BOY'S VOICE [*Off-stage*]. Red Rover! Red Rover! Let Mary come over!

[*As* MISS CUSHING *enters the house,* SHIRLEY KAPLAN *appears at the ground-floor window, at the extreme right, with a glass of steaming tea in her hand. She is a dark, unattractive Jewess, past thirty. She wears a light house-dress.* KAPLAN *goes on reading.*]

SHIRLEY [*to the neighbors outside; she speaks with the faintest trace of accent*]. Good evening.

THE OTHERS [*not very cordially*]. Good evenin'.

SHIRLEY. It's been a terrible day, hasn't it?

JONES *and* MRS. JONES. Yeah.

SHIRLEY [*going to the other window*]. Papa, here's your tea. Haven't you finished your paper yet? It makes it so hot, with the lights on.

KAPLAN [*lowering his newspaper*]. Oll right! Oll right! Put it out! Put it out! There is anahoo notting to read in de papers. Notting but deevorce, skendal, and moiders. [*He speaks with a strong accent, over-emphatically, and with much gesticulation. He puts his paper away, removes his glasses, and starts to drink his tea.*]

[*No one answers.* SHIRLEY *goes away from the window and puts out the lights.*]

SHIRLEY. There doesn't seem to be a breath of air anywhere.

MRS. JONES [*sotto voce*]. You wouldn't think anybody would want to read that Hebrew writin', would ya? I don't see how they make head or tail out of it, me-self.

JONES. I guess if you learn it when you're a kid—

MRS. JONES [*suddenly*]. Well, will you look at your hubby, Mrs. F.! He's sure got his hands full! [*She looks towards the left, greatly amused.* SHIRLEY *reappears at the window at the extreme right, and seats herself on the sill.*]

MRS. FIORENTINO [*leaning far out*]. Joost look at him! [*Calling.*] Lippo, be careful you don't drop any!

LIPPO [*off-stage*]. 'Allo, Margherita!

[*They all watch in amusement, as* FILIPPO FIORENTINO, *a fat Italian, with thick black hair and moustache, comes on at the left. He is clutching a violin in his left arm and balancing five ice-cream cones in his right hand.*]

LIPPO [*shouting*]. Who wanta da ice-cream cone? Nica fresha ice-cream cone!

MRS. FIORENTINO. Lippo, you will drop them!

MRS. JONES [*going up to him*]. Here, gimme your violin. [*She relieves him of the violin and he shifts two of the cones to his left hand.*]

LIPPO [*as* MRS. JONES *hands the violin to* MRS. FIORENTINO]. T'ank you, Meeses Jones. 'Ere's for you a nica, fresha ice-cream cone.

[MRS. FIORENTINO *puts the violin on a chair behind her.*]

MRS. JONES [*taking a cone*]. Why thank you very much, Mr. F.

LIPPO [*going up to the window*]. Meeses Fiorentino, 'ere's for you a nica, fresha ice-cream cone.

MRS. FIORENTINO [*taking the cone*]. It makes me too fat.

LIPPO. Ah, no! Five, ten poun' more, nobody can tell da deef! [*He laughs aloud at his own joke and crosses to the stoop.*]

MRS. JONES [*enjoying her cone*]. Ain't he a sketch, though?

LIPPO. Meester Jones, you eata da cone, ha?

JONES. Why, yeah, I will at that. Thanks. Thanks.

LIPPO. Meester Maurrant?

MAURRANT. Naw; I got me pipe.

LIPPO. You lika betta da pipe den da ice-cream? [*Crossing the stoop.*] Meesa Kaplan, nica, fresha cone, yes?

SHIRLEY. No, thanks. I really don't want any.

LIPPO. Meester Kaplan, yes?

KAPLAN [*waving his hand*]. No, no! Tenks, tenks!

MRS. JONES [*to* JONES]. You oughta pay Mr. F. for the cones.

JONES [*reluctantly reaching into his pocket*]. Why, sure.

LIPPO [*excitedly*]. Ah, no, no! I don' taka da mon'. I'm treata da whole crowd. I deedn' know was gona be such a biga crowd or I bringa doz'. [*Crossing to* OL-SEN.] Meester Olsen, you lika da cone, ha?

OLSEN. Sure. Much oblige'. [*He takes the pipe from his mouth and stolidly licks the cone.*]

LIPPO [*seating himself on the stoop, with a long sigh of relaxation*]. Aaah! [*He tastes the cone and smacking his lips, looks about for approval.*] Ees tasta good, ha?

JONES [*his mouth full*]. You betcha!

MRS. JONES. It cools you off a little.

LIPPO. Sure. Dassa right. Cool you off. [*He pulls at his clothing and sits on the stoop.*] I'ma wat, wat—like I jus' come outa da bad-tub. Ees' 'ota like hal in da Park. Two, t'ree t'ousan' people, everybody sweatin' —ees smal lika menageria.

[*While he is speaking,* ALICE SIMPSON, *a tall, spare spinster, appears at the right. She goes up the steps, enters the vestibule, and is about to push one of the buttons on the side wall.*]

MRS. JONES [*sotto voce*]. She's from the Charities. [*Coming over to the stoop and calling into the vestibule.*] If you're lookin' for Mrs. Hildebrand, she ain't home yet.

MISS SIMPSON [*coming to the doorway*]. Do you know when she'll be back?

MRS. JONES. Well, she oughta be here by now. She jus'
went aroun' to the Livingston. That's the pitcher-
theayter.

MISS SIMPSON [*outraged*]. You mean she's gone to a
moving-picture show?

OLSEN [*calmly*]. She's comin' now.

LIPPO [*rising to his feet and calling vehemently*]. Mees
Hil'brand! Hurry up! Hurry up! Ees a lady here. [*He
motions violently to her to hurry.* LAURA HILDEBRAND
appears at the right, with her two children, CHARLIE
and MARY. *She is a small, rather young woman, with
a manner of perpetual bewilderment. Both children
are chewing gum, and* MARY *comes on skipping a
rope and chanting: "Apple, peach, pear, plum, ba-
nana."* CHARLIE *carefuly avoids all the cracks in the
sidewalk.*]

MISS SIMPSON [*coming out on the steps*]. Well, good evening, Mrs. Hildebrand!

MRS. HILDEBRAND [*flustered*]. Good evening, Miss Simpson.

MISS SIMPSON. Where have you been?—to a moving-picture show?

MRS. HILDEBRAND. Yes, ma'am.

MISS SIMPSON. And where did you get the money?

MRS. HILDEBRAND. It was only seventy-five cents.

MISS SIMPSON. Seventy-five cents is a lot, when you're
being dispossessed and dependent upon charity. I
suppose it came out of the money I gave you to buy
groceries with.

MRS. HILDEBRAND. We always went, Thursday nights, to
the pictures when my husband was home.

MISS SIMPSON. Yes, but your husband isn't home. And
as far as anybody knows, he has no intention of coming home.

KAPLAN [*leaning forward out of his window*]. Ees dis
your conception of cherity?

SHIRLEY. Papa, why do you interfere?

MISS SIMPSON [*to* KAPLAN]. You'll please be good enough

to mind your own business.

KAPLAN. You should go home and read in your Bible de life of Christ.

MRS. JONES [*to* MRS. FIORENTINO]. Will you listen to who's talkin' about Christ!

MISS SIMPSON [*turning her back on* KAPLAN *and speaking to* MRS. HILDEBRAND]. You may as well understand right now that nobody's going to give you any money to spend on moving-picture shows.

LIPPO. Ah, wotsa da matter, lady? [*He thrusts his hand into his pocket and takes out a fistful of coins.*] 'Ere, you taka da mon', you go to da pitcha, ever' night. [*He forces the coins into* MRS. HILDEBRAND'S *hand.*] An' here's for da bambini. [*He gives each child a nickel.*]

MRS. FIORENTINO [*to* MRS. JONES]. Dot's why we never have money.

MRS. HILDEBRAND [*bewildered*]. I really oughtn't to take it.

LIPPO. Sure! Sure! I got plenta mon'.

MISS SIMPSON [*disgustedly*]. We'd better go inside. I can't talk to you here, with all these people.

MRS. HILDEBRAND [*meekly*]. Yes, ma'am. [*She follows* MISS SIMPSON *into the house, her children clinging to her.*]

MRS. JONES. Wouldn't she give you a pain?

LIPPO. I tella you da whola troub'. She's a don' gotta nobody to sleepa wit'.

[*The men laugh.*]

MRS. JONES [*to* MRS FIORENTINO]. Ain't he the limit!

MRS. FIORENTINO [*greatly pleased*]. Tt!

LIPPO. Somebody go sleepa wit' her, she's alla right. Meester Jones, 'ow 'bout you?

[SHIRLEY, *embarrassed, leaves the window.*]

JONES [*with a sheepish grin*]. Naw, I guess not.

LIPPO. Wot'sa matter? You 'fraid you' wife, ha? Meester Maurrant, how 'bout you?

[MAURRANT *emits a short laugh.*]

MRS. FIORENTINO [*delighted*]. Lippo, you're joost awful.

LIPPO [*enjoying himself hugely*]. Alla ri'. Ah'ma gonna go myself! [*He laughs boisterously. The others laugh too.*]

MRS. JONES [*suddenly*]. Here's your wife now, Mr. Maurrant.

[*A sudden silence falls upon them all, as* MRS. MAURRANT *approaches at the left. A swift glance appraises her of* MAURRANT'S *presence.*]

LIPPO. 'Allo, Meeses Maurrant. Why you don' come to da concerto?

MRS. MAURRANT. Well, I was waiting for Rose, but she didn't get home. [*To* MAURRANT, *as she starts to go up the steps.*] Is she home yet, Frank?

MAURRANT. No, she ain't. Where you been all this while?

MRS. MAURRANT. Why, I've been out looking for Willie.

MAURRANT. I'll give him a good fannin', when I get hold of him.

MRS. MAURRANT. Ah, don't whip him, Frank, please don't. All boys are wild like that, when they're that age.

JONES. Sure! My boy Vincent was the same way. An' look at him today—drivin' his own taxi an' makin' a good livin'.

LIPPO [*leaning on the balustrade*]. Ees jussa same t'ing wit' me. W'en Ah'm twelva year, I run away—I don' never see my parent again.

MAURRANT. That's all right about that. But it ain't gonna be that way in my family.

MRS. MAURRANT [*as* MISS SIMPSON *comes out of the house*]. Look out, Frank. Let the lady pass.

MISS SIMPSON. Excuse me.

[*They make way for her, as she comes down the steps.* MRS. MAURRANT *seats herself on the stoop.*]

LIPPO. Meeses Hil'brand, she gotta de tougha luck, ha? To-morra, dey gonna t'row 'er out in da street, ha?

MISS SIMPSON [*stopping at the right of the stoop and*

turning towards him]. Yes, they are. And if she has any place to sleep, it will only be because the Charities find her a place. And you'd be doing her a much more neighborly act, if you helped her to realize the value of money, instead of encouraging her to throw it away.

LIPPO [*with a deprecatory shrug*]. Ah, lady, no! I give 'er coupla dollar, maka 'er feel good, maka me feel good—dat don' 'urt nobody.

[SHIRLEY *reappears at the window.*]

MISS SIMPSON. Yes it does. It's bad for her character.

KAPLAN [*throwing away his cigarette and laughing aloud*]. Ha! You mek me leff!

MISS SIMPSON [*turning, angrily*]. Nobody's asking your opinion.

KAPLAN. Dot's all right. I'm taling you wit'out esking. You hoid maybe already dot poem:
      "Organized cherity, measured and iced,
      In der name of a kushus, stetistical Christ."

MISS SIMPSON [*fiercely*]. All the same, you Jews are the first to run to the Charities. [*She strides angrily off at the right.* LIPPO, *affecting a mincing gait, pretends to follow her.*]

KAPLAN [*leaning out of the window*]. Come back and I'll tal you somet'ing will maybe do good your kerecter.

MRS. FIORENTINO. Lippo!

MRS. JONES [*highly amused*]. Look at him, will ya?

LIPPO [*laughing and waving his hand*]. Goodbye, lady! [*He comes back to the stoop.*]

KAPLAN [*to the others*]. Dey toin out in de street a mudder vit' two children, and dis female comes and preaches to her bourgeois morility.

MRS. JONES [*to* MRS. FIORENTINO]. He's shootin' off his face again.

SHIRLEY. Papa, it's time to go to bed!

KAPLAN [*irritably*]. Lat me alone, Shoiley. [*Rising and addressing the others.*] Dees cherities are notting but anudder dewise for popperizing de verking-klesses. W'en de lendlords steal from de verkers a million dollars, dey give to de Cherities a t'ousand.

MAURRANT. Yeah! Well, who's puttin' her out on the street? What about the lan'lord here? He's a Jew, ain't he?

MRS. JONES. I'll say he's a Jew! Isaac Cohen!

KAPLAN. Jews oder not Jews—wot has dis got to do vit' de quastion? I'm not toking releegion, I'm toking economics. So long as de ke*pit*alist klesses—

MAURRANT [*interrupting*]. I'm talkin' about if you don't pay your rent, you gotta move.

MRS. MAURRANT. It doesn't seem right, though, to put a poor woman out of her home.

MRS. FIORENTINO. And for her husband to run away— dot vos not right either.

LIPPO. I betcha 'e's got 'nudder woman. He find a nice blonda chicken, 'e run away.

MRS. JONES. There ought to be a law against women goin' around, stealin' other women's husbands.

MRS. FIORENTINO. Yes, dot's right, Mrs. Jones.

MAURRANT. Well, what I'm sayin' is, it ain't the land-lord's fault.

KAPLAN. Eet's de folt of our economic system. So long as de institution of priwate property exeests, de verkers vill be at de moicy of de property-owning klesses.

MAURRANT. That's a lot o' bushwa! I'm a woikin' man, see? I been payin' dues for twenty-two years in the Stage-Hands Union. If we're not gettin' what we want, we call a strike, see?—and then we get it.

LIPPO. Sure! Ees same wit' me. We gotta Musician Union. We getta pay for da rehears', we getta pay for da overtime—

SHIRLEY. That's all right when you belong to a strong union. But when a union is weak, like the Teachers' Union, it doesn't do you any good.

MRS. JONES [*to* MRS. FIORENTINO]. Can y' imagine that?— teachers belongin' to a union!

KAPLAN [*impatiently*]. Oll dese unions eccomplish notting wotever. Oll dis does not toch de fondamental problem. So long as de tuls of industry are in de hands of de ke*pit*alist klesses, ve vill hev exploitation and sloms and—

MAURRANT. T' hell wit' all dat hooey! I'm makin' a good livin' an' I'm not doin' any kickin'.

OLSEN [*removing his pipe from his mouth*]. Ve got prosperity, dis coontry.

JONES. You said somethin'!

KAPLAN. Sure, for de reech is plenty prosperity! Mister Morgan rides in his yacht and upstairs dey toin a woman vit' two children in de street.

MAURRANT. And if you was to elect a Socialist president to-morra, it would be the same thing.

MRS. FIORENTINO. Yes, dot's right, Mr. Maurrant.

JONES. You're right!

KAPLAN. Who's toking about electing presidents? Ve must put de tuls of industry in de hends of de vorking-klesses and dis ken be accomplished only by a sushal revolution!

MAURRANT. Yeah? Well, we don't want no revolutions in this country, see?

[*General chorus of assent.*]

MRS. JONES. I know all about that stuff—teachin' kids there ain't no Gawd an' that their gran'fathers was monkeys.

JONES [*rising, angrily*]. Free love, like they got in Russia, huh?

[KAPLAN *makes a gesture of impatient disgust, and sinks back into his chair.*]

MAURRANT. There's too goddam many o' you Bolshevikis runnin' aroun' loose. If you don't like the way things is run here, why in hell don't you go back where you came from?

SHIRLEY. Everybody has a right to his own opinion, Mr. Maurrant.

MAURRANT. Not if they're against law and order, they

ain't. We don't want no foreigners comin' in, tellin' us how to run things.

MRS. FIORENTINO. It's nothing wrong to be a foreigner. Many good people are foreigners.

LIPPO. Sure! Looka Eetalians. Looka Cristoforo Colombo! 'E'sa firs' man discov' America—'e's Eetalian, jussa like me.

MAURRANT. I'm not sayin' anythin' about that—

OLSEN [*removing his pipe*]. Firs' man is Lief Ericson.

LIPPO [*excitedly, going towards* OLSEN]. Wassa dat?

OLSEN. Firs' man is Lief Ericson.

LIPPO. No! No! Colombo! Cristoforo Colomb'—'e'sa firs' man discov' America—ever'body knowa dat! [*He looks about appealingly.*]

MRS. JONES. Why, sure, everybody knows that.

JONES. Every kid learns that in school.

SHIRLEY. Ericson was really the first discoverer—

LIPPO [*yelling*]. No! Colomb'!

SHIRLEY. But Columbus was the first to open America to settlement.

LIPPO [*happily, as he goes back to the stoop*]. Sure, dassa wot Ah'm say—Colomb' is firs'.

OLSEN. Firs' man is Lief Ericson.

[LIPPO *taps his forehead, significantly.*]

LIPPO. Looka wot Eetalian do for America—'e build bridge, 'e build railroad, 'e build subway, 'e dig sewer. Wit'out Eetalian, ees no America.

JONES. Like I heard a feller sayin': the Eye-talians built New York, the Irish run it an' the Jews own it.

[*Laughter.*]

MRS. FIORENTINO [*convulsed*]. Oh! Dot's funny!

JONES [*pleased with his success*]. Yep; the Jews own it all right.

MAURRANT. Yeah, an' they're the ones that's doin' all the kickin'.

SHIRLEY. It's no disgrace to be a Jew, Mr. Maurrant.

MAURRANT. I'm not sayin' it is. All I'm sayin' is, what

we need in this country is a little more respect for law an' order. Look at what's happenin' to people's homes, with all this divorce an' one thing an' another. Young girls goin' around smokin' cigarettes an' their skirts up around their necks. An' a lot o' long-haired guys talkin' about free love an' birth control an' breakin' up decent people's homes. I tell you it's time somethin' was done to put the fear o' God into people!

MRS. JONES. Good for you, Mr. Maurrant!

JONES. You're damn right.

MRS. FIORENTINO. Dot's right, Mr. Maurrant!

MRS. MAURRANT. Sometimes, I think maybe they're only trying to get something out of life.

MAURRANT. Get somethin' huh? Somethin' they oughtn't to have, is that it?

MRS. MAURRANT. No; I was only thinking—

MAURRANT. Yeah, you were only thinkin', huh?

KAPLAN [*rising to his feet again*]. De family is primerily an economic institution.

MRS. JONES [*to* MRS. FIORENTINO]. He's in again.

KAPLAN. W'en priwate property is ebolished, de femily will no longer hev eny reason to exeest.

SHIRLEY. Can't you keep quiet, papa?

MAURRANT [*belligerently*]. Yeah? Is that so? No reason to exist, huh? Well, it's gonna exist, see? Children respectin' their parents an' doin' what they're told, get me? An' husbands an' wives, lovin' an' honorin' each other, like they said they would, when they was spliced—an' any dirty sheeny that says different is li'ble to get his head busted open, see?

MRS. MAURRANT [*springing to her feet*]. Frank!

SHIRLEY [*trying to restrain* KAPLAN]. Papa!

KAPLAN. Oll right! I should argue vit' a low-kless gengster.

MAURRANT [*raging*]. Who's a gangster? Why, you goddamn—! [*He makes for the balustrade.*]

MRS. MAURRANT [*seizing his arm*]. Frank!

JONES [*seizing the other arm*]. Hey! Wait a minute!
Wait a minute!

MAURRANT. Lemme go!

SHIRLEY [*interposing herself*]. You should be ashamed
to talk like that to an old man! [*She slams down the
window.*]

MAURRANT. Yeah? [*To* MRS. MAURRANT *and* JONES.] All
right, lemme go! I ain't gonna do nothin'.

[*They release him.* SHIRLEY *expostulates with* KAPLAN
and leads him away from the window.]

MRS. JONES [*who has run over to the right of the stoop*].
Maybe if somebody handed him one, he'd shut up
with his talk for a while.

LIPPO. 'E talka lika dat een Eetaly, Mussolini's gonna
geeve 'eem da castor-oil.

MRS. JONES [*laughing*]. Yeah? Say, that's a funny idea!
[*Still chuckling, she goes back to the railing at the
left of the stoop.*]

JONES. No kiddin', is that what they do?

MRS. FIORENTINO. Yes, dot's true. My husband read it to
me in the Italian paper.

MRS. MAURRANT. Why must people always be hurting
and injuring each other? Why can't they live together in peace?

MAURRANT [*mockingly*]. Live in peace! You're always
talkin' about livin' in peace!

MRS. MAURRANT. Well, it's true, Frank. Why can't people just as well be kind to each other?

MAURRANT. Then let 'im go live with his own kind.

JONES [*coming down the steps*]. Yeah, that's what I
say. [*As* MRS. JONES *laughs aloud.*] What's eatin' you?

MRS. JONES. I was just thinkin' about the castor-oil.

[MAURRANT *seats himself on the right balustrade.*]

LIPPO. Sure, 'esa funny fell', Mussolini. [*Doubling up
in mock pain.*] 'E geeve 'em da pain in da belly, dey
no can talk. [*Suddenly.*] Look! 'Eresa da boy. 'Esa
walk along da street an' reada da book. Datsa da

whola troub': reada too much book.

[*While* LIPPO *is speaking,* SAMUEL KAPLAN *appears at the left. He is twenty-one, slender, with dark, unruly hair and a sensitive, mobile face. He is hatless, and his coat is slung over one shoulder. He walks along slowly, absorbed in a book. As he approaches the stoop,* SHIRLEY, *in a kimono, appears at the closed window, opens it, and is about to go away again, when she sees* SAM.]

SHIRLEY [*calling*]. Sam!

SAM [*looking up*]. Hello, Shirley.

SHIRLEY. Are you coming in?

SAM. No, not yet. It's too hot to go to bed.

SHIRLEY. Well, I'm tired. And papa's going to bed, too. So don't make a noise when you come in.

SAM. I won't.

SHIRLEY. Good night.

SAM. Good night.

[SHIRLEY *goes away from the window.*]

SAM [*to the others, as he seats himself on the curb to the right of the stoop*]. Good evening!

SEVERAL. 'Evening.

LIPPO [*approaching* SAM]. 'Ow you lika da concerto? I see you sittin' in da fronta seat.

SAM. I didn't like it. Why don't they play some real music, instead of all those Italian organ-grinder's tunes?

LIPPO [*excitedly*]. Wotsa da matter? You don't lika da Verdi?

SAM. No, I don't. It's not music!

LIPPO. Wot you call music—da Tschaikov', ha? [*He hums derisively a few bars from the first movement of the "Symphonie Pathétique."*]

SAM. Yes, Tschaikovsky—and Beethoven. Music that comes from the soul.

MRS. MAURRANT. The one I like is— [*She hums the opening bars of Mendelssohn's "Spring Song."*]

LIPPO. Dotsa da Spreeng Song from da Mendelson.

MRS. MAURRANT. Yes! I love that. [*She goes on humming softly.*]

MRS. FIORENTINO. And the walzer von Johann Strauss. [*She hums the "Wienerwald Waltz."*]

MRS. JONES. Well, gimme a good jazz band, every time.

LIPPO [*protesting*]. Ah no! Ees not music, da jazz. Ees breaka your ear. [*He imitates the discordant blaring of a saxophone.*]

JONES [*bored*]. Well, I guess I'll be on me way.

MRS. JONES. Where are you goin'?

JONES. Just around to Callahan's to shoot a little pool. Are you comin' along, Mr. Maurrant?

MAURRANT. I'm gonna wait awhile.

[*A* MAN, *with a club-foot, appears at the right and crosses the stage.*]

MRS. JONES [*as* JONES *goes toward the right*]. Don't be comin' home lit, at all hours o' the mornin'.

JONES [*over his shoulder*]. Aw, lay off dat stuff! I'll be back in a half-an-hour. [*He goes off at the right.*]

A VOICE [*off-stage*]. Char-lie!

MRS. JONES. Him an' his pool! Tomorra he won't be fit to go to work again.

SAM [*who has been awaiting a chance to interrupt*]. When you hear Beethoven, it expresses the struggles and emotions of the human soul.

LIPPO [*waving him aside*]. Ah, ees no good, da Beethoven. Ees alla time sad, sad. Ees wanna maka you cry. I don' wanna cry, I wanna laugh. Eetalian music ees make you 'appy. Ees make you feel good. [*He sings several bars of Donna è mobile.*]

MRS. MAURRANT [*applauding*]. Yes, I like that, too.

LIPPO. Ah, ees bew-tiful! Ees maka you feela fine. Ees maka you wanna dance. [*He executes several dance steps.*]

MRS. FIORENTINO [*rising*]. Vait, Lippo, I vill give you music. [*She goes away from the window. The lights go on, in the Fiorentino apartment.*]

LIPPO [*calling after her*]. Playa Puccini, Margherita!

[*He hums an air from* "Madame Butterfly." *Then as* MRS. FIORENTINO *begins to play the waltz from* "La Bohème" *on the piano.*] Ah! "La Bohème"! Bewtiful! Whosa gona dance wit' me? Meeses Maurrant, 'ow 'bout you?

MRS. MAURRANT [*with an embarrassed laugh*]. Well, I don't know. [*She looks timidly at* MAURRANT, *who gives no sign.*]

LIPPO. Ah, come on! Dansa wit' me! [*He takes her by the hand.*]

MRS. MAURRANT. Well, all right, I will.

LIPPO. Sure, we have nica dance.

[*They begin to dance on the sidewalk.*]

LIPPO [*to* MAURRANT]. Your wife ees dansa swell.

MRS. MAURRANT [*laughing*]. Oh, go on, Mr. Fiorentino! But I always loved to dance!

[*They dance on.* SANKEY *appears, at the left, carrying a paper-bag, from which the neck of a ginger-ale bottle protrudes.* MAURRANT *sees him and rises.*]

MRS. JONES [*following* MAURRANT'S *stare and seeing* SANKEY]. Look out! You're blockin' traffic!

SANKEY [*stopping at the left of the stoop*]. I see you're having a little dance. [MRS. MAURRANT *sees him and stops dancing.* LIPPO *leans against the right balustrade, panting. The music goes on.*]

SANKEY. Say, go right ahead. Don't let me stop you.

MRS. MAURRANT. Oh, that's all right. I guess we've danced about enough. [*She goes up the steps, ill at ease.*]

SANKEY. It's a pretty hot night for dancing.

MRS. MAURRANT. Yes, it is.

SANKEY [*going towards the right*]. Well, I got to be going along. Good night, folks.

THE OTHERS [*except* MAURRANT]. Good night.

LIPPO [*as he seats himself at the left of the stoop*]. Stoppa da music, Margherita! [*The music stops.*]

[SANKEY *goes off at the right.* MRS. MAURRANT *goes quickly up the steps.*]

MAURRANT [*stopping her*]. Who's that bird?

MRS. MAURRANT. Why, that's Mr. Sankey. He's the milk-collector.

MAURRANT. Oh, he is, is he? Well, what's he hangin' around here for?

MRS. MAURRANT. Well, he lives just down the block somewhere.

MRS. JONES. He's just been down to the drug-store, gettin' some ginger-ale for his wife.

MAURRANT. Yeah? Well, what I want to know is, why ain't Rose home yet?

MRS. MAURRANT. I told you, Frank—

MAURRANT. I know all about what you told me. What I'm sayin' is, you oughta be lookin' after your kids, instead of doin' so much dancin'.

MRS. MAURRANT. Why, it's the first time I've danced in I don't know when.

MAURRANT. That's all right about that. But I want 'em home, instead o' battin' around the streets, hear me?

[*While he is speaking,* WILLIE *appears sobbing at the left, his clothes torn and his face scratched. He is carrying his skates.*]

MRS. MAURRANT [*coming down the steps*]. Why, Willie, what's the matter? [*Reproachfully, as* WILLIE *comes up to her, sniffling.*] Have you been fighting again?

WILLIE [*with a burst of indignation*]. Well, dat big bum ain't gonna say dat to me. I'll knock da stuffin's out o' him, dat's what I'll do!

MAURRANT [*tensely, as he comes down the steps*]. Who's been sayin' things to you?

WILLIE. Dat big bum, Joe Connolly, dat's who! [*Blubbering.*] I'll knock his goddam eye out, next time!

MRS. MAURRANT. Willie!

MAURRANT [*seizing* WILLIE's *arm*]. Shut up your swearin', do you hear?—or I'll give you somethin' to bawl for. What did he say to you, huh? What did he say to you?

WILLIE [*struggling*]. Ow! Leggo my arm!

MRS. MAURRANT. What difference does it make what a little street-loafer like that says?

MAURRANT. Nobody's askin' you! [*To* WILLIE.] What did he say? [*He and* MRS. MAURRANT *exchange a swift involuntary look; then* MAURRANT *releases the boy.*] G'wan up to bed now, an' don't let me hear no more out o' you. [*Raising his hand.*] G'wan now. Beat it!

[WILLIE *ducks past* MAURRANT *and hurries up the steps and into the vestibule.*]

MRS. MAURRANT. Wait, Willie, I'll go with you. [*She goes up the steps, then stops and turns.*] Are you coming up, Frank?

MAURRANT. No I ain't. I'm goin' around to Callahan's for a drink, an' if Rose ain't home when I get back, there's gonna be trouble. [*Without another glance or word, he goes off at the right.* MRS. MAURRANT *looks after him for a moment with a troubled expression.*]

MRS. MAURRANT [*entering the vestibule*]. Well, good night, all.

THE OTHERS. Good night.

[SAM *rises. As* MRS. MAURRANT *and* WILLIE *enter the house,* MRS. FIORENTINO *reappears at the window.*]

MRS. FIORENTINO. Lippo! [*She sees that something is wrong.*]

MRS. JONES. Say, you missed it all! [SAM, *about to go up the steps, stops at the right of the stoop.*]

MRS. FIORENTINO [*eagerly*]. Vat?

MRS. JONES [*volubly*]. Well, they were dancin', see? An' who should come along but Sankey!

MRS. FIORENTINO. Tt!

[*A light appears in the Maurrant apartment.*]

MRS. JONES. Well, there was the three o' them—Mr. Maurrant lookin' at Sankey as if he was ready to kill him, an' Mrs. Maurrant as white as a sheet, an' Sankey as innocent as the babe unborn.

MRS. FIORENTINO. Did he say something?

MRS. JONES. No, not till after Sankey was gone. Then he wanted to know who he was an' what he was doin' here. "He's the milk-collector," she says.

MRS. FIORENTINO. It's joost awful.

MRS. JONES. Oh, an' then Willie comes home.

LIPPO. Da boy tella 'eem 'is mamma ees a whore an' Weelie leeck 'im.

MRS. JONES. Well, an' what else is she?

SAM [*unable longer to restrain himself*]. Stop it! Stop it! Can't you let her alone? Have you no hearts? Why do you tear her to pieces like a pack of wolves? It's cruel, cruel! [*He chokes back a sob, then dashes abruptly into the house.*]

LIPPO [*rising to his feet and yelling after him*]. Wotsa matter you?

MRS. JONES. Well, listen to him, will you! He must be goin' off his nut, too.

LIPPO. 'Esa reada too mucha book. Ees bad for you.

MRS. FIORENTINO. I think he is loving the girl.

MRS. JONES. Yeah? Well, that's all the Maurrants need is to have their daughter get hooked up wit' a Jew. It's a fine house to be livin' in, ain't it, between the Maurrants upstairs, an' that bunch o' crazy Jews down here.

[*A* GIRL *appears at the left, glancing apprehensively, over her shoulder, at a* MAN *who is walking down the street behind her. They cross the stage and go off at the right.*]

MRS. JONES [*as* MRS. OLSEN *comes up the cellar steps and over to the stoop*]. Well, good night.

MRS. FIORENTINO. Good night, Mrs. Jones.

LIPPO. Goo' night, Meeses Jones.

MRS. JONES. Wait a minute, Mrs. Olsen. I'll go with you.

[MRS. JONES *and* MRS. OLSEN *enter the house.* OLSEN *yawns mightily, knocks the ashes from his pipe, and goes down the cellar steps.* WILLIE MAURRANT *leans out of the window and spits into the areaway. Then he leaves the window and turns out the light. A*

POLICEMAN *appears, at the right, and strolls across the stage.*]

LIPPO [*who has gone up the steps*]. Margherita, eef I ever ketcha you sleepin' wit' da meelkaman, Ah'm gonna breaka your neck.

MRS. FIORENTINO [*yawning*]. Stop your foolishness, Lippo, and come to bed!

[LIPPO *laughs and enters the house.* MRS. FIORENTINO *takes the pillow off the windowsill, closes the window, and starts to pull down the shade.* ROSE MAURRANT *and* HARRY EASTER *appear at the left.* ROSE *is a pretty girl of twenty, cheaply but rather tastefully dressed.* EASTER *is about thirty-five, good-looking, and obviously prosperous.*]

MRS. FIORENTINO. Good evening, Miss Maurrant.

ROSE [*as they pass the window*]. Oh, good evening, Mrs. Fiorentino.

[ROSE *and* EASTER *cross to the stoop.* MRS. FIORENTINO *looks at them a moment, then pulls down the shade and turns out the lights.*]

ROSE [*stopping at the foot of the steps*]. Well, this is where I live, Mr. Easter. [*She extends her hand.*] I've had a lovely time.

EASTER [*taking her hand*] Why, you're not going to leave me like this, are you? I've hardly had a chance to talk to you.

ROSE [*laughing*]. We've been doing nothing but talking since six o'clock. [*She tries gently to extricate her hand.*]

EASTER [*still holding it*]. No, we haven't. We've been eating and dancing. And now, just when I want to talk to you—[*He puts his other arm around her.*] Rose—

ROSE [*rather nervously*]. Please don't, Mr. Easter. Please let go. I think there's somebody coming. [*She frees herself as the house-door opens and* MRS. OLSEN *appears in the vestibule. They stand in silence, as* MRS.

OLSEN *puts the door off the latch, tries it to see that it is locked, dims the light in the vestibule and comes out on the stoop.*]

MRS. OLSEN [*as she comes down the steps*]. Goot evening, Miss Maurrant. [*She darts a swift look at* EASTER *and crosses to the cellar steps.*]

ROSE. Good evening, Mrs. Olsen. How's the baby?

MRS. OLSEN. She vas cryin' all the time. I tank she **vas** gettin' new teet'.

ROSE. Oh, the poor little thing! What a shame!

MRS. OLSEN [*as she goes down the steps*]. Yes, ma'am. Goot night, Miss Maurrant.

ROSE. Good night, Mrs. Olsen. [*To* EASTER.] She's got the cutest little baby you ever saw.

EASTER [*rather peevishly*]. Yeah? That's great. [*Taking* ROSE's *hand again.*] Rose, listen—

ROSE. I've really got to go upstairs now, Mr. Easter. It's awfully late.

EASTER. Well, can't I come up with you for a minute?

ROSE [*positively*]. No, of course not!

EASTER. Why not?

ROSE. Why, we'd wake everybody up. Anyhow, my father wouldn't like it.

EASTER. Aren't you old enough to do what you like?

ROSE. It's not that. Only I think when you're living with people, there's no use doing things you know they don't like. [*Embarrassed.*] Anyhow, there's only the front room and my little brother sleeps there. So good night, Mr. Easter.

EASTER [*taking both her hands*]. Rose—I'm crazy about you.

ROSE. Please let me go now.

EASTER. Kiss me good-night.

ROSE. No.

EASTER. Why not, hm?

ROSE. I don't want to.

EASTER. Just one kiss.

ROSE. No.

EASTER. Yes! [*He takes her in his arms and kisses her.* ROSE *frees herself and goes to the right of the stoop.*]

ROSE [*her bosom heaving.*] It wasn't nice of you to do that.

EASTER [*going over to her*]. Why not? Didn't you like it? Hm?

ROSE. Oh, it's not that.

EASTER. Then what is it, hm?

ROSE [*turning and facing him*]. You know very well what it is. You've got a wife, haven't you?

EASTER. What of it? I tell you I'm clean off my nut about you.

ROSE [*nervously, as the house-door opens*]. Look out! Somebody's coming.

[EASTER *goes to the other side of the stoop and they fall into a self-conscious silence, as* MRS. JONES *comes out of the house, leading an ill-conditioned dog.*]

MRS. JONES [*as she comes down the steps*]. Oh, good evenin' [*She stares at* EASTER, *then goes towards the right.*]

ROSE. Good evening, Mrs. Jones. It's been a terrible day, hasn't it?

MRS. JONES. Yeah. Awful. [*Stopping.*] I think your father's been kinda worried about you.

ROSE. Oh, has he?

MRS. JONES. Yeah. Well, I gotta give Queenie her exercise. Good night. [*She stares at* EASTER *again, then goes off at right.*]

ROSE. Good night, Mrs. Jones. [*To* EASTER.] I'll soon have all the neighbors talking about me.

EASTER [*going over to her again*]. What can they say, hm?—that they saw you saying good night to somebody on the front door-step?

ROSE. They can say worse than that—and what's more, they will, too.

EASTER. Well, why not snap out of it all?

ROSE. Out of what?

EASTER [*indicating the house*]. This! The whole business. Living in a dirty old tenement like this; working all day in a real-estate office, for a measly twenty-five a week. You're not going to try to tell me you like living this way, are you?

ROSE. No, I can't say that I like it especially. But maybe it won't always be this way. Anyhow, I guess I'm not so much better than anybody else.

EASTER [*taking her hand*]. Do you know what's the matter with you? You're not wise to yourself. Why, you've got just about everything, you have. You've got looks and personality and a bean on your shoulders—there's nothing you haven't got. You've got It, I tell you.

ROSE. You shouldn't keep looking at me, all the time, at the office. The other girls are beginning to pass hints about it.

EASTER [*releasing her hand, genuinely perturbed*]. Is that a fact? You see, that shows you! I never even knew I was looking at you. I guess I just can't keep my eyes off you. Well, we've got to do something about it.

ROSE [*nervously snapping the clasp of her handbag*]. I guess the only thing for me to do is to look for another job.

EASTER. Yes, that's what I've been thinking, too. [*As she is about to demur.*] Wait a minute, honey! I've been doing a little thinking and I've got it all doped out. The first thing you do is throw up your job, see?

ROSE. But—

EASTER. Then you find yourself a nice, cozy little apartment somewhere. [*As she is about to interrupt again.*] Just a minute, now! Then you get yourself a job on the stage.

ROSE. How could I get a job on the stage?

EASTER. Why, as easy as walking around the block. I've got three or four friends in the show-business. Ever hear of Harry Porkins?

ROSE. No.

EASTER. Well, he's the boy that put on Mademoiselle
Marie last year. He's an old pal of mine, and all I'd
have to say to him is: [*Putting his arm around her
shoulder.*] "Harry, here's a little girl I'm interested
in," and he'd sign you up in a minute.

ROSE. I don't think I'd be any good on the stage.

EASTER. Why, what are you talking about, sweetheart?
There's a dozen girls, right now, with their names
up in electric lights, that haven't got half your stuff.
All you got to do is go about in the right way—put
up a little front, see? Why, half the game is nothing
but bluff. Get yourself a classy little apartment, and
fill it up with trick furniture, see? Then you doll
yourself up in a flock of Paris clothes and you throw
a couple or three parties and you're all set. [*Taking
her arm.*] Wouldn't you *like* to be on Broadway?

ROSE. I don't believe I ever could be.

EASTER. Isn't it worth trying? What have you got here,
hm? This is no kind of a racket for a girl like you.
[*Taking her hand.*] You do like me a little, don't
you?

ROSE. I don't know if I do or not.

EASTER. Why, sure you do. And once you get to know
me better, you'd like me even more. I'm no Valen-
tino, but I'm not a bad scout. Why, think of all the
good times we could have together—you with a little
apartment and all. And maybe we could get us a little car—

ROSE. And what about your wife?

EASTER [*letting go her hand*]. The way I figure it is,
she doesn't have to know anything about it. She
stays up there in Bronxville, and there are lots of
times when business keeps me in New York. Then,
in the summer, she goes to the mountains. Matter
of fact, she's going next week and won't be back
until September.

ROSE [*shaking her head and going towards the stoop*].

I don't think it's the way I'd want things to be.

EASTER. Why, there's nothing really wrong about it.

ROSE. Maybe there isn't. But it's just the way I feel about it, I guess.

EASTER. Why, you'd get over that in no time. There's lots of girls—

ROSE. Yes, I know there are. But you've been telling me all along I'm different.

EASTER. Sure, you're different. You're in a class by yourself. Why, sweetheart— [*He tries to take her in his arms.*]

ROSE [*pushing him away*]. No. And you mustn't call me sweetheart.

EASTER. Why not?

ROSE. Because I'm not your sweetheart.

EASTER. I want you to be—

[*A sudden yell of pain is heard from upstairs. They both look up, greatly startled.*]

EASTER. My God, what's that—a murder?

ROSE. It must be poor Mrs. Buchanan. She's expecting a baby.

EASTER. Why does she yell like that? God, I thought somebody was being killed.

ROSE. The poor thing! [*With sudden impatience she starts up the steps.*] I've got to go now. Good night.

EASTER [*taking her hand*]. But, Rose—

ROSE [*freeing her hand quickly*]. No, I've got to go. [*Suddenly.*] Look, there's my father. There'll only be an argument if he sees you.

EASTER. All right, I'll go. [*He goes toward the left, as* MAURRANT *appears at the right.*]

ROSE [*going up to the top step*]. Good night.

EASTER. Good night. [*He goes off at the left.* ROSE *begins searching in her hand-bag for her latchkey.*]

ROSE [*as* MAURRANT *approaches*]. Hello, pop.

MAURRANT [*stopping at the foot of the steps*]. Who was that you was talkin' to?

ROSE. That's Mr. Easter. He's the manager of the office.

MAURRANT. What's he doin' here? You been out wit' him?

ROSE. Yes, he took me out to dinner.

MAURRANT. Oh, he did, huh?

ROSE. Yes, I had to stay late to get out some letters. You see, pop, the office is closed tomorrow, on account of Mr. Jacobson's funeral—

MAURRANT. Yeah, I know all about that. This is a hell of a time to be gettin' home from dinner.

ROSE. Well, we danced afterwards.

MAURRANT. Oh, you danced, huh? With a little pettin' on the side, is that it?

ROSE [*rather angrily, as she seats herself on the left balustrade*]. I don't see why you can never talk to me in a nice way.

MAURRANT. So you're startin' to go on pettin' parties, are you?

ROSE. Who said I was on a petting party?

MAURRANT. I suppose he didn't kiss you or nothin', huh?

ROSE. No, he didn't! And if he did—

MAURRANT. It's your own business, is that it? [*Going up the steps.*] Well, I'm gonna make it my business, see? Is this bird married? [ROSE *does not answer.*] I t'ought so! They're all alike, them guys—all after the one thing. Well, get this straight. No married men ain't gonna come nosin' around my family, get me?

ROSE [*rising agitatedly as the house-door opens*]. Be quiet, pop! There's somebody coming.

MAURRANT. I don't care!

[BUCHANAN *hurries out of the house. He is a small and pasty young man—a typical "white-collar slave." He has hastily put on his coat and trousers over his pajamas and his bare feet are in slippers.*]

BUCHANAN [*as he comes down the steps*]. I think the baby's coming!

ROSE [*solicitously*]. Can I do anything, Mr. Buchanan?

BUCHANAN [*as he hurries towards the left*]. No, I'm just

going to phone for the doctor.

ROSE [*coming down the steps*]. Let me do it, and you go back to your wife.

BUCHANAN. Well, if you wouldn't mind. It's Doctor John Wilson. [*Handing her a slip of paper.*] Here's his number. And the other number is her sister, Mrs. Thomas. And here's two nickels. Tell them both to come right away. She's got terrible pains. [*Another scream from upstairs.*] Listen to her! I better go back. [*He dashes up the steps and into the house.*]

ROSE. Oh, the poor woman! Pop, tell ma to go up to her. Hurry!

MAURRANT. Aw, all right. [*He follows* BUCHANAN *into the house.* ROSE *hurries off at the left, just as* MAE JONES *and* DICK MCGANN *appear.* MAE *is a vulgar shop-girl of twenty one;* DICK, *a vacuous youth of about the same age.* MAE *is wearing* DICK'S *straw hat and they are both quite drunk.*]

MAE [*to* ROSE]. Hello, Rose. What's your hurry?

ROSE [*without stopping*]. It's Mrs. Buchanan. I've got to phone to the doctor. [*She hurries off.*]

DICK [*as they approach the stoop*]. Say, who's your little friend?

MAE. Oh, that's Rose Maurrant. She lives in the house.

DICK. She's kinda cute, ain't she?

MAE [*seating herself on the stoop*]. Say, accordin' to you, anythin' in a skirt is kinda cute—providin' the skirt is short enough.

DICK. Yeah, but they ain't any of 'em as cute as you, Mae.

MAE [*yawning and scratching her leg*]. Yeah?

DICK. Honest, I mean it. How 'bout a little kiss? [*He puts his arms about her and plants a long kiss upon her lips. She submits with an air of intense boredom.*]

DICK [*removing his lips*]. Say, you might show a little en-thoo-siasm.

MAE [*rouging her lips*]. Say, you seem to think I oughta hang out a flag every time some bozo decides to wipe off his mouth on me.

DICK. De trouble wit' you is you need another little snifter. [*He reaches for his flask.*]

MAE. Nope! I can't swaller any more o' that rotten gin o' yours.

DICK. Why, it ain't so worse. I don't mind it no more since I had that brass linin' put in me stomach. Well, happy days! [*He takes a long drink.*]

MAE [*rising indignantly*]. Hey, for God's sake, what are you doin'—emptyin' the flask?

DICK [*removing the flask from his lips*]. I t'ought you didn't want none.

MAE. Can't you take a joke? [*She snatches the flask from him and drains it, kicking out at* DICK, *to prevent his taking it from her.*]

DICK [*snatching the empty flask*]. Say, you wanna watch your step, baby, or you're li'ble to go right up in a puff o' smoke.

MAE [*whistling*]. Phew! Boy! I feel like a t'ree alarm fire! Say, what de hell do dey make dat stuff out of?

DICK. T'ree parts dynamite an' one part army-mule. Dey use it for blastin' out West.

MAE [*bursting raucously into a jazz tune*]. Da-da-da-da-dee! Da-da-da-da-dee! [*She executes some dance steps.*]

DICK. Say, shut up, will ya'? You'll be wakin' the whole neighborhood.

MAE [*boisterously*]. What the hell do I care? Da-da-da-da-dee! Da-da-da-da-dee! [*Suddenly amorous, as she turns an unsteady pirouette.*] Kiss me, kid!

DICK. I'll say!

[*They lock in a long embrace.* SAM, *coatless, his shirt-collar open, appears at the window, watches the pair for a moment, and then turns away, obviously disgusted. They do not see him.*]

DICK [*taking* MAE's *arm*]. Come on!

MAE. Wait a minute! Where y' goin'?

DICK. Come on, I'm tellin' ya! Fred Hennessy gimme

de key to his apartment. Dere won't be nobody dere.

MAE [*protesting feebly*]. I oughta go home. [*Her hand to her head.*] Oh, baby! Say, nail down dat sidewalk, will ya?

DICK. Come on!

[ROSE *appears at the left.*]

MAE. Sweet papa! [*She kisses* DICK *noisily; then bursts into song again.*]. Da-da-da-da-dee! Da-da-da-da-dee! [*As they pass* ROSE.] Hello, Rose. How's de milkman?

DICK [*raising his hat with drunken politeness*]. Goo' night, sweetheart.

[*They go off at the left,* MAE'S *snatches of song dying away in the distance.* ROSE *stands still, for a moment, choking back her mortification.*]

BUCHANAN'S VOICE. Miss Maurrant, did you get them?

ROSE [*looking up*]. Why yes, I did. The doctor will be here right away. And Mrs. Thomas said it would take her about an hour.

[VINCENT JONES *appears at the right and stops near the stoop. He is a typical New York taxicab driver, in a cap.* ROSE *does not see him.*]

BUCHANAN'S VOICE. She's got terrible pains. Your mother's up here with her. [MRS. BUCHANAN *is heard calling faintly.*] I think she's calling me.

[ROSE *goes towards the stoop and sees* VINCENT.]

VINCENT. Hello, Rosie.

ROSE. Good evening. [*She tries to pass, but he blocks her way.*]

VINCENT. What's your hurry?

ROSE. It's late.

VINCENT. You don't wanna go to bed, yet. Come on, I'll take you for a ride in me hack. [*He puts his arm about her.*]

ROSE. Please let me pass.

[SAM *appears at the window. They do not see him.*]

VINCENT [*enjoying* ROSE'S *struggle to escape*]. You got a lot o' stren'th, ain't you? Say, do you know you're gettin' fat? [*He passes one hand over her body.*]

ROSE. Let me go, you big tough.

SAM [*simultaneously*]. Take your hands off her! [*He climbs quickly out of the window and onto the stoop.* VINCENT, *surprised, releases* ROSE *and steps to the sidewalk.* ROSE *goes up the steps.* SAM, *trembling with excitement and fear, stands on the top step.* VINCENT *glowers up at him.*]

VINCENT. Well, look who's here! [*Mockingly.*] Haster gesehn de fish in de Bowery? [*Menacingly.*] What de hell do you want?

SAM [*chokingly*]. You keep your hands off her!

VINCENT. Yeah? [*Sawing the air with his hands.*] Oi, Jakie! [*He suddenly lunges forward, seizes* SAM'S *arm, pulls him violently by the right hand down the steps and swings him about, so that they stand face to face, to the left of the stoop.* ROSE *comes down between them.*] Now what o' ya got t' say?

ROSE. Let him alone!

SAM [*inarticulately*]. If you touch her again—

VINCENT [*mockingly*]. If I touch her again—! [*Savagely.*] Aw, shut up, you little kike bastard! [*He brushes* ROSE *aside and putting his open hand against* SAM'S *face, sends him sprawling to the pavement.*]

ROSE [*her fists clenched*]. You big coward.

VINCENT [*standing over* SAM]. Get up, why don't you?

ROSE [*crossing to* SAM]. If you hit him again, I'll call my father.

VINCENT [*as* MRS. JONES *and the dog appear at the right*]. Gee, don't frighten me like dat. I got a weak heart. [*He is sobered, nevertheless.* SAM *picks himself up.*]

VINCENT [*as* MRS. JONES *approaches*]. Hello, ma.

MRS. JONES [*with maternal pride*]. Hello, Vincent. What's goin' on here?

VINCENT. Oh, just a little friendly argument. Ikey Finkelstein don't like me to say good evenin' to his girl friend.

ROSE. You'd better keep your hands to yourself here-after.

VINCENT. Is dat so? Who said so, huh?

MRS. JONES. Come on, Vincent. Come on upstairs. I saved some stew for you.

VINCENT. All right, I'm comin'. [*To* ROSE.] Good night, dearie. [*He makes a feint at* SAM, *who starts back in terror.* VINCENT *laughs.*]

MRS. JONES. Aw, let 'im alone, Vincent.

VINCENT [*as he goes up the steps*]. Who's touchin' him? A little cockroach like dat ain't woit' my time. [*To* ROSE.] Some sheik you picked out for yourself! [*He enters the vestibule and opens the door with his latchkey.*]

MRS. JONES [*going up the steps*]. You seem to have plenty of admirers, Miss Maurrant. [*Passing on the top step.*] But I guess you come by it natural.

[ROSE *does not reply.* MRS. JONES *follows* VINCENT *into the house.* ROSE *averts her head to keep back the tears.* SAM *stands facing the house, his whole body quivering with emotion. Suddenly he raises his arms, his fists clenched.*]

SAM [*hysterically, as he rushes to the foot of the stoop*]. The dirty bum! I'll kill him!

ROSE [*turning and going to him*]. It's all right, Sam. Never mind.

SAM [*sobbing*]. I'll kill him! I'll kill him! [*He throws himself on the stoop and, burying his head in his arms, sobs hysterically.* ROSE *sits beside him and puts her arm about him.*]

ROSE. It's all right, Sam. Everything's all right. Why should you pay any attention to a big tough like that? [SAM *does not answer.* ROSE *caresses his hair and he grows calmer.*] He's nothing but a loafer, you know that. What do you care what he says?

SAM [*without raising his head*]. I'm a coward.

ROSE. Why no, you're not, Sam.

SAM. Yes, I am. I'm a coward.

ROSE. Why, he's not worth your little finger, Sam. You wait and see. Ten years from now, he'll still be driving a taxi and you—why, you'll be so far above him, you won't even remember he's alive.

SAM. I'll never be anything.

ROSE. Why, don't talk like that, Sam. A boy with your brains and ability. Graduating from college with honors and all that! Why, if I were half as smart as you, I'd be just so proud of myself!

SAM. What's the good of having brains, if nobody ever looks at you—if nobody knows you exist?

ROSE [*gently*]. I know you exist, Sam.

SAM. It wouldn't take much to make you forget me.

ROSE. I'm not so sure about that. Why do you say that, Sam?

SAM. Because I know. It's different with you. You have beauty—people look at you—you have a place in the world—

ROSE. I don't know. It's not always so easy, being a girl —I often wish I were a man. It seems to me that when you're a man, it's so much easier to sort of—be yourself, to kind of be the way you feel. But when you're a girl, it's different. It doesn't seem to matter what you are, or what you're thinking or feeling—all that men seem to care about is just the one thing. And when you're sort of trying to find out just where you're at, it makes it hard. Do you see what I mean? [*Hesitantly.*] Sam, there's something I want to ask you— [*She stops.*]

SAM [*turning to her*]. What is it, Rose?

ROSE. I wouldn't dream of asking anybody but you. [*With a great effort.*] Sam, do you think it's true— what they're saying about my mother?

[SAM *averts his head, without answering.*]

ROSE [*wretchedly*]. I guess it is, isn't it?

SAM [*agitatedly*]. They were talking here, before—I couldn't stand it any more! [*He clasps his head and, springing to his feet, goes to the right of the stoop.*] Oh, God, why do we go on living in this sewer?

ROSE [*appealingly*]. What can I do, Sam? [SAM *makes a helpless gesture.*] You see, my father means well enough, and all that, but he's always been sort of strict and—I don't know—sort of making you freeze up, when you really wanted to be nice and loving. That's the whole trouble, I guess; my mother never had anybody to really love her. She's sort of gay and happy-like—you know, she likes having a good time and all that. But my father is different. Only—the way things are now—everybody talking and making remarks, all the neighbors spying and whispering—it sort of makes me feel— [*She shudders.*] I don't know—!

SAM [*coming over to her again*]. I wish I could help you, Rose.

ROSE. You do help me, Sam—just by being nice and sympathetic and talking things over with me. There's so few people you can really talk to, do you know what I mean? Sometimes, I get the feeling that I'm all alone in the world and that—

[*A scream of pain from* MRS. BUCHANAN.]

ROSE [*springing to her feet*]. Oh, just listen to her!

SAM. Oh, God!

ROSE. The poor thing! She must be having terrible pains.

SAM. That's all there is in life—nothing but pain. From before we're born, until we die! Everywhere you look, oppression and cruelty! If it doesn't come from Nature, it comes from humanity—humanity trampling on itself and tearing at its own throat. The whole world is nothing but a blood-stained arena, filled with misery and suffering. It's too high a price to pay for life—life isn't worth it! [*He seats himself despairingly on the stoop.*]

ROSE [*putting her hand on his shoulder*]. Oh, I don't know, Sam. I feel blue and discouraged sometimes,

too. And I get a sort of feeling of, oh, what's the use.
Like last night. I hardly slept all night, on account of
the heat and on account of thinking about—well, all
sorts of things. And this morning, when I got up, I
felt so miserable. Well, all of a sudden, I decided I'd
walk to the office. And when I got to the Park, everything looked so green and fresh, that I got a kind of
feeling of, well, maybe it's not so bad, after all. And
then, what do you think?—all of a sudden, I saw a
big lilac-bush, with some flowers still on it. It made
me think about the poem you said for me—remember?—the one about the lilacs.

SAM [*quoting*].

> "When lilacs last in the dooryard bloom'd
>   And the great star early droop'd in the west-
>   ern sky in the night,
>   I mourn'd and yet shall mourn, with ever-
>   returning Spring."

[*He repeats the last line.*]

>   I mourn'd and yet shall mourn, with ever-
>   returning Spring? Yes!

ROSE. No, not that part. I mean the part about the
farmhouse. Say it for me, Sam. [*She sits at his feet.*]

SAM.

> "In the door-yard, fronting an old farm-house,
>   near the white-washed palings,
>   Stands the lilac-bush, tall-growing, with
>   heart-shaped leaves of rich green,
>   With many a pointed blossom, rising delicate,
>   with the perfume strong I love,
>   With every leaf a miracle—and from this bush
>   in the door-yard,
>   With delicate-color'd blossoms and heart-
>   shaped leaves of rich green,
>   A sprig with its flower I break."

ROSE [*eagerly*]. Yes, that's it! That's just what I felt like
doing—breaking off a little bunch of the flowers. But
then I thought, maybe a policeman or somebody

would see me, and then I'd get into trouble; so I didn't.

BUCHANAN'S VOICE. Miss Maurrant! Miss Maurrant!

[SAM *and* ROSE *spring to their feet and look up.*]

ROSE. Yes?

BUCHANAN'S VOICE. Do you mind phoning to the doctor again? She's getting worse.

ROSE. Yes, sure I will. [*She starts to go.*] Wait! Maybe this is the doctor now.

BUCHANAN'S VOICE [*excitedly as* DR. WILSON *appears at the left*]. Yes, that's him. Mrs. Maurrant! Tell her the doctor's here! Doctor, I guess you're none too soon.

DR. WILSON [*a seedy, middle-aged man in a crumpled Panama*]. Plenty of time. Just don't get excited.

[*He throws away his cigarette and enters the vestibule. The mechanical clicking of the door-latch is heard as* DR. WILSON *goes into the house.*]

ROSE. I hope she won't have to suffer much longer.

MAURRANT [*appearing at the window, in his undershirt*]. Rose!

ROSE [*rather startled*]. Yes, pop, I'll be right up.

MAURRANT. Well, don't be makin' me call you again, d'ya hear?

ROSE. I'm coming right away.

[MAURRANT *leaves the window.*]

ROSE. I'd better go up now, Sam.

SAM. Do you have to go to bed when you're told, like a child?

ROSE. I know, Sam, but there's so much wrangling goes on all the time, as it is, what's the use of having any more? Good night, Sam. There was something I wanted to talk to you about, but it will have to be another time.

[*She holds out her hand.* SAM *takes it and holds it in his.*]

SAM [*trembling and rising to his feet*]. Rose, will you kiss me?

ROSE [*simply*]. Why, of course I will, Sam.

[*She offers him her lips. He clasps her in a fervent embrace, to which she submits but does not respond.*]

ROSE [*freeing herself gently*]. Don't be discouraged about things, Sam. You wait and see—you're going to do big things some day. I've got lots of confidence in you.

SAM [*turning away his head*]. I wonder if you really have, Rose?

ROSE. Why, of course, I have! And don't forget it! Good night. I hope it won't be too hot to sleep.

SAM. Good night, Rose.

[*He watches her, as she opens the door with her latch-key and goes into the house. Then he goes to the stoop and seating himself, falls into a reverie. A PO-LICEMAN appears at the right and strolls across, but SAM is oblivious to him. In the distance, a home-comer sings drunkenly. A light appears in the MAUR-RANT hall-bedroom, and a moment later ROSE comes to the window and leans out.*]

ROSE [*calling softly*]. Hoo-hoo! Sam! [SAM *looks up, then rises.*] Good night, Sam.

[*She wafts him a kiss.*]

SAM [*with deep feeling*]. Good night, Rose dear.

[*She smiles at him. Then she pulls down the shade. SAM looks up for a moment, then resumes his seat. A scream from* MRS. BUCHANAN *makes him shudder. A deep rhythmic snoring emanates from the Fiorentino apartment. A steamboat whistle is heard. The snoring in the Fiorentino apartment continues. SAM raises his clenched hands to heaven. A distant clock begins to strike twelve.* SAM'S *arms and head drop forward.*]

THE CURTAIN FALLS SLOWLY

Act two

*Daybreak, the next morning. It is still quite dark and
comparatively quiet. The rhythmic snoring in the* FIOR-
ENTINO *apartment is still heard, and now and then a
distant "L" train or speeding automobile. A moment
after the rise of the curtain,* JONES *appears, at the
right on his way home from the speakeasy. He reels
slightly, but negotiates the steps and entrance-door
without too much difficulty. It grows lighter—and nois-
ier. The street-light goes out. The* OLSEN *baby begins to
cry. An alarm clock rings. A dog barks. A canary begins
to sing. Voices are heard in the distance. They die out
and other voices are heard.*

The house-door opens and DR. WILSON *comes out,
passing* JONES *at the top of the stoop.* DR. WILSON *stands
on the steps and yawns the yawn of an over-tired man.
Then he lights a cigarette and goes towards the left.*

BUCHANAN'S VOICE. Doctor!

DR. WILSON [*stopping and looking up*]. Well?

BUCHANAN'S VOICE. What if she does wake up?

DR. WILSON [*sharply*]. She won't, I've told you! She's too
exhausted. The best thing you can do is lie down and
get some sleep yourself.

[*As he goes off at the left,* MAE *and* DICK *appear. They
walk slowly and listlessly and far apart.*]

DICK [*as they reach the stoop*]. Well, goo' night.

MAE [*with a yawn, as she finds her latch-key*]. Goo'
night. [*Going up the steps and looking towards the
Fiorentino apartment.*] Aw, shut up, you wop!

DICK [*his dignity wounded*]. How 'bout kissin' me good
night?

MAE [*venomously, from the top step*]. For God's sake,

ain't you had enough kissin' for one night!

[*She enters the vestibule and puts the key in the lock. The ringing of an alarm clock is heard.*]

DICK [*raising his voice*]. Well, say, if that's the way you feel about it—

MAE. Aw, go to hell!

[*She enters the house. The alarm clock has stopped ringing.*]

DICK. You dirty little tart!

[*He stands muttering to himself for a moment, then goes off at the right, passing the* POLICEMAN, *who looks at him suspiciously. The sounds of a Swedish quarrel are heard from the janitor's apartment. The baby is still crying. As the* POLICEMAN *goes left, a* MILKMAN *appears, whistling and carrying a rack of full milk-bottles.*]

THE POLICEMAN. Hello, Louie.

[*The snoring in the Fiorentino apartment stops.*]

THE MILKMAN. Hello, Harry. Goin' to be another scorcher.

THE POLICEMAN. You said it.

[*He goes off at the left.*]

[*The* MILKMAN *crosses to the cellar steps.* MAE *appears, at the hall bedroom window of the Jones apartment, and removes her dress over her head. The* MILKMAN, *about to go down the steps, sees her and stops to watch.* MAE, *about to slip out of her step-ins, sees him, throws him an angry look and pulls down the shade. The* MILKMAN *grins and goes down the cellar steps.* CHARLIE HILDEBRAND *comes out of the house. He is chewing gum and as he comes out to the top of the stoop, he scatters the wrappings of the stick of gum on the stoop. Then he jumps down the four steps of the stoop in one jump, and goes off at the left, pulling the chewing-gum out in a long ribbon, and carefully avoiding all the cracks in the pavement. A* YOUNG WORKMAN, *carrying a kit of tools and a tin lunch-box, appears at the left, extinguishes the red*

*light on the excavation, and opening the door, goes
in. A* TRAMP *comes on at the right and shuffles across.
He sees a cigar butt on the pavement, picks it up and
pockets it, as he exits at the left.* ROSE, *in her nightgown, appears at the window, yawns slightly and disappears. It is daylight now. The baby stops crying.*
MRS. OLSEN *comes up the cellar steps. She goes up the
stoop, turns out the light in the vestibule, and takes
the door off the latch. The* MILKMAN *comes up the
cellar steps, his tray laden with empty bottles and
goes off, whistling, at the left.* SAM, *coatless, a book
in his hand, appears at the window. He looks out for
a moment, then climbs out on the stoop, looks up at*
ROSE'S *window, then seats himself and begins to read.*
WILLIE *comes out of the house.*]

WILLIE [*chanting, as he comes down the steps*]. Fat, Fat,
the water-rat, Fifty bullets in his hat.

SAM. Hello, Willie. Is Rose up yet?

WILLIE [*without stopping or looking at him*]. Yeah. I
don't know. I guess so.

[*He turns a somersault and goes off at left, continuing
his chanting.* SAM *glances up at* ROSE'S *window again,
then resumes his book.* MRS. JONES *and her dog come
out of the house.*]

MRS. JONES [*haughtily, as she comes down the steps*].
Mornin'.

SAM [*scarcely looking up from his book*]. Good morning.

[MRS. JONES *and the dog go off at the right. A middle-
aged workman, carrying a large coil of wire, appears
at the left and goes to the door of the excavation.*
MRS. OLSEN *comes out of the house and exits into the
basement.*]

THE WORKMAN [*calling*]. You down there, Eddie?

A VOICE [*from the depths*]. Yeah!

THE WORKMAN. All right!

[*He climbs down into the excavation.* ROSE *comes to*

window and pulls up the shade. WILLIE *and* CHARLIE *can be heard, offstage left, engaged in an earnest conversation.*]

CHARLIE [*offstage*]. He could not!

WILLIE [*offstage*]. He could so!

[*They appear at left. Each has under his arm a paper-bag, from which a loaf of bread protrudes.*]

CHARLIE. I'll betcha he couldn't.

WILLIE. I'll betcha he could.

CHARLIE. I'll betcha a million dollars he couldn't.

WILLIE. I'll betcha five million dollars he could. Hold that! [*He hands* CHARLIE *his loaf of bread and turns a cart-wheel.*] Bet you can't do it.

CHARLIE. Bet I can.

[*He puts both loaves of bread on the pavement, attempts a cart-wheel and fails.*]

WILLIE [*laughing raucously*]. Haw-haw! Told you you couldn't!

CHARLIE. Can you do this?

[*He turns a back somersault.*]

WILLIE. Sure—easy! [*He turns a back somersault. They pick up their loaves again.* WILLIE'S *drops out of the bag, but he dusts it with his hand and replaces it.*] How many steps can you jump up?

CHARLIE. Three. [*He jumps up three steps.*]

WILLIE. I can do four.

CHARLIE. Let's see you.

[WILLIE, *the bread under his arm, jumps up the four steps, undisturbed by* SAM'S *presence. He drops the bread, and is about to replace it in the bag, but gets a better idea. He inflates the bag and explodes it with a blow of his fist.* CHARLIE *looks on, in admiration and envy.*]

ROSE [*appearing at the window*]. Willie, we're waiting for the bread.

WILLIE [*holding it up*]. All right! Can'tcha see I got it?

[*He enters the house followed by* CHARLIE.]

SAM [*rising*]. Hello, Rose.

ROSE. Hello, Sam.

SAM. Come down.

ROSE. I haven't had breakfast yet. [*Calling into the room.*] Yes! He's on his way up.

MISS CUSHING [*coming out of the house*]. Good morning.

[*She looks inquiringly from* SAM *to* ROSE.]

SAM [*impatiently*]. Good morning.

[*A middle-aged nun appears at the right, accompanied by a scrawny child of about fourteen. They walk across the stage.*]

ROSE. I'm going to Mr. Jacobson's funeral. [*Calling into the room.*] Yes, I'm coming. [*To* SAM.] Breakfast's ready. I'll be down as soon as the dishes are done.

[*She disappears.* SAM *looks up at the window for a moment, then begins to read again.* MRS. FIORENTINO *appears at the window, at the extreme left, with a double armful of bedding, which she deposits upon the window-sill. Then she goes away again.*]

SHIRLEY [*appearing at the window*]. Sam, breakfast is ready.

SAM. I don't want any breakfast.

SHIRLEY. What do you mean, you don't want any breakfast? What kind of a business is that, not to eat breakfast?

SAM. Do I have to eat breakfast, if I don't want to?

SHIRLEY. You've got your head so full of that Rose Maurrant upstairs that you don't want to eat or sleep or anything any more.

SAM. If I don't feel like eating, why should I eat? [*Bursting out.*] You're always telling me: "Eat!" "Don't eat!" "Get up!" "Go to bed!" I know what I want to do, without being told.

SHIRLEY. I don't see, just when you're graduating from college, why you want to get mixed up with a little batzimer like that!

SAM. It's always the same thing over again with you. You never can get over your race prejudice. I've told you a hundred times that the Jews are no better than anybody else.

SHIRLEY. I'm not talking about that! Look at the kind of family she comes from. What's her father? Nothing but an illiterate rough-neck. And her mother—

SAM [*indignantly*]. Are you starting, too?

KAPLAN'S VOICE. Shoi-ley!

SHIRLEY. Wait a minute, papa's calling. [*Into the room.*] All right, papa! [*To* SAM.] Come in, Sam, or papa will be making long speeches again.

SAM [*impatiently*]. All right! All right! I'll come.

[*A young shopgirl, smiling to herself, appears at the right and walks across the stage.* SAM *rises and goes into the house.* SHIRLEY *leaves the window.* BU-CHANAN, *emerging from the house, collarless and un-shaven, encounters* SAM *in the vestibule.*]

BUCHANAN [*eagerly*]. Good morning!

SAM [*abruptly*]. Good morning.

[*He enters the house.* BUCHANAN *looks back at him, then comes down the steps.* MRS. FIORENTINO *raises the drawn shade and opens the window.*]

MRS. FIORENTINO. Good morning, Mr. Buchanan.

BUCHANAN. Oh, good morning, Mrs. Fiorentino. [*Going over to the left balustrade.*] I guess you know that the baby came last night, don't you?

MRS. FIORENTINO. No! I did not hear a vord about it.

BUCHANAN. Why, I thought she'd wake up the whole neighborhood, the way she was yelling. Three-thirty this morning the baby came. I been up the whole night.

[*An old* LETTER-CARRIER, *coatless, appears at the right.*]

MRS. FIORENTINO. A boy, is it?

BUCHANAN. No, it's a little girl. I guess we'll call her Mary, after my mother.

LETTER-CARRIER [*going up the steps*]. Mornin'.

MRS. FIORENTINO. Good morning. Any letters for me?

LETTER-CARRIER [*from the top of the steps*]. No, not a thing.

BUCHANAN [*turning toward him*]. I was just telling Mrs. Fiorentino, I had a little addition to my family last night.

LETTER-CARRIER. Your first, is it?

BUCHANAN [*hastening to explain*]. Well, we've only been married a little over a year.

LETTER-CARRIER. Well, I've had seven, an' I'm still luggin' a mail-bag at sixty-two.

[*He goes into the vestibule and puts the mail into the letter-boxes.*]

MRS. FIORENTINO. How is your wife?

BUCHANAN. Well, she had a pretty hard time of it. Her sister's up there with her. And Mrs. Maurrant was up, nearly all night. I don't know what we'd have done without her.

LETTER-CARRIER [*coming down the steps*]. It don't pay to let 'em have their own way too much. That's where I made my mistake.

[*As the* LETTER-CARRIER *goes off at the left,* LIPPO *appears at the window behind his wife, and tickles her.*]

MRS. FIORENTINO [*startled*]. Lippo!

BUCHANAN. Morning. I was just telling your wife—

MRS. FIORENTINO. Lippo, what do you think? Mr. Buchanan has a little girl!

LIPPO. Ah, dotsa fine! Margherita, why you don' have da baby, ha?

MRS. FIORENTINO [*abruptly*]. I must go and make the coffee.

[*She goes away from the window.* OLSEN *comes half-way up the steps and leans against the railing, smoking his pipe.*]

A VOICE [*offstage left*]. Oh-h! Corn! Sweet corn!

LIPPO. Ees funny t'ing. You gotta de leetle, skeeny wife and she's hava da baby. My Margherita she's beeg an' fat an' she no can hava da baby.

BUCHANAN. Well, that's the way o' the world, I guess.

[*As he goes off, at the left, an* ICE-MAN *appears, trundling a three-wheeled cart, filled with ice.*]

LIPPO. Buon giorno, Mike.

MIKE. Buon giorno, signore. Come sta?

LIPPO. Benissimo. Fa molto caldo ancora, oggi.

MIKE. Si, si, signore. Bisognera abbastanza ghiaccio. Twen'y fi' cent, ha?

LIPPO. No, no, è troppo.

MIKE. Twen'y cent? Eesa melta fas'.

LIPPO. Alla right. Gimme twen'y cent.

MIKE. Si, si, signore. Sure.

[*As he wheels the cart to the cellar-entrance and begins to chop a block of ice, a man in shirt-sleeves strides in from the left and stops at the curb, as though seeing someone in a house across the street.*]

THE MAN [*angrily*]. Well, what about it? We've been waiting a half an hour!

A VOICE. I'll be right over!

THE MAN. Yeah? Well, make it snappy! [*He strides off at the left, muttering angrily.* ROSE *comes out of the house and stands in the doorway, looking for* SAM. *Then she comes out on the stoop and peers into the Kaplan apartment. As she turns away, she sees* LIPPO.]

ROSE [*crossing to the left of the stoop*]. Good morning.

LIPPO. Gooda mornin', Meesa Maurrant.

[MIKE *goes down into the cellar, with a chunk of ice.*]

ROSE. It's awful hot again, isn't it?

LIPPO. You don' like?

ROSE. I don't sleep very well, when it's so hot.

LIPPO. No? Ah'm sleepa fine. Een Eetaly, where Ah'm born, is much more 'ot like 'era. Een summer, ees too 'ot for workin'. Ees too 'ot only for sleepin'. W'en Ah'm leetla boy, Ah'm sleepa, sleepa, whola day. I don't wear no clo's—nawthin' only leetle short pair pants. I lay down on groun' under da lemon-tree, Ah'm sleepa whola day.

ROSE. Under a lemon-tree! That must have been nice.

LIPPO. Ees smella sweet, lemon-tree. Where Ah'm born ees t'ousan' lemon-tree. Lemon an' olive an' arancia.

ROSE. Oh, that must be lovely!

LIPPO. Ah, ees bew-tiful! Ees most bew-tiful place in whole worl'. You hear about Sorrent', ha?

ROSE. No, I don't think I ever did.

LIPPO [*incredulously*]. You never hear about Sorrent'?

ROSE. No, I don't know much about geography. Is it a big place?

LIPPO. Ees not vera beeg—but ever'body know Sorrent'. Sorrento gentile! La bella Sorrento! You hear about Napoli—Baia di Napoli?

ROSE. Oh yes, the Bay of Naples! Is it near there?

LIPPO. Sure, ees on Bay of Napoli. Ees bew-tiful! Ees alla blue. Sky blue, water blue, sun ees shina alla time.

ROSE. Oh, how lovely.

[MIKE *comes up the cellar steps, chops another block of ice, and goes down the cellar steps with it.*]

LIPPO. An' ees Vesuvio, too. You hear about Vesuvio?— ees beeg volcano.

ROSE. Oh yes, sure. I saw a picture once, called The Last Days of Pompeii, and it showed Mount Vesuvius, with smoke coming out of the top.

LIPPO. Da's right. An' night-time, ees fire come out, maka da sky red.

ROSE. Didn't it frighten you?

LIPPO. Ah no, ees nawthin' to be afraid. Ees jus' volcano.

ROSE. I'd love to go to Italy. It must be awfully pretty. But I don't suppose I ever will.

LIPPO. W'y sure! Some day you gonna marry reech feller; 'e's take you Eetaly—ever'where.

ROSE. I guess there's not much chance of that. Rich fellows aren't going around looking for girls like me to marry. Anyhow, I don't think money is everything, do you?

LIPPO. Ees good to hava money. Da's w'y Ah'm come to America. Een Eetaly, ees bewtiful, but ees no money. 'Ere ees not bewtiful, but ees plenty money. Ees better to 'ave money.

[*An elderly* MAN, *in the gray uniform of a special officer, comes out of the house, filling his pipe from a tobacco-box.*]

THE MAN. Good mornin'.

ROSE. Good morning, Mr. Callahan. [*The* MAN *drops the empty tobacco-tin on the sidewalk and goes off slowly at the left.*] I don't think I'd be happy, just marrying a man with money, if I didn't care for him, too.

LIPPO [*laughing*]. Wotsa matter, ha? You lova da leetla kike, ha?

ROSE. Why no, I don't. I don't love anybody—at least, I don't think I do. But it's not on account of his being a Jew.

LIPPO. No, ees no good—Jew. 'E's only t'ink about money, money—alla time money.

ROSE. But Sam isn't like that, a bit. He's only interested in poetry and things like that.

[*The* ICE-MAN *comes up out of the cellar and trundles off his cart at the right.*]

MRS. FIORENTINO [*calling*]. Lippo! Breakfast!

LIPPO [*calling*]. Alla right, Margherita! [*To* ROSE.] You marry fella wit' lot o' money. Ees much better.

[*He goes away from the window as* MISS CUSHING *appears at the left, carrying a paper-bag.*]

ROSE. How's your mother today, Miss Cushing?

MISS CUSHING. She's not feeling so good today.

ROSE. It's too bad she's not feeling well.

MISS CUSHING. I'm afraid it's her heart. At her age, you know—!

[*As she enters the house,* TWO COLLEGE GIRLS *of nineteen appear at the right.*]

FIRST GIRL [*as they appear*]. I don't understand it.

SECOND GIRL. Convex is this way; and concave is this way.

FIRST GIRL. That I know.

SECOND GIRL. When you're near-sighted, they give you convex glasses, and when you're far-sighted, they give you concave.

FIRST GIRL. That I didn't know.

SECOND GIRL. Of course, you know it. Didn't we have it in psychology?

FIRST GIRL [*as they disappear at the left*]. I don't remember.

[WILLIE *comes out of the house on his way to school. He is hatless, and carries his books under his arm.*]

ROSE [*intercepting him at the top of the stoop*]. Why, Willie, the way you look! Your collar's all open.

WILLIE. I know it! De button came off.

ROSE. Why didn't you ask ma to sew it on for you?

WILLIE. She ain't dere. She's up at Buchanan's.

ROSE. Well, wait till I see if I have a pin. [*She searches in her hand-bag.*]

WILLIE [*starting down the steps*]. Aw, it's all right de way it is.

ROSE [*following him to the sidewalk*]. No, it isn't. You can't go to school like that. [*Producing a safety-pin.*] Now, hold still while I fix it.

WILLIE [*squirming*]. Aw, fer de love o' Mike—!

ROSE. You'll get stuck, if you don't hold still. There, that looks better now. And you didn't comb your hair, either.

WILLIE [*trying to escape*]. Say, lemme alone, can'tcha?

ROSE [*taking a comb out of her hand-bag and combing his hair*]. You can't go to school looking like a little street-loafer.

WILLIE. Aw, you gimme a pain in de—

ROSE. You're getting big enough to comb your own hair, without being told. There! Now, you look very nice.

WILLIE. So's your old man!

[*He runs towards the left kicking the empty tobacco tin ahead of him, then stops, turns, and deliberately rumples his hair.*]

ROSE [*indignantly, as* WILLIE *runs off*]. Why, Willie!

[MRS. JONES *and the dog appear at right.* OLSEN *knocks the ashes out of his pipe and goes down into the cellar.* MRS. MAURRANT *comes out of the house.*]

ROSE. Hello, ma.

MRS. JONES [*at the steps*]. Good mornin'.

ROSE *and* MRS. MAURRANT. Good morning, Mrs. Jones.

MRS. JONES. How's little Mrs. Buchanan gettin' on?

MRS. MAURRANT. Well, she's sleeping now, poor thing. She was so worn out she just went off into a sound sleep. I really didn't think, last night, she'd have the strength to pull through it.

MRS. JONES. Well, it's somethin' we all got to go through. I been through enough with mine, I hope to tell you. Not that they didn't turn out all right.

MRS. MAURRANT. I wouldn't give up having mine for anything in the world.

MRS. JONES. Well, after all, what more does any woman want than watchin' her kids grow up an' a husband to look out for her?

MRS. MAURRANT. Yes, that's true.

MRS. JONES. Yes, and the world would be a whole lot better off, if there was more that lived up to it. [*Starting up the steps.*] Well, I gotta get my Mae up out o' bed. Gawd knows what time she got in this mornin'. [*She enters the vestibule, then stops and turns.*] If you don't mind my bein' so bold, Mrs. Maurrant— an' I don't mind sayin' it in front of your daughter, either—I'd think twice before I'd let any child o' mine bring a Jew into the family.

ROSE [*with a show of temper*]. I don't see what it has to do with you, Mrs. Jones.

MRS. JONES. There's no need to get huffy about it. I'm only advisin' you for your own good. I'm sure it don't make no difference to me what you do. Come on, Queenie. [*She goes into the house.*]

ROSE. Well, of all the nerve I ever heard in my life—! She and those wonderful children of hers!

MRS. MAURRANT [*coming half way down the steps*]. The best way is not to pay any attention to her. There's lots of people like that in the world—they never seem to be happy, unless they're making trouble for somebody. Did Willie go to school?

ROSE. Yes, he did. It's awful the way he goes around, looking like a little tough. And the language he uses, too.

MRS. MAURRANT. I know. I just don't seem able to manage him any more.

ROSE. I sometimes wonder if it wouldn't be better for us all, if we moved out to the suburbs somewhere—you know, some place in Jersey or Staten Island.

MRS. MAURRANT. I don't think pop would do it. [*As* MAURRANT *comes out of the house, carrying a much-battered satchel.*] Are you leaving now, Frank?

MAURRANT [*from the top of the stoop*]. Looks like it, don't it? Where you been all this while?

MRS. MAURRANT. Why, you know where I've been, Frank—up to Mrs. Buchanan's.

MAURRANT. Yeah? An' where you goin' now?

MRS. MAURRANT. Just around to Kraus's to get a chicken. I thought I'd make her some chicken-soup, to give her strength.

MAURRANT. Say, how about lookin' after your own home an' lettin' the Buchanans look after theirs?

MRS. MAURRANT. All I'm trying to do is to be a little neighborly. It's the least anybody can do, with the poor thing hardly able to lift her hand.

MAURRANT. That's all right about that! [*Coming down the steps.*] A woman's got a right to stay in her own home, lookin' after her husband an' children.

MRS. MAURRANT [*going towards him*]. What else have I been doing all these years, I'd like to know?

MAURRANT. Well, just see that you don't forget it, that's all—or there's li'ble to be trouble.

MRS. MAURRANT [*putting her hand on his arm*]. All right, Frank. Don't say any more, please. When will you be back—to-morrow?

MAURRANT. I don't know when I'll be back. Whenever I'm t'roo wit' me work—that's when. What are you so anxious to know for, huh?

MRS. MAURRANT. Why, I just asked, that's all.

MAURRANT. Oh, you just asked, huh? Just in case somebody wanted to come aroun' callin', is that it?

MRS. MAURRANT. No, it isn't. It isn't anything of the kind. You got no right to talk to me like that in front of my own daughter. You got no right. No, you haven't! [*She turns away and hurries off abruptly at the left.*]

ROSE. Ma! [*She starts to run after her mother.*]

MAURRANT [*imperiously*]. Come back here, you! [ROSE *hesitates.*] Come back, hear me? [ROSE *turns and comes slowly back.*] You stay right here.

[*He puts down his satchel and takes a flask from his pocket.*]

ROSE. Why do you talk to her like that?

MAURRANT. Nobody's askin' you.

ROSE. If you were only a little nicer to her, maybe everything would be different.

MAURRANT. Yeah? Where's she got any kick comin'? Ain't I always been a good husband to her? Ain't I always looked after her?

[*He takes a drink.*]

ROSE. It's not that, pop. It's somebody to be sort of nice to her that she wants—sort of nice and gentle, the way she is to you. That's all it is.

MAURRANT [*turning to her*]. So she's got you headed the same way, has she? Goin' out nights with married men, huh?

ROSE. You don't need to worry about me, pop. I can take care of myself, all right.

MAURRANT. No daughter o' mine ain't gonna go that way. I seen too many o' those kind around the theayter.

ROSE. Things are different nowadays, pop. I guess maybe you don't realize that. Girls aren't the way they used to be—sort of soft and helpless. A girl nowadays knows how to look out for herself. But not her, pop; she needs somebody to look after her.

MAURRANT. Aw, can all that talk! You been listenin' to them Bolshevikis, that's the trouble. But I'm gonna keep you straight, by God, or I'll know the reason why.

ROSE. I guess I've got a right to think about things for myself.

MAURRANT. Yeah? Well, don't let me ketch that other bozo comin' around here, either—that's all I got to say.

ROSE [*hesitantly, going up to him*]. Pop, listen—couldn't we get a little house somewhere—Queens or somewhere like that?

MAURRANT. What's the idea?

ROSE. Well, I don't know. I sort of thought it would be nice for all of us. And maybe if ma had a nice little home and some real nice neighbors—do you see what I mean?

MAURRANT. This place suits me all right.

ROSE. You can get some real nice little houses that don't cost such an awful lot. And I wouldn't mind helping to pay for it. And once we had it all fixed up—

MAURRANT. Forget it! I don' know when I'll be back. [*As he starts to go right.*] An' remember what I tol' you, hear?

MRS. JONES [*appearing at her window with a tin dustpan*]. Good mornin', Mr. Maurrant. You off on a little trip?

MAURRANT [*curtly*]. Yeah. [*He goes off.* MRS. JONES *empties the dustpan out of the window and goes away.* KAPLAN *comes out of the house, a bundle of news-*

*papers under his arm. He walks slowly and painfully,
with the aid of a heavy stick.*]

KAPLAN [*at the foot of the steps*]. Vy do you look so sed,
hm?

ROSE [*turning and sitting on the right balustrade*]. Oh,
good morning, Mr. Kaplan.

KAPLAN. A young girl, like you, should not look so sed.

ROSE. I'm not sad, especially, only—

KAPLAN. You got troubles, hm?

ROSE. I don't know. It's just sort of everything.

KAPLAN. Velt-schmerz you got, hm? Vit' my boy Sem
is de same t'ing. Dees vay you feel only ven you are
young. Ven you gat old like me, you tink only:
"Moch longer I von't be here."

ROSE. Why should things be the way they are, Mr. Kaplan? Why must people always be fighting and having
troubles, instead of just sort of being happy together?

KAPLAN. My dear young leddy, ef I could enser dis quastion, I would be de greatest benefactor thet de verld
hes ever known. Dees is som't'ing vich all de phi-
losophers hev been unable to enser. De ones thet believe in God, say de davil is responsible; and de ones
thet don't believe in God, say 'uman nature is responsible. It is my opinion thet most unheppiness
can be traced to economic cosses and thet—

[CHARLIE *and* MARY HILDEBRAND *have come out of the
house, carrying their school-books.*]

MARY. Hello.

ROSE. Hello, Mary. Hello, Charlie.

CHARLIE. Hello.

MARY [*chattily, as they reach the sidewalk*]. We're going to be dispossessed today.

ROSE. What a shame!

MARY. Yes, ma'am. My father went away and so we
couldn't pay the rent.

CHARLIE [*tugging at her arm*]. Aw, come on, Mary.

ROSE. Have you another place to live, Mary?

MARY. No, ma'am. But Miss Simpson, from the Charities, says she'll find us a place. She says we must learn to be less extravagant.

CHARLIE. Come ahead, will you?

MARY. I'm going to school now. Good-bye.

ROSE. Good-bye.

[*The children go off, at the left.*]

KAPLAN. More trobles!

ROSE. I know. Isn't it awful to think of them being turned out in the street like that?

KAPLAN. In a ciwilized verld, soch t'ings could not heppen.

ROSE. You mean if there were different laws?

KAPLAN. Not laws! We got already too many laws. Ve must hev ection, not laws. De verking-klesses must t'row off de yoke of ke*pit*alism, and ebolish wage-slavery.

ROSE. But wouldn't people still be unkind to each other and fight and quarrel among themselves?

KAPLAN. My dear young leddy, so long as ve keep men in slevery, dey vill behave like sleves. But wance ve establish a verld based upon 'uman needs and not upon 'uman greed—

ROSE. You mean people will begin being nice to each other and making allowances and all?

KAPLAN. All dees vill come. Wot ve hev now is a wicious soicle. On de one hend, we hev a rotten economic system—

ROSE. Excuse me, here's my mother. [*She goes towards the left as* MRS. MAURRANT *approaches, a paper package in her hand.* KAPLAN *goes off at the right.*]

MRS. MAURRANT [*as* ROSE *comes up to her*]. Did he go? [*They stop on the pavement, at the left of the stoop.*]

ROSE. Yes.

MRS. MAURRANT. I got a little chicken, to make Mrs. Buchanan some soup.

ROSE. He had a flask with him, ma. I hope he doesn't start drinking.

MRS. MAURRANT. What did he say—anything?

ROSE. No, only the way he always talks. I tried to talk to him about buying a house somewheres, but he wouldn't listen.

MRS. MAURRANT. No, I knew he wouldn't.

ROSE. It doesn't seem to be any use trying to get him to listen to anything.

MRS. MAURRANT. It's always been that way. I've always tried to be a good wife to him, Rose. But it never seemed to make any difference to him.

ROSE. I know, ma.

MRS. MAURRANT. And I've tried to be a good mother, too.

ROSE. I know, ma. I know just the way you feel about it.

MRS. MAURRANT [*appealingly*]. Do you, Rose?

ROSE. Yes, ma, I do. Honest I do.

MRS. MAURRANT. I've always tried to make a nice home for him and to do what's right. But it doesn't seem to be any use.

ROSE. I know, ma. [*Hesitantly.*] But it's on account of— [*She stops.*]

MRS. MAURRANT. Are you going to start, too? Are you going to start like all the others? [*She turns away and bursts into tears.*]

ROSE [*fondling her*]. Don't, ma. Please don't.

MRS. MAURRANT. I thought you'd be one that would feel different.

ROSE. I do, ma—really I do.

MRS. MAURRANT. What's the good of being alive, if you can't get a little something out of life? You might just as well be dead.

ROSE. Look out, ma. Somebody's coming.

[*A smartly-dressed girl, with one side of her face covered with cotton and adhesive tape, appears at the left and crosses the stage. At the same time,* JONES *comes out of the house.* ROSE *and* MRS. MAURRANT *stand in awkward silence, as he comes down the stoop and approaches them.*]

JONES. Well, is it hot enough for you today?

ROSE. It's awful, isn't it?

JONES [*as he goes towards the left*]. You said it. Still along about January, we'll all be wishin' we had a little o' this weather. [*He exits.* MRS. MAURRANT *goes towards the stoop.*]

ROSE. Ma, listen. If I say something, will you listen to me?

MRS. MAURRANT. Yes, sure I will, Rose. I'll listen to anything you say, only—

ROSE. Well, what I was thinking was, if he didn't come around here so much, maybe. Do you see what I mean, ma?

MRS. MAURRANT [*constrainedly*]. Yes, Rose.

ROSE [*putting her arm around her*]. It's on account of all that's going around—everybody in the whole house. You see what I mean, don't you, ma?

MRS. MAURRANT. Every person in the world has to have somebody to talk to. You can't live without somebody to talk to. I'm not saying that I can't talk to you, Rose, but you're only a young girl and it's not the same thing.

ROSE. It's only on account of pop. I'm scared of what he's likely to do, if he starts drinking.

MRS. MAURRANT. Well, I'll see, Rose. Sometimes I think I'd be better off if I was dead.

ROSE. If there was only something I could do.

MRS. MAURRANT. There isn't anything anybody could do. It's just the way things are, that's all.

[BUCHANAN *appears at the left. They turn and face him as he approaches.*]

MRS. MAURRANT. Oh, Mr. Buchanan, I got a little chicken, so that I could make her some good, nourishing soup.

BUCHANAN. Well, say, you got to let me pay you for it.

MRS. MAURRANT. Oh, never mind about that. We'll have the chicken for supper tonight. Did you have her medicine made up?

BUCHANAN. Yes, I got it right here. I called up the office and they told me not to come down today.

MRS. MAURRANT. Well, that's very nice. It'll be a comfort to her to have you around.

BUCHANAN. Yes, that's what I thought, too. Well, I'd better be getting upstairs. [*He goes up the steps.*]

MRS. MAURRANT. I'll be up later, with the soup.

BUCHANAN. Well, thanks. [*Stopping at the top of the stoop and turning to her.*] You've been a mighty good neighbor, Mrs. Maurrant. [*He enters the house.*]

MRS. MAURRANT. He's an awful nice young feller—so nice and gentle. And he's always trying to be so helpful. It makes you feel sort of sorry for him.

[SHIRLEY *comes out of the house, carrying a large wicker bag, which contains her lunch and school-books. She takes a postcard out of the mail-box.*]

MRS. MAURRANT [*going up the steps*]. Well, I'd better go and start this chicken. Are you coming home for lunch, Rose?

ROSE. Yes. I'll be back as soon as the funeral's over.

MRS. MAURRANT. Oh, all right. [*As she sees* SHIRLEY.] Good morning.

SHIRLEY [*coming out of the vestibule, reading the postcard*]. Good morning.

ROSE. Good morning.

[MRS. MAURRANT *goes into the house. The shade of* MAE'S *window flies up and she is seen, for an instant, dressed only in her step-ins. She yawns noisily and turns away from the window.*]

ROSE [*seating herself on the stoop*]. It's another awful day, isn't it?

SHIRLEY. Yes, and when you have to keep forty children quiet—! Well, thank goodness, in two weeks, school closes. Otherwise, I think I'd go crazy.

ROSE. Well, you get a nice long vacation, anyhow.

SHIRLEY. Not much vacation for me. I'm taking Summer courses at Teachers' College. [*She looks at* ROSE *a moment, hesitates, and then comes down the steps.*]

Miss Maurrant, if you don't mind, I want to talk to you about my brother, Sam.

ROSE. Why certainly, Miss Kaplan.

SHIRLEY. I guess you know he's only finishing college this month—

ROSE. Yes, of course, I do.

SHIRLEY. Then he has to go three years to law-school and pass the bar examination, before he can be a full-fledged lawyer.

ROSE. Yes, it takes a long time.

SHIRLEY. A long time and lots of money. And before a young lawyer begins to make his own living, that takes a long time, too. It will be ten years, maybe, before he's making enough to support himself and a family. [*Looking away.*] Then it's time enough for him to think about marriage.

ROSE. You don't mean me and Sam, Miss Kaplan?

SHIRLEY. Yes, that's just what I mean.

ROSE. Why, we're just good friends, that's all.

SHIRLEY. I know how it is with a boy like Sam, Miss Maurrant. He thinks he's a man already; but he's nothing but a boy. If you're such a good friend, you shouldn't take his mind away from his work.

ROSE. But I haven't meant to, Miss Kaplan—honest I haven't.

SHIRLEY. I've had to work hard enough to get him as far as he is. And I have my father to take care of, too. The few dollars he makes, writing for the radical papers, don't even pay the rent. Believe me, every dollar I make goes.

ROSE. I know. Sam's often told me how much he owes to you.

SHIRLEY. He doesn't owe me anything. I don't care about the money. Only he should be thinking about his work and not about other things.

ROSE. Yes, he should be thinking about his work. But don't you think there are other things in the world, too, besides just work?

SHIRLEY. Don't you think I know that? I know that just as well as you do. Maybe you think I'm only an old-maid school-teacher, without any feelings.

ROSE. Oh. I don't—really I don't!

SHIRLEY [*turning her head away*]. Maybe I'm not a movie vamp, with dimples—but I could have had my chances, too. Only, I wanted to give Sam an education.

ROSE. I haven't tried to vamp Sam, honestly I haven't. We just seemed sort of naturally to like each other.

SHIRLEY. Why must you pick out Sam? You could get other fellows. Anyhow, it's much better to marry with your own kind. When you marry outside your own people, nothing good ever comes of it. You can't mix oil and water.

ROSE. I don't know. I think if people really care about each other—

SHIRLEY. He's nothing but a baby. He sees a pretty face and, right away, he forgets about everything else.

ROSE [*with a flash of temper*]. I know I haven't as much brains as Sam, or as you, either, if that's what you mean.

SHIRLEY [*contritely, going towards her*]. I didn't mean to hurt your feelings. I haven't got anything against you. Only, he's all I've got in the world. What else have I got to live for?

SAM [*appearing at the extreme right window, with a cup of coffee and a piece of coffee-cake*]. Hello, Rose.

ROSE. Hello, Sam.

SHIRLEY [*in a low tone*]. Please don't tell him what I said. [SAM *goes to the other window*.]

ROSE. Oh no, I won't.

[SHIRLEY *hurries off at the left*.]

ROSE [*rising and turning towards* SAM]. Sam—

SAM [*holding out the coffee-cake*]. Want some coffee-cake?

ROSE. No. [*Going up the steps*.] Sam, there's something I want to ask you, before I forget. Is there any special way you have to act in a synagogue?

SAM [*eating throughout*]. In a synagogue?

ROSE. Yes. The funeral I'm going to is in a synagogue, and I thought there might be some special thing you have to do. Like in church, you know, a girl is always supposed to keep her hat on.

SAM. I don't know. I've never in my life been in a synagogue.

ROSE. Didn't you ever go to Sunday-school, or anything like that?

SAM. No.

ROSE. That's funny. I thought everybody went once in a while. How about when your mother died?

SAM. She was cremated. My parents were always rationalists.

ROSE. Didn't they believe in God or anything?

SAM. What do you mean by God?

ROSE [*puzzled*]. Well—you know what I mean. What anybody means—God. Somebody that sort of loves us and looks after us, when we're in trouble.

SAM [*sitting on the window-sill*]. That's nothing but superstition—the lies that people tell themselves, because reality is too terrible for them to face.

ROSE. But, Sam, don't you think it's better to believe in something that makes you a little happy, than not to believe in anything and be miserable all the time?

SAM. There's no such thing as happiness. That's an illusion, like all the rest.

ROSE. Then, what's the use of living?

SAM [*brushing the last crumbs off his hands*]. Yes, what is the use?

ROSE. Why, you oughtn't to talk like that, Sam—a person with all the talent and brains that you've got. I know things aren't just the way you want them to be. But they aren't for anybody. They aren't for me, either.

SAM. Then, why don't we get out of it, together?

ROSE. I don't see just how we could do that, Sam.

SAM. It would be easy enough—ten cents' worth of carbolic acid.

ROSE. Why, Sam, you don't mean kill ourselves!

SAM. Is your life so precious to you that you want to cling to it?

ROSE. Well, yes. I guess it is.

SAM. Why? Why? What is there in life to compensate for the pain of living?

ROSE. There's a lot. Just being alive—breathing and walking around. Just looking at the faces of people you like and hearing them laugh. And seeing the pretty things in the store-windows. And rough-housing with your kid brother. And—oh, I don't know— listening to a good band, and dancing—Oh, I'd hate to die! [*Earnestly.*] Sam, promise you won't talk about killing yourself, any more.

SAM. What difference would it make to you, if I did?

ROSE. Don't talk like that, Sam! You're the best friend I've ever had. [*She puts her hand on his.*]

SAM. I can't think of anything but you.

ROSE. There's something I want to ask your advice about, Sam. It's about what I started to tell you about, last night. A man I know wants to put me on the stage.

SAM [*releasing her hand and drawing back*]. What man?

ROSE. A man that works in the office. He knows a manager and he says he'll help me get started. You see, what I thought was, that if I could only get out of here and have a decent place to live and make a lot of money, maybe everything would be different, not only for me, but for ma and pop and Willie.

SAM. But don't you know what he wants, this man?

ROSE. Nobody gives you anything for nothing, Sam. If you don't pay for things in one way, you do in another.

SAM. Rose, for God's sake, you mustn't!

[VINCENT JONES *comes out of the house.*]

ROSE [*seeing* VINCENT *in the vestibule*]. Look out, Sam,

here's that tough from upstairs. [*She goes over to the left of the stoop.*]

VINCENT [*in the doorway*]. Hello, Rosie. Been here all night, talkin' to the little yid?

[ROSE *does not answer.*]

VINCENT [*turning to* SAM]. Hello, motzers! Shake! [*He leans over the balustrade and seizes* SAM's *hand in a crushing grip.*]

SAM [*writhing with pain*]. Let me go!

ROSE. Let him alone!

[VINCENT *gives* SAM's *hand another vicious squeeze and then releases him.* SAM *cowers back in the window, nursing his hand.*]

VINCENT [*waving his hand about in mock pain*]. Jesus, what a grip dat little kike's got! I'd hate to get into a mix-up wit' him. [*To* ROSE.] Got a date to-night, kid?

ROSE. Yes, I have.

VINCENT. Yeah? Gee, ain't dat too bad. I'll give you two dollars, if you let me snap your garter.

ROSE. Shut up, you!

[VINCENT *laughs.* SAM *makes an inarticulate sound.*]

VINCENT [*threateningly*]. Whadja say? I tought I hoid you say sumpin. [*He makes a threatening gesture.* SAM *shrinks back.*]

VINCENT [*with a loud laugh, as he goes down the steps*]. Fightin' Kaplan, de pride o' Jerusalem! [*He looks at them both, then laughs again.*] Fer cryin' out loud! [*He goes off at the left.*]

ROSE. Oh, if there was only some way of getting out of here! [SAM *puts the back of his hand to his forehead and turns away.*] I sometimes think I'd just like to run away.

SAM [*without turning*]. Yes!

ROSE. Anywhere—it wouldn't matter where—just to get out of this.

SAM [*turning*]. Why shouldn't we do it?

ROSE [*rather startled, coming over to the right balustrade*]. Would you go with me, Sam?

SAM. Yes—anywhere.

ROSE. I've heard that people are much nicer and friend-
lier, when you get outside of New York. There's not
so much of a mad rush, other places. And being
alone, you could sort of work things out for yourself.
[*Suddenly*]. Only, what would you do, Sam?

SAM. I could get a job, too.

ROSE. And give up your law-work?

SAM. I'd give up everything, to be with you.

ROSE. No. I wouldn't let you do that, Sam. It's different
with me—

[EASTER *appears at the right.*]

EASTER [*stopping at the right of the stoop*]. Good morning, Miss Maurrant. [*Startled,* ROSE *turns and sees
him, for the first time.*]

ROSE [*none too pleased*]. Oh, good morning, Mr. Easter.
What brings you in this neighborhood?

EASTER [*not very plausibly*]. Well, I just happened to
have a little business right around the corner. So, I
thought as long as you were going to the funeral, we
might just as well go together.

ROSE. Well, I hardly expected to see you around here.
[*An awkward pause.*] Oh, I'd like you to meet my
friend, Mr. Kaplan.

EASTER. How do you do, Mr. Kaplan? Glad to know
you.

[SAM *murmurs something inaudible. An awkward silence.*]

ROSE [*to* SAM]. Mr. Easter is the manager of the office.

[SAM *does not reply. Another silence.*]

ROSE [*to* EASTER]. It's awful hot again, isn't it?

EASTER. Worse than yesterday. [*Approaching the stoop.*]
Tell you what I was thinking. I was thinking that
after the funeral, we might take a run down to the
beach, somewhere, and cool off a little.

ROSE. I can't today. I've got a lot of things I want to do.

EASTER. Oh, you can do 'em some other day.

ROSE. No, really, I can't. [*Looking at her watch.*] Well,

I guess it's time we got started. [*She comes down the steps.*]

EASTER. Yes, it is. We'll pick up a cab at the corner.

[MRS. MAURRANT *appears at her window, looks out, and sees* ROSE *and* EASTER.]

ROSE. Why, I thought I'd walk. It's not far.

EASTER. Too hot today for any walking.

ROSE [*starting to go towards the left*]. Not if you keep in the shade.

EASTER. Much more comfortable taking a cab.

ROSE. I'd rather walk.

EASTER. Well, whatever you say. Good morning, **Mr.** Kaplan. Glad to have met you.

[SAM *murmurs an inaudible reply.*]

ROSE. Good-bye, Sam, I'll see you later. [SAM *does not answer.* ROSE *and* EASTER *go towards the left, in silence.* SAM *watches them intently, trembling with jealousy.* MRS. MAURRANT, *surprised and disturbed, watches* ROSE *and* EASTER.]

ROSE [*to* EASTER, *as they disappear*]. It's a lucky thing my father wasn't around.

[SAM *suddenly turns and disappears into the house.* MRS. MAURRANT *remains at the window, looking out with obvious expectancy.*]

A DISTANT VOICE. [*Off-stage left.*] Straw-berries! Straw-berries!

[*An anemic girl of eighteen, with a music-roll under her arm, appears at the left. She enters the house and pushes one of the buttons in the vestibule, then goes to the entrance-door and waits. A moment later* MRS. FIORENTINO *appears hastily at the window, and whisks away the bedclothes. After another moment the latch clicks and the girl enters the house.*]

THE VOICE [*a little nearer.*]. Oh-h! Straw-berries! Straw-berries!

[SANKEY *appears at the right. He carries a pencil behind his ear, wears a round cap with a metal name-plate and a stiff visor, and carries a large black-covered bill-holder. He and* MRS. MAURRANT *see each other and both become tense with excitement.* MRS. MAURRANT *beckons to him and he comes over to the railing under her window.*]

MRS. MAURRANT [*in a low, tense voice*]. Come up.

SANKEY [*looking about nervously*]. Now?

MRS. MAURRANT. Yes. I got to talk to you.

SANKEY. Is it all right?

MRS. MAURRANT. Yes. He's gone to Stamford.

SANKEY. How about later?

MRS. MAURRANT. No. Rose'll be home in an hour. She's not working today.

SANKEY. All right. [*He looks about again, then goes quickly towards the steps.* SAM *appears at the entrance-door. He is about to step out, when he sees* SANKEY. *He stops and looks at him.* SANKEY *sees* SAM, *hesitates a moment, then goes quickly into the house. Meanwhile,* MRS. MAURRANT *has closed both windows and pulled down the shades.* SAM *takes a periodical out of the mailbox, then comes out of the house and down the steps. He looks up at the* MAURRANT *windows, sees the drawn shades, and looks about in perturbed perplexity, not knowing what to do. At length, he sits down on the steps of the stoop, tears the wrapper off the periodical—The Nation—and begins to read. The girl in* LIPPO'S *apartment begins playing the piano. This continues throughout the scene. Two untidy and rather coarse-looking men appear at the left and approach the stoop:* JAMES HENRY, *a city-marshal, and* FRED CULLEN, *his assistant. They stop in front of the house.* SAM *pays no attention to them.*]

THE MARSHAL [*crossing to the left of the stoop, and taking a paper from his pocket*]. Dis is it. [*To* SAM.] Hildebrand live here?

SAM [*startled*]. What?

THE MARSHAL. I'm askin' you if Hildebrand lives here.

SAM. Yes. Fourth floor.

THE MARSHAL. Better give de janitor a buzz, Fred.

[FRED *goes up the steps and rings the janitor's bell, then leans over the left balustrade.*]

FRED [*bawling*]. Hey, janitor.

OLSEN [*below*]. Vell?

FRED. Come on out a minute. [*As* OLSEN *appears below.*] We got a warrant for Hildebrand.

OLSEN. Fourt' floor—Hildebrand.

FRED. Yeah, I know. We got a warrant for her.

THE MARSHAL. I'm City Marshal Henry. We got a dispossess warrant.

OLSEN [*coming up the steps*]. Oh, sure. You gonna put 'em out?

THE MARSHAL. Yeah, dat's it. Has she got anybody to take de foinicher away?

OLSEN [*with a shrug*]. I don't know.

THE MARSHAL. Well, we'll have t' dump it on de sidewalk, den. Go ahead, Fred. [*They enter the house.* OLSEN *leans his elbows on the coping, and smokes his pipe.* SAM *sits on the steps, deep in troubled thought. A grocery boy, with a full basket, appears at the right, and goes down the cellar-steps.* MAE JONES *comes out of the house. She stands on the top step, yawns noisily, and goes off at left. She and* SAM *do not pay the slightest attention to each other.*]

A VOICE [*a little nearer*]. Straw-berries! Straw-*berries!*

[MRS. OLSEN *comes up the cellar-steps with a heavy pail of water.* OLSEN *leans forward to make room for her. She staggers over to the stoop, almost dropping the pail, and goes up the steps into the vestibule.* OLSEN *yawns and goes down into the cellar.* MRS. JONES *appears at the window, her hair wet and stringy, a towel pinned about her shoulders, and leans out to dry her hair.*]

AN OLD-CLOTHES MAN [*appearing at left*]. I kesh ko! I

kesh ko! [*He wears a battered derby and carries a folded newspaper under his arm.* MRS. OLSEN, *on her knees, begins washing up the vestibule.* FRED *comes out of the house, carrying a worn chair and a large gilt-framed picture, which he deposits on the sidewalk, against the railing to the left of the stoop.*]

AN OLD-CLOTHES MAN [*as if to someone across the street*]. Kesh ko? [*To* SAM.] Any old klose, mister?

[SAM *pays no attention to him.* FRED *re-enters the house.*]

THE OLD-CLOTHES MAN [*to* MRS. JONES]. Any ol' klose, leddy?

MRS. JONES. Naw, nawthin'.

THE OLD-CLOTHES MAN. Hets? Shoes? Ol' stockings?

MRS. JONES. Nawthin', I tell you.

[*As the* OLD-CLOTHES MAN *goes off at the right,* MAURRANT *appears, still carrying his satchel.*]

MRS. JONES. Why, hello, Mr. Maurrant. [MAURRANT *looks up without replying and comes over to the stoop.*] I thought you was off to Stamford.

MAURRANT. I changed me— [*He stops, to the right of the stoop, and looks up at the drawn shades of his apartment.* SAM *rises, slowly and rigidly, his eyes glued in fascination upon* MAURRANT. MAURRANT'S *movements take on a lithe and cat-like quality. Then, slowly and deliberately, he goes towards the steps, his back arched, like a tiger ready to spring.*]

SAM [*suddenly blocking the steps*]. No! No! For God's sake—!

MAURRANT [*raging*]. Out o' me way, you goddam little rat! [*He flings* SAM *violently aside, almost knocking him down.* MRS. OLSEN, *terrified, rises and shrinks into a corner as* MAURRANT *with swift stealthiness enters the house.* MRS. JONES *leans out to see what is wrong.* SAM *rushes down the steps and stands under the* MAURRANT *windows. The* MARSHAL *comes out of the house, carrying a wash-boiler filled with pots.*]

SAM [*hysterically*]. Mrs. Maurrant! Mrs. Maurrant!

MRS. JONES. What's the matter.

[*The* MARSHAL *puts the wash-boiler on the balustrade and looks on in amazement.*]

SAM [*to* MRS. JONES]. Quick! Run and tell her! Quick!

MRS. JONES. What is it? [*Suddenly.*] Oh, Gawd, is he in there? [*She leaves the windows hastily.*]

SAM. Yes! Mrs. Maurrant! Mrs. Maurrant!

[*A scream of terror is heard from the* MAURRANT *apartment.*]

MRS. MAURRANT'S VOICE. Frank! Frank! [*Two shots are heard, in quick succession, and then a heavy fall.* MRS. OLSEN *runs out of the vestibule and down into the cellar.* SANKEY'S *voice is heard, inarticulate with fear. Then one of the shades shoots up, and* SANKEY *appears at the window, coatless, his face deformed by terror. He tries to open the window, but succeeds only in shattering the pane with his elbow.* MAURRANT *appears behind him and pulls him away from the window. Then another shot is heard.*]

THE MARSHAL. For Chris' sake, what's happenin'? Get an ambulance, you! [*He pushes* SAM *towards the left, then hurries off at the right. As* SAM *runs off, a crowd begins to form.* OLSEN *comes up from the cellar, followed by the* GROCERY-BOY. *The two workmen come up out of the excavation. Two or three of the workmen from the demolished building run on at the right.*]

A WORKMAN. What's happening?

A MAN. What is it? A murder?

[*Still others join the crowd: A huckster, a janitor from a neighboring house, a mulatto girl, six or eight women of the neighborhood, some in street-dresses, others in house-dresses or dingy wrappers.* LIPPO'S *pupil appears at the window, badly frightened. The crowd surges about uncertainly, not knowing what has happened, and buzzing with questions which nobody can answer. While the crowd is still forming,*

FRED, *the* MARSHAL'S *assistant, appears at the broken window.*]

FRED [*excitedly*]. Grab dat boid! He's comin' down!

A WORKMAN. What boid?

A MAN. Here he is, now!

[*The crowd murmurs with excitement and surges about the stoop as the house-door opens and* MAUR-RANT *appears. His coat is open and his shirt is torn almost to shreds. His face, hands, and clothing are covered with blood. He stands in the door-way for a moment, surveying the crowd, his eyes glaring.*]

FRED. Grab him! Don't let him get away!

[*As the crowd makes a concerted movement towards* MAURRANT, *he whips out an automatic revolver and levels it. The crowd shrinks back. Some of the women scream.*]

MAURRANT. Git back! Git back, all o' you!

[*The crowd falls back towards the left to make way for him. With his back to the balustrade, he comes quickly down the steps, and still leveling his revolver at the crowd, retreats backwards to the cellar steps. A man, approaching at the right, comes stealthily up behind him, but* MAURRANT *senses his presence in time, wheels quickly, menaces the man with his re-volver, then rushes down the cellar steps. While all this is happening, the other shade in the* MAURRANT *apartment flies up and* MISS CUSHING *opens the win-dow and leans out.*]

MISS CUSHING. Hurry up! Get an ambulance!

[*No one pays any attention to her, as they are all watch-ing* MAURRANT. *As* MAURRANT *runs down the cellar steps, the crowd surges forward to the railing on both sides of the stoop and leans over. A scream from* MRS. OLSEN *is heard from the basement.* FRED *goes away from the window.*]

MISS CUSHING. Get an ambulance, somebody! [*Unable to attract anyone's attention, she leaves the window.*]

OLSEN. Olga! [*He hurries down the cellar steps.*]

A MAN [*calling*]. Here's a cop! [*The crowd looks to the right.*] Hey! Hurry up!

[*A* POLICEMAN *runs on from the right.*]

THE POLICEMAN. Where is he?

VOICES IN THE CROWD. He's down the cellar! He ran down the cellar! He went down the steps!

THE POLICEMAN. Get out of the way!

[*The* POLICEMAN *and two* MEN *in the crowd go down the cellar steps.*]

VOICES IN THE CROWD. Watch yourself! Look out, he's got a gun! He's a big guy with his shirt torn!

[*The rest of the crowd peers over the railing.*]

MISS CUSHING [*leaning out of* ROSE'S *window*]. Hey, don't you hear me? Get an ambulance!

ANOTHER MAN [*looking up*]. What's de matter? You want de ambulance?

MISS CUSHING. Yes! Right away!

ANOTHER MAN [*to the* GROCERY-BOY]. Run aroun' de corner to de horspital, Johnny, an' tell 'em to send de ambulance!

THE GROCERY-BOY. Sure!

MISS CUSHING. Run!

[*The* GROCERY-BOY *runs off swiftly at the left.* MISS CUSHING *leaves the window. Meanwhile, as the* POLICEMAN *and the two* MEN *have gone down the cellar steps, the* MARSHAL *has run on from the right, panting.*]

THE MARSHAL [*as the* GROCERY-BOY *runs off*]. Did dey git 'm?

A MAN. He beat it down de cellar.

A WORKMAN. De cop's gone after him.

THE MARSHAL. Why de hell didn' you stop 'im?

[FRED *comes out of the house.*]

A WORKMAN. He had a gun.

FRED. Did somebody go for de ambulance?

A MAN. Yeah. De kid went.

A WOMAN. It's only aroun' de corner.

ANOTHER MAN. Dey'll be here, right away.

[*The crowd moves over towards* FRED.]

THE MARSHAL [*pushing his way through the crowd and up the steps*]. What de hell happened, Fred?

FRED [*as the crowd moves toward the stoop*]. It's a moider. Dis boid's wife an' some other guy. Jesus, you oughta see de blood.

[*Another* POLICEMAN *runs up at the left, closely followed by* SAM.]

FRED. Upstairs, officer! Dere's two of 'em got shot.

THE POLICEMAN [*elbowing his way through the crowd*]. Look out o' de way, youse! [*He goes up the stoop and crosses to the door.*] Where's de guy dat did it?

VOICES IN THE CROWD. Down de cellar! He beat it down de steps!

FRED. Dere's another cop after 'im. You better look after dem upstairs. Foist floor.

SAM [*agonized*]. Are they dead?

[*No one pays any attention to him.*]

THE MARSHAL [*stopping the* POLICEMAN, *and exhibiting his badge*]. I'm City Marshal Henry. Kin I do anythin'?

POLICEMAN. Don' let anybody in or out! Hear?

THE MARSHAL. Yeah, sure!

[*The* POLICEMAN *exits quickly into the house.*]

SAM. Are they dead?

[*No one notices him. The* MARSHAL *takes up his position in the doorway.*]

BUCHANAN [*appearing at the* MAURRANT *window*]. Where's the ambulance?

THE MARSHAL. It'll be here right away. Dere's a cop on his way up.

SAM. Mr. Buchanan! Mr. Buchanan! Are they dead?

[*But* BUCHANAN *has already disappeared. The two* MEN *who followed the first* POLICEMAN *into the cellar now come up the steps. The crowd moves over to the railing at the right.*]

THE MARSHAL. Did you get him, boys?

ONE OF THE MEN. He must be hidin' somewheres. De cop's lookin' for 'im.

ANOTHER MAN. Somebody better call de resoives.

[SAM *runs up the steps and tries to enter the house.*]

THE MARSHAL [*seizing him roughly*]. You can't get in now! Get back dere! [*He pushes* SAM *back into the crowd at the foot of the steps.*]

THE POLICEMAN [*appearing at the* MAURRANT *window*]. Hey, call up headquarters an' tell 'em to send the resoives. Make it quick! [*He goes away from the window.*]

THE MARSHAL. You go, Fred.

FRED. Sure!

A MAN. Dere's a phone in de warehouse.

[*An ambulance bell is heard at the left, as* FRED *goes quickly towards the left. Another spectator hurries on and joins the crowd.*]

VOICES IN THE CROWD. Dere it is! Dere's de ambulance now! Here dey come!

[*The crowd moves over towards the left.*]

A MAN. Dey won't be able to git past.

THE POLICEMAN [*reappearing at the window*]. Is dat de ambulance?

THE MARSHAL. Yeah.

[BUCHANAN *and* MRS. JONES *crowd to the window, behind the* POLICEMAN, *and at the other window,* LIPPO, MISS CUSHING, *and* MRS. HILDEBRAND *appear. A hospital interne and an ambulance-driver come on at the left.*]

THE POLICEMAN. Hurry up, doc! She's still breathin'.

THE INTERNE [*forcing his way through the crowd*]. All right! Better bring the stretcher, Harry.

THE AMBULANCE-DRIVER. Yes, sir. [*He hurries off at the left. The* INTERNE *goes quickly into the house. The crowd attempts to follow, several of its members going up the steps.*]

THE MARSHAL [*pushing them back*]. Keep back, now! Back off de stoop, everybody!

[*The crowd forms a compact mass about the foot of the steps. The persons at the* MAURRANT *windows have disappeared.* FRED *hurries on at the left.*]

FRED [*pushing his way through the crowd and up the steps*]. I got 'em. Dey'll be right up. Anudder cop jes' wen' in t'roo de warehouse cellar.

THE MARSHAL. Dey'll git 'im all right. [*Looking at his watch.*] Better git busy wit' dat foinicher, Fred. We got two udder jobs today.

FRED. Yeah, sure, Jimmy. [*He enters the house. The* AMBULANCE-DRIVER *appears at the left, carrying a canvas stretcher.*]

THE AMBULANCE-DRIVER. Get out o' the way!

THE MARSHAL. Git back, can't youse? What de hell's de matter wit' youse? [*He comes down the steps and violently pushes the crowd back. The* AMBULANCE-DRIVER *enters the house.*]

THE POLICEMAN [*at the window*]. Are dey bringin' dat stretcher?

THE MARSHAL. On de way up! [*To the crowd.*] Keep back!

[*The* POLICEMAN *leaves the window.* LIPPO'S PUPIL, *her music-roll under her arm, appears timidly in the doorway.*]

THE MARSHAL [*grabbing her arm roughly*]. Where you goin'?

THE GIRL [*nervously*]. I'm going home.

THE MARSHAL. Home? Where do you live?

THE GIRL. Ninety-first Street.

THE MARSHAL. What are you doin' here?

THE GIRL. I just came for a music-lesson, that's all.

THE MARSHAL. Yeah? Well, you can't go now.

THE GIRL [*beginning to whimper*]. I want to go home.

THE MARSHAL. You can't go now. Nobody can't leave de house now.

THE POLICEMAN [*coming out of the house*]. Who's dis kid?

THE MARSHAL. Says she come here to take a music-lesson

an' she wants to go home.

THE POLICEMAN [*to the girl*]. Do you know anythin' about this killin'?

THE GIRL. No, I don't. I just heard some shooting, that's all. My mother will be worried, if I don't come home.

THE POLICEMAN. Well, you can't go now. Get inside dere, out o' de way. Dey'll be bringin' her down in a minute. [*He pushes the girl inside the house and comes down the steps.*]

THE POLICEMAN. Come on, git back from dem steps! Back now, all o' youse! [*He and the* MARSHAL *push the crowd back to the right of the stoop, leaving the steps and the side-walk in front of them clear. Then he goes up the steps again.*]

THE MARSHAL. What did he do? Shoot two of 'em?

THE POLICEMAN. I'll say he did! His wife an' her sweetie. A guy named Sankey. He was dead when I got up dere.

THE MARSHAL. I seen him tryin' to climb out t'roo de winder. An' dis guy grabs 'im an' pulls 'im back.

THE INTERNE [*from the* MAURRANT *window*]. Officer! Come on up! [*He leaves the window, as the* POLICE-MAN *exits into the house. Suddenly* SAM *utters an exclamation of anguish and, pushing his way out of the crowd, hurries over to the left.*]

THE MARSHAL. Hey you! Where you goin'?

[SAM *ignores him and hurries on.*]

A WOMAN. Look! There's the Maurrant girl!

ANOTHER WOMAN. Who?

A WOMAN. It's her daughter.

[*The crowd murmurs excitedly, as* ROSE *comes on quickly at the left.*]

ROSE. What's the matter, Sam? What's the ambulance for? Did anybody get hurt?

SAM. Go away, Rose. Go away.

ROSE. Who is it, Sam? What's the matter? Is it my

mother? It's not my mother, is it? [*Clinging to him.*] Sam, is it?

SAM. There's been an accident. Go away. Rose. [*He tries to force her away.*]

ROSE. Tell me what's happened! Tell me!

MISS CUSHING [*appearing at the window*]. They're bringing her down!

ROSE [*with a cry*]. It *is* my mother!

MISS CUSHING [*seeing her*]. Oh, my God, there's Rose!

[MRS. FIORENTINO, MRS. JONES, MRS. HILDEBRAND, LIPPO, *and* BUCHANAN *crowd to the* MAURRANT *windows.*]

SAM. Rose! Go away!

[*She pays no attention to him, but stands watching the door, transfixed. The* INTERNE *comes briskly out of the house.*]

THE INTERNE [*to the* MARSHAL]. Hold the door open, will you? [*He comes down the steps.*]

THE MARSHAL. Sure, doc! [*He hurries into the vestibule.*]

THE INTERNE [*to the crowd*]. Keep back, now!

ROSE [*seizing the* INTERNE'S *arm*]. Doctor! Is she dead?

THE INTERNE. Who are you? Her daughter?

ROSE. Yes, sir. I'm her daughter.

THE INTERNE. She's pretty badly hurt. Step aside, now!

[*They step aside, as the* AMBULANCE-DRIVER *and the* POLICEMAN *come out of the house, carrying* MRS. MAURRANT *on the stretcher. There is a low murmur from the crowd.*]

THE AMBULANCE-DRIVER. Easy, now.

THE POLICEMAN. All right.

[*They come down the steps and go towards the left.*]

ROSE [*running forward and gripping the side of the stretcher*]. Mother! Mother!

MRS. MAURRANT [*opening her eyes, feebly*]. Rose! [*She tries to lift her hand, but it falls back.*]

THE INTERNE [*pulling* ROSE *back*]. You mustn't talk to her now.

[SAM *takes her about the shoulders. They and the* IN-
TERNE *follow the stretcher off at the left. The crowd
swarms after them.* FRED *comes out of the house, carrying one end of an iron bedstead.*]

CURTAIN

Act three

*Mid-afternoon of the same day. At the left of the stoop
is a large roll of bedding. Before the rise of the curtain,
and continuing faintly thereafter, a woman can be
heard singing scales.* OLSEN, *pipe in mouth, is leaning
against the railing. Two* MEN, *furniture-movers, appear
at the left.*

ONE OF THE MEN [*picking up the bedding*]. All right.
Dat's all, Charlie!
[*The* MEN *exit left. A* POLICEMAN *comes out of the
house, carrying the blood-stained dress of* MRS. MAUR-
RANT, *and* SANKEY'S *coat, cap, and bill-holder. He
comes down the steps, and exits at the right. At the
left, two young* NURSE-MAIDS, *in smart uniforms, ap-
pear, each wheeling a de-luxe baby-carriage.*]
FIRST NURSE-MAID [*seeing the house-number*]. This
must be the place, right here—346.
[*They stop, under the* MAURRANT *windows.*]
SECOND NURSE-MAID. Yes, I guess it is.
FIRST NURSE-MAID. Yes, this is it, all right. [*Looking up.*]
Must be right up there, on the first floor, see?
SECOND NURSE-MAID. Yes, sure. [*Excitedly.*] Say, look!
You can see where the glass is out of the window.
That's where this feller What's-his-name tried to
climb out.

FIRST NURSE-MAID. Oh, yes, I see it! Say, what do you know about that!

SECOND NURSE-MAID [*taking a pink tabloid newspaper from under the hood of the baby-buggy*]. Wait! There's a picture of it somewhere. [*Turning the pages.*] Here it is. [*They excitedly examine it together, as she reads.*] "Composograph showing Sankey, scantily clad, in a last vain attempt to escape the vengeance of the jealousy-crazed husband whose home he had destroyed." And there's Maurrant pulling him back. And Mrs. Maurrant trying to get the pistol away from him, see? Look at the blood running down her face, will you?

FIRST NURSE-MAID. It's worse than awful! Can you *imagine* what those two must have felt like, when he walked in on them like that?

SECOND NURSE-MAID. Well, he just happened to be one of the ones that finds out! Believe me, there's lots and lots of husbands that don't know the half of what goes on up-town, while they're down-town making a living.

FIRST NURSE-MAID. Say, you're not telling me, are you? If I was to spill all I know, there'd be many a happy home busted up. I wonder if they caught him.

SECOND NURSE-MAID [*as her* BABY *begins a thin wailing*]. Oh, God, he's in again! [*To the unseen* BABY.] Shut up a little while, can't you? [*She shakes the carriage.*]

A POLICEMAN [*appearing at the* MAURRANT *windows, a tabloid in his hand*]. Keep movin', ladies. No loiterin' aroun' here.

FIRST NURSE-MAID [*eagerly*]. Say, have they caught him yet?

THE POLICEMAN. Why, ain't you hoid? He was last seen flyin' over Nova Scotia, on his way to Paris.

FIRST NURSE-MAID. Who are you trying to string, anyhow?

SECOND NURSE-MAID [*coquettishly*]. Say, will you let us

come up and look around?

THE POLICEMAN. Why, sure, sure! Bring de babies, too. De commissioner is soivin' tea up here at four-thoity.

SECOND NURSE-MAID. You're awful smart, aren't you?

THE POLICEMAN. Yeah, that's why dey put me on de entertainment committee. I'm Handsome Harry Moiphy, de boy comedian o' Brooklyn.

FIRST NURSE-MAID [*looking at her watch*]. Oh, say, I ought to be getting back. [*Turning her carriage.*] Clarice darling would throw a duck-fit, if she knew I brought her precious Dumplings to a neighborhood like this.

SECOND NURSE-MAID [*turning her carriage*]. There's not so much to see, anyhow. It's nothing but a cheap, common dump.

[*They go towards the left.*]

THE POLICEMAN. Over de river, goils. See you in de funny paper.

SECOND NURSE-MAID. Don't you get so fresh.

THE POLICEMAN. Drop in again, when you're in de neighborhood. An' tell Mrs. Vanderbilt, Harry was askin' for her.

[*As the* NURSE-MAIDS *go off at the left,* EASTER *hurries on at the right, several folded newspapers under his arm.*]

EASTER [*to the* POLICEMAN, *going to the left of the stoop*]. Is Miss Maurrant up there, officer?

THE POLICEMAN. No. There ain't nobody up here but me.

EASTER. You don't happen to know where she is, do you?

THE POLICEMAN. No, I don't. Are you a reporter?

EASTER. Who, me? I'm just a friend of hers. I've got to see her.

THE POLICEMAN. Well, I ain't seen her since she went off to the horspital this mornin'. She ain't been back since. [*He starts to leave the window.*]

EASTER. Oh, officer!

THE POLICEMAN. Yeah?

EASTER. Have they caught him yet?

THE POLICEMAN. Naw, not yet. But we'll get 'im, all right! [*He leaves the window.* EASTER *remains at the left of the stoop, uncertain whether to go or not.* MRS. JONES *appears, at the right, carrying several newspapers.*]

MRS. JONES [*to* OLSEN]. Have they caught him yet?

OLSEN [*shaking his head*]. No.

MRS. JONES. I been down at Police Headquarters all this while—[*Breaking off, as she notices* EASTER.] Say, what's he want here?

[OLSEN *shrugs his shoulders.*]

EASTER [*approaching them*]. Pardon me, but maybe you can tell me where I can find Miss Maurrant?

[OLSEN *shakes his head.*]

MRS. JONES. Why no, I can't. I jus' this minute got back from Police Headquarters. Maybe she's aroun' at the horspital.

EASTER. No, I just came from there.

MRS. JONES. Well, I really couldn't say where she is. Was there somethin' special you wanted to see her about?

EASTER. I'm a friend of hers—

MRS. JONES. Yeah, I noticed you talkin' to her last night, when I took the dog out. [*Staring at him.*] Well, I guess she'll need all the friends she's got, now. Imagine a thing like that happenin' right here in this house, at ten o'clock in the mornin'! Everythin' goin' on just as usual, and then, all of a sudden, before you know it, there's two people murdered.

OLSEN. I tal everybody some day he kill her.

MRS. JONES. Well, I ain't sayin' it's right to kill anybody, but if anybody had a reason, he certainly had. You oughta heard some o' the questions they was askin' me down at the Police. I could feel myself gettin' redder an' redder. "Say," I says, "how do you expect me to know things like that?" [*Suddenly, as she looks left.*] Here's Rose now!

EASTER. Where? [*He turns quickly and hurries to the left, as* ROSE *appears, carrying four or five packages.*]

MRS. JONES [*to* OLSEN]. He seems to take a pretty friendly interest in her.

[OLSEN *nods.*]

ROSE [*anxiously, as she comes up to* EASTER *at the left of the stoop*]. Have they caught him yet?

EASTER. Why no, they haven't. I just asked the officer upstairs.

ROSE. Oh, I hope he got away! If they get him, there's no telling what they'll do to him. And what would be the good of that? He never would have done it, if he'd been in his right mind.

EASTER. I only heard about it a little while ago. So I went right around to the hospital. But they said you'd left.

ROSE [*going to the steps*]. She never opened her eyes again. They did everything they could for her, but it didn't help.

EASTER. Here, let me take your bundles.

ROSE. No, it's all right. I think I'll just sit down for a minute. [*She sits on the stoop and puts the packages beside her.*]

EASTER. Can't I get you something? A drink or something?

ROSE. No, I'm all right. It's so hot. [*She puts her hand to her head.*] And all those people asking me a lot of questions.

MRS. JONES [*approaching the stoop*]. Are you feelin' dizzy or anythin'?

ROSE. No, I'll be all right in a minute.

MRS. JONES. Well, I was gonna say, if you want to go up to my flat an' lay down for a minute—

ROSE. No, thanks; I don't want to lie down. I've got to go upstairs to get some things.

EASTER. Why, say, you don't want to go up there!

ROSE. I've got to; there's some things I need.

EASTER. Well, let me get them for you. Or this lady here.

MRS. JONES. Yeah, sure. The place is a sight up there. You're li'ble to go into a faint or somethin'.

ROSE. I guess nothing can be any worse than what's happened already. [*Indicating the bundles.*] I got to change my dress. I bought a white dress for her. And white silk stockings. I want her to look pretty.

MRS. JONES. Yeah, white is the nicest.

ROSE. She looks so quiet and natural. You'd think she was asleep.

MRS. JONES. It was the same way with my mother. You'd of thought she was gonna get up the next minute. [*Starting to go up the steps.*] Well, I gotta go up an' get me some lunch. Between everythin' happenin' an' goin' down to Police Headquarters an' all, I ain't had a bite to eat since breakfast. [*Stopping on the top step, and looking from* ROSE *to* EASTER.] Well, you certainly never know, when you get up in the mornin', what the day is gonna bring. [*She enters the house.*]

ROSE [*rising*]. Well, I'd better be going up, too. There's a lot of things to attend to.

EASTER. You better let me come up with you.

ROSE. Why thanks, Mr. Easter. But I'd rather go alone, if you don't mind.

EASTER. But, listen here—you can't go through all this alone—a kid like you. That's why I came around. I knew you'd be needing a helping hand.

ROSE. That's awfully nice of you, Mr. Easter. But I don't need any help, honest I don't. [*She opens one of the packages.*]

EASTER. Why, you can't handle everything yourself! What about a place to live and all that?

ROSE [*taking a rosette of black crape out of the package*]. Well, I don't exactly know, yet. I'll have to find some place where Willie and I can live. I'd like it to be some place where he wouldn't be running around the streets all the time. You see, there's nobody but me to look out for him now.

[OLSEN *crosses to the cellar.* MRS. JONES *appears at her window and furtively peeps out at* ROSE *and* EASTER.]

ROSE [*as she sees that* OLSEN *is about to descend the cellar steps*]. Oh, Mr. Olsen!

OLSEN [*stopping*]. Yes, ma'am.

ROSE. Would you mind lending me a hammer and some tacks? I want to put up this crape.

OLSEN. Yes, ma'am; I bring 'em right away. [*He goes down into the cellar.* MRS. JONES *leaves the window.*]

EASTER [*insistently*]. But why won't you let me help you out?

ROSE. It's terribly nice of you, Mr. Easter. But I'll be able to manage alone, really I will. It isn't as if I wasn't young and strong and able to take care of myself. But as it is, I'd sort of rather not be under obligations.

EASTER. Why, you wouldn't be under any obligations. I just mean it in a friendly way, that's all.

ROSE. You've been very nice to me and all that, Mr. Easter. But—well, I've been sort of thinking things over—you know, about what we talked about last night and all. And I honestly don't think I'd care about going on the stage.

EASTER. Say, you've got me all wrong, Rose! Just forget all about that, will you? I just want to help you out, that's all. [*Taking a step towards her.*] I think you're one swell kid, and I want to do something for you. I'm not trying to put anything over on you.

[SHIRLEY *appears, at the left, carrying her school-bag, from which a newspaper protrudes.*]

ROSE. Well, that's nice and friendly of you, Mr. Easter. And if I ever do need any help—

SHIRLEY [*catching sight of* ROSE]. Rose! You poor thing!

[*She runs up to* ROSE *and throws her arms about her.*] It's terrible—terrible!

ROSE. Yes, it is. But I sort of had a feeling, all along, that something terrible was going to happen.

[OLSEN *comes up the steps, with a hammer and a box of tacks.*]

SHIRLEY. How could he do such a thing! I couldn't believe it when I read it.

ROSE. He was out of his mind, when he did it. Oh, I only hope he got away! [*As* OLSEN *approaches.*] Oh, thanks, Mr. Olsen.

OLSEN. I do it.

ROSE [*giving him the crape*]. Oh, would you, please? Right up there, I think. [*She indicates the left of the doorway.*]

OLSEN [*going up the steps*]. Sure.

ROSE [*going to* EASTER *and extending her hand*]. Thanks for coming around, Mr. Easter. I don't know when I'll be able to get back to the office.

EASTER. Why, that's all right about that. Only, in the meantime, I wish—

ROSE. If I need any help, I'll let you know. [*With a tone of finality in her voice.*] Good-bye.

EASTER. All right; but don't forget. [*He hesitates, then decides to go.*] Well, good-bye. [*He goes off at left.*]

ROSE. I've got to go up and get some things that Willie and I need. Sam went to call for him at school and take him around to my aunt's. You see, I didn't want him coming back here. He's only a little kid, after all.

SHIRLEY. Oh, it's such a terrible thing! I can't believe it yet.

OLSEN [*holding up the crape*]. Dis vay?

ROSE. Yes, like that. [*Hesitantly, as she picks up her bundles.*] Miss Kaplan, it's sort of silly of me, I guess. But I'm kind of afraid to go up there alone. I wonder if you'd mind coming up with me.

[OLSEN *tacks up the crape.*]

SHIRLEY. Anything I can do for you, poor child! [*She and* ROSE *go up the steps.*]

ROSE. Thanks ever so much. [*To* OLSEN.] Thanks, Mr. Olsen. It's awfully nice of you. [*She and* SHIRLEY *enter the house.* OLSEN *exits down the cellar steps.* KAPLAN *appears at his window, and seating himself, begins to read a newspaper. An undersized* MAN *and a tall, athletic* WOMAN *appear at the right. They are dressed for tennis, and carry tennis rackets.*]

MAN [*as they cross*]. He *would* say that.

WOMAN. So I just looked at him for a moment, without saying anything. And then, I said: "My dear boy," I said. "What do you expect anyhow, in this day and age?" I said, "Why even Frankl has to do a black bathroom occasionally," I said.

MAN [*as they disappear at the left*]. Exactly! And what did he say to that?

[BUCHANAN *comes out of the house, and, seeing* KAPLAN *at the window, stops at the right balustrade.*]

BUCHANAN. Well, there's been *some* excitement around here to-day.

KAPLAN [*looking up from his paper*]. Dees is a terrible t'ing vich hes heppened.

BUCHANAN. I'll say it is! You know, the way I look at it, he didn't have a right to kill the both of them like that. Of course I'm not saying what she did was right, either.

KAPLAN. How ken ve call ourselves ciwilized, ven ve see that sax jealousy hes de power to avaken in us de primitive pessions of de sevege?

BUCHANAN [*rather bewildered by this*]. Yes, that's true, too. Of course, you can't expect a man to stand by and see his home broken up. But murdering them, like that, is going a little too far. Well, I got to go and phone the doctor. This thing's given my wife a kind of a *re*lapse. She thought a lot of Mrs. Maurrant. [*He goes down the steps, and off at the left, as*

LIPPO *appears at the right*.]

LIPPO [*stopping in front of* KAPLAN's *window*]. Dey don' ketch Maurrant, ha?

KAPLAN. I hevn't hoid anyt'ing foider.

LIPPO. He'sa gonna gat da 'lectrica chair, ha?

KAPLAN. De blood-lust of our enlightened population must be setisfied! De Chreestian state will kerry out to de last letter de Mosaic law.

LIPPO. Eef Ah'm ketcha my wife sleepin' wit' 'nudder man, Ah'm gonna kella 'er, too.

[SAM *hurries on at the left*.]

KAPLAN. So you t'ink thet merriage should give to de hosband de power of life and det' and thet—

SAM [*going up the steps*]. Papa, is there any news of Maurrant?

KAPLAN. I hev heard notting.

SAM. The police are going to make me testify against him. What can I do, papa?

KAPLAN. You ken do notting.

SAM. How can I send a man to the electric chair? How can I? I tried to stop him, papa. I tried to warn her— [*He stops short, as several shots are heard offstage at the left*.] What's that.

LIPPO [*excitedly*]. Dey finda 'im! [*He runs off at the left, followed by* SAM. KAPLAN *leans out of the window. At the same moment,* MRS. JONES *leans out of her window and, a moment later,* MRS. FIORENTINO *out of hers. In the* MAURRANT *apartment, the* POLICEMAN *leans out and* ROSE *and* SHIRLEY *appear in the hall bedroom window.* ROSE *is wearing a mourning-dress.* OLSEN *comes up the cellar steps and runs off at the left.* MRS. OLSEN *comes up the steps. Several* MEN *and* WOMEN *appear at the right, and run off at the left*.]

ROSE [*agitatedly*]. Is that him?

THE POLICEMAN. Must be!

[*Voices are heard shouting in the distance, and then another shot. The* POLICEMAN *leaves the window*.]

ROSE. Oh, God! They wouldn't shoot him, would they? [*She leaves the window.*]

SHIRLEY [*following her*]. Rose!

[*Two or three more persons appear at the right and run off at the left. The* POLICEMEN *runs out of the house, as* BUCHANAN *appears at the left.*]

BUCHANAN [*excitedly*]. They got him!

[*The* POLICEMAN *runs off at the left.* SHIRLEY *reappears at the* MAURRANT *window.*]

MRS. JONES [*calling*]. Have they got him?

BUCHANAN. Yes! He was hiding in the furnace down at 322. [*As* ROSE *comes out of the house.*] They found him, Miss Maurrant!

ROSE [*her hand to her heart*]. Oh! Is he hurt?

BUCHANAN. I don't know. He fired at the cops and they fired back at him. I was just passing the house when it happened.

MRS. JONES [*leaning far out*]. Here they come! [*She leaves the window. The low murmur of the approaching crowd can be heard, off-stage left.*]

ROSE. Where? [*She comes down the stoop and looks off at the left.*] Oh! [*She covers her eyes and turns away.*]

MRS. FIORENTINO. You better come inside.

SHIRLEY. Come up, Rose.

BUCHANAN. Yes, you better. [*He takes her by the arm.*]

ROSE [*resisting*]. No. No. Please let me alone. I want to see him. [*She leans against the railing. Meanwhile, the murmur and tramp of the approaching crowd has grown nearer and nearer.*]

MRS. FIORENTINO. Look at him, vill you! [MISS CUSHING *comes out of the house and stands on the stoop, followed a moment later by* MRS. JONES. MAURRANT *appears at the left, between two policemen. Behind him a third* POLICEMAN *holds back a swarming crowd, which includes* SAM *and* LIPPO. MAURRANT'S *clothes are torn, and his right arm is in a crude sling. Sweat, blood, and grime have made him almost unrecog-*

nizable. The POLICEMEN, *too, show evidences of a struggle.*]

ROSE [*running forward*]. Pop! Are you hurt?

MAURRANT [*seeing her for the first time*]. Rose!

ONE OF THE POLICEMEN [*to whom* MAURRANT *is manacled*]. Keep back, miss!

MAURRANT. It's me daughter! Fer Chris' sake, boys, lemme talk to me daughter! Maybe I'll never be seein' her again!

FIRST POLICEMAN. Give 'im a woid wit' her. [*He is the* OFFICER *who was on duty in the Maurrant apartment.*]

SECOND POLICEMAN [*after a moment's hesitation*]. Well, all right. [*Savagely to* MAURRANT.] But don't try to pull nothin', hear?

[*There is a forward movement in the crowd.*]

FIRST POLICEMAN [*to the crowd*]. Keep back, youse!

MAURRANT. Rose! You're wearin' a black dress, Rose!

ROSE. Oh, pop, why did you do it? Why did you?

MAURRANT. I must o' been out o' me head, Rose. Did she say anythin'?

ROSE. She never opened her eyes again.

MAURRANT. I'd been drinkin', Rose— see what I mean?— an' all the talk that was goin' around. I just went clean off me nut, that's all.

ROSE. What'll they do to you, pop?

MAURRANT. It's the chair for me, I guess. But I don't care—let 'em give me the chair. I deserve it all right. But it's her I'm thinkin' of, Rose—the way she looked at me. I oughtn't to done it, Rose.

ROSE. She was always so good and sweet.

MAURRANT. Don't I know it? I ain't no murderer—you ought to be the one to know that, Rose. I just went out o' me head, that's all it was.

SECOND POLICEMAN. All right, that's all now. Come on!

MAURRANT. Gimme a minute, can't you? She's me daughter. Gimme a chance, can't you? What's gonna happen to you, Rose?

ROSE. I'll be all right, pop. You don't need to worry about me.

MAURRANT. I ain't been a very good father, have I?

ROSE. Don't worry about that, pop.

MAURRANT. It ain't that I ain't meant to be. It's just the way things happened to turn out, that's all. Keep your eye on Willie, Rose. Don't let Willie grow up to be a murderer, like his pop.

ROSE. I'm going to do all I can for him, pop.

MAURRANT. You're a good girl, Rose. You was always a good girl.

ROSE [*breaking down*]. Oh, pop! [*She throws her arms about his neck and buries her head against him.* MAURRANT *sobs hoarsely.*]

FIRST POLICEMAN [*gently*]. Come on now, miss. [*He and* SAM *take* ROSE *away from* MAURRANT.]

SECOND POLICEMAN. All right. Come on, Charlie.

[THEY *go towards the right, the crowd swarming behind them. Straggling along at the very end of the crowd is an unkempt* WOMAN, *wheeling a ramshackle baby-carriage.* MRS. JONES *and* MISS CUSHING *fall in with the crowd.* ROSE *gradually recovers her self-control, and stands at the stoop with* SAM *beside her. The others watch the receding crowd for a moment. Then* KAPLAN *and* MRS. FIORENTINO *leave their windows. The* FIRST POLICEMAN *enters the house, followed by* LIPPO. MRS. OLSEN *goes to the cellar.* SHIRLEY *looks down at* ROSE *and* SAM *for a moment, then abruptly leaves the window.*]

SAM [*taking* ROSE *by the arm*]. Rose, you better come inside.

ROSE. No, I'm all right again, Sam—honestly I am. [*Trying to regain her self-composure.*] What about Willie, Sam?

SAM. I told him an accident had happened.

ROSE. It's better to break it to him that way. But I'll have to tell him, I guess. He'd only find it out himself to-morrow, with the papers all full of it. I saw

Mrs. Sankey down at Police Headquarters. It's terrible for her, with two little children.

SHIRLEY [*appearing at the* MAURRANT *window, a covered pot in her hand*]. Rose!

ROSE [*looking up*]. Yes, Miss Kaplan?

SHIRLEY. There's a chicken here that I found on the gas-stove.

ROSE. A chicken?

SHIRLEY. Yes. The policeman says he smelt it cooking this morning, so he turned out the gas.

ROSE. Oh, I remember now. My mother said she was going to make some soup for poor Mrs. Buchanan, upstairs.

SHIRLEY. It won't keep long, in this weather.

ROSE. No. I really think Mrs. Buchanan ought to have the good of it.

SHIRLEY. All right. I'll take it up to her.

ROSE. Thanks ever so much, Miss Kaplan. [SHIRLEY *leaves the window.*] It's only a few hours ago that she was standing right here, telling me about the chicken. And then she went upstairs, and the next I saw of her, they were carrying her out. [*Abruptly, as she starts to go up the steps.*] Well, I've got to go up and get my things.

SAM. I must talk to you! What are you going to do, Rose?

ROSE. Well, I haven't really had any time to do much thinking. But I really think the best thing I could do, would be to get out of New York. You know, like we were saying this morning—how things might be different, if you only had a chance to breathe and spread out a little. Only when I said it, I never dreamt it would be this way.

SAM. If you go, I'll go with you.

ROSE. But, Sam dear—

SAM. I don't care anything about my career. It's you—you—I care about. Do you think I can stay here, stifling to death, in this slum, and never seeing you? Do you think my life means anything to me without you?

ROSE. But, Sam, we've got to be practical about it. How would we manage?

SAM. I don't care what I do. I'll be a day-laborer; I'll dig sewers—anything. [*Taking her passionately in his arms.*] Rose, don't leave me!

ROSE. I like you so much, Sam. I like you better than anybody I know.

SAM. I love you, Rose. Let me go with you!

ROSE. It would be so nice to be with you. You're different from anybody I know. But I'm just wondering how it would work out.

SAM. If we have each other, that's the vital thing, isn't it? What else matters but that?

ROSE. Lots of things, Sam. There's lots of things to be considered. Suppose something was to happen—well, suppose I was to have a baby, say. That sometimes happens, even when you don't want it to. What would we do, then? We'd be tied down then, for life, just like all the other people around here. They all start out loving each other and thinking that everything is going to be fine—and before you know it, they find out they haven't got anything and they wish they could do it all over again—only it's too late.

SAM. It's to escape all that, that we must be together. It's only because we love each other and belong to each other, that we can find the strength to escape.

ROSE [*shaking her head*]. No, Sam.

SAM. Why do you say no?

ROSE. It's what you said just now—about people belonging to each other. I don't think people ought to belong to anybody but themselves. I was thinking that if my mother had really belonged to herself, and that if my father had really belonged to himself, it never would have happened. It was only because they were always depending on somebody else for what they ought to have had inside themselves. Do you see what I mean, Sam? That's why I don't want to belong to anybody, and why I don't want anybody to belong to me.

SAM. You want to go through life alone?—never loving anyone, never having anyone love you?

ROSE. Why, of course not, Sam! I want love more than anything else in the world. But loving and belonging aren't the same thing. [*Putting her arms about him.*] Sam dear, listen. If we say good-bye now, it doesn't mean that it has to be forever. Maybe some day, when we're older and wiser, things will be different. Don't look as if it was the end of the world, Sam!

SAM. It *is* the end of my world.

ROSE. It isn't, Sam! If you'd only believe in yourself a little more, things wouldn't look nearly so bad. Because once you're sure of yourself, the things that happen to you aren't so important. The way I look at it, it's not what you do that matters so much; it's what you are. [*Warmly.*] I'm so fond of you, Sam. And I've got such a lot of confidence in you. [*Impulsively.*] Give me a nice kiss!

[SAM *takes her in his arms and kisses her passionately. A gawky* GIRL *of seventeen—one of* LIPPO'S *pupils, appears at the left, and looks at them, scandalized. Then she goes into the vestibule and rings the bell. The door clicks and she enters the house, as* SHIRLEY *comes out, carrying a wicker suit-case.* SHIRLEY *looks at* SAM *and* ROSE.]

ROSE [*to* SHIRLEY]. I was just telling Sam that I think I'll soon be going away from New York.

[SAM *looks at her for a moment, in agony, then goes abruptly into the house.*]

SHIRLEY. I put your things in this suitcase. [*She comes down to the pavement. The* GIRL, *in the Fiorentino apartment, begins tuning her violin.*]

ROSE [*taking the suit-case*]. You've been awfully nice to me. Don't worry about Sam, Miss Kaplan. Everything will be all right with him.

SHIRLEY. I hope so.

[*From the Fiorentino apartment come the strains of Dvořák's "Humoresque," jerkily played on a violin.*]

ROSE. Oh, I just know it will! [*Extending her hand.*] Good-bye, Miss Kaplan.

SHIRLEY. Good-bye, Rose. [*Impulsively.*] You're a sweet girl. [*She hugs and kisses her.*]

ROSE. I hope I'll see you again.

SHIRLEY [*crying*]. I hope so, Rose.

[ROSE *takes up the suit-case and goes off at left.* SHIRLEY *stands watching her.*]

KAPLAN [*re-appearing at his window*]. Shoiley, vot's de metter again vit Sem? He's crying on de bed.

SHIRLEY. Let him alone, papa, can't you? [*She turns and enters the house.* KAPLAN *sighs and, seating himself at the window, opens a newspaper. A shabby, middle-aged* COUPLE *appear at the right, and approach the stoop.*]

THE MAN [*reading the To-Let sign*]. Here's a place. Six rooms. Want to take a look at it?

[*A* GROUP OF CHILDREN *off-stage left begin singing "The Farmer in the Dell." This continues until after the curtain is down.*]

THE WOMAN. All right. No harm lookin'. Ring for the janitor. [*The* MAN *goes up the stoop and rings the janitor's bell.*] Somebody must o' just died.

THE MAN. Yeah, maybe that's why they're movin' out. [*Wiping his face with a handkerchief.*] Phoo! Seems to be gettin' hotter every minute.

[MRS. FIORENTINO *seats herself at her window, a sewing-basket in her lap.* MRS. JONES *and* MISS CUSHING *appear at the right, busily engaged in conversation.*]

MISS CUSHING. The poor little thing!

MRS. JONES [*as they go up the steps*]. Well, you never can tell with them quiet ones. It wouldn't surprise me a bit, if she turned out the same way as her mother. She's got a gentleman friend, that I guess ain't hangin' around for nothin'. I seen him late last night, and this afternoon, when I come home from the police— [*She is still talking, as they enter the house.* MRS. OLSEN *comes up the cellar steps.* A SAILOR *appears at the left with two girls, an arm about the waist of each. They stroll slowly across.*]

CURTAIN

HOLIDAY

by Philip Barry

First production, November 26, 1928,
at the Plymouth Theatre, New York City,
with the following cast:

LINDA SETON, *Hope Williams*
JOHNNY CASE, *Ben Smith*
JULIA SETON, *Dorothy Tree*
NED SETON, *Monroe Owsley*
SUSAN POTTER, *Barbara White*
NICK POTTER, *Donald Ogden Stewart*
EDWARD SETON, *Walter Walker*
LAURA CRAM, *Rosalie Norman*
SETON CRAM, *Thaddeus Clancy*
HENRY, *Cameron Clemens*
CHARLES, *J. Ascher Smith*
DELIA, *Beatrice Ames*

SCENES

ACT I *Room on the Third Floor of Edward Seton's House*
   in New York.
ACT II *Room on the Top Floor.*
ACT III *Room on the Third Floor.*

Act one

SCENE: *A room on the third floor of* EDWARD SETON'S *house in New York. The only entrance is at Left. It is a very large rectangular room of the Stanford White period. The panelling is heavy, the mouldings are heavy, the three long windows looking out over the park at Back are hung with heavy curtains. The portrait of* SETON'S *father, by a contemporary English master, hangs over the fireplace, at the right. It is a handsome room, and quite a comfortable room, but rich, very rich. At Right and Left are two comfortable sofas, a table behind each. On one table are two telephones, one for the house, the second for outside. On the other table, magazines and newspaper, and a cigarette-box. This side of the sofa, near Center, are two upholstered benches, and at Right and Left of each a large chair. In the corners of the room, at Back, stand two more chairs, a table and lamp beside each.*

TIME: *It is about twelve o'clock on a bright, cold Sunday morning in mid-December, this year.*

AT RISE: *A fire is burning in the fireplace. Sunday papers are strewn upon a low table and beside a chair near it.*
JULIA SETON *is seated at a desk, Right, writing a note. She is twenty-eight, and quite beautiful. She writes in silence for a few minutes, then calls, in response to a knock at the door:*

JULIA. Yes? [HENRY *enters from Left.* HENRY *is the butler. He is fifty, of pleasant appearance, of pleasant manner.*] Oh, hello, Henry. How have you been? [*She seals the note.*]

HENRY. Well, thank you, Miss. We're very glad to have you back again.

JULIA. It was a lovely trip.

HENRY. A Mr. Case to see you, Miss. He said you expected him, so Charles is bringing him up.

JULIA. That's right. How many are we for lunch?

HENRY. Six, I believe. Only Mr. and Mrs. Cram are expected.

JULIA. Hasn't Miss Linda friends, too?

HENRY. Not as we've been told, Miss.

JULIA. Have an extra place set, will you?

HENRY. Yes, Miss. [HENRY *collects the newspapers from the floor and chairs, and piles them in a neat pile upon a table. After a moment* CHARLES, *a younger man-servant, appears in the doorway.*]

CHARLES. Mr. Case, Miss.

JULIA [*rises from the desk and calls in the direction of the hall*]. Come in, Johnny! Quick!—Of all slow people. [CHARLES *stands aside to admit* JOHNNY CASE, *and enters after him.* JOHNNY *is thirty, medium-tall, slight, attractive-looking, luckily not quite handsome. He goes at once to* JULIA.]

JOHNNY. There was a traffic-jam. Men were dying like flies.—Did you really go to church?

JULIA. Yes, but I ducked the sermon. I was sure you'd get here before me. You're staying for lunch, you know.

JOHNNY. Thanks, I'd love to. [BOTH *look warily at the* TWO MEN *tidying up the room.*] I'm actually hungry again. Those same old shooting-pains.

JULIA. Isn't it extraordinary the appetite that place gives you? You should have seen the breakfast I ate on the train.

JOHNNY. Why wouldn't you join me? You were invited.

JULIA. Miss Talcott would have swooned away. She's the world's worriedest chaperon as it is. [HENRY *goes out.* CHARLES *has begun to gather ashtrays upon a larger tray.*] —You can leave the trays till later, Charles.

CHARLES. Very well, Miss. [*He moves toward the door.* JULIA *talks against his exit.*]

JULIA [*to* JOHNNY]. Have you ever known such cold?

JOHNNY. Never.

JULIA. It's hard to believe it was twenty degrees lower at Placid.

JOHNNY. You don't feel it, there.

JULIA. That's what they say.—And you can close the door, Charles. It makes a draught.

CHARLES. Yes, Miss.

JULIA. When Mr. Seton comes in, would you ring this room from the door? Two short ones.

CHARLES. Very good, Miss. [*He goes out, closing the door after him. For a moment* JULIA *and* JOHNNY *stand transfixed, looking at each other. Then* JULIA *smiles slightly and says:*]

JULIA. Hello, Sweet— [*In an instant* JOHNNY *is beside her and she is in his arms, being kissed. At length she stands off from him, murmuring*] Johnny— Johnny—mind your manners.

JOHNNY. But, dear, where are we?

JULIA. We're here, all right. [JOHNNY *moves away from her and looks about him.*]

JOHNNY. But where's "here"?

JULIA. Where I live. Don't you like it?

JOHNNY. But Julia, seriously, what *is* all this?

JULIA. All what?

JOHNNY. All this house—and armies of men underfoot picking up newspapers, and—

JULIA. Aren't you silly, Johnny. I told you where I

lived. [*She seats herself upon a sofa.*]—I wrote it on the back of an envelope for you.

JOHNNY. But it's enormous. I'm overcome. It's the Grand Central. How can you stand it?

JULIA. I seem to manage.

JOHNNY. Don't you find you rattle around a good deal in it?

JULIA. I hadn't noticed that I did.

JOHNNY [*cups his hands and calls through them*]. Hoo! [*then*]: There's a bad echo.

JULIA. You stop criticizing this house, or I'll call the bouncer.

JOHNNY. But you must all be so *rich*, Julia!

JULIA. Well, we aren't poor.

JOHNNY. You should have told me, you really should.

JULIA. Would it have made any difference?

JOHNNY [*laughs*]. Lord, yes! I'd have asked you to marry me in two days, instead of ten.

JULIA [*a pause, then*]. How do you mean?

JOHNNY. I went through an awful struggle. You've no idea. I had very definite plans for the next few years, and at first a wife looked like quite a complication.

JULIA. What were the plans?

JOHNNY. For one thing, I was worried about having enough for both of us. If I'd known, I'd have spared myself. It's simply swell now. Good Julia.

JULIA. Aren't you funny, Johnny.

JOHNNY. Why?

JULIA. To talk about it.

JOHNNY. It? Money? Why? Is it so sacred?

JULIA. Of course not. But—

JOHNNY. I'm simply delighted, that's all.

JULIA. —That I have—uh—money?

JOHNNY. Yes. Sure. [*She laughs.*]

JULIA. You're amazing.

JOHNNY. But why not?—If I'd suddenly discovered you could play the piano I'd be delighted, wouldn't I?

JULIA. Is it like knowing how to play the piano?

JOHNNY. Well, they're both very pleasant accomplishments in a girl.

JULIA. But, my dear, you're going to make millions, yourself!

JOHNNY. Oh, no, I'm not.

JULIA. You are too!

JOHNNY. —Am not.

JULIA. Are too. [*A brief pause.*]

JOHNNY. How did you happen to decide I'd do, Julia?

JULIA. I fell in love with you, silly.

JOHNNY. You might have done that, and still not have wanted to marry me.

JULIA. I do, though.

JOHNNY. You know awfully little about me.

JULIA. *I* know enough.—You aren't trying to get out of anything, are you, Johnny?

JOHNNY. Watch me.

JULIA. Because you haven't a chance, you know. [*She rises and goes to the window at Back.*]

JOHNNY. But what's there different about me? What did it?

JULIA. You're utterly, utterly different.

JOHNNY. —I am a man of the pee-pul—

JULIA. That might be one reason.

JOHNNY. I began life with these two bare hands.

JULIA. —So did the gentleman over the fireplace. [JOHNNY *looks at the portrait above the mantel.*] —Take heart from Grandfather.

JOHNNY. You wouldn't tell me you're *those* Setons!

JULIA. Forgive us, Johnny, but we are.

JOHNNY [*overwhelmed, lowers his head*]. It's too much.

JULIA [*lightly*]. —What man has done, man can do—or words to that effect. [*She is looking out the window, down into the street.*]

JOHNNY. See here, child—if you think I'm a budding young Captain of Industry, or—

JULIA. Sh—wait a minute.

JOHNNY. What's the matter?

JULIA. It's the motor. At least I think—yes, it is.

JOHNNY. Him?

JULIA. Wait a minute— No—it's only Linda. **Father** must have decided to walk home with Ned.

JOHNNY. Did you tell him, as you planned to?

JULIA [*again moves toward the sofa*]. Father? Just exactly as I planned to.

JOHNNY. I'm still not sure that church was a good place.

JULIA. I wanted to give him a chance to think, before he started talking. He never talks in church.

JOHNNY. What did you say?

JULIA. I said, "Look here, Father: I'm going to marry Johnny Case." And he said, "What's that?" and I said, "I said, I'm going to marry Johnny Case."

JOHNNY. And he never even peeped?

JULIA. Oh, yes.—"And who may Johnny Chase be?" "Case," I said. "Not Chase." "Well, Case, then?"—I told him I'd met you at Placid, that he'd meet you at luncheon and that you were with Sloan, Hobson, Hunt and Sloan.—That was right, wasn't it?

JOHNNY. Sloan, Hobson, *Hunter* and Sloan.

JULIA. It was near enough. He said, "I know Sam Hobson," and began to pray rapidly—and that was all there was to it.

JOHNNY. But probably there'll be more.

JULIA. Yes, probably a lot more—I hope you're feeling strong. [*They seat themselves together upon the sofa at Right.*]

JOHNNY. Seriously, how do you think he'll take it?

JULIA [*laughs*].—Seriously! [*then*]: You'll have one big thing in your favor, Johnny.

JOHNNY. What?

JULIA. You'll see.

JOHNNY. I know: It's this necktie.

JULIA. Johnny—

JOHNNY. Julia—

JULIA. Don't jest, boy.

JOHNNY. Oh, darling, let's not let the fun go out of it!

JULIA. Is it likely to?

JOHNNY. No, but—

JULIA. Say it.

JOHNNY. What was the point of spilling it so quickly?

JULIA. I had to tell Father. It would be different if Mother were alive. I could have broken it gently through her, I suppose. But as it is—

JOHNNY. —Eventually, I know. But why the rush?

JULIA. I had to tell him. He'd never have forgiven me.

JOHNNY. It could have been such a swell guilty secret for awhile.

JULIA. I can't see what particular fun a secret would have been.

JOHNNY. Can't you, dear?

JULIA. No.

JOHNNY. All right.

JULIA. Oh, don't say "all right" that way! You don't mean "all right."

JOHNNY [*smiles*]. All right.

JULIA. You're the most outspoken, direct man I've ever known, and you sit there, sobbing over—

JOHNNY. It's all right, dear. Really it is.

JULIA. I thought you wanted us to be married as soon as possible.

JOHNNY. I do.

JULIA. Well, then.

JOHNNY. When shall we?

JULIA. There's another place Father comes in.

JOHNNY. I should think it would be pretty much up to you.

JULIA. You don't know Father.

JOHNNY. But let's not have an elaborate one—wedding, I mean.

JULIA. I doubt if we can avoid it. We've got to think of Father.

JOHNNY. It's getting pretty complicated.

JULIA. You didn't think it would be simple, did you?

JOHNNY. I suppose I just didn't think.

JULIA. You couldn't have. [*In sudden exasperation.*] Oh, Johnny, *Johnny*—what's the matter with you?

JOHNNY. I just hate the thought of sitting down with a man and being practical about you—so soon, I mean. [JULIA *softens.*]

JULIA. —Angel. [*She kisses him, lightly.*] It's got to be done, though.

JOHNNY. All right. I'll gird up my loins.—You know, I'll bet he'll hate this necktie. It doesn't look substantial.

JULIA. You might sit like this—covering it with your hand.

JOHNNY. I love you, Julia.

JULIA. I love you, Johnny.

JOHNNY. That's the main thing, isn't it?

JULIA. Darling, that's everything—

JOHNNY. Kiss?

JULIA. With pleasure— [*They kiss.*]

JOHNNY. —Don't go.

JULIA. I wouldn't think of it.

JOHNNY. It'd be swell to have this whole day free with no ordeals to face.

JULIA. It'll be over soon.—I think we'll have Ned and Linda on our side.

JOHNNY. Lord, do they have to mix in, too?

JULIA. Well, they're my brother and sister.

JOHNNY. Are they good guys?

JULIA. —Dears. Ned's a little inclined to drink too much, but I think he'll outgrow it. You ought to be able to help him, I think. Linda's a curious girl. She's developed the queerest—I don't know—attitude toward life. I can't make her out. She doesn't think as we do at all, any more.

JOHNNY. We?

JULIA. —The family. Father's worried sick about her. I think *we* can help her a lot, though—I hope we can.

JOHNNY [*rises and goes to the fireplace*]. She might prefer to work it out for herself. So might Ned.

JULIA. You *are* strange this morning, Johnny.

JOHNNY. How?

JULIA. You seem—not to like things quite as much as you might.

JOHNNY. Oh, yes, I do!

JULIA. We can't just wander forever up snowy mountains through pine woods with never a care, you know.

JOHNNY. Come here, darling. [*He goes to her, she to him. They meet.*] —We can do better than that.

JULIA. Do you suppose?

JOHNNY. *I know.* [JULIA's *head drops.*]

JULIA. Oh, I feel so awfully sad all at once.

JOHNNY. Don't—*don't*. Don't ever— [*His grasp tightens upon her shoulders.*] Look up here—! [*With an effort, she looks up.*] —Now please kiss me several times. [*She kisses him, once, twice, lightly.*]

JULIA. Is that all right?

JOHNNY. All right, hell. It's perfect. [*He bends to kiss her again, when the door suddenly opens and* LINDA SETON *enters, in hat and fur coat.* LINDA *is twenty-seven, and looks about twenty-two. She is slim, rather boyish, exceedingly fresh. She is smart, she is pretty, but beside* JULIA's *grace,* JULIA's *beauty, she seems a trifle gauche, and almost plain. She is pulling off her hat.*]

LINDA. I must say, that of all the boring— [*She stops at the sight of* JULIA *and* JOHNNY.] Why, Julia. For shame, Julia. [JULIA *and* JOHNNY *part.* LINDA *throws her hat and gloves upon a chair.*] Is this a way to spend Sunday morning? Who's your partner? Anyone I know?

JULIA. It's— [*She recovers her composure.*] —This is Mr. Case—my sister, Linda.

JOHNNY. How do you do?

LINDA. Well, thanks.—And you?

JOHNNY. I couldn't be better.

LINDA. Good.

JULIA [*with dignity*]. —*Johnny* Case, his name is. I'm going to marry him.

LINDA. That makes it all right, then. [*She takes off her coat.*] Who's coming to lunch? Susan and Nick didn't telephone, did they?

JULIA. —In just one month I'm going to marry him.—

LINDA. .Stand over here in the light, will you, Case? [JOHNNY *turns to her scrutiny.*] —But I've never even seen you before.

JULIA. Neither had I, until ten days ago at Placid.

LINDA. [*to* JOHNNY, *with hope*]. You aren't a guide, are you?

JOHNNY. No. I'm a lawyer.

LINDA. Wouldn't you know it.

JULIA [*seats herself upon a chair at Right*]. I want you to be maid-of-honor, Linda.

LINDA. I accept. What'll we wear? [*She sits upon the bench at Left, and* JOHNNY *upon the sofa facing her.*] Listen: is this what came over Father in church?

JULIA. I imagine so.

LINDA. Then you've told him already.

JULIA. Yes.

LINDA. Tsch-tsch, this modern generation. [*To* JOHNNY.] Well, young man, I hope you realize what you're getting in for.

[DELIA, *a housemaid of about thirty-five, comes in, takes* LINDA'S *coat, hat and gloves, and goes out with them.*]

JULIA. That's pleasant.

LINDA. I don't mean you. You're divine. I mean Father and Cousin Seton Cram and Laura and the rest of the outlying Setons—and the general atmosphere of plenty, with the top riveted down on the cornucopia—

JULIA. Johnny will try to bear up, won't you, Johnny?

JOHNNY. I'll do my best.

LINDA [*goes to* JULIA *and seats herself upon the bench*

facing her]. But how *did* you happen to get together?
Tell Linda everything.

JULIA. Well, I was walking along the road with Miss
Talcott one morning on the way to the rink and who
should I see but—

LINDA. —*Whom* should I see but—

JULIA. —And who should I see but this man coming
along, carrying skiis.

LINDA. Fancy that. A downright romance. Go on, dear—

JULIA. Do you really want to know?

LINDA. I'm hungry for romance, Sister. If you knew the
way my little heart is beating against its bars right
this minute.

JULIA. He had a queer look on his face.

LINDA. I can believe that. His eyes must have been
burning.

JULIA. As a matter of fact, the trouble was with his
nose. So I stopped him and said: "I suppose you
don't realize it, but your nose is frozen." And he
said: "Thanks, I hadn't realized it." And I said:
"Well, it is." And he said: "I don't suppose there's
anything you personally could do about it."

LINDA. Fresh.

JULIA. I thought so too.

JOHNNY. She was fresh to mention it. It looked to me
like an out-and-out pick-up.

LINDA. Obviously.

JULIA. I know a good thing when I see it.

LINDA [*to* JOHNNY]. —So you swept her off her snow-
shoes?

JOHNNY. It was touch-and-go with us.

LINDA [*to* JULIA]. I think I like this man.

JULIA. I was sure you would.

LINDA. Well, my dears, take your happiness while you
may.

JOHNNY. Watch us.

JULIA [*laughs*]. No—*don't* watch us! Hello, Ned—

[NED SETON *enters from the hall. He is twenty-six. He is as handsome in his way as* JULIA *is in hers. His features are fine, a little too fine. He displaces very little, but no one minds: he is a nice boy.* JOHNNY *rises.* NED *goes to* JULIA.]

NED. Oh, *you're* back.—Then it was you who took that shaker out of my room.

JULIA. This is Mr. Case—my brother Ned. [JOHNNY *moves to* NED. *They shake hands briefly.*]

NED. How do you do?—It was you who took it, Julia, and I'm sick of your meddling in my affairs.

JULIA. I'm going to marry him. [NED *turns slowly, as* JULIA's *words penetrate, and regards* JOHNNY.]

NED. You've got a familiar look about you.

JOHNNY. That's good.

NED. Is your name Johnny Case?

JOHNNY. Johnny Case.

NED. —One Saturday, quite a while ago, I went down to New Haven for a game. Afterwards, you took me all the way home from the Field, and put me to bed somewhere.

LINDA. How sweet.

JOHNNY. Call me Nana. [*He goes to the sofa at Right.*]

NED. I never got a chance to thank you. Thanks.

JOHNNY. It's all right.—Any time.

NED [*settles down with a newspaper on the sofa at Left*]. He's a good man, this Case fellow.

LINDA. The point is, there's no moss apparent, nor yet the slighest touch of decay.

NED. I expect Father'll be a job. When do they come to grips?

JULIA. Before luncheon, I suppose.

LINDA [*rises*]. That soon? See here, Case, *I* think you need some coaching.

JOHNNY. I'd be grateful for anything in this trouble.

LINDA. Have you anything at all but your winning way to your credit?

JOHNNY. Not a thing.

JULIA. Oh, hasn't he, though!

LINDA. The first thing Father will want to know is, how are you fixed?

JOHNNY. Fixed?

LINDA [*firmly*]. —Fixed.—Are you a man of means, and if so, how much?

JULIA. Linda!

LINDA. Be still, Beauty. [*To* JOHNNY.] I know you wouldn't expect that of a man in Father's position, but the fact is, money is our god here.

JULIA. Linda, I'll—! —Johnny, it isn't true at all.

NED [*looks up from his paper*]. No?—What is, then?

LINDA. Well, young man?

JOHNNY [*goes to her*]. I have in my pocket now, thirty-four dollars, and a package of Lucky Strikes. Will you have one?

LINDA. Thanks. [*She takes a cigarette from him.*] —But no gilt-edged securities? No rolling woodlands?

JOHNNY. I've got a few shares of common stock tucked away in a warm place.

LINDA. —Common? Don't say the word. [*She accepts a light from him.*] I'm afraid it won't do, Julia.—He's a comely boy, but probably just another of the vast army of clock-watchers. [*She moves toward the window.* JOHNNY *laughs and seats himself on the sofa at Right.*]

NED [*from behind his newspaper*]. How are you socially?

JOHNNY. Nothing there, either.

LINDA [*turning*]. You mean to say your mother wasn't even a Whoozis?

JOHNNY. Not even that.

JULIA. Linda, I do wish you'd shut up.

NED. Maybe he's got a judge somewhere in the family.

LINDA. Yes, that might help. Old Judge Case's boy. White pillars. Guitars a-strummin'. Evenin', Massa.

NED. You must know some prominent people. Drop a few names.

LINDA. —Just casually, you know: "When I was to Mrs.
Onderdonk's cock-fight last Tuesday, whom should I
see but Mrs. Marble. Well, sir, I thought we'd die
laughing—"

JULIA [*to* JOHNNY]. This is a lot of rot, you know.

JOHNNY. I'm having a grand time.

LINDA. " 'Johnny,' she says to me—she calls me
'Johnny'—"

JULIA. Oh, will you be *quiet!* What on earth has set
you off this time?

LINDA. But it's dreadful, Sister. [*To* JOHNNY.] —Just
what do you think you're going to prove with Edward Seton, financier and cotillion-leader?

JOHNNY. Well, I'll tell you: when I find myself in a position like this, I ask myself: What would General
Motors do? Then I do the opposite.

LINDA [*laughs and reseats herself. To* JULIA]. It'll be a
pity, if it doesn't come off. It'll be a real pity.

JULIA. It will come off. [*To* JOHNNY.] Father isn't at all
as they say he is.

JOHNNY. No?

JULIA. Not in the least.—Ned, where is he? Didn't he
come in with you?

JOHNNY. Don't hurry him. There's no hurry.

NED. He said he had to stop to see Sam Hobson about
something.

JULIA [*to* JOHNNY]. You.

JOHNNY. That's nice. I hope I get a good character.

LINDA. If it does go through all right, are you really
going to make it quick?

JULIA. The second week in January. The tenth.

LINDA. —Announcing when?

JULIA. Right away—next Saturday, say.

LINDA [*eagerly*]. Oh, darling, let me give a party for it!

JULIA [*puzzled*]. Do you want to? I thought you hated
the thought of—

LINDA. *I* want to! Not Father. *I* want to.

JULIA. Why, of course, dear. We'd love it.

NED. Who'd like a drink? [*No one bothers with him.*]

LINDA. —Father's to have nothing to do with it. And we *won't* send out cards. I'll telephone people.—Saturday's New Year's Eve, do you know it? Oh, Lord, Lord—let's have some fun in this house before you leave it!

JULIA. Why, Linda—

LINDA. I mean it! Let me, won't you?

JULIA. If Father doesn't mind.

LINDA. No ifs at all!—And just a few people—very few. Not a single bank of pink roses and no String Quartet during supper. All I want by way of entertainment is just one good tap-dancer. Let me plan it. Let me give it. Julia, let *me* do something for you once— —*me,* Julia.

JULIA. I'd love it, dear. I really would.

LINDA. It won't be a ball, it'll be a simple sit-down supper—and you know where?—The old playroom.

JULIA. Why, not the—

LINDA. —Because the playroom's the one room in this house anyone's ever had fun in!

NED. I haven't been up there for ten years.

LINDA. That's your loss, Neddy. I've installed a new fangled gramophone, and I sit and play to myself by the hour. Come up some time. It's worth the trip. [*She turns suddenly to* JOHNNY.] —Do you know any living people, Case? That's a cry from the heart.

JOHNNY. One or two.

LINDA. Give me a list. [*To* JULIA.] —Seton and Laura can't have a look-in—is that understood? [*To* JOHNNY.] —A terrible cousin and his wife—the Seton Crams. They're coming for lunch today. I hope your digestion's good. [*To* JULIA.] —Not a look-in, remember.

JULIA. I don't know how you'll keep them out.

LINDA [*rises abruptly*]. Oh, Julia—this is important to me!—No one must touch my party but me, do you hear?

JULIA. All right, darling.

LINDA. If anyone does, I won't come to it.

NED. —At that, you might have a better time. [*He rises.*] Look here, Case—

JOHNNY. Yes?

NED. Cocktails aren't allowed at mid-day, so just before luncheon's announced I'll ask you if you care to brush up.

JOHNNY. And guess what I'll say.

JULIA. There'll be wine with lunch, Ned.

NED. You have to give it something to build on, don't you? [*A buzzer sounds twice.* JULIA *and* JOHNNY *rise.*]

JULIA. —It's Father! He's home.

LINDA. He'll go up to his sitting-room first.

JULIA [*moves toward the door*]. I know. Come on with me, Ned.

NED. I don't want to see him.

JULIA. Please come with me. [NED *goes out. She turns to* JOHNNY.] You wait here with Linda a moment. I'll either come down again or send word. Just talk a while. [*She follows* NED *out. A brief pause. Then* LINDA *goes to the bench at Left, and* JOHNNY *to the one at Right.*]

LINDA. However do you do, Mr. Case?

JOHNNY. —And you, Miss—uh—?

LINDA. Seton is the name.

JOHNNY. Not one of the bank Setons!

LINDA. The same.

JOHNNY. Fancy!—I hear a shipment of earmarked gold is due in on Monday. [*Now they are seated.*]

LINDA [*in her most social manner*]. Have you been to the Opera much lately?

JOHNNY. Only in fits and starts, I'm afraid.

LINDA. But, my dear, we must do *something* for them! They entertained us in Rome.

JOHNNY. —And you *really* saw Mount Everest?

LINDA. Chit.

JOHNNY. Chat.

LINDA. Chit-chat.

JOHNNY. Chit-chat.

LINDA. Will that go for the preliminaries?

JOHNNY. It's all right with me.

LINDA. I love my sister Julia more than anything else in this world.

JOHNNY. I don't blame you. So do I.

LINDA. She's so sweet, you don't know.

JOHNNY. Yes, I do.

LINDA. She's beautiful.

JOHNNY. She's all of that.

LINDA. —And exciting, too—don't you think?

JOHNNY. —Don't. I'll start jittering.

LINDA. It's terribly important that she should marry the right person.

JOHNNY. That's important for everyone.

LINDA. It's particularly so for Julia.—I suppose you realize you're a rather strange bird in these parts.

JOHNNY. How's that?

LINDA. You don't know the kind of men we see as a rule. —Where have you been?

JOHNNY. Oh—working hard.

LINDA. Nights?

JOHNNY. Nights too.

LINDA. What about these little jaunts to Placid? Come clean, Case.

JOHNNY. That's the first holiday I've ever had.

LINDA [*unconvinced*]. Yes.

JOHNNY. You heard what I said.

LINDA. Then you can't have been working long.

JOHNNY. Just since I was ten. [*She frowns, puzzled.*]

LINDA. —Ten. At what?

JOHNNY. —Anything I could get. Law, the last few years.

LINDA. —Must be ambitious.

JOHNNY [*expels his breath in a long, tired jet*]. I am. Not for that, though.

LINDA. For what, then?

JOHNNY. Oh—to live. Do you mind? [*There is a pause.*]

LINDA. What is it you've been doing?

JOHNNY. I don't call what I've been doing, living.

LINDA. No? [*He shakes his head.*]

JOHNNY. —A while ago you asked me if I knew any living people. I know damn few.

LINDA. There aren't but damn few.

JOHNNY. Well, I mean to be one of them some day. Johnny's dream.

LINDA. So do I. Linda's longing.

JOHNNY. There's a pair called Nick and Susan Potter—

LINDA. So you know Nick and Susan?

JOHNNY. I should say I do.

LINDA. So that's where I've heard your name. Aren't they grand?

JOHNNY. It seems to me they know just about everything. Maybe I'm wrong.

LINDA. You're not, though.

JOHNNY. Life must be swell when you have some idea of what goes on, the way they do.

LINDA. They get more fun out of nothing than anyone I know.

JOHNNY. You don't have such a bad time yourself, do you?

LINDA [*leaning forward*]. Case, are you drawing me out? [JOHNNY *laughs.*]

JOHNNY. Sure! Come on!

LINDA. Well, compared to the time I have, the last man in a chain-gang thoroughly enjoys himself.

JOHNNY. But how does that happen?

LINDA. You tell me, and I'll give you a rosy red apple.

JOHNNY. It seems to me you've got everything.

LINDA. Oh, it does, does it?

JOHNNY. What's the matter? Are you fed up?

LINDA. —To the neck.—Now tell me about *your* operation.

JOHNNY. I had been ailing for years—I don't know—life

seemed to have lost its savor—

LINDA. Couldn't you do your housework?

JOHNNY. Every time I ran upstairs I got all rundown. [LINDA *laughs.* JOHNNY *leans forward.*] You'd better come on a party with Julia and me.

LINDA. Any time you need an extra girl, give me a ring. —When?

JOHNNY. How's Tuesday?

LINDA. Splendid, thanks.—And how's Thursday?

JOHNNY. Blooming.

LINDA [*reflectively*]. —Looked badly the last time we met.

JOHNNY. —Just nerves, nothing but nerves.

LINDA [*a moment's pause, then*]: —Do I seem to you to complain a good deal?

JOHNNY. I hadn't noticed it.

LINDA. Then I can let myself go a little: this is a hell of a life, Case.

JOHNNY [*looks about him*]. What do you mean? All this luxe? All this—?

LINDA. You took the words right out of my mouth.

JOHNNY. Well, for that matter, so's mine.

LINDA. What's the answer?

JOHNNY. Maybe you need some time off, too—I mean from what you're doing, day in, day out—

LINDA. *Days* out, please—*years* out—

JOHNNY. All right: take it. Take the time—

LINDA. —And of course *that's* so easy.

JOHNNY. —It can be done. *I* intend to do it. I intend to take quite a lot of it—when I'm not so busy just making the wherewithal.

LINDA. Case, you astonish me. I thought you were a Willing Worker.

JOHNNY. I am, if I can get what I'm working for.

LINDA. And what would that be?

JOHNNY. Mine is a simple story: I just want to save part of my life for myself. There's a catch to it, though. It's got to be part of the young part.

LINDA. You'll never get on and up that way.

JOHNNY. All right, but I want *my* time while I'm young. And let me tell you, the minute I get hold of just about twenty nice round thousands, I'm going to knock off for as long as they last, and—

LINDA. Quit?

JOHNNY. Quit. Retire young, and work old. That's what I want to do.

LINDA. —Grand. Does Julia know about it?

JOHNNY. No—there's no use getting her hopes up until it happens.—Don't tell her, will you?

LINDA. She has enough of her own for two right now—or ten, for that matter. Mother and Grandfather did us pretty pretty.

JOHNNY [*shakes his head*]. Thanks, but I've got to do myself—only just pretty enough.

LINDA. I see. That's foolish—but you're all right, Case. You haven't been bitten with it yet—you haven't been caught by it.

JOHNNY. By what?

LINDA [*so reverently*]. The reverence for riches.

JOHNNY [*laughs*]. You *are* a funny girl.

LINDA. —Funny, am I? And what about you, you big stiff?

JOHNNY [*laughs, and rises*]. —Just take Johnny's hand, and come into the Light, sister. [JULIA *enters.* JOHNNY *turns to her.*] Did you see him?

JULIA. I saw him.

LINDA. Julia! How was he?

JULIA. I don't know yet.—Johnny, you go up to Ned's room. You haven't arrived yet. Take the elevator—Father's coming down the stairs. Quick, will you?

JOHNNY. When do I arrive?

JULIA. One o'clock. It's quarter to.

JOHNNY. This is getting a little complicated, if you ask me.

JULIA. Nobody asked you. Go on! Do as you're told.

JOHNNY [*turns*]. See here, you saucy—

LINDA [*goes to the fireplace*]. Go on, Case. Don't expect simplicity here—just think of our Fifth Avenue frontage. [JOHNNY *laughs and goes out.* LINDA *turns to* JULIA.] Tell me: was Father awful?

JULIA. —The same old story, of course: I'm being married for my money.

LINDA. That's always flattering.—But Case didn't know our foul secret, did he?

JULIA. No.

LINDA. Even if he had, what of it?—And what good's all this jack we've got, anyway—unless to get us a superior type of husband?

JULIA. I hate you to talk like that! I hate it!

LINDA. Listen to me, Julia: I'm sore all the way through. I've been sore for a long time now, ever since I really saw how it—oh, never mind. Anyway, I don't doubt that if Case *had* known he'd still be running. You're in luck there.

JULIA. You do like him, don't you?

LINDA. She asks me if I like him!—My dear girl, do you realize that *life* walked into this house this morning? Marry him quick. Don't let him get away. And if Father starts the usual—where *is* Big Business, anyhow?

JULIA. He said he'd be right down.

LINDA. Stand your ground, Julia. If you don't know your own mind by now, you haven't got a mind. Name your date and stick to it. I'm telling you.

JULIA [*slowly*]. I want Father to see that Johnny has the selfsame qualities Grandfather had,—and that there's no reason why he shouldn't arrive just where he did.

LINDA. —If he wants to.

JULIA. —Wants to! You don't know Johnny. You don't know how far he's come already—and from what—

LINDA. —Or where he's going.

JULIA. *I* do! *I* know! I can see it clear as day! [*A moment, then*]: Linda—

LINDA. What?

JULIA. It'll be awful to leave you.

LINDA. I don't know exactly what I'll do, when you go. I've got to do something—get out—quit on it—change somehow, or I'll go mad. I could curl up and die right now.

JULIA [*touched*]. Why, darling—

LINDA. Why, my foot. I don't look sick, do I? [*She moves to the fireplace.*] Oh, Lord, if I could only get *warm* in this barn! [*She crouches before the fire and holds her hands to it.*] —Never mind about me. I'll be all right. Look out for yourself. When Big Business comes down, just watch you don't let him— [*The door opens. She looks over her shoulder and sees her Father.*] —But by a strange coincidence, here he is now.

JULIA. Did you see Mr. Hobson, Father?

[EDWARD SETON *enters. He is fifty-eight, large, nervous, distinguished. He wears a black morning coat, a white carnation in the buttonhole, and gray striped trousers. He takes nose glasses from his nose and folds them away in a silver case.*]

EDWARD. Yes.—Of course, my dear, there is another thing to be considered: What is the young man's background? Is he the sort of person that—? Ah, good morning, Linda.

LINDA. You saw me in church, Father. What's on your mind? You look worried.

EDWARD. I presume Julia has told you her story?

LINDA. Story? She's told me the facts.

EDWARD. But we mustn't rush into things, must we? [*A glance passes between JULIA and LINDA.*]

JULIA [*goes to him*]. I want to be married on January tenth, Father. That's—that's just two weeks from Tuesday.

EDWARD [*moves to the table behind the sofa at Right, and begins to search through the newspapers*]. Quite impossible.

LINDA. Why?

JULIA. Yes, why? I—I'm sure I couldn't stand a long engagement.

EDWARD. As yet, there is no engagement to stand.

LINDA. The boy has loads of charm, Father.

EDWARD [*quickly*]. You know him?

LINDA. I've heard tell of him.

EDWARD [*tastes the word*]. Charm.

LINDA. —I suppose it's solid merit you're after. Well, the rumor is he's got that, too. Sterling chap, on the whole. A catch, in fact. [NED *wanders in and seats himself upon the sofa at Left, with a newspaper.*]

JULIA. What did Mr. Hobson say, Father?

EDWARD. We must find out about the young man's background.

JULIA. What did he say?

EDWARD. Have you the financial section of the *Times,* Ned?

NED. No, I try to take Sundays off, when I can.

EDWARD. —Which reminds me: I should like you to make a practice of remaining in the office until six o'clock.

NED. Six!—What for?

EDWARD. As an example to the other men.

NED. But there's nothing for me to do after three.

EDWARD. You will find something.

NED. Look here, Father—if you think I'm going to fake a lot of—

EDWARD. Did you understand me, Ned? [*A moment:* NED *loses.*]

NED. —Oh, all right.

JULIA. What did Mr. Hobson say about Johnny, Father?

EDWARD [*settles himself upon the sofa with the financial section, now happily found*]. His report was not at all unfavorable.

LINDA. That must have been a blow.

JULIA. —But what did he *say?*

EDWARD. We must find out more about the young man,

JULIA. He seems to have some business ability—he has put through what looks like a successful reorganization of Seaboard Utilities. He holds some of the stock.

NED. Seaboard! Poor fellow—

EDWARD. —Shrewd fellow, perhaps. Hobson says signs are not unfavorable for Seaboard.—We'll buy some in the morning, Ned.

LINDA. Just another ill wind blowing money to Da-Da.

EDWARD. But we *must* know more about Mr. Chase's background.

JULIA. Case, Father, Case.

LINDA. Let it go. Chase has such a sweet banking sound.

JULIA. He's from Baltimore.

LINDA. Fine old pre-war stock, I imagine.

NED. Wasn't there a Judge Case somewhere?

EDWARD. We shall see. We shall take steps to—

LINDA. Father, if you reach for a Social Register, I'll cry out with pain.

EDWARD [*with decision*]. Well, I most certainly intend to know more about the young man than his name and his birthplace.—He does not, of course, realize that you have spoken to me, as yet?

NED. Of course not.

LINDA. Julia works fast, but not *that* fast, do you, Julia? [JULIA *does not answer.*]

EDWARD. I propose not to allow the subject of an engagement to come up in my first talk with him. I believe I am competent to direct the conversation.— You and Ned, Julia, may excuse yourselves on one pretext or another. I should like you to stay, Linda.

LINDA. I *knew* I should have learned shorthand. [EDWARD *smiles.* HENRY *enters.*]

EDWARD. I shall trust your memory.—Yes, Henry?

HENRY. Mr. Case wishes to be announced, sir.

EDWARD. Yes. [HENRY *goes out, closing the door after him.* EDWARD *arranges his cuffs, and takes a firmer seat in his chair.*]

LINDA. —So does Mr. Case's engagement. I want to give a party for it New Year's Eve, Father.

JULIA. Wait a minute, dear—

EDWARD [*watching the doorway*]. You may give a party if you like, Linda, but whether to announce an engagement, we shall see—

LINDA. —Another point about my party is that it's *my* party—mine.

EDWARD. Yes?

LINDA. Yes—and as such, I'd like to run it. I can do quite well without your secretary this time, darling —and without Seton's and Laura's helpful hints, I can do brilliantly.—There's someone at the door.

NED. Keep a stiff upper lip, Father. No doubt the fellow is an impostor.

EDWARD [*laughs*]. Oh, we shall learn many things this morning! He is not the first young man to be interviewed by me.

JULIA. Father—

EDWARD. Yes, daughter?

JULIA. Remember: I know what I want. [JOHNNY *enters*.] Oh, here you are!

JOHNNY. Here I am.

JULIA. Father, this is—Mr. Case. [JOHNNY *goes to* EDWARD. *They shake hands.* NED *rises*.]

EDWARD. How do you do, Mr. Case?

JOHNNY. How do you do, sir?

EDWARD. —My daughter, Linda.

LINDA. How do you do?

JOHNNY. How do you do?

EDWARD. And my son, Ned.

JOHNNY. How do you do?

NED. I recall your face, but your figure puzzles me.

EDWARD. Julia, if you and Ned will do the telephoning I spoke of, Linda and I will try to entertain Mr. Case until the others come—won't we, Linda?

LINDA. Sure. I'm game.

JULIA [*moves toward the door*]. —Coming, Ned?

NED [*following her*]. I wonder what we'd do without the telephone. [*They go out.*]

EDWARD. Sit down, Mr. Case.

JOHNNY. Thank you. [*He seats himself upon the bench, Left, and* LINDA *upon a small stool at the fireplace.*]

EDWARD. I presume, like all young people, you have the bad habit of smoking before luncheon?

JOHNNY. I'm afraid I have.

EDWARD. —A cigar?

JOHNNY. Not right now, thank you.

EDWARD [*lets himself down into a sofa*]. We've been quite at the mercy of the snow these days, haven't we?

JOHNNY. It doesn't seem much after Placid.

EDWARD. Placid—ah, yes! My daughter Julia has just come from there.

JOHNNY. I know.

EDWARD [*a brief pause, then*]: —You are in business in New York, Mr. Case?

JOHNNY. Yes, I'm in the Law. I'm with Sloan, Hobson.

EDWARD. An excellent firm.—And a born New Yorker?

JOHNNY. No. I was born in Baltimore.—In eighteen ninety-seven. July sixth. I'm thirty.

EDWARD. Baltimore—I used to have many friends in Baltimore.—The Whites—the Clarence Whites—Possibly you knew them.

JOHNNY. No, I don't believe I ever did.

EDWARD. —And then there was Archie Fuller's family—

JOHNNY. I'm afraid not.

EDWARD. —And let me see now—Colonel Evans—old Philip Evans—

JOHNNY. Nope. [*There is a silence, then*]: I haven't been there in some years. And I shouldn't be likely to know them, anyway. My mother and father died when I was quite young. My father had a small grocery story in Baltimore, which he was never able to make a go of. He left a number of debts which my mother worked very hard to clear up. I was the

JULIA. Oh, so do I!

LINDA. Come on, Father, be an angel. *I* think he's a very good number.

EDWARD. I am afraid it is too important a matter to be decided off-hand.

JULIA. But I want to be married on the—

EDWARD [*with sudden sharpness*]. You will be married, Julia, when I have reached a favorable decision—and upon a day which I will name.

JULIA. I—our plan was—the tenth, and sail that night on—

EDWARD. The tenth is out of the question.

JULIA. Oh, but Father—! I—

EDWARD. —And we shall let it rest at that, for the moment.

LINDA. But you'll come round, Father! I have a swell hunch you'll come round. Oh, Lordy, Lordy, what fun! Let's all join hands and— [*Voices are heard from the hall.*]

EDWARD. Seton?—Laura?—Is that you I hear?

LINDA. You bet it is.—Let's *not* join hands.

[SETON CRAM *and his wife,* LAURA, *enter.* SETON *is thirty-six, somewhat bald, inclined to a waistline, but well turned out in a morning coat, striped trousers and spats.* LAURA *is thirty-two, a shade taller than* SETON, *with a rather handsome, rather disagreeable face. She is as smartly dressed as a poor figure will allow.*]

SETON. Hello, hello!

EDWARD. —How are you, young man?

SETON. Blooming, thanks. We walked all the way up. [*They shake hands with* EDWARD.]

LAURA. I do hope we're not late, Uncle Ned.

EDWARD. No, indeed!

LINDA. You're early.

LAURA. Julia, my dear, you're back. [*She kisses her and then bears down upon* LINDA.] —And Linda! How simply stunning!

LINDA [*wards off the impending kiss*]. Careful, Laura—
I've got the most terrible cold.

LAURA. [*returning.*] But I never saw you looking better!
—Hello, Ned.

NED. Hello.

EDWARD. This is—uh—Mr. Case—my nephew, Mr. Cram,
and Mrs. Cram. [LAURA *inclines her head.*]

SETON. How do you do?

JOHNNY. How do you do? [NED *edges away from* LAURA.
EDWARD, *still stunned, stares in front of himself.*]

LAURA. —Isn't it horrid how chapped one's hands get
this weather? I don't know *what* to do. How was
Placid, Julia?—You must have had *such* a divine
time. Were there loads of amusing people there?—
And lots of beaux, too— Oh, you needn't deny it!—
We know Julia, don't we, Seton?—And you, Linda—
we haven't seen *you* for ages— [*She seats herself upon
the bench at Right*] —Now sit right down and tell us
everything you've been doing—

LINDA. Well, take the average day: I get up about eight-
thirty, bathe, dress, and have my coffee.—Aren't you
going to brush up before lunch, Ned?

NED. —Would you care to brush up before lunch, Case?

JOHNNY. I think I shall, if I may. [*He follows* NED *to
the door.*]

LINDA. —Julia?

JULIA. I'm all right, thanks.

LINDA. But look at *me*, will you! [*She moves quickly
across the room after* NED *and* JOHNNY, *flecking imaginary dust from her dress as she goes.*]—Simply *covered* with dust!—Wait, boys!

CURTAIN

Act two

SCENE—*The Playroom on the top floor is a long and spacious low-ceilinged room with white woodwork and pale blue walls upon which are lightly traced storybook designs in silver, white and green.*

At Right and Left there are two windows with window seats below them, curtained in a white-starred cretonne of a deeper blue than the walls.

The only entrance is from the hall at Back.

At Right there is a low platform for horizontal bars and a punching-bag, above which a pair of trapezes swing from the ceiling. At present they are tied up. Against the back wall behind them is a glass cabinet containing a collection of old toys, arranged on shelves in orderly rows.

Also at Right is a table, with tablecloth spread, and four small chairs. Against the back wall at Left is an old-fashioned music-box, and in the corner near it a small electric gramophone. Also at Left is a low couch and a table, a miniature easy-chair and a folding cushion.

TIME: *New Year's Eve, this year.*

AT RISE: *The Playroom is empty, and lit only by a pale night glow from the windows. A moment, then* JULIA *opens the door, and calls:*

JULIA. Linda! [*There is no answer. Dance music is heard from downstairs.*] She isn't here.

NED [*reaches past her to an electric button and lights the room*]. I didn't say she was. All I said was it's where she comes, as a rule, when she finds herself in a jam. [*They come into the room.* BOTH *are in evening clothes. In one hand* NED *carries two whisky and sodas. He puts one glass on the table and retains the other.*]

JULIA. I don't believe she's in the house.

NED [*takes a swallow of his drink*]. Maybe not.

JULIA. I told them all at dinner that she had a blinding headache, but expected to come down later.

NED. That's as good as anything— [*And another swallow*]. Let's get out of here. This room gives me a funny feeling.

JULIA. Wait a minute.—You know how furious Father was when she wasn't there for dinner— [*She goes and shuts the door, closing out the music.*] What can we do, Ned?

NED. Search me.

JULIA [*she moves to a chair and seats herself*]. But it's her party!

NED. Don't make me laugh, Julia. It was, maybe, until you and Father took it over.

JULIA. *I* did?

NED. You stood by and saw it done. Then the Crams got hold of it. Among you, you asked the whole list— which was just what Linda didn't want. You threw out the team of dancers she'd engaged for supper, and got in that troupe of Scotch Songbirds. You let Farley, with his Flower Fancies, turn it into a house of mourning. Among you, you made Linda's funny little bust into a first-class funeral. I can't say I blame her, no. However—[*He raises his glass.*]—drink to Linda.

JULIA. Well, I do! She should have realized that Father couldn't announce my engagement without *some* fuss.

NED. She should have, yes. But unlike me, Linda always hopes. [*Again his glass is raised.*] Bottoms up to Linda.

JULIA. Don't, Ned.

NED. Don't what?

JULIA. You've been drinking steadily since eight o'clock.

NED. Yes?—Funny old Ned. On New Year's Eve, too. [*He drains his glass and takes up the other.*]

JULIA. Will you kindly stop it?

NED. Darling sister, I shall drink as much as I like at any party I agree to attend. [*She turns from him with an exclamation.*] —And as much as I like is as much as I can hold. It's my protection against your tiresome friends. Linda's out of luck, she hasn't one.

JOHNNY [*comes in. Music and voices are heard from downstairs*]. —Believe it or not, I've been talking politics with an Admiral. [*He looks about him.*] —What a nice room!

NED. It's too full of ghosts for me. It gives me the creeps.

JULIA. She isn't here, Johnny.

JOHNNY. Linda?

JULIA. Yes, of course.

JOHNNY. Did you expect she would be?

JULIA. Ned thought so.

NED. Ned was wrong.

[HENRY *and* CHARLES *enter.* HENRY *carries table linen and silver and a tray of plates and glasses;* CHARLES *a pail of ice containing two bottles of champagne and a plate of sandwiches. They go to the table.*]

JULIA. Isn't there room for everyone downstairs, Henry?

HENRY. Miss Linda telephoned to serve supper here for six at half-past eleven, Miss.

NED. Ned was right.

JULIA. From where did she telephone, do you know?

HENRY. She didn't say, Miss. [*There is a pause.* HENRY *and* CHARLES *proceed to set the table.*]

JOHNNY [*to* JULIA]. I think I know where she is, if that's any help.

JULIA. You? Where—?

JOHNNY. With Nick and Susan Potter.

JULIA. What's she doing with them?

JOHNNY. Dining, I imagine.

NED. It's eleven-twenty now.

JULIA. Where did you get your information, Johnny?

JOHNNY. I met her coming in this afternoon. She said she wouldn't stay in the house tonight. Apparently it meant more to her than anyone thought.

NED. Not than I thought. I warned Father.

JOHNNY. It was no use talking to her. She was going out to dine somewhere by herself. I knew that Nick and Susan were having Pete Jessup and Mary Hedges, so I telephoned Susan and asked her to ask Linda, too.

JULIA. I wish you had spoken to me first.

JOHNNY. Why?

JULIA. People like that aren't good for Linda.

JOHNNY [*looks at her for a moment, puzzled, and then laughs*]. What are you talking about Julia?

JULIA. They make her even more discontented than she is. Heavens knows why, but they do.

NED. Apparently she's bringing them back with her. [HENRY *and.* CHARLES *go out, closing the door after them.*]

JULIA. Well, they certainly can't expect to have supper up here by themselves.

NED. No? Why not?

JULIA. They simply can't, that's all.

NED. What is this conspiracy against Linda, anyway? Are you all afraid she might cause a good time here, for once—and if she did, the walls might fall down? Is that it? [JULIA *does not reply.* JOHNNY *seats himself near her.*]

JOHNNY. I do love this room, don't you, Julia?

JULIA [*briefly*]. Yes.—It was Mother's idea for us.

JOHNNY. She must have been sweet.

JULIA. She was.

NED. —Father wanted a big family, you know. So she had Julia straight off, to oblige him. But Julia was a girl, so she promptly had Linda. But Linda was a girl

—it looked hopeless. [*His voice rises.*] —So the next year she had me, and there was much joy in the land. —It was a boy, and the fair name of Seton would flourish. [JULIA *looks at him in alarm.*] —It must have been a great consolation to Father. Drink to Mother, Johnny—she tried to be a Seton for a while, then gave up and died.—Drink to Mother—

JOHNNY [*laughs uneasily*]. You're talking through your hat, Ned.

NED. But I'm not.

JULIA [*to* JOHNNY]. Can't you possibly persuade him that he's had enough?

NED. It's all right, Julia: you heard what I said. —There's a bar in my room, if you want anything, Johnny. Tell as many of the men as you think need it. It's all very pleasant and hole-in-the-wall like everything else that's any relief in this house.—Drink to Father. [*He drains his glass, sets it down upon a table, turns on his heel and goes out, closing the door after him.*]

JULIA. We must do something about them—we *must*, Johnny!

JOHNNY. —Him and Linda.

JULIA. Yes, yes!

JOHNNY. I don't see what.—It seems a lot more goes on inside them than we've any idea of. Linda must be at the end of some rope or other. As for Ned—

JULIA. He always does this—always—

JOHNNY [*rises*]. He began some time.—I'll keep an eye on him, though, and if he stops making sense I'll get him to bed somehow.

JULIA. —And Linda's got to bring her friends downstairs.—People know there's something wrong, now— they must know.—She's simply *got* to!

JOHNNY. All right, darling. Only—

JULIA. Only what—

JOHNNY. —Do try to enjoy tonight, won't you?

JULIA. But I am, Johnny. I think it's a lovely party!

JOHNNY. Then how about getting that frown from between your eyes and not feeling personally responsible for three hundred guests, and a brother and sister?

JULIA. —Someone's got to be.

JOHNNY. —Let your Father, then.

JULIA. Poor man. Reporters have been after him all day long.

JOHNNY. Me, too. I've never felt so important.

JULIA. I hope you didn't talk.

JOHNNY. I just asked for offers for the story of how I wooed and won you. Farm Boy Weds Heiress as Blizzard Grips City.

JULIA [*laughs*]. What *did* you say?

JOHNNY. I didn't see them.

JULIA. That's right. Father was awfully anxious that nothing be added to what he sent in—except, of course, what they're bound to add themselves.

JOHNNY. Evidently it's a good deal.

JULIA. Well, that we can't help.

JOHNNY. The French Line wrote me. They want to give us a suite, in place of the cabin.

JULIA. I doubt if we ought to accept it.

JOHNNY. No? Why not?

JULIA. I think it might not look so well. I'll ask Father.

JOHNNY [*a brief pause, then*]: Perhaps we oughtn't to go abroad at all. Perhaps *that's* too great an evidence of wealth.

JULIA. Now, Johnny—

JOHNNY. —But we're going, my dear, and in the most comfortable quarters they choose to provide.

JULIA. What a curious tone for you to take. [*He looks at her in amazement, then laughs genuinely.*]

JOHNNY. Julia, don't be ridiculous! "Tone to take." [*She turns from him.*] —We may be suddenly and unexpectedly important to the world, but I don't see that we're quite important enough to bend over backwards.

JULIA [*a silence, then*]: Of course, I'll do whatever you like about it.

JOHNNY. It would be nice if you'd like it too.

JULIA [*she returns to him*]. And I'll like it too, Johnny. [*He bends and kisses her lightly.*]

JOHNNY. —Sweet. [*He takes her by the hand and draws her toward the door*]. —Come on, let's go below and break into a gavotte.

JULIA [*stops*]. —Do something for me, will you?

JOHNNY. Sure.

JULIA. —Stay here till Linda arrives, then make her come down. I can't wait. *Some* female member of the household's got to be around, if it's only the cook.

JOHNNY. —I'll *ask* her to come down.

JULIA. Insist on it!

JOHNNY. Well, I'll do whatever a gent can in the circumstances.

JULIA. You're *so* irritating! Honestly, I hate the sight of you.

JOHNNY. Julia—

JULIA. What?

JOHNNY. Like hell you do.

JULIA. I know. It's hopeless. [*She goes to the door, opens it, then turns to him again. Laughter is heard from downstairs.*] Do as you like—I love you very much.

JOHNNY. —You get through that door quick and close it after you, or you won't get out at all.

JULIA. —Just to look at you makes my spine feel like—feel like— [*He moves swiftly toward her, but finds the door closed. He stands for a moment staring at it, transfixed, then pulls it open, calling "Darling!"— But instead of* JULIA, *he finds* NICK POTTER.]

NICK. Hey! What is this?

JOHNNY. Nick! [NICK *moves away from him, scowling, and straightening his coat. He is about thirty-four, with an attractive, amusing face.*]

NICK. —Get fresh with me, and I'll knock your block

off. [*He sees the champagne and goes to it.*] What have we here—some kind of a grape beverage?

JOHNNY. Mumm's the word.—Where's Susan?

NICK. Coming.—I hear you're engaged. Many happy returns. Is it announced yet?

JOHNNY. Thanks.—No, it's to come with a roll of drums at midnight—"A lady has lost a diamond and platinum wrist watch."

NICK. —With that gifted entertainer, Mr. Edward Seton, at the microphone—

JOHNNY. That's the plan.

NICK. I heard about his work with this party.—He has the true ashman's touch, that man.

JOHNNY. He's been all right to me.

NICK. Oh, sure—he believes you're a comer. That's what won him over so quickly—the same stuff as Grandpa Seton himself—up-from-nothing—hew to the line—eat yeast. Me—of course I'm God's great social menace because I never got out and did Big Things.

JOHNNY. I really like him. I like him a lot.

NICK. Keep your men on him, though. Don't relax your vigilance. [*He is opening the bottles and filling the glasses. Music and voices are heard through the open door.*]

JOHNNY. —You think, for instance, that if *I* should quit business—

NICK. Just try it once. Why, he'd come down on you like Grant took Bourbon.

JOHNNY. You've got him all wrong, Nick.

NICK. Maybe.—Anyhow, you're not really thinking of it, are you?

JOHNNY [*goes to the couch*]. I am, you know!

NICK. On what, may I ask?

JOHNNY. Well, I've got a nice little mess of common stock that's begun to move about two years before I thought it would. And if it goes where I think it will—

NICK. —Haven't you and Julia a pretty good life ahead as it is, Johnny?

JOHNNY. You and Susan have a better one.

NICK. Listen, baby—I don't think I'd try any enlightened living stuff on this family. They wouldn't know what you were talking about.

JOHNNY. Julia would.

NICK. —Might. But the old man's a terror, Johnny. Honestly—you don't *know*.

JOHNNY. Enough of your jibes, Potter. You answer to me for your slurs on a Seton.

NICK [*moves toward him*]. —Seats on a Slurton—I want to get three seats on a Slurton for Tuesday night. [—*And confronts him with an empty bottle.*] Go on, hit me, why don't you? Just hit me. Take off your glasses—[*And returns to the table.*]—I was dragged against my will to this function. And somehow I don't seem to so well.

JOHNNY. What?

NICK. —Function.

[LINDA *and* SUSAN *enter.* SUSAN *is thirty, smart and attractive. She goes straight to* JOHNNY *and kisses him.*]

SUSAN. Cheers from me, Johnny.

JOHNNY. Thanks, Susan.

SUSAN *and* NICK [*together*]. We only hope that you will be as happy as we have been. [LINDA *closes the door. Voices and music cease to be heard.* NICK *continues to fill the glasses.*]

JOHNNY [*to* LINDA]. What did you do with Pete and Mary?

LINDA. They're coming in a heated barouche.

JOHNNY. Linda, I'm to inform you that there's another party going on in the house.

LINDA. You mean that low-class dance hall downstairs? [*She moves toward* NICK.] Don't speak of it. [NICK *gives her a glass of wine, and then one to* SUSAN.]

NICK. Here, Pearl, wet your pretty whistle with this.

[NICK *and* JOHNNY *take glasses.* SUSAN *raises hers.*]

SUSAN. —To Johnny and his Julia.

JOHNNY. Julia— [*They drink.* LINDA *seats herself in a chair near the table.*]

SUSAN. —Merry Christmas, from Dan to Beersheba.

NICK. [*examining the table*]. —Only sandwiches? What a house!

LINDA. There's solid food on the way.

NICK. I'll trade twenty marbles and a jack-knife for the carcass of one chicken, in good repair.

LINDA. You should have been with us, Johnny. Not one word of sense was spoken from eight to eleven.

SUSAN. —When Linda got homesick.

LINDA. I'm a die-hard about this evening and this room. I only hope nobody else wanders in. [JOHNNY *seats himself near* LINDA.]

NICK. I tell you who'd be fun.

LINDA. Who?

NICK. Seton and Laura.

LINDA. They wouldn't stay long.—You see those trapezes?

NICK. Yes?

LINDA. Time was when Seton and I used to swing from them by our knees, and spit at each other.

NICK. Great!

LINDA. I'm happy to say now, I rarely missed.

JOHNNY. But aren't we going downstairs?

LINDA. No, Angel, we're not.

NICK. It's grand here. It takes sixty years off these old shoulders. [*He looks at his watch.*] Eleven-forty.— Doctor Stork's on the way, dears, with Little Baby New Year. [*He goes and seats himself with* JOHNNY *and* LINDA.]

LINDA. I wish someone would tell me what *I'm* to do next year—and the year after—and the year after that—

SUSAN. What you need is a husband, Linda. [*She joins the group.*]

LINDA. Have you got any addresses?

SUSAN. He'll arrive. I only hope you'll know how to act when he does.

LINDA. Well, I won't take No for an answer.

NICK. Don't you do it.

LINDA. And in the meanwhile what? Hot-foot it around the world with a maid and a dog? Lie on one beach after another, getting brown?

NICK. Oo, I *love* to play in the sand.

SUSAN. [*to* LINDA]. —You just won't stay put, will you, child?

LINDA. And grow up to be a committee-woman and sit on Boards? Excuse me, Susan, but from now on any charity work *I* do will be for the rich. They need it more. [NICK, SUSAN *and* JOHNNY *are eating sandwiches and sipping their wine.*]

NICK. Now look, Linda—let me tell you about yourself, will you?

LINDA. Go ahead.

NICK. There's more of your grandfather in you than you think.

LINDA. Boo.

NICK. There is, though. He wasn't satisfied with the life he was born into, so he made one for himself. Now, you don't like *his* five-story log cabin so you're out in the woods again with your own little hatchet.

SUSAN. The Little Pioneer, with Linda Seton.

JOHNNY. —Linda's off on the wrong foot, though. She's headed up the fun-alley. She thinks having fun is the whole answer to life.

LINDA. *I* do?

JOHNNY. You do.—Me—it's not just entertainment *I'm* after—oh, no—I want all of it—inside, outside—smooth and rough—let 'er come!

NICK. You're right, too.—Life's a grand little ride, if you take it yourself.

JOHNNY. —And no good at all if someone else takes you on it. Damn it, there's *no* life any good but the one you make for yourself.

SUSAN [*a protest*]. Hey, hey—

JOHNNY. —Except yours and Nick's, maybe.

LINDA. But they *have* made theirs!—Haven't you, Susan?

SUSAN. About half-and-half, I should say. I don't know quite what we'd do if we had to earn our own living.

NICK. Earn it.—Is it settled about the wedding, Johnny?

JOHNNY. The twelfth—a week from Friday.

LINDA. Why not the tenth?

JOHNNY. Your father had a corporation meeting.—Ushers' dinner on Monday, Nick.

NICK [*to* SUSAN]. Don't wait lunch for me Tuesday.

SUSAN. Just come as you are.—Oh, I gave a scream.

LINDA. What's the matter?

SUSAN [*to* JOHNNY]. —Then you've put off your sailing, too?

JOHNNY. We had to.

SUSAN. Don't tell me it's the *Paris* now?

JOHNNY. Yes. Why?

SUSAN. But we changed ours from the tenth to the *Paris* so as not to bump into your wedding trip!

NICK. Well, we'll change back again.

JOHNNY. Don't think of it. It'll be great fun.

LINDA. Guess what *I* did in a wild moment this morning—

NICK. What?

LINDA. —Had my passport renewed—and Ned's. I want to get him away.

SUSAN. You're sailing then too?—It's a field-day!

LINDA. No—not till a week or so after.

JOHNNY. Come along with us, Linda. It'd be grand. We'd own the boat.

LINDA. You'll have had plenty of family by then, little man. We'll join up later.

JOHNNY. How long do you plan to stay over, Nick?

NICK. Oh—June—August—September—like the dirty loafers we are.

LINDA. Loafers nothing!

JOHNNY. You've got the life, you two.

LINDA. Haven't they? [*To* SUSAN.] You know, you've always seemed to me the rightest, wisest, happiest people ever I've known.

SUSAN. Why, Linda, thanks!

LINDA. You're my one real hope in the world.

JOHNNY. Mine, too.

SUSAN. Well, when we're with a pair like you—shall I say it, Nick?

NICK. Just let them look at us: Beam, darling—

SUSAN [*beams*]. —The Beaming Potters.

NICK. —In ten minutes of clean fun—

NICK *and* SUSAN [*together*]. We hope you'll like us! [*then*]:

NICK. —And what about you, Johnny? How long will you and Julia be there? [*A moment.* JOHNNY *smiles. then*]:

JOHNNY. Well—maybe indefinitely.

LINDA. How do you mean? Julia said March.

JOHNNY. Julia doesn't know yet.

LINDA. Johnny, what *is* this? !

JOHNNY. Well, some stock that I got at about eight was kind enough to touch fifteen today. And if a deal I think's going through does go through, it'll do twice that.

SUSAN [*puzzled*]. I must be dumb, but—

JOHNNY. Friends, there's a very fair chance I'll quit business next Saturday.

LINDA. Johnny!

NICK. For good?

JOHNNY. —For as long as it lasts.

SUSAN. As what lasts? Have you made some money?

JOHNNY. I think I shall have, by Saturday.

SUSAN. Good boy!

LINDA. Oh, very good boy!

NICK. —And Julia doesn't know your little plan?

JOHNNY. I haven't breathed a word of it to her. I wanted to be sure first. It all depends on what a

Boston crowd called Bay State Power does about it.
I'll know that Monday.

LINDA. They'll do it! I don't know what it is, but I know
they'll do it! Oh, Lord, am I happy! [*A moment.
then*]: But, Johnny—

JOHNNY. What?

LINDA. I'm scared.

JOHNNY. Of what?

LINDA. Listen to me a moment: Father and Julia— [*She
stops, as* SETON *and* LAURA *appear in the doorway,
and exclaims in disgust.*] My God, it's Winnie-the-
Pooh! [JOHNNY *and* NICK *rise.* LAURA *gazes about her.*]

LAURA. But isn't this lovely!

SETON. Well, well, so here you are! [*He comes into the
room.* LAURA *follows.*]

NICK. So we are.

SETON. Hello, Nick—Hello, Susan!

NICK. How are you?

LAURA [*to* SUSAN]. My dear, what fun! We simply never
meet any more.

SUSAN. —Just a pair of parallel lines, I expect.

LAURA. I must say you're a picture, Susan.

SUSAN [*rises and goes to the couch*]. —Madame is in a
tin bed-jacket by Hammacher-Schlemmer.

LAURA. May we sit down a minute? [*She seats herself
in* NICK'S *chair.*]

LINDA. Why not?

LAURA. I've never been up here. It's awfully pleasant.

LINDA. We like it.

NICK. Of course, it's rather far from the car-line—

SUSAN. And the water isn't all it might be—

NICK *and* SUSAN [*together*]. —But *we* like it!

JOHNNY. Don't change it, friends. It's the poor man's
club.

LAURA. What on earth are you all talking about?

LINDA [*rises and goes to the table*]. Oh, just banter—
airy nothings—give and take—

NICK. It's our defense against the ashman's touch.

LAURA. I *love* the decorations.

LINDA. They *love* to be loved.

LAURA. I'm afraid I don't follow you. You're not all tight, are you?

LINDA. On the continent, dear, on the continent.

NICK. We have a very high boiling-point.

SETON [*leans over and plucks* JOHNNY'S *sleeve*]. You old fox, you.

JOHNNY. Yes? How's that?

SETON. Sam Hobson's downstairs. He's just been telling me about your little haul in Seaboard. You might have let your friends in on it.

JOHNNY. There's still time. Climb aboard if you like.

SETON. I have already.—Do you know there's an order in our office to buy sixty thousand shares for Ross, of Bay State Power, all the way up to thirty?

JOHNNY [*quickly*]. Are you sure of that?

SETON. I took the order myself.

JOHNNY. Then that cinches it.

SUSAN. Is it a real killing, Johnny?

JOHNNY. For me it is!

SETON [*impressively*]. —Just thirty or forty thousand, that's all.

SUSAN. —No odd cents?

LINDA. Johnny—Johnny—

NICK. Let this be a lesson to you, young man.

SETON. —Anyone mind if I talk a little business?—The impression in our part of town is, it's you who put Seaboard on the map.

JOHNNY. I wouldn't go so far as that.

SETON. Ross said so himself.—Look here: we'd damn well like to have you with us, in Pritchard, Ames.

JOHNNY. Thanks, I've heard about that.

SETON. The Chief's told you already?

JOHNNY. I saw him this afternoon.

SETON [*to* NICK]. —To begin at twice what he gets now —and probably a directorship in Seaboard, to boot.

NICK. Well, well—to boot, eh?

SETON [*to* JOHNNY]. I hope you said yes.

JOHNNY. I told him I'd let him know.

SETON. Believe me when I tell you the first fifty thousand is the hardest.—It's plain sailing after that.

LINDA [*suddenly*]. Look out, Johnny!

SETON. —In two years we'll make your forty thousand, eighty—in five, two hundred.

NICK [*edges over to* JOHNNY]. —Lend a fellow a dime for a cup of coffee, mister? [JOHNNY *laughs.*]

SETON. Well, how about it?

JOHNNY. I'll let him know.

SETON. You couldn't do better than to come with us—not possibly.

JOHNNY [*rises and puts his glass on the table*]. It's awfully nice of you, it really is.

LINDA. Look out, look *out!*

JOHNNY. Don't worry, Linda.

SETON. —Just let me give you a brief outline of the possibilities—

LINDA. That will do for business tonight, Seton.

SETON. I just want to tell Johnny—

LINDA. It's enough, really.

SETON [*laughs, and rises*]. You're the hostess!—Then let's all go downstairs and celebrate, shall we?

LAURA [*rises*]. Yes, let's.—It's such a wonderful party.

LINDA. I'm not going downstairs.

SETON. Oh, come along, Linda—don't be foolish.

LAURA. Do come, dear. Your father said to tell you he—

LINDA. Yes—I thought so.—But I'm not going downstairs.

NICK [*moves away from them to the other side of the room*]. Where's the old music-box we used to play, Linda?

LINDA. Over there—but I've got something better— [*She goes to the gramophone in the corner.*] Listen—it's electric—it'll melt your heart with its—

NICK. Take it away. [SUSAN *rises.* SETON *and* LAURA *move toward the door.*]

SUSAN. Nick—you wouldn't go whimsical on us!

NICK. Oh, God, for the old scenes—the old times—

SETON. It's a quarter to twelve now, you know—

NICK [*is examining the music-box*]. Welcome, little New Year—

LAURA. Linda, I really think that—

LINDA. I know, Laura.

NICK [*reads the music-box's repertory from a card*]. "Sweet Marie"—"Fatal Wedding"—"Southern Roses"—

SUSAN. —And *this* is the way they used to dance when Grandmamma was a girl.

NICK [*covers his eyes, and gulps*]. Don't. My old eyes can scarcely see for the tears.

LAURA. You're all absolutely mad.

[HENRY *and* CHARLES *enter, with a chafing-dish and a platter of cold meats. A chorus of male voices is heard from downstairs.*]

SUSAN. Heavens, what would that be?

LINDA. It's the Scottish Singers, the little dears— [*She is watching* JOHNNY.]

NICK. I wouldn't have come if I'd known the Campbells were coming— [CHARLES *closes the door.* LINDA *starts a loud new dance-record on the gramophone.*]

SETON [*angrily*]. What do you think this gets you, anyway?

LINDA. Peace and quiet!

NICK [*huddles himself in his arms*]. What a night! What a night!

SUSAN. What Nick really wants is some nice beer to cry into.

LINDA. Will everybody please stop sobbing! Stop it!— Take some wine, will you, Case?

JOHNNY. Thanks.

LINDA [*intensely*]. If you weaken now—!

JOHNNY. I never felt stronger.

LINDA [*turns to* SUSAN]. Peter and Mary—they couldn't have ditched us, could they?

SUSAN. Oh, no, they'll be along—

NICK. Eleven forty-seven—what *can* be keeping old Doctor Stork? [HENRY *and* CHARLES, *having placed the platter and chafing-dish upon the table, go out.*]

LAURA [*at the door*]. Linda—really—people are beginning to wonder a little—

LINDA. I am *not going downstairs.*

LAURA [*laughs unpleasantly*]. Well, of course, if—

LINDA. But I wouldn't dream of keeping anyone who wants to—

LAURA [*stares a moment, then turns to* SETON]. Apparently we aren't welcome here.

SETON. I gathered that some time ago.—Linda, I think your conduct toward your guests tonight is outrageous.

LAURA. And so do I.

LINDA. I imagined that was what brought you up, you sweet things.

SETON. If you ask me, it's one of the worst cases of downright rudeness I've ever seen.

LINDA. And has someone asked you?

LAURA. —When a girl invites three hundred people to her house, and then proceeds to—

LINDA. I invited six people—three of whom you see before you. The others came on someone else's say-so —yours and Father's, I believe.

LAURA. Perhaps we'd better go home, Seton.

LINDA. Oh, you're here now. Stay, if you like. I'd prefer it, however, if you'd do your commenting on my behavior not to my face, but behind my back as usual—

LAURA [*opens the door*]. Come, Seton— [*She goes out, with all the hauteur she can command.*]

SETON [*to* LINDA]. When I think of the—

LINDA. —Before you go, you wouldn't care to swing on the old trapeze a while, would you—? [*He stares. She turns away.*] I suppose not. [SETON *goes out, closing*

the door after him. LINDA *moves toward the table.*]
Oh, the cheek, the cheek!

NICK. Some day they'll draw themselves up like that
and won't be able to get down again. [*He goes to*
JOHNNY.] Well, Johnny—!

JOHNNY [*at the table*]. Lord, it's the grandest feeling—
Oh, wait till Julia hears! On tonight of all nights,
too! What a break that is!

LINDA. I've never been so happy for anyone in my life.

NICK. Go to it, boy!

JOHNNY. Oh, won't I? Watch me! [*then*]: —Where'll
we spend the Spring?—Let's all spend the Spring together!

NICK. What do you say, Susan? Do you think we could
stand them?

SUSAN. There'll always be a curse and a blow for you
with us, Johnny.

LINDA. Can I come? Please, can I come, too—? [*She trots
in among them.*]

NICK. Don't leave us, darling. We want you. We need
you. [SUSAN *joins them. She sits at the end of the
table, opposite* NICK, *and* JOHNNY *and* LINDA *behind
it, facing the front.* JOHNNY *refills the glasses and*
SUSAN *and* LINDA *serve the food.*]

SUSAN. How about the south of France?

JOHNNY. Why not?

LINDA. No, no—the air reeks of roses and the nightin-
gales make the nights hideous.

JOHNNY [*overcome*]. Don't—don't— [*He gives each of
them a glass of wine.*]

NICK [*a suggestion*]. If we went to Norway, we could
all paint a house at midnight.

JOHNNY. —Norway's out. It's got to be some place you
can swim all day long.—You know, it's just dawned
on me that I've never swum enough. That's one of
the things I want to do: *swim*.

NICK [*rises and leans upon the table*]. Young man, in

the bright lexicon of youth there is no such word.
Swimming is for idlers.

SUSAN. —And Hawaiians.

LINDA. —And fish.

NICK. Are you a fish? Answer me that.—Can you look
yourself squarely in the eye and say "I am a fish"?
No. You cannot.

JOHNNY. You are a hard man, sir.

NICK. It is life that has made me hard, son.

JOHNNY. —But I want only to be like you, Daddy—how
can I be like you?

NICK. You ask me for the story of my success?—Well,
I'll tell you—

LINDA. Come—gather close, children. [*They turn their
chairs and face him.*]

NICK. —I arrived in this country at the age of three
months, with nothing in my pockets but five cents
and an old hat-check. I had no friends, little or no
education, and sex to me was still the Great Mystery. But when I came down the gang-plank of that
little sailing-vessel—steam was then unknown, except
to the very rich— Friends, can you picture that manly
little figure without a tug at your heart strings, and
a faint wave of nausea? But I just pulled my belt a
little tighter, and told myself, "Don't forget you're
a Potter, Nick"—I called myself "Nick"—and so I
found myself at my first job, in the glass works. Glass
was in its infancy then—we had barely scratched the
surface—but I have never shirked work—and if there
was an errand to be run, I ran five errands. If someone wanted to get off at the third floor, I took him
to the tenth floor.—Then one day came my big
chance. I was in the glass-blowing department then
—now Miss Murphy's department—and a very cap-
able little woman she is—

LINDA. Why, Mr. Potter, I'm no such thing.

NICK. Oh, yes, you are, Miss Murphy! Well, sir, I was
blowing glass like a two-year-old, whistling as I blew.

Suddenly I looked down and found in my hand—*a bottle*—or what we now know as a bottle. I rushed to my employer, a Mr. Grandgent, and said, "Look, Mr. Grandgent—I think I've got something here." Mr. Grandgent looked—and laughed—*laughed,* do you understand?—I went from city to city like some hunted thing, that laugh still in my ears. But with me went my bottle. They called it Potter's Folly. They said it would never work. Well, time has shown how right they were. Now the bottle is in every home. I have made the bottle a National Institution! —and that, my dears, is how I met your grandmother. [*He bows.*]

LINDA [*rises, champagne-glass in hand*]. —To one who, in the face of every difficulty, has proved himself a Christian gentleman.—Music, music! [*She goes to the gramophone and starts a record.*]

SUSAN [*rises*]. —To one who has been friend to rich and poor alike—

JOHNNY [*rises*]. —To one who, as soldier—

LINDA. —As statesman—

SUSAN. —As navigator—

JOHNNY. —As man about town—

LINDA. —As scout-leader—

NICK. —As Third Vice-President of the second largest spat factory in East St. Louis—

JOHNNY. On behalf of the hook-and-ladder company of the First Reformed Church, I want to say a few words about our brave Fire Laddies. Has it occurred to you— [*The door opens and* JULIA *and* EDWARD *enter.*]

EDWARD. Linda!

LINDA. Yes?

EDWARD. Please turn that machine off. [SUSAN *goes to* NICK.]

LINDA. You know Mr. and Mrs. Potter, Father—

EDWARD [*curtly*]. How do you do? [*Then to* LINDA.] Turn it off, Linda— [LINDA *stops the record.*]

NICK [*to* SUSAN]. —Fell, or was pushed.

JOHNNY [*moves eagerly toward* JULIA]. Julia! Listen, darling! I've got a grand surprise for you—

EDWARD. Just a moment!—You must all come down, now. It's nearly twelve, and we want the entire party together to see the New Year in.

LINDA. But there are two parties, Father—the one down there and mine—*here*.

EDWARD. Please do as I say, Linda.

LINDA. I asked for permission to have a few of my friends here tonight. You said I might. I've got some of them, now, and—

EDWARD. —I noticed you had.

LINDA. —And more are coming.

JULIA. They've come, haven't they?

LINDA. How do you mean?

JULIA. Peter Jessup and what's-her-name—Mary Hedges—

LINDA. What about them?

JULIA. They're downstairs.

LINDA. They—?—How long have they been there?

JULIA. Twenty minutes or so. I said you'd be down.

LINDA. Oh, you did, did you?

JULIA. —They're being very amusing. I said we expected them to be. Jessup has done his trained-seal act to perfection, and now I think Mary Hedges is about to give her imitations. [*There is a silence.* LINDA *stares at her, speechless.*] They're a great success, really.

LINDA [*without turning*]. Nick—will you and Susan bring them up to my sitting-room? I'll be there in a minute.

SUSAN. All right, Linda. [*She moves toward the door.* NICK *follows, gazing anxiously at the ceiling as he goes.*]

NICK. —The New Year ought to be just about passing over Stamford. [*They go out, closing the door after them.*]

JOHNNY [*goes to* JULIA]. Julia! Big news, dear—guess what's happened?

LINDA [*to* EDWARD *and* JULIA, *before* JULIA *can reply*]. Oh, this is so humiliating.—Peter and Mary are my guests, do you understand? Not paid entertainers— [*She moves away from them.*]

JULIA. I'm sorry. I simply couldn't imagine mixing in people like that to no purpose.

LINDA. Couldn't you?

JULIA. No.—But of course I can't follow your reasoning these days, Linda. I can't follow it at all.

EDWARD [*to* LINDA]. There's no cause for temper, child. Just run along now, and we'll follow. Julia and I want to talk to Johnny for a moment.

JULIA [*turns again to* JOHNNY]. What is it, Johnny? Quick, tell me!

LINDA. —Listen to me, Father: tonight means a good deal to me—I don't know what, precisely—and I don't know how. Something is trying to take it away from me, and I can't let it go. I'll put in an appearance downstairs, if you like. Then I want to bring a few people up here—the few people in the world I can talk to, and feel something for. And I want to sit with them and have supper with them, and we won't disturb anyone. That's all right with you, isn't it?

EDWARD. Your place is downstairs.

LINDA. Once more, Father: this is important to me. Don't ask me why. I don't know. It has something to do with—when I was a child here—and this room —and good times in it—and—

EDWARD. What special virtue this room has, I'm sure I don't see.

LINDA. You don't, do you—no—you can't. Well, I'll tell you this room's my home. It's the only home I've got. There's something here that I understand, and that understands me. Maybe it's Mother.

EDWARD. Please do as I have told you, Linda.

LINDA. I suppose you know it's the end of us, then.

EDWARD. Don't talk nonsense. Do as I say.

LINDA. It *is* the end. But all the same, I'm going to have supper here tonight in my home with my friends.

EDWARD. I have told you—

LINDA. —You thought I'd come around, didn't you? You always think people will come around. Not me: not tonight. And I shan't be bothered here, either. Because if there's one thing you can't stand it's a scene. I can promise you one, if you interfere. I can promise you a beauty. [EDWARD *turns from her.* LINDA *looks about her, at the room.*]

EDWARD. —Well, Johnny, so there's good news, is there?

LINDA [*suddenly*]. Was Mother a sweet soul, Father? Was she exciting?

EDWARD [*to* JOHNNY]. —A happy day all around, eh? An engagement to be announced, New Year's to celebrate—and now—

LINDA. Was Mother a sweet soul, Father? Was she exciting?

EDWARD. Your mother was a very beautiful and distinguished woman. [*To* JOHNNY.] Naturally, I am delighted that—

LINDA. Was she a sweet soul, Father? Was she exciting? [*For an instant* EDWARD *loses control of himself.*]

EDWARD. Linda, if you are not happy here, why don't you go away? I should be glad if next month you would take your maid and Miss Talcott and go on a trip somewhere. You distress me. You cause nothing but trouble and upsets. You—

LINDA. All right, Father. That's just what I'm going to do, after the wedding. No maid and no Miss Talcott, though. Just me—Linda—the kid herself—

EDWARD. As you wish.

LINDA. I've wanted to get out for years. I've never known it so well as tonight. I can't bear it here any longer. It's doing terrible things to me.

EDWARD. —And will you leave this room now, please?

LINDA. This room—this room—I don't think you'll be able to stand it long. I'll come back when you've left it— [*She goes out. There is a silence, then*]:

JULIA. She's dreadful tonight. She's made one situation after another.

EDWARD. Never mind, my dear. Things will settle themselves. [*He seats himself in a chair at Right*]. Well, Johnny—I don't think I need worry about the way *you'll* take care of Julia, need I?

JOHNNY [*laughs, uncertainly*]. We'll try to manage!

EDWARD. I consider what you've done a fine piece of work. I congratulate you.

JULIA. Oh, and so do I—so do *I*, dear! [*She sits near her father.*]

JOHNNY. —But you don't know yet, do you?

EDWARD. The fact is, Seton has just now told us.

JULIA. Isn't it marvelous?—Oh, what a New Year!

EDWARD. —Your stock is going up with a rush, it seems. It's time to make hay, I think.

JOHNNY. Hay?

EDWARD [*with relish*]. Money! Money!

JULIA. *Now* all those years you worked so hard—they'll pay interest now, Johnny! [*The frown grows between* JOHNNY's *eyes.*]

EDWARD. Of course, I could put you into the Bank tomorrow—but I am not sure that that would be advisable at present.

JULIA. —That will come, won't it, Johnny? [*To* EDWARD.] You'd better not wait *too* long, though—he may cost you too much!

EDWARD [*smiles*]. We'll have to risk that. People always do. [*Then seriously.*] Pritchard, Ames is an excellent house. In my opinion, you could not do better than to go with them. Then, in five or six years, you come to us on your own merit. After that, as the children put it, "the sky's the limit." You're in a fair way to be a man of means at forty-five. I'm proud of you.

JOHNNY [*there is a pause, finally*]: But—I'd made up
my mind not to take the Pritchard, Ames offer.

EDWARD. What? And why not?

JOHNNY. I don't want to get tied up for life quite so
soon. You see, I'm a kind of a queer duck, in a way.
I'm afraid I'm not as anxious as I might be for the
things most people work toward. I don't *want* too
much money.

EDWARD. Too *much* money?

JOHNNY. Well, more than I need to live by. [*He seats
himself facing them and begins eagerly, hopefully,
to tell them his plan.*] —You see, it's always been my
plan to make a few thousands early in the game, if
I could, and then quit for as long as they last, and
try to find out who I am and what I am and what
goes on and what about it—now, while I'm young,
and feel good all the time.—I'm sure Julia understands what I'm getting at—don't you, Julia?

JULIA [*laughs, uncertainly*]. I'm not sure I do, Johnny.

EDWARD. You wish to occupy yourself otherwise, is that
it?—with some—er—art or other, say—

JOHNNY. Oh, no, I've got no abilities that way. I'm not
one of the frail ones with a longing to get away from
it all and indulge a few tastes, either. I haven't any
tastes. Old china and first editions and gate-legged
tables don't do a thing to me. I don't want to live any
way or in any time but my own—now—in New York
—and Detroit—and Chicago—and Phoenix—any
place here—but I do want to live!

EDWARD. —As a gentleman of leisure.

JOHNNY. —As a man whose time, for a while at least,
is his own. That's what I've been plugging for ever
since I was ten. Please don't make me feel guilty
about it, sir. Whether I'm right or wrong, it's more
important to me than anything in the world but
Julia. Even if it turns out to be just one of those
fool ideas that people dream about and then go flat
on—even if I find I've had enough of it in three

months, still I want it. I've got a feeling that if I let this chance go by, there'll never be another for me. So I don't think anyone will mind if I—just have a go at it—will they, Julia? [JULIA *is silent.*]—Will they, dear? [JULIA *rises.* JOHNNY *rises with her.*]

JULIA [*after a moment*]. Father—will you let Johnny and me talk a while?

EDWARD. Just a moment— [*He rises and turns to* JOHNNY.] —As I understand it, you have some objection, perhaps, to our manner of living—

JOHNNY. Not for you, sir. I haven't the slightest doubt it's all right for you—or that it's the answer for a lot of people. But for me—well, you see I don't *want* to live in what they call "a certain way." In the first place I'd be no good at it and besides that I don't want to be identified with any one class of people. I want to live every whichway, among all kinds—and know them—and understand them—and love them —*that's* what I want!—Don't you, Julia?

JULIA. Why I— It sounds—

EDWARD. In all my experience, I have never heard such a—

JOHNNY. I want those years now, sir.

JULIA. Father—please— [*He turns to her. Their eyes meet.*] —It will be all right, I promise you.

EDWARD [*moves toward the door, where he turns once more to* JOHNNY]. Case, it strikes me that you chose a strange time to tell us this, a very strange time.

JOHNNY [*puzzled*]. I don't quite—

EDWARD. —In fact, if I had not already sent the announcement to the newspapers—asked a number of our friends here tonight to—

JULIA. Father!

JOHNNY [*very quietly*]. Oh, I see.

JULIA. Father—please go down. We'll come in a minute. [EDWARD *hesitates an instant, then goes out.*]

JOHNNY [*still hopeful, turns to* JULIA]. —Darling, he didn't get what I'm driving at, at all! My plan is—

JULIA. Oh, Johnny, Johnny, why did you do it?

JOHNNY. Do what?

JULIA. You knew how all that talk would antagonize him.

JOHNNY [*a moment*]. You think talk is all it was?

JULIA. I think it was less than that! I'm furious with you.

JOHNNY. It wasn't just talk, Julia.

JULIA. Well, if you think you can persuade me that a man of your energy and your ability possibly *could* quit at thirty for *any* length of time, you're mistaken.

JOHNNY. I'd like a try at it.

JULIA. It's ridiculous—and why you chose tonight of all nights to go on that way to Father—

JOHNNY. Wait a minute, dear: we'd better get clear on this—

JULIA. I'm clear on it now! If you're tired, and need a holiday, we'll have it. We'll take two months instead of one, if you like. We'll—

JOHNNY. That wouldn't settle anything.

JULIA. Johnny, I've known quite a few men who don't work—and of all the footling, unhappy existences— it's inconceivable that you could stand it—it's unthinkable you could!

JOHNNY. —I might do it differently.

JULIA. Differently!

JOHNNY [*a moment, then*]: Julia, do you love me? [*She looks at him swiftly, then looks away.*]

JULIA [*slowly*]. You—you have a great time standing me against a wall and throwing knives around me, don't you? [*In an instant he has taken her in his arms.*]

JOHNNY. Oh, sweet—

JULIA [*against his shoulder*]. What do you do things like that for? What's the matter with you, anyway?

JOHNNY [*he stands off and looks at her*]. Haven't you the remotest idea of what I'm after? [*She looks at him, startled.*] I'm after—all that's in me, all I am.

I want to get it out—where I can look at it, know it.
That takes time.—Can't you understand that?

JULIA. But you haven't an idea yet of how exciting
business can be—you're just beginning! Oh, Johnny,
see it through! You'll love it. I know you will.
There's no such thrill in the world as making
money. It's the most—what are you staring at?

JOHNNY. Your face.

JULIA [*she turns away*]. Oh—you won't listen to me—
you won't hear me—

JOHNNY. Yes, I will.

JULIA [*a pause. Then* JULIA *speaks in another voice*].
And you'd expect me to live on—this money you've
made, too, would you?

JOHNNY. Why, of course not. You have all you'll ever
need for anything you'd want, haven't you?

JULIA [*another pause, then*]: —I suppose it doesn't oc-
cur to you how badly it would *look* for you to stop
now, does it—?

JOHNNY. Look? How? [*She does not answer.*] —Oh—you
mean there'd be those who'd think I'd married
money and called it a day—

JULIA. There would be. There'd be plenty of them.

JOHNNY. —And you'd mind that, would you?

JULIA. Well, I'm not precisely anxious to have it
thought of you.

JOHNNY. —Because *I* shouldn't mind it—and I think
that lookout's mine. Oh, darling, you don't see what
I'm aiming at, either—but try a little blind faith for
a while, won't you? Come along with me—

JULIA. Johnny— [*She reaches for his hand.*]

JOHNNY. —The whole way, dear.

JULIA. —Wait till next year—or two years, and we'll
think about it again. If it's right, it can be done, then
as well as now.—You can do that for me—for us—
can't you? [*A moment. Then he slowly brings her
around and looks into her eyes.*]

JOHNNY. You think by then I'd have "come around"—

that's what you think, isn't it?—I'd have "come around"—

JULIA. But surely you can at least see that if—! [*She stops, as* LINDA *re-enters.*]

LINDA. It lacks six minutes of the New Year, if anyone's interested. [*A moment, then* JULIA *moves toward the door.*]

JULIA. Come on, Johnny.

JOHNNY [*to* LINDA]. Where are the others?

LINDA. My pretty new friends? Well, it seems they've ditched me. [*She starts a tune on the music-box.*] —*This* won't make too much noise, do you think?

JOHNNY. How do you mean, Linda?

LINDA. I imagine Peter and Mary got tired of being put through their tricks, and slid out when they could. Nick and Susan left a message upstairs with Delia saying that they had to go after them. I'm supposed to follow, but I don't think I will, somehow.

JULIA. Oh, I *am* sorry.

LINDA. Are you, Julia? That's a help. [*She goes to the supper-table.*] —Anyone care for a few cold cuts before the fun starts?

JOHNNY. You're not going to stay up here all alone—

LINDA. Why not? I'm just full of resources. I crack all kinds of jokes with myself—and they say the food's good. [*She takes a bite of a sandwich and puts it down again.*] Ugh! Kiki—

JULIA. Linda, this is plain stubbornness, and you know it.

LINDA [*wheels about sharply*]. Listen, Julia—! [*She stops, and turns away.*] No—that gets you nowhere, does it?

JULIA [*to* JOHNNY]. Are you coming?

JOHNNY. I think I'll wait a moment with Linda, if you don't mind.

JULIA. But I do mind!—Will you come, please?

JOHNNY. —In a moment, Julia. [JULIA *looks at him. He*

meets her gaze steadily. She turns and goes out.
There is a pause, then]:

LINDA. You'd better run on down, don't you think?

JOHNNY. Not right away. [*Another pause.*]

LINDA. I'm afraid I don't know how to entertain you.
I've done all my stuff.

JOHNNY. I don't need entertaining.

LINDA [*another pause, a very long one.* LINDA *looks uncertainly toward the music-box, finally*]: —You
wouldn't care to step into a waltz, Mr. Case?

JOHNNY. I'd love it. [*She extends her arms. He takes
her in his. They begin to waltz slowly to the music-
box.*] —There's a conspiracy against you and me,
child.

LINDA. What's that?

JOHNNY. The Vested Interests—

LINDA. I know.

JOHNNY. —They won't let you have any fun, and they
won't give me time to think.

LINDA. I suppose, like the great fathead you are, you
told them all your little hopes and dreams.

JOHNNY. Um.

LINDA. —Pretty disappointing?

JOHNNY. Bad enough.

LINDA. Poor boy.

JOHNNY. How about your own evening?

LINDA. Not so good, either.

JOHNNY. Poor girl.

LINDA. But we won't mind, will we?

JOHNNY. Hell, no, we won't mind.

LINDA. We'll get there—

JOHNNY. We'll get there! [*She stops in the dance and
looks up at him for a moment, curiously. Then he
smiles at her and she smiles back.*]

JOHNNY. —Place head, A, against cheek, B, and proceed as before— [*They begin to dance again.*] —Of
course they may be right.

LINDA. Don't you believe it!

JOHNNY. They seem—awfully sure.

LINDA. It's your ride still, isn't it? You know where you want to go, don't you?

JOHNNY. Well, I thought I did.

LINDA. So did I.—Pathetic, wasn't it—all my fuss and fury over anything so unimportant as this party.

JOHNNY. Maybe it was important.

LINDA. Well, if it was, I'm not. And I guess that's the answer.

JOHNNY. Not quite.

LINDA. —Me and my little what-do-you-call-it—defense mechanism—so pathetic. Yes, I'm just chock-full of pathos, I am.

JOHNNY. You're a brick, Linda.

LINDA. Oh, shut your silly face— [*then*]: You're right, you know—there *is* nothing up the fun-alley.

JOHNNY. Fun-alley?

LINDA. I had a nice little seven-word motto for my life, but I guess she don't work—

JOHNNY. What was it?

LINDA. "Not very important—but pretty good entertainment."

JOHNNY. H'm—

LINDA. For "pretty good" read "rotten." [*They dance for a few moments, silently. Then* LINDA *stops.*] There. That's enough. I'm getting excited.

JOHNNY. —What?

LINDA. —It was grand. Thanks. You can go now. [*She has not yet left his arms. Suddenly from outside comes the sound of bells tolling. Her grasp tightens upon his arm.*] Listen! [*She looks over her shoulder toward the window. Horns begin to be heard from the distance, long-drawn-out, insistent.*]

JOHNNY. It's it, all right.

LINDA [*again she turns her face to his*]. Happy New Year, Johnny.

JOHNNY [*he bends and kisses her*]. Happy New Year,

dear. [*For an instant she clings to him, then averts her face.*]

LINDA [*in a breath*]. Oh, Johnny, you're so attractive—

JOHNNY [*with difficulty*]. You're—you're all right yourself— [*There is a dead silence. Then she leaves his arms, turns and smiles to him.*]

LINDA. —You can count on Sister Linda.—Run on down now—quick! They'll be waiting.

JOHNNY [*hesitates*]. Linda—

LINDA. What?

JOHNNY. They've—your father—I've been put in a position that—

LINDA. Do you love Julia, Johnny? [*He turns away.*]

JOHNNY. Of course I do.

[NED *enters silently, another glass in hand. He stands in the shadow at Left, watching them, swaying almost imperceptibly.*]

LINDA. —Well, if ever she needed you, she needs you now. Once it's announced she'll go through with it. Then you can help her. I can't do anything any more. I've tried for twenty years. You're all that's left. Go on, Johnny— [*He goes to the door. From downstairs a swelling chorus of male voices begins "Auld Lang Syne."*] —And tell those choir-boys for me that I'll be in Scotland before them.

[JOHNNY *goes out, closing the door after him.* LINDA *stops the music-box, then moves slowly to the window, Right, where she stands silently for a moment, looking out.* NED *is still watching her, immobile. At length she turns to him*]:

LINDA. —Just take any place, Ned. [*He goes to the couch and sits there.*]

NED. —Rum party down there, isn't it?

LINDA. A hundred million dollars knocking together never made many sparks that I could see. [*She takes a glass of wine from the table.*] What's it like to get drunk, Ned?

NED. It's— How drunk?

LINDA. Good and drunk.

NED. Grand.

LINDA. [*She seats herself near the table, facing him.*] *How* is it?

NED. Well, to begin with, it brings you to life.

LINDA. Does it?

NED. Yes.—And after a little while you begin to know all about it. You feel—I don't know—important—

LINDA. That must be good.

NED. It is.—Then pretty soon the game starts.

LINDA. What game?

NED. —That you play with yourself. It's a swell game—there's not a sweller game on this earth, really—

LINDA [*sips her wine*]. How does it go?

NED. Well, you think clear as crystal, but every move, every sentence is a problem. That—gets pretty interesting.

LINDA. I see.

NED. Swell game. Most terribly exciting game.

LINDA. You—get beaten, though, don't you?

NED. Sure. But that's good, too. Then you don't mind anything—not anything at all. Then you sleep.

LINDA [*she is watching him, fascinated*]. How—long can you keep it up?

NED. A long while. As long as you last.

LINDA. Oh, Ned—that's awful!

NED. Think so?—Other things are worse.

LINDA. But—but where do you end up?

NED. Where does everybody end up? You die.—And that's all right, too.

LINDA [*a pause, then*]: Ned, can you do it on champagne?

NED. Why— [*He stops and looks at her, intently.*] —What's the matter, Linda?

LINDA [*she finishes her glass and sets it down*]. Nothing.

NED. I know.

LINDA. Yes?

NED. Johnny.

LINDA. Give me some more wine, Ned.

NED [*rises and goes over to her*]. He's a funny guy, isn't he?

LINDA. Give me some, Ned—

NED [*he goes to the table, refills her glass, returns, and gives it to her*]. —You can tell me about it, dear.

LINDA [*looks up at him. A moment, then*]: I love the boy, Neddy.

NED. I thought so.—Hell, isn't it?

LINDA. I guess it will be.

NED [*raises his glass*]. Here's luck to you—

LINDA [*stares at her glass*]. I don't want any luck. [*NED moves away from her to the table near the couch. He finishes his drink, leaves it there and sinks down upon the couch. LINDA carefully sets her glass of wine, untouched, upon the supper table, and rises.*] I think what I'd better do is— [*She moves slowly to the door, and opens it. The song is just finishing. It is applauded. LINDA hesitates at the door.*] Ned— [*He does not answer. Suddenly, from downstairs, comes a long roll of drums. LINDA stiffens. She starts to close the door, but is held there, her hand upon the knob. EDWARD's voice begins to be heard*]:

EDWARD. Ladies and gentlemen—my very good friends: I have the honor to announce to you the engagement of my daughter, Julia, to Mr. John Case—an event which doubles the pleasure I take in wishing you— and them—a most happy and prosperous New Year. [*There is prolonged applause and through it congratulations and laughter. Slowly she closes the door, but still stands with her hand upon it. Finally she speaks without turning*]:

LINDA. Ned— [*He does not answer.*] Ned—maybe I ought to go down and—I'm not sure I *will* stay up here—do you mind? [*He is silent. She turns and sees him.*] Ned! [*He is asleep. She goes to him swiftly, speaking again, in a low voice.*] Ned— [*A moment, then*]: Poor lamb. [*She bends and kisses him. She goes to the doorway, turns off the lights in the Play-room, and opens the door. A confusion of excited voices is heard from downstairs. In the lighted hall-way* LINDA *turns to the stairs, raises her head and goes out, calling above the voices.*] Hello!—Hello, everyone!

CURTAIN

Act three

SCENE: *The same as Act I.*

TIME: *Twelve days later. Ten o'clock at night.*
The curtains are drawn and the lamps lighted. Cof-fee service is on a small table near the fireplace. NICK *and* SUSAN *are taking their coffee.* LINDA's *cup is on the table. She stands near the sofa at Left Center, frowning at* NICK.

LINDA. No?
NICK [*shakes his head*]. Not possibly. [*He is behind the sofa at Right, upon which* SUSAN *is seated.*]
SUSAN. Why should Johnny pick a place like that?
LINDA. Why should he go away at all?
NICK. I'd have done the same thing—I'd have just giv' 'er a look, I would, and flounced out.
SUSAN. Hush, Nick. This is no time for fooling.
LINDA [*thinks a minute, then head down, eyes on the floor, she paces across the room and back, and across again. She stops opposite them and turns*]. —Atlantic City.
SUSAN. You don't go to Atlantic City for six days to think.
NICK. Old Chinese proverb.
LINDA. But where can he be, then?—*Where?*

SUSAN. Don't worry, Linda. I'm sure he's all right.

NICK. Susan and I parted forever at least forty times. [*To* SUSAN.] —Or was it forty-seven?

SUSAN. Of course. —And they haven't even done that. They've just put off the wedding a while.

LINDA. I know, but— [*She looks away, anxiously.*] Oh, Lordy, Lordy—

NICK. Johnny will come around, Linda. He's up against the old fight between spirit and matter—anyone want to take a hundred on spirit?

LINDA. I will! I'll take two hundred!

NICK. It's a bet, Madam. [*He looks at his watch.*]

SUSAN. Don't forget we have to go back to the house for our bags, Nick.

NICK. There's lots of time. She doesn't sail until midnight. "She"—a boat that size, "she"—the big nance. [*To* LINDA.] —You don't really want to see us off, do you?

LINDA. Oh, yes! But can you stop back for me on your way down?

SUSAN. If you like.

LINDA. I don't want to leave here till the last minute. I keep feeling that something may happen.

SUSAN. Where's Julia now?

LINDA. She went to dine some place with Father. He won't let her out of his sight—or into mine.

NICK. No wonder Johnny took to the woods.

LINDA [*quickly*]. —The woods?

NICK. —Or wherever he did take to.

LINDA. Now I know!

SUSAN. Yes?

LINDA. It was at Placid they met. It was at Placid they— of course! [*She goes to the telephone behind the sofa, at Left.*]

NICK [*to* SUSAN]. It may be. They say they always return to the scene of the crime.

LINDA. Long distance, please.

SUSAN. —In which case, I suppose Julia wins.

NICK. I don't know. It's pretty cold at Placid. There's nothing for a rapid pulse like a little wet snow up the sleeve.

LINDA. Long distance, please—

SUSAN [*to* NICK]. Would you mind telling me how a man like Johnny is attracted to a girl like that, in the first place?

NICK [*to* SUSAN]. You're too young to know, Susan.

LINDA [*at the telephone*]. —Long distance?

SUSAN. I can think of several people who'd be better for Johnny than Julia.

LINDA. I want to speak with Lake Placid, New York—

NICK. I can think of one, anyway.

LINDA. —Placid—the Lake Placid Club.

SUSAN. Do you suppose she's in love with him?

NICK. Suppose? I know. Look at her.

LINDA. "P-l-a-c-i-d"—

NICK. Tiger, Tiger, Tiger.

LINDA. Quiet a minute, will you? [*To the telephone.*] —Placid—calm—peaceful. Yes. And I'd like to speak with Mr. John Case.

SUSAN. If I could grab you the way I did, she can—

NICK. But there's more in this than meets the ear, darling—Julia.

LINDA. Quiet! [*Then, to the telephone.*] —Miss Seton. *Linda Seton.* [*To* SUSAN.] —I don't want to give him heart-failure, thinking it's— [*To the telephone.*] —John Case—Lake Placid Club—Linda Seton. Thanks. [*She replaces the receiver and returns to* NICK *and* SUSAN.] I'm sure he's there. I feel it in my bones.

NICK [*a pause, then*]: Linda, Johnny asked me not to tell anyone, but I think you ought to know something: the fact is, he's got a single cabin on the *Paris* for himself tonight.

LINDA. He—? How do you know?

NICK. Because I got it for him.

LINDA. You don't seriously think he'd do it?

NICK. No—I can't say I do.

LINDA. Well, *I* do! Oh, Lord—then he's in New York now!

NICK. Maybe so.

LINDA. He can't be, or he'd be here.—Where did he go to, Nick?

NICK. Of that, I wasn't informed.

LINDA. You know, this is ageing me.

SUSAN. We know something else you don't know, Linda.

LINDA. Oh! What is it?

NICK. —Look out, Susan. Steady, girl.

LINDA [*glances at them quickly, then lights a cigarette*]. What is it?

SUSAN. How did you happen to decide not to come abroad, as you planned?

LINDA. Why, I—well, I thought probably Johnny and Julia—they'd rather not have any family tagging along, and besides that, I want to get Ned off on a trip with me—out West, if I can.

SUSAN. I know. But—

NICK [*again* NICK *cuts across her*]. —I saw Ned in Jimmy's last night. He was—well, if I may use the word—

SUSAN. Look here, Linda—

LINDA [*to* NICK]. —I think he's all right tonight. He went to a show with the Wheelers.

NICK [*reflects*]. I wonder if they're really in love with each other.

LINDA. They're terribly in love.

SUSAN. What makes you think so?

LINDA. I know it. Johnny couldn't help but be, and Julia—

SUSAN [*glances at* NICK]. You meant the Wheelers, didn't you?

NICK. Why, I—yes, I did.

LINDA. I don't know about them. [*She moves away from them, then back again.*]

SUSAN. Can't *you* do anything with her, Linda?

LINDA. Who—Julia?

SUSAN. Yes.

LINDA. I've talked myself blue in the face. It's no good.
She won't listen. I've had the cold-shoulder and the
deaf-ear so long now I'm all hoarse and half frozen.

SUSAN. I thought she's always depended on you.

LINDA. Well, she doesn't any more.

SUSAN. You love her a great deal, don't you?

LINDA [*laughs shortly*]. I expect I do!

SUSAN. —But my dear child, don't you see that if she
thinks just as your father does—

LINDA. Johnny'll fix that. Johnny'll fix everything.

SUSAN. He'll never change *them*, Linda.

LINDA. Susan, you don't know that man.

NICK. —It'd be a pity to deprive your father of the
pleasure he'd take in putting him over on the town.

LINDA. Don't speak of it. That's one thing Johnny's
been spared so far. I don't think he's had an inkling
of *it* yet.

NICK. It will come: Mr. and Mrs. John Sebastian Case
have closed their Sixty-fourth Street house and gone
to Coney Island for the hunting. Mrs. Case will be
remembered as Julia Seton, of Seton Pretty.

SUSAN. I'd like a picture of him, when it happens.

NICK. I wouldn't.

LINDA. —If they'd only listen to me—I've got to make
them listen!—And he's so sweet, he's so attractive.
What's the matter with the girl, anyway? She ought
to know by now that men like Johnny don't grow
on every bush.

SUSAN. —But you see, the things you like in him are
just what she can't stand, Linda. And the fate you
say he'll save her from is the one fate in this whole
world she wants.

LINDA. I don't believe it.—Even so, she loves him—
and there's been a break—and wouldn't you think
she'd at least be woman enough to hang on—*hang
on!*

SUSAN. I don't know. There's another who isn't woman enough to grab.

LINDA [*there is a silence. Finally* LINDA *speaks*]. —I don't quite get you, Susan.

SUSAN. Well, to make it plain, no man's lost this side of the altar.

NICK. She's talking a lot of— [*Then, to* SUSAN.] Come on, Pearl—ups-a-daisy.

LINDA. Susan—

SUSAN. Yes, dear?

LINDA. Julia has never in her life loved anyone but Johnny.

SUSAN. —And you.

LINDA. —And me.

NICK [*in spite of himself*]. —And herself.

LINDA [*turns on him sharply*]. That's not true! —Even in this it's of him she's thinking—she may be mistaken, but it *is* of him!

SUSAN. I've no doubt she believes that.

LINDA. Well, I believe it too!

NICK. —Come on, will you, Susan?

LINDA. I think it's rotten of you to suspect things of Julia that aren't Julia at all, and I think it's worse of you to—

NICK. We're sorry, Linda, really we are.

LINDA. You aren't sorry! You're— [*Suddenly she covers her face with her hands.*] Oh, what's the matter with me?

SUSAN. Linda, I could shake you.

LINDA. I wish you would.—I wish someone would, till there was nothing left to shake.

SUSAN. —And there's not a thing to do about it?

LINDA. What there is to do, I'm doing. [*She goes to the window at Back. A silence, then*]:

SUSAN. —And if you did anything else, I expect you wouldn't be Linda.

NICK. Linda. I think you're just about the— [*But that*

is as close as he can get to a declaration of faith.]
—Oh, hell— [*He turns to* SUSAN.] Will you come,
dear? It's ten-thirty.

SUSAN [*rises and moves toward* LINDA. NICK *follows*].
But if Johnny should— [LINDA *faces her.*]—Promise
us one thing, Linda.

LINDA. What?

SUSAN [*after a moment*]. Nothing.

LINDA. I love you two.

SUSAN. —And so do we love you.

LINDA. —Call back for me when?

SUSAN. In half an hour.

NICK. Less.

LINDA. —Then could your car possibly take me out to
Mary Hedges'?

SUSAN. But of course! What a good idea—

LINDA. Mary asked if— I'll have a bag packed. [JULIA
comes in.] Oh, hello, dear.—Are you back already?

JULIA. Isn't it late? Hello, Susan. Hello, Nick. I thought
you were sailing. [*She leaves her evening wrap on the
sofa, Left, and moves toward the writing table at
Right.*]

SUSAN. We are.

NICK. At the crack of twelve. On the way now, in fact.

JULIA. I hope you have a grand trip.

SUSAN. Thanks. [DELIA *enters and takes* JULIA'S *wrap
from the sofa.*]

LINDA. —Delia, will you pack a bag for me, please? I'm
going to Mrs. Hedges until Tuesday.

DELIA. Yes, Miss. [*She goes out.* NICK *and* SUSAN *stand
at Center, facing* JULIA.]

SUSAN. I'm sorry we won't be here for the wedding,
Julia.

JULIA. I'm sorry too, Susan.

NICK. When's it to be?

JULIA. We haven't quite—set a date, yet.

SUSAN. —In the Spring, some time?

JULIA. Possibly before.

NICK. Let us know, won't you?

JULIA. Of course.

NICK [*a brief pause, then*]: —Then you're not coming down to the boat tonight?

JULIA. I'm afraid I can't. Bon voyage, though.

NICK [*thinks rapidly*]. Thanks. Can we take any word to Johnny for you?

JULIA. To Johnny?

NICK. Yes.—Or a basket of fruit, maybe?

JULIA. He'll be there, will he?

NICK [*this, at any rate,* NICK *can do*]. I should imagine so, if he's sailing.

JULIA. Sailing!

NICK. Isn't he?

JULIA. I wasn't aware of it.

NICK. Well, all I know is that the morning he left for wherever he went to, he telephoned me to get him a single cabin through Andrews, of the French Line. I don't believe it's been given up, or I'd have heard from them. I thought of course you knew, or I—

JULIA. I think I should—if he were going.

NICK. Yes, I suppose so. [*To* SUSAN.] We won't expect him, then.

SUSAN. No.—Goodbye, Julia. [*They move together toward the door.*]

NICK. Look us up, when you arrive. Immigrant's Bank. —We'll see you later, Linda.

LINDA. I'll be ready.

SUSAN. Thanks. Lovely evening—

NICK *and* SUSAN [*together*]. —And you must come and see *us* some time! [*They go out. There is a silence.* JULIA *looks for a cigarette.*]

LINDA. It may be true, Julia. I think the chances are it is.

JULIA. What?

LINDA. —That Johnny's going with them.

JULIA [*laughs*]. Not possibly, darling!—Why don't they keep these cigarette boxes filled—

LINDA. Stop it, Julia!

JULIA. Stop it?

LINDA. —Pretending you don't give a damn.

JULIA [*finds and lights a cigarette*]. You seem to be taking my little difficulty more seriously than I am. [*She moves toward the sofa at Left.*]

LINDA. If you don't want Johnny to go off tonight and make a hash of both your lives, you'd better send him some word to the boat.

JULIA [*smiles*]. Somehow, I don't think that's necessary.

LINDA. Why not?

JULIA. Well, for one reason, because he won't be there. He's no more sailing tonight than I am.

LINDA. You don't know that he's not!

JULIA. I don't know that he is, so I think I'm safe in assuming it.—Do you want to go to the Todds' dinner on Wednesday? They telephoned—

LINDA. —Julia, why do you want to shut me out in the cold like this?

JULIA. I wasn't aware that I was.

LINDA. —But won't you just *talk* to me! Oh, please, Julia—

JULIA. I don't know what there is to say.

LINDA. Never so long as I remember has there been anything we couldn't—

JULIA. If there's been any shutting out done, it's you who've done it, Linda.

LINDA. Me?!

JULIA. Johnny and I have had a difference of opinion, and you're siding with him, aren't you?

LINDA. But he's right! He's right for you as well as for himself—

JULIA. I think that's for me to decide.

LINDA. Not Father?

JULIA. Father has nothing to do with it—

LINDA. Oh, no!

JULIA. He happens to agree with me where you don't, that's all.

LINDA. We've always agreed before—always.

JULIA. No—I think quite often I've given in, in order to avoid scenes and upsets and—oh, well—

LINDA [*a silence, then*]: —Is that true, Julia?

JULIA. You've always been the "stronger character," haven't you? At least people have always thought so. You've made all the decisions, you've always had the ideas—

LINDA. —And you've been resenting me right from the very— [*She moves away from her, toward the fireplace.*] Oh—I can't believe it—

JULIA. It's nothing to get in a state about—and I didn't say I resented you. You've been an immense help, often. But when it comes to determining my future, and the future of the man I'm going to marry—

LINDA [*turns on her sharply*]. —Your future! What do you want, Julia—just security? Sit back in your feather-boa among the Worthies of the World?

JULIA. Well, I'm certain that one thing I *don't* want is to start this endless, aimless discussion all over again.

LINDA. But I tell you you can't *stand* this sort of life forever—not if you're the person I think you are. And when it starts going thin on you, what'll you have to hold on to?—Lois Evans shot herself—why? Fanny Grant's up the Hudson in a sanitarium—why?

JULIA. I'm sure I don't know.

LINDA. —Nothing left to do or have or want—that's why —and no insides! There's not a poor girl in town who isn't happier than we are—at least they still *want* what we've got—*they* think it's good. [*She turns away.*] —If they knew!

JULIA. —And *I* think it's good.

LINDA. Lord, Julia, don't tell me that you *want* it!

JULIA. I want it, and it's all I want.

LINDA [*there is a silence, then*]: —Then it's goodbye, Julia.

JULIA. Oh, Linda, for Heaven's sake don't be so ridiculous! If you're so damn set on being violent, get a

few Russians in and talk life with a great big L
to them.

EDWARD [*comes in, an admonishing finger raised*]. Ah—
ah—ah!

LINDA [*turns to him*]. —Father, I think you're both giving Johnny the rottenest kind of a deal.

EDWARD. In what way?

LINDA. Every way! Why do you do it? It can't be that
you think he's out to marry for money. You must
realize how simple it would have been for him—to
conform to specifications now, and then just not
get up some fine morning.

EDWARD [*moves to the table behind the sofa at Right*].
I don't regard the young man as a fortune-hunter,
Linda.

LINDA. Well, what is it, then?

EDWARD [*finds a cigarette and comes forward with it*].
—I think his outlook has merely become—somewhat
confused, shall we say, and—

LINDA. —And you'll straighten it out for him.

EDWARD [*to* JULIA]. We shall try, shan't we, daughter?

LINDA. Why hasn't he a right to spend some part of
his life as he wants to? He can afford it. What's he
got to do? Pile up so much that he can be comfortable on the income of his income?

EDWARD [*seats himself in a chair near the sofa*]. —That
would be an excellent aim, but I think we shall
hardly require it of him.

LINDA. I'd like to hear the requirements.

EDWARD. Any self-respecting young man wishes to earn
enough to support his wife and his family.

LINDA. Even when his wife already has—? Even when
there's no possible need of it?

EDWARD. Even then.

LINDA. Oh, Father, what a fake idea that is!

EDWARD. I don't think so. Nor does Julia.—In addition,
he has somehow developed a very curious attitude toward work—

LINDA. It seems to me saner than most. He wants his leisure at this end—good sense, I call it.—Which is harder to do, anyway—? Go to an office and rustle paper about or sit under a tree and look at your own soul?

JULIA [*contemptuously*]. Heavens!—the office, I should say.

LINDA. Then you've never looked, Julia.

JULIA. You can't talk to her, Father.

EDWARD. I should like to understand what he—and you—are aiming at, Linda, but I must confess I cannot. [NED *comes in.*] —I consider his whole attitude deliberately un-American.

LINDA [*stares at* EDWARD]. Are you serious?

EDWARD. Entirely.

LINDA [*she stares for a moment more*]. —You're right. I believe it is.

NED [*seats himself on the sofa, at Left*]. I've always said the Americans were a great little people.

LINDA. —Then he's a bad one, and will go to hell when he dies. Because apparently he can't quite believe that a life devoted to piling up money is all it's cracked up to be.—That's strange, isn't it—when he has us, right before his eyes, for such a shining example?

JULIA. I thought *you* were the one who found leisure so empty.

LINDA. —You think I call this, leisure? A life-sentence to *this?*—Or that he does?

JULIA. I think any variety of it he'd find quite as empty.

LINDA. —Even if it should be, he's got a right to discover it for himself! Can't you see that?

JULIA. I can see the discovery would come, quick enough.

LINDA. —And you don't want to be with him to lend a hand, if it should? [JULIA *is silent.*]

EDWARD. Linda, I listened most attentively to our young dreamer the other day. I have listened quite as at-

tentively to you this evening. I am not entirely
without intelligence, but I must still confess that
most of your talk seems to me to be of the seven-
teen-year-old variety.

LINDA. I'm glad if it is! We're all grand at seventeen.
It's after that that the—sickness sets in.

EDWARD [*chuckles, shakes his head and rises*]. —I feel
very well, myself—and you look in perfect health,
my dear. [*He moves toward the door.*]

LINDA. —You both think he'll come around, Father—
compromise, anyway. You'll get fooled. He won't
give way one little inch.

EDWARD [*at the door* EDWARD *turns, smiling*]. Stub-
born—?

LINDA. Right! And sure he's right!

EDWARD. We shall see— [*He goes out, victor.*]

JULIA. —Is that all, Linda?

LINDA. Where are you going?

JULIA. To bed.

LINDA. Now?

JULIA. Yes. Have you any objections?

LINDA. You actually won't lift a finger to keep him off
that boat tonight?

JULIA. He has no idea of taking it.

LINDA. You don't know him!

JULIA. Well, I think I know him a little better than
you. I happen to be engaged to him.

[HENRY *has entered with a tray containing a decanter
of whisky, ice, a bottle of soda, and one glass.*]

NED. Thanks, Henry. [HENRY *bows and goes out.*]

JULIA. Ned, I thought you went to the theatre with the
Wheelers—

NED. I did, but it was so bad I left. [*He rises, goes behind the table and makes himself a drink.*]

JULIA. Wasn't that just a trifle rude?

NED. I don't know, Julia. Look it up under R in the
book of etiquette, will you?

JULIA. I can't imagine what you're thinking of these

days.—Drinking alone—that's pretty too, isn't it?

NED. I never thought of the aesthetic side, but I see what you mean. [*He takes a long swallow of his drink.*]

JULIA [*regards him contemptuously, then, to* LINDA]. If there's any message of any sort, I wish you'd ring my room.

LINDA. All right. [JULIA *goes out.* LINDA *seats herself and stares moodily in front of her.*]

NED. —Like a drink?

LINDA. No, thanks.

NED [*again settles down upon the sofa*]. —You know, most people, including Johnny and yourself, make a big mistake about Julia.

LINDA. What's that?

NED. They're taken in by her looks. At bottom she's a very dull girl, and the life she pictures for herself is the life she belongs in. [*The telephone rings.* LINDA *goes to it.*]

LINDA. —You've never hit it off, that's all. [*At the telephone.*] Hello.—Yes.—Yes.—What? When, do you know?—Well, ask, will you? [*To* NED.] He *was* there.

NED. Who and where?

LINDA. Johnny—Placid. [*To the telephone.*] Yes? This—? I see. No. No. That's right. Thanks. [*She puts down the telephone and turns again to* NED.] —And left this noon.

NED. Then he'll be around tonight.

LINDA. You think so? This late?

NED. He'll be around.

LINDA [*a moment, then*]: Ned—

NED. What?

LINDA. Do you remember what we talked about New Year's Eve?

NED [*a brief pause, then*]: Sure—I remember.

LINDA. Tell me something—

NED. Sure.

LINDA. Does it stand out all over me?

NED. Why?

LINDA. Nick and Susan—I think they got it.

NED. Anyone who loves you would, Linda.

LINDA. Oh, that's awful. I'm so ashamed— [*Then she raises her head.*] I'm not, though!

NED. Why should you be?

LINDA [*suddenly*]. Look here, Ned—you're in a jam too, aren't you?

NED. Me?

LINDA. You.

NED. Sure, I suppose so.

LINDA. Is it that you hate this— [*Her gesture includes the house and all it represents.*] —Or that you love that— [*She indicates his drink.*]

NED. H'm— [*He looks about him.*] Well, God knows I hate all this—[*And lifts the glass before his eyes.*] —And God knows I'm crazy mad over this— [*He takes a deep swallow and sets the glass down.*] I guess it's both.

LINDA. What are we going to do?

NED. Nothing, that I know of.

LINDA. But we must!

NED [*hunches down into the sofa*]. I'm all right.

LINDA. You're not—but you'll pull out of it—and *I'll* pull out of it.

NED. I'm all right. I don't mind any more.

LINDA. You've got to mind. We can't just let go, can we?

NED. *I* can. I have.

LINDA. No. No!

NED. Listen, Linda: I've had the whole thing out with myself, see? All of it. A lot of times. And I've developed my what-do-you-call-it—technique. I'm all right. There's no reason for stewing over me. I'm—[*He squints at his glass.*] —very happy.

LINDA. There must be some sort of life for you—

NED. —But there *is!* Haven't I got the swell Seton name to uphold? [*He laughs shortly.*] —Only that's where I'll fox it. I'll make *it* uphold me.

LINDA. Neddy—listen: After the wedding we'll go out to Boulder, both of us.—We'll live on horseback and in trout streams all day long every day until we're in hand again. We'll get so damn tired that we won't be able to want anything or think of anything but sleep.

NED. You make it too hard. Come on—have a drink—

LINDA. Oh, you're dying, Neddy!

NED [*very patiently*]. All right, Linda.

LINDA. Won't you do that with me?

NED. Thanks, but uh-uh. Nope.

LINDA [*moves away from him to the other side of the room*]. Oh, won't anyone ever again do what I *know* they should do?

NED. That's what's the matter with you, Linda. You worry so much over other people's troubles you don't get anywhere with your own. [HENRY *enters.* LINDA *is staring at* NED.]

HENRY. —Mr. Case, Miss.

LINDA [*a silence, then* LINDA *recovers herself*]. Yes?— Have him come up, will you? [HENRY *bows and goes out. A moment.* NED *watches her, then*]:

NED. —Are you sure you *want* to get over him?

LINDA. No. I'm not. And that's what scares me most. I feel alive, and I love it. I feel at last something's happening to me. But it can't get anywhere, so it's like living on—*your* stuff. I've *got* to get over it.

NED. —Because it seems so hopeless, is that it?

LINDA. Seems! What do you mean?

NED. Don't you know? [LINDA *can only look at him. He goes to her.*] —Then let me tell you something: you're twice as attractive as Julia ever thought of being. You've got twice the looks, and twice the mind, and ten times the guts. You've lived in her shade for years now, and there's nothing to it. You could charm a bird off a tree, if you would. And why not? If you were in her way, she'd ride you down like a rabbit.

LINDA [*softly*]. Oh, you stinker—knowing the way she

loves him—you stinker, Ned.

NED [*shrugs*]. All right. [*He wanders in the direction of the door.*] —Tell him Hello for me, will you?

LINDA [LINDA's *voice rises*]. —If there's one thing I'll do in my life, it'll be to let the fresh air back into you again, hear me?—I'll do it if I have to shoot you.

NED [*turns and smiles back at her*]. —All right. [*He goes out. With an exclamation* LINDA *goes to the window and looks out, huddling herself in her arms.*]

JOHNNY [*enters. A moment, then*]: Hello, Linda.

LINDA. Hello, Johnny.

JOHNNY. Is—? [LINDA *moves to the telephone.*]

LINDA. I'll send for her.

JOHNNY. Wait a minute. [*A silence. He looks about him.*] I feel as if I'd—been away quite a while.

LINDA. Yes.

JOHNNY. I went to Placid.

LINDA. I see.

JOHNNY. It was horrible there.

LINDA. I can imagine it.

JOHNNY. Oh, Linda, I love her so—

LINDA. Of course you do, Johnny.

JOHNNY. It—makes anything else—any plans—ideas—anything—

LINDA. —Seem so unimportant, of course.

JOHNNY. But I know they are important! I know that!

LINDA [*smiles*]. Still—

JOHNNY [*turns away*]. That's it—*still*—

LINDA [*a moment*]. I think it'll come out all right, Johnny.

JOHNNY. Maybe, in the long run.

LINDA. Have you—I suppose you've decided something or other—

JOHNNY. I'm going to stay at my job, if that's what you mean.

LINDA [*after a moment, very quietly*]. I see.

JOHNNY. But only for a while! Only a couple of years, say—just until I can get through to her that—well, it's what she asked, and after all, a couple of years isn't a lifetime.

LINDA. No, of course not.

JOHNNY. I can see the way they look at it—I could hardly expect them suddenly to do a complete about-face, and—but hang it, they ought at least to see what I'm getting at!

LINDA. Perhaps eventually they will.

JOHNNY. That's what I'm counting on.

LINDA [*another silence, then*]: The fun's gone out of you, Johnny. That's too bad.

JOHNNY [*stares at the floor*]. It'll be back.

LINDA. I hope.

JOHNNY [*looks up suddenly*]. Linda—you agree that there's only the one thing for me to do now—

LINDA [*smiles again*]. Compromise—

JOHNNY. Yes, damn it! But *you* think that's right, don't you?

LINDA. I don't think it matters a bit what I think—

JOHNNY [*goes to her suddenly and seizes her wrists*]. It does, though! You think it's right, don't you? Say you think it's right!

LINDA. Shall I send for Julia?

JOHNNY. Say it first!

LINDA [*with difficulty*]. Johnny—when two people love each other as much as you, anything that keeps them apart must be wrong.—Will that do? [JOHNNY *drops her hand and moves away from her.*] —And shall I send for her now?

JOHNNY. Go ahead.

LINDA [*goes to the telephone and presses a button in the box beside it*]. With luck, we'll manage not to include Father this time.

JOHNNY. Oh, Lord, yes! [LINDA *again presses the button, again several times.*] Asleep, probably—

LINDA. Of course not. [*She presses it again, then*]: Julia —yes—would you come down a minute? No—but there's no telegram *to* send up. Will you come, Julia?

[*Her voice changes.*] Julia, it's terribly important that you come down here at once. [*She replaces the telephone and turns to* JOHNNY.] She'll be right down.

JOHNNY. If she doesn't fall asleep again.

LINDA. Johnny—don't talk like that. I can't stand to hear your voice do that.

JOHNNY. You care more what happens to me than she does.

LINDA [*startled*]. What? Don't be silly. [*Then, with difficulty.*] Maybe I feel things about you that she doesn't because—well, maybe just because *I'm* not in love with you.

JOHNNY. You know what I think of you, don't you?

LINDA [*smiles*]. I'd be glad to hear.

JOHNNY. I like you better than anyone else in the world.

LINDA. That's very nice, Johnny—because I like you a good deal, too. [*For a long moment their eyes hold them together. Then* EDWARD *comes in and, with a start,* LINDA *sees him.*] Oh, for the love of Pete—

EDWARD [*advances to* JOHNNY, *hand outstretched*]. Well, well—good evening!

JOHNNY. Good evening, sir. [*They shake hands.*]

LINDA [*turns away*]. —Both members of this club.

EDWARD. They tell me you've been away. Very pleasant, having you back.

JOHNNY. It's pleasant to be back.

EDWARD. —Quite at the mercy of the snow these days, aren't we?

JOHNNY. Quite.

EDWARD [*moves toward the fireplace*]. Still, they say Americans need four seasons, so I suppose we oughtn't to complain, eh?

JOHNNY. I suppose not.

LINDA. Father—Johnny came tonight to see Julia—

EDWARD. —That doesn't surprise me a great deal, Daughter—not a great deal!

LINDA. —Julia—not you and me.—Come on—let's go byebye.

JULIA [*enters*]. Linda, what's the idea of—? [*She sees* JOHNNY.] Oh—

JOHNNY [*goes to her swiftly*]. Get a wrap, will you? We're going out—

JULIA [*hesitates*]. Father—you won't mind if Johnny and I—

EDWARD. Please close the door. I wish to speak with both of you. [JULIA *gestures helplessly to* JOHNNY *and closes the door.*] —You insist upon putting me in a position that I don't in the least relish— [JULIA *seats herself upon the bench at Left. The door is opened again, tentatively.*] Who's that?—Oh, come in, Ned, come in.

NED [*enters and moves toward his drink*]. Sorry.—I just wanted—

EDWARD. Sit down, Son— [NED *seats himself upon the sofa Left.* EDWARD *continues to* JULIA *and* JOHNNY]. —Coming between two young people in love is furthest from my wish and intention.—Love, true love, is a very rare and beautiful thing, and— [NED *rises and moves silently toward the door.*] Where are you going? Please sit down! [*He waits until* NED *has returned to his place, then continues.*] —And I believe its path—that is to say, the path of true love, contrary to the adage, *should* run smooth. But in order that it may—I am a man of fifty-eight years, and speak from a long experience and observation— it is of paramount importance that—

JOHNNY. I beg your pardon, sir.

EDWARD. Yes?

JOHNNY. If Pritchard, Ames still want me, I'll go with them when we get back from our wedding-trip— about March first, say. [LINDA *turns away. There is a silence, then*]:

JULIA [*softly*]. Oh, Johnny— [*She goes to him.*]

JOHNNY. I'm still not convinced—I still don't believe in

it, but it's what Julia wishes and—and I'm—glad to defer to her wish.

LINDA. And now, in Heaven's name, may they be left alone—or shall we all move over to Madison Square Garden?

EDWARD [*disregarding her*]. You are not convinced, you say— [LINDA *exclaims impatiently.*]

JOHNNY. Would you like me to lie to you, sir?

JULIA. It's enough for me, Father.

JOHNNY. Julia said a year or two. I'll stay with them three years. I'll work harder than ever I've worked before. I'll do everything I can to make a success of it. I only ask that if at the end of the three years I still feel that it's wise to quit for a while, there won't be any more objections.

EDWARD. I doubt if by that time there'll be reason for any.

JOHNNY. We'll have to see about that, sir.

JULIA. Well, Father?

EDWARD [*a pause, then*]: When is it you wish to be married?

JULIA. As soon as possible.

JOHNNY. Sooner.

EDWARD. The invitations must be out for ten days at least.—How would two weeks from Wednesday suit you?

JULIA. That would be perfect.

EDWARD. No doubt there will be a sailing later that week.—Well, now, the sun's shining once more, isn't it?—And we're all friends again, eh?

LINDA. Just one big family.

EDWARD. —And what are your plans for your wedding-trip, may I ask?

JOHNNY. We haven't any very definite ones. Mostly France, I expect.

EDWARD. It's well to arrange even honeymoons a bit in advance.—Now let me suggest a little itinerary: You'll land at Plymouth or Southampton, and proceed straight to London. I'll cable my sister tomorrow. She and her husband will be delighted to have you stay with them.

LINDA. Good Lord, Father—

EDWARD [*to* JOHNNY]. He is Sir Horace Porter—one of the most important men in British banking circles.

JULIA. Father, I'm not sure—

EDWARD. You can scarcely go abroad and not stop with your Aunt Helen, Julia. In addition, it will save hotel expense and Johnny will be able to learn something of British methods.—Then I shall cable the Bouviers in Paris.—He was expert adviser to the Minister of Finance in the late war—a very good man for you to know. If they aren't already in Cannes, they will be very glad to have you visit them. And if they are, you could not do better than go straight to the South yourselves and—

JOHNNY. I had thought of this as more of a lark than a business trip, sir.

EDWARD. —But there's no harm in combining a little business with pleasure, is there? I've never found there was.

JULIA [*to* JOHNNY]. They have a lovely place in Cannes.

EDWARD. A week in London—a week in Paris—

LINDA. An hour in the Louvre—

EDWARD. —Ten days in Cannes—ideal! Then you might sail from Genoa and return by the Southern route. [*To* JULIA.] I'll arrange to have your house ready for you to go into March first.

JULIA. —Thanks, dear.

JOHNNY. What house is that, Julia?

JULIA. Father's lending us the sweetest little place on Sixty-fourth Street.

NED [*to* LINDA]. Would you call the Sixty-fourth Street house little?

LINDA [*watching* JOHNNY]. —By comparison.

EDWARD [*to* JULIA]. And I have also decided to turn the cottage at The Poplars over to you for the summers.

JULIA. Father, you shouldn't—you really should not!
[*She goes to him and takes his hand.*]

NED. Now there *is* a small place—hasn't even got a ball-room.

JULIA. Oh, Johnny—wait till you see it!

EDWARD [*is beaming*]. This is not a deed of gift, you know—not yet. Perhaps when you have occupied them for—er—five years or so, my hard old heart may soften.

JULIA. —Listen to him—*his* hard old heart! [*To* JOHNNY.] —Have you ever known of anyone so sweet?

JOHNNY [*after a moment*]. Julia—I'm sorry—but I can't stand it.

JULIA [*a silence, then*]: Would you—mind telling me what you mean?

JOHNNY. If we begin loaded down with possessions, obligations, responsibilities, how would we ever get out from under them? We never would.

EDWARD. Ah?

JOHNNY. —No. You're extremely generous—and kind—but it's not for me.

EDWARD. And may I ask what *is* for you?

JOHNNY. I don't know yet, but I do know it's not this.

EDWARD [*very quietly*]. We are to understand, then, that you are *not* returning to work.

JOHNNY. That work? For this? [*He shakes his head*]. —No.

JULIA. But you said—!

JOHNNY. —I'm back where I was, now. I can see now that it's got to be a clean break, it's simply got to.

EDWARD. But the other day, if I remember correctly, you intimated that you might follow some occupation—

JOHNNY. Eventually, yes. I think I may still be fairly active at thirty-five or forty.

EDWARD. —And in the meantime you expect just to lie fallow, is that it?

JOHNNY. Not lie—be! I expect to dig and plow and water for all I'm worth.

EDWARD. Toward the—er—eventual occupation which is to overtake you—

JOHNNY. Exactly.

EDWARD. I see.—Julia, if you marry this young man now, I doubt if he will ever again earn one penny. [*He moves to the table behind the sofa, at Right.*]

JOHNNY [*advances*]. Julia, if it's important to you, I'll promise you I shall always earn my own living. And what's more, if there's need of it, I'll always earn yours.

JULIA. Thanks.

JOHNNY. Oh, my dear, we've got to make our own life—there's nothing to it if we don't—there's no other way to live it!—Let's forget wedding invitations and two weeks from Wednesday. Let's go now. Let's be married tonight. [EDWARD *turns, in amazement.*]

JULIA. I must decide now, must I?

JOHNNY. Please—

JULIA. —And if I say No—not unless you—?

JOHNNY. —Then I'm going tonight, by myself.

JULIA [*a moment, then*]: Very well—you can go. Because I don't quite see myself with an idler for a husband.

JOHNNY [*a silence, then* JOHNNY *speaks slowly.*] I suppose the fact is, I love feeling free inside even better than I love you, Julia.

JULIA. Apparently—or what you call feeling free.

JOHNNY [*turns to* EDWARD]. Goodbye, sir. I'm sorry we couldn't make a go of it. Thanks for trying, anyhow. [*He goes to* LINDA *and takes both her hands*]. —Goodbye to you, Linda. You've been sweet.

LINDA. Goodbye, Johnny. So have you.—I hope you find what you're looking for.

JOHNNY. I hope *you* do.

LINDA. You did want someone along with you on the big search, didn't you?

JOHNNY. I did, you know.

LINDA. Poor boy.

JOHNNY. —But we won't mind, will we?

LINDA. Hell, no—*we* won't mind.

JOHNNY. We'll get there—

LINDA. Sure! *We'll* get there!

JOHNNY. Linda—

LINDA. [*She leans toward him*]. Oh, please do—

JOHNNY [*bends, kisses her briefly, and moves toward the door*]. Goodbye, Ned. [NED *attempts a goodbye, but cannot say it.* JOHNNY *goes out. There is a complete silence for a moment. Then* LINDA *murmurs*]:

LINDA. I'll miss that man. [*Another silence, which* JULIA *finally breaks*]:

JULIA [*half to herself*]. —He's really gone, then.

EDWARD. Yes.—And in my opinion—

LINDA [*turns sharply*]. —Good riddance, eh? [EDWARD *nods sagely.*]

JULIA. —Really gone—

LINDA [*goes to her*]. —Oh, never mind, dear, never mind. If he loves you, he'll be back!

JULIA [*turns upon her*]. —Be back? Be *back,* did you say? What do you think I am? Do you think all I've got to do with my time is to persuade a—a lightweight like him that there's something to life but having fun and more fun? [LINDA *stares, unable to speak.*]

EDWARD. I hope, Julia, that this experience, hard as it may have been, will teach you that—

JULIA. Oh, don't worry about me! I'm all right. [*She laughs briefly.*] —Even a little more than all right, I should say.

NED [*rises*]. —Um.—Narrow squeak, wasn't it? [*Suddenly* LINDA *grasps* JULIA's *arm.*]

JULIA. What's the matter with you?

LINDA. You don't love him.

JULIA. Will you kindly let go my arm?

LINDA. You don't love him!

JULIA. Will you *please*—

LINDA. Answer me! Do you or do you not?

JULIA. And what's that to you, may I ask?

EDWARD. Now, children—

LINDA. What's it to me! Oh, what's it to me! [*Her grasp tightens on* JULIA's *arm.*] Answer me!

JULIA. Father—what's the matter with her?

LINDA. You don't, do you? I can *see* you don't. It's written all over you. You're relieved he's gone—re-lieved!

JULIA. And suppose I am?

LINDA. —She asks me suppose she is! [*Again she confronts* JULIA.] Are you? Say it!

JULIA [*wrenches herself free*]. —I'm so relieved I could sing with it.—Is that what you want?

LINDA. Yes!—Thanks! [*She throws back her head and laughs with joy, and moves quickly to the table behind the sofa at Left.*] Oh, Lordy, Lordy—have I got a job now! [*From her handbag on the table she takes two brown envelopes, goes to* NED *and gives him one of them.*]

NED. What is it? [*He sees.*] Passport—

LINDA. What do you say?

NED. When?

LINDA. Now. Tonight.

NED. Oh, I couldn't tonight.

LINDA. Of course you could! If I can, you can.

EDWARD [*advances*]. Linda, where are you off to?

LINDA [*to* NED]. Will you come?

NED. Well, you know I'd like to, but—

LINDA. Then come!

EDWARD. Linda, where are you going? Tell me instantly.

LINDA. —On a trip. On a big ride. Oh, what a ride! Do you mind?

NED. Listen, Father, I'd—

EDWARD. A trip now is out of the question. Please remember you have a position to fill. You are not an idler. [*To* LINDA.] —A trip where?

LINDA [*to* NED]. You won't?

NED. I can't.

LINDA. —Caught.

NED. Maybe.

LINDA. —I'll be back for you, Ned.

NED [*almost inaudibly*]. I'll—be here—

DELIA [*enters*]. Excuse me, Miss Linda—Mr. and Mrs. Potter are waiting in the car. Your bag has gone down.

LINDA. Bring my fur coat, will you, Delia?—And throw a couple of hats in the hatbox and take it down, too.

DELIA. Very well, Miss. [DELIA *goes out*.]

LINDA [*turns to* JULIA]. —You've got no faith in Johnny, have you, Julia? His little dream may fall flat, you think—yes! So it may! What about it? What if it should? There'll be another—the point is, he *does* dream! Oh, I've got all the faith in the world in Johnny. Whatever he does is all right with me. If he wants to sit on his tail, he can sit on his tail. If he wants to come back and sell peanuts, Lord how I'll believe in those peanuts!—Goodbye, Julia.—Goodbye, Father. [*She leaves them and goes to* NED.] Goodbye, Neddy—

NED. Goodbye, kid—good luck— [*For a moment they cling together, then*]:

LINDA. Oh, never you fear, I'll be back for you, my fine bucko!

NED. All right, kid. [*She moves toward the door.* NED *is drawn after her.* DELIA *enters with the fur coat.* LINDA *takes it from her.* DELIA *goes out*.]

EDWARD. As yet you have not said where it is you are—

JULIA [*exclaims suddenly*]. I know!

LINDA [*going out*]. —And try to stop me, someone! Oh, please—someone try to stop me! [*She is gone.*]

NED [*stands looking after her, murmuring softly*]. Oh, God, oh, God—

EDWARD. I shall not permit it! I shall—

NED. —Permit it!—Permit Linda?—Don't make me laugh, Father.

JULIA [*advancing*]. She's going *with* them, isn't she? *Isn't* she?

NED [*smiles and picks up his glass again*]. —Going to get her Johnny.

JULIA [*laughs shortly*]. A fine chance she's got!

NED. —Any bets? [*Then savagely.*] —Any bets, Julia? [*He raises his glass.*] —To Linda— [*The portrait above the fireplace catches his eye.*] —And while we're at it—Grandfather! [*He drinks.*]

CURTAIN